Middle School 3-1

기말고사 완벽대비

적중 100

영어 기출 문제집

중 3

미래 | 최연희

Best Collection

구성과 특징

교과서의 주요 학습 내용을 중심으로 학습 영역별 특성에 맞춰 단계별로 다양한 학습 기회를 제공하여
단원별 학습능력 평가는 물론 중간 및 기말고사 시험 등에 완벽하게 대비할 수 있도록 내용을 구성

Words & Expressions

Step1　Key Words 단원별 핵심 단어 설명 및 풀이
　　　　Key Expression 단원별 핵심 숙어 및 관용어 설명
　　　　Word Power 반대 또는 비슷한 뜻 단어 배우기
　　　　English Dictionary 영어로 배우는 영어 단어

Step2　실력평가 단원별 수시평가 대비 주관식, 객관식 문제풀이

Step3　서술형 대비 학업성취도 및 수행능력평가 대비 서술형 문제풀이

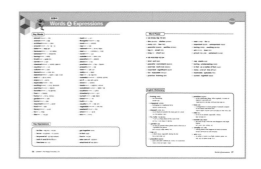

Conversation

Step1　핵심 의사소통 소통에 필요한 주요 표현 방법 요약
　　　　핵심 Check 기본적인 표현 방법 및 활용능력 확인

Step2　대화문 익히기 교과서 대화문 심층 분석 및 확인

Step3　교과서 확인학습 빈칸 채우기를 통한 문장 완성 능력 확인

Step4　기본평가 시험대비 기초 학습 능력 평가

Step5　실력평가 단원별 수시평가 대비 주관식, 객관식 문제풀이

Step6　서술형 대비 학업성취도 및 수행능력평가 대비 서술형 문제풀이

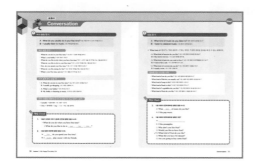

Grammar

Step1　주요 문법 단원별 주요 문법 사항과 예문을 알기 쉽게 설명
　　　　핵심 Check 기본 문법사항에 대한 이해 여부 확인

Step2　기본평가 시험대비 기초 학습 능력 평가

Step3　실력평가 단원별 수시평가 대비 주관식, 객관식 문제풀이

Step4　서술형 대비 학업성취도 및 수행능력평가 대비 서술형 문제풀이

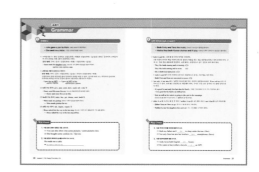

Reading

Step1　구문 분석 단원별로 제시된 문장에 대한 구문별 분석과 내용 설명
　　　　확인문제 문장에 대한 기본적인 이해와 인지능력 확인

Step2　확인학습A 빈칸 채우기를 통한 문장 완성 능력 확인

Step3　확인학습B 제시된 우리말을 영어로 완성하여 작문 능력 키우기

Step4　실력평가 단원별 수시평가 대비 주관식, 객관식 문제풀이

Step5　서술형 대비 학업성취도 및 수행능력평가 대비 서술형 문제풀이
　　　　교과서 구석구석 교과서에 나오는 기타 문장까지 완벽 학습

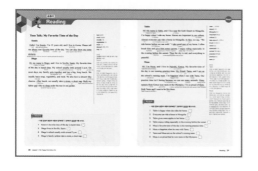

Composition

|영역별 핵심문제|

단어 및 어휘, 대화문, 문법, 독해 등 각 영역별 기출문제의 출제 유형을 분석하여 실전에 대비하고 연습할 수 있도록 문제를 배열

|단원별 예상문제|

기출문제를 분석한 후 새로운 시험 출제 경향을 더하여 새롭게 출제될 수 있는 문제를 포함하여 시험에 완벽하게 대비할 수 있도록 준비

|서술형 실전 및 창의사고력 문제|

학교 시험에서 점차 늘어나는 서술형 시험에 집중 대비하고 고득점을 취득하는데 만전을 기하기 위한 학습 코너

|단원별 모의고사|

영역별, 단계별 학습을 모두 마친 후 실전 연습을 위한 모의고사

교과서 파헤치기

- **단어Test1~3** 영어 단어 우리말 쓰기, 우리말을 영어 단어로 쓰기, 영영풀이에 해당하는 단어와 우리말 쓰기
- **대화문Test1~2** 대화문 빈칸 완성 및 전체 대화문 쓰기
- **본문Test1~5** 빈칸 완성, 우리말 쓰기, 문장 배열연습, 영어 작문하기 복습 등 단계별 반복 학습을 통해 교과서 지문에 대한 완벽한 습득
- **구석구석지문Test1~2** 지문 빈칸 완성 및 전문 영어로 쓰기

Contents

Lesson 3

Plants That Feed Us

의사소통 기능

- 안부 묻고 답하기
  A: Is something wrong?
  B: I have a bad fever.

- 조언 구하기
  What do you think I should do?

언어 형식

- 분사
  He ate a basket of tomatoes in front of many people **watching** him.

- 동사의 강조
  Spinach **does have** a lot of nutrients.

Words & Expressions

Key Words

- **absorb** [əbsɔ́:rb] 동 흡수하다
- **actually** [ǽktʃuəli] 부 실제로
- **article** [á:rtikl] 명 기사, 논문
- **battleship** [bǽtlʃ̃ip] 명 전함
- **bean** [bi:n] 명 콩
- **bloom** [blu:m] 동 꽃을 피우다
- **British** [brítiʃ] 형 영국의
- **capital** [kǽpətl] 명 수도
- **cartoon** [kɑːrtú:n] 명 만화
- **character** [kǽriktər] 명 등장인물
- **characteristic** [kæriktərístik] 명 특성, 특징 형 특징적인
- **consider** [kənsídər] 동 고려하다, 여기다
- **contain** [kəntéin] 동 포함하다, 담고 있다
- **crush** [krʌʃ] 동 으스러뜨리다
- **defeat** [difí:t] 동 물리치다, 패배시키다
- **discover** [diskʌ́vər] 동 발견하다
- **erase** [iréis] 동 지우다
- **expect** [ikspékt] 동 기대하다
- **face** [feis] 동 향하다
- **fighter** [fáitər] 명 전투기, 투사
- **German** [dʒə́:rmən] 형 독일의 명 독일어
- **government** [gʌ́vərnmənt] 명 정부, 국가
- **happen** [hǽpən] 동 일어나다
- **healthy** [hélθi] 형 건강한
- **hidden** [hídn] 형 숨겨진
- **hide** [haid] 동 숨다, 숨기다
- **however** [hauévər] 부 그러나
- **improve** [imprú:v] 동 개선하다, 향상시키다
- **insect** [ínsekt] 명 곤충, 벌레
- **lower** [lóuər] 동 낮추다
- **material** [mətíəriəl] 명 물질, 재료
- **nutrient** [njú:triənt] 명 영양소, 영양분
- **pilot** [páilət] 명 비행사, 조종사
- **place** [pleis] 동 두다, 놓다
- **planet** [plǽnit] 명 행성, 혹성
- **poisonous** [pɔ́izənəs] 형 유독한, 독성의
- **prove** [pru:v] 동 증명하다
- **publish** [pʌ́bliʃ] 동 출판하다
- **radar** [réida:r] 명 레이더, 전파 탐지기
- **researcher** [risə́:rtʃər] 명 연구원, 조사원
- **Scottish** [skátiʃ] 형 스코틀랜드의
- **secret** [sí:krit] 명 비밀
- **sensor** [sénsər] 명 감지기, 센서
- **snowboard** [snóubɔ̀:rd] 명 스노보드
- **soak** [souk] 동 담그다, 적시다
- **soil** [sɔil] 명 흙, 토양
- **solve** [sɑlv] 동 해결하다
- **spinach** [spínitʃ] 명 시금치
- **statue** [stǽtʃu:] 명 조각상, 동상
- **stomachache** [stʌ́məkèik] 명 복통
- **system** [sístəm] 명 시스템, 체계, 장치
- **surprising** [sərpráiziŋ] 형 놀라운
- **technology** [teknálədʒi] 명 기술
- **trace** [treis] 명 흔적 동 추적하다
- **truth** [tru:θ] 명 사실, 진실
- **vision** [víʒən] 명 시력
- **vitamin** [váitəmin] 명 비타민
- **world-famous** [wə̀:rldféiməs] 형 세계적으로 유명한

Key Expressions

- **be afraid of** ~을 두려워하다
- **be good for** ~에 유익하다
- **be scared of** ~을 무서워하다
- **by -ing** ~함으로써
- **get some fresh air** 신선한 공기를 마시다
- **give it a try** 시도해 보다
- **have a fever** 몸에 열이 있다
- **in addition** 게다가
- **keep a secret** 비밀을 지키다
- **keep ~ away from ...** ~을 …로부터 멀리하다
- **Royal Air Force** 영국 공군
- **lose weight** 살을 빼다
- **no longer** 더 이상 ~가 아닌
- **soak up** 흡수하다, 빨아들이다
- **sore throat** 인후염
- **stay full** 포만감을 가지다
- **take medicine** 약을 먹다
- **turn A into B** A를 B로 바꾸다

Word Power

※ 서로 비슷한 뜻을 가진 어휘

- □ **absorb** 흡수하다 : **soak up** 빨아들이다, 적시다
- □ **cartoon** 만화 : **comic strip** 만화
- □ **consider** 여기다 : **regard** 간주하다

- □ **improve** 개선하다 : **upgrade** 개선하다
- □ **contain** 포함하다 : **involve** 포함하다
- □ **improve** 개선하다 : **get better** 좋아지다

※ 서로 반대되는 뜻을 가진 어휘

- □ **hide** 숨기다 ↔ **uncover** 밝혀내다

- □ **defeat** 물리치다 ↔ **yield** 굴복하다

※ 동사 – 동사+er/or = 명사(사람)

- □ **act** 행동하다 – **actor** 배우
- □ **fight** 싸우다 – **fighter** 전사, 전투기
- □ **invent** 발명하다 – **inventor** 발명가
- □ **research** 조사하다 – **researcher** 조사원

- □ **direct** 감독하다, 지휘하다 – **director** 감독
- □ **interview** 인터뷰하다 – **interviewer** 면접관
- □ **paint** 그리다 – **painter** 화가
- □ **visit** 방문하다 – **visitor** 방문자

※ 명사 – 명사+ist = 명사(사람)

- □ **art** 예술 – **artist** 예술가
- □ **science** 과학 – **scientist** 과학자

- □ **cartoon** 만화 – **cartoonist** 만화가
- □ **tour** 여행 – **tourist** 여행자

※ keep을 포함한 표현

- □ **keep ～ a secret** ～을 비밀로 하다
- □ **keep away** 멀리하다
- □ **keep in touch** 연락하다

- □ **keep a diary** 일기를 쓰다
- □ **keep ～ in mind** ～을 명심하다
- □ **keep track of** ～을 기록하다

English Dictionary

- □ **battleship** 전함
  - → the largest type of ship used in war, with very big guns and heavy armour
  - 중무장을 하고 대형 대포를 가진 전쟁에 사용되는 가장 큰 형태의 선박

- □ **carrot** 당근
  - → a long pointed orange vegetable that grows under the ground
  - 땅 밑에서 자라는 길고 뾰족한 오렌지색 채소

- □ **cartoon** 만화
  - → a funny drawing in a newspaper or magazine
  - 신문이나 잡지에 실린 우스운 그림

- □ **character** 등장인물
  - → a person in a book, play, film etc.
  - 책, 연극, 영화 등에 등장하는 사람

- □ **hide** 숨기다
  - → to cover something so that it cannot be seen clearly
  - 명확하게 보이지 않도록 감추다

- □ **insect** 곤충
  - → a small creature such as a fly or ant, that has six legs
  - 여섯 개의 다리를 가진 파리나 개미 같은 작은 생물

- □ **nutrient** 영양분
  - → a chemical or food that provides what is needed for plants or animals to live and grow
  - 식물이나 동물이 살고 성장하기 위하여 필요한 것을 제공해 주는 화학 물질이나 음식

- □ **secret** 비밀
  - → a fact that is known by only a small number of people, and is not told to anyone else
  - 소수의 사람들에 의해서만 알려진 사실이며 다른 누구에게도 말해지지 않는 어떤 것

- □ **statue** 동상
  - → an image of a person or animal that is made in solid material such as stone or metal
  - 돌이나 금속 같은 단단한 재료로 만들어진 사람이나 동물의 이미지

01 다음 중 주어진 단어의 관계와 같은 것은?

> lower – raise

① similar – alike
② necessary – essential
③ truth – falsehood
④ unusual – uncommon
⑤ advantage – benefit

02 다음 영영풀이에 해당하는 단어로 가장 적절한 것은?

> a fact that is known by only a small number of people, and is not told to anyone else

① diary   ② newspaper
③ secret   ④ politician
⑤ news

★중요
03 다음 중 밑줄 친 단어의 쓰임이 바르지 <u>않은</u> 것은?

① Jamie is a <u>dancer</u>. He dances very well.
② Polly is a <u>diver</u>. She can dive deep in the sea.
③ Chris is a <u>swimmer</u>. He swims like a fish.
④ Dave is an <u>actor</u>. He acts in a movie.
⑤ Jill is a <u>composor</u>. She composes beautiful music.

서답형
04 다음 우리말에 맞게 빈칸에 알맞은 말을 쓰시오. (3 단어)

> 그 곰을 두려워하지 마.
> ➡ Don't _____ the bear.

➡ _____

05 다음은 각 영영풀이에 알맞은 단어를 빈칸으로 표시한 것이다. 모형 '★' 안에 들어갈 알파벳을 순서대로 배열한 것은?

> • ___ ___ ___ ___ ★ : a person who is trained to fly an aircraft
> • ___ ★ ___ ___ : to put something into a liquid and leave it there
> • ___ ___ ___ ★ ___ ___ : to press something very hard to break it into pieces
> • ___ ___ ___ ___ ★ : someone whose job is acting in plays or films

① hide   ② tone   ③ town
④ hold   ⑤ tour

서답형
06 다음 문장의 빈칸에 들어갈 말을 〈보기〉에서 골라 쓰시오.

> ┤ 보기 ├
> material   statue   bloom   character

(1) Flowers _____ every April.
(2) The white _____ of Kim Koo looks good.
(3) The _____ can be divided into two parts, iron and plastic.
(4) The main _____ in this book is very famous all around the world.

★중요
07 다음 빈칸에 공통으로 들어갈 말로 가장 적절한 것은? (대 · 소문자 무시)

> • Do you see the house _____ the river?
> • He used to travel _____ train.
> • _____ doing this, I can help her.

① on   ② in   ③ at
④ about   ⑤ by

01 주어진 단어의 관계와 같도록 빈칸에 알맞은 말을 쓰시오.

> fight – fighter : invent – _____

02 다음 영영풀이에 해당하는 단어를 〈보기〉에서 찾아 쓰시오.

> ┤ 보기 ├
>
> statue   insect   expect

(1) _____ : to believe that something will happen

(2) _____ : an image of a person or animal that is made in solid material such as stone or metal

(3) _____ : a small creature such as a fly or ant, that has six legs

03 우리말 의미에 맞게 주어진 단어를 바르게 나열하시오. (필요하다면 어형을 바꾸시오.)

(1) 졸업 후에, 나는 조사원으로서 NASA에 직장을 얻었다.

(research / graduation / with NASA / got / after / a job / I / as / a)

➡ _____

   _____

(2) 그 면접관은 내게 나의 미래 계획에 관해 물었다.

(plans / asked / about / the / future / me / my / interview)

➡ _____

   _____

(3) 나는 만화가인 것이 자랑스러워.

(cartoon / I / proud / being / a / am / of)

➡ _____

   _____

04 (A)~(C)에 각각 공통으로 들어가는 말을 순서대로 쓰시오.

> (A) I think I _____ a fever.
>   They _____ difficulty in reading books.
> (B) I want you to _____ it a secret.
>   Dave used to _____ a diary.
> (C) I will _____ the medicine tonight.
>   Shall we _____ a walk?

➡ (A) _____ (B) _____ (C) _____

05 주어진 우리말에 맞게 빈칸에 알맞은 말을 쓰시오.

(1) 운동은 우리의 몸과 마음에 유익하다.

➡ Exercise _____ _____ _____ our body and mind.

(2) 그 법은 더 이상 효력이 없습니다.

➡ The law is _____ _____ effective.

(3) 게다가, 나는 너무 어려요.

➡ _____ _____, I am too young.

(4) 여러분은 매일 계획을 세움으로써 이것을 할 수 있습니다.

➡ You can do this _____ _____ plans every day.

(5) 그것은 독성이 강한 물질로 만들어졌어요.

➡ It was made with a _____ _____.

06 다음 빈칸에 알맞은 말을 쓰시오.

> A: What do you want to be in the future?
> B: I want to be an _____. I like inventing things. Edison is my role model.

Conversation

① 안부 묻고 답하기

> **A** Is something wrong? 무슨 문제 있어?
>
> **B** I have a bad fever. 열이 심하게 나요.

- 상대방의 안부를 묻는 표현에는 우리가 잘 알고 있는 'How are you?'(잘 지내니?) 이외에도 'How have you been?'(어떻게 지냈니?) 또는 'What's up?', 'What's going on?'(무슨 일 있니?) 등의 다양한 표현들이 있다.

- 안부를 물을 때 상대방이 좋지 않아 보여서 걱정이 되는 상황일 때는 '무슨 문제가 있니?'라는 의미로 'Is something wrong?'(무슨 일 있니?), 'Is there anything wrong with you?' 또는 'What's wrong (with you)?' 등으로 물어본다.

- 상대방의 안부를 물을 때 대답은 본인의 상황에 따라서 'Great, very well. Thank you.', 'Fine, thanks.', 'Not bad.', 'I hurt ~.' 등으로 하면 되고, 'How about you?'로 되물을 수도 있다. 'How have you been?'(어떻게 지냈니?)에 대하여 응답할 때는 'I've been'은 생략하고 '(I've been) Good.', 'Fine.', 'Great.' 등을 쓸 수 있다.

안부 묻기

- Is something wrong? 무슨 문제 있어?
- What's wrong with you? 무슨 일 있니?
- How are you doing? 어떻게 지내니?
- What's the matter? 무슨 일 있어?
- How have you been? 그동안 어떻게 지냈어?
- How's it going? 어떻게 지내니?

핵심 Check

1. 다음 대화의 빈칸에 들어가기에 적절하지 <u>않은</u> 것은?

> **B:** Bomi, do you have some medicine?
> **G:** Why? _____
> **B:** I have a stomachache. I think I ate too much for lunch.
> **G:** Why don't you go for a walk?
> **B:** O.K. I'll give it a try.

① What's the matter?
② Is something wrong?
③ What's wrong?
④ Where have you been?
⑤ Is there anything wrong with you?

② 조언 구하기

> • **What do you think I should do?** 내가 뭘 해야 한다고 생각해?

- 어려운 일이나 안 좋은 일이 있어서 상대에게 조언을 구해야 할 때는 '무엇을 해야 할까요?'의 의미로 'What do you think I should do?'(제가 무엇을 해야 한다고 생각하세요?) 또는 'How can I ~?'(어떻게 ~할까요?) 등으로 물어본다.

- 조언을 구할 때 방법을 물어보는 의미로 'How can I ~?', 'What can I ~?'라고 할 수 있고, 'What can I do to ~?', 'What should I do to ~?'라고 하거나 'What's your advice?', 'What do you suggest?' 등으로 물어볼 수도 있다.

- 상대방에게 조언을 할 때는 '(I think) You should ~.', 'Make sure you ~.', 'I suggest (that) you ~.', 'You need to ~.', 'You have to ~.' 등으로 대답할 수 있으며, 'Why don't you ~?' 또는 'How/What about ~?' 등의 제안하는 표현을 이용하여 조언을 할 수도 있다.

조언 구하기

- **What do you think I should do?** 내가 뭘 해야 한다고 생각해요?
- **What should I do to ~?** ~하려면 뭘 해야 할까요?
- **What do you suggest?** 제안하는 게 뭔가요?
- **What do you advise me to do?** 무엇을 할지 조언해 주시겠습니까?
- **If you were me, what would you do?** 만약 제 입장이면 어떻게 하실 겁니까?

조언하기

- **(I think) You should ~.** ~해야 한다고 생각해.
- **I suggest you ~.** ~하라고 하고 싶어.
- **Why don't you ~?** ~하는 것이 어떠니?

- **Make sure you ~.** 반드시 ~해라.
- **You need to ~. / You have to ~.** 너는 ~해야 해.
- **How about ~? / What about ~?** ~하면 어때?

핵심 Check

2. 다음 대화의 내용에 어울리도록 빈칸에 주어진 단어를 적절하게 배열하시오.

B: It's so hard to lose weight. (you, I, what, do, do, think, should)?

G: Well, why don't you walk your dog every day?

B: My dog would love it, but would it help me lose weight?

G: Sure. When you walk your dog, you're actually exercising, too.

B: O.K. I'll think about it.

➡ _____

Listen and Speak 1 A-1

B: Bomi, do you have ❶some medicine?

G: Why? ❷Is something wrong?

B: I ❸have a stomachache. I think I ate too much for lunch.

G: ❹Why don't you go for a walk?

B: O.K. I'll ❺give it a try.

B: 보미야, 약 좀 있니?
G: 왜? 무슨 문제 있어?
B: 배가 아파. 점심을 너무 많이 먹었나 봐.
G: 산책을 좀 하는 게 어때?
B: 알겠어. 한번 해 볼게.

❶ some은 셀 수 있는 명사와 없는 명사를 모두 수식할 수 있다.
❷ 주로 상대방이 좋지 않아 보여서 걱정이 되는 상황일 때 쓰는 말로 'What's the matter?', 'Is anything wrong with you?'와 같다.
❸ 병이 있다고 말할 때는 주로 동사 have를 사용하여 말한다.
❹ 조언하는 말로 'How about ~?', '(I think) You should ~.' 등으로 대체하여 쓸 수 있다.
❺ give it a try: 시도하다, 한번 해 보다

Check(√) True or False

(1) Bomi ate too much for lunch.   T ☐ F ☐

(2) The boy will try going for a walk.   T ☐ F ☐

Listen and Speak 2 A-1

B: It's so hard to lose weight. ❶What do you think I should do?

G: Well, ❷why don't you walk your dog every day?

B: My dog would love it, but would it help me ❸lose weight?

G: Sure. When you walk your dog, you're actually exercising, ❹too.

B: O.K. I'll think about it.

B: 몸무게를 줄이는 건 너무 어려워. 내가 뭘 해야 한다고 생각해?
G: 글쎄, 매일 너의 개를 산책시키는 건 어때?
B: 우리 개는 좋아하겠지만, 그게 살을 빼는 데 도움이 될까?
G: 물론이지. 네가 개를 산책시키면, 사실은 너도 운동하는 거잖아.
B: 좋아. 생각해 볼게.

❶ 조언을 구하는 말로 'What should I do to ~?', 'What do you advise me to do?' 등으로 대체하여 쓸 수 있다.
❷ 조언하는 말로 'How about ~?', '(I think) You should ~.' 등으로 대체하여 쓸 수 있다.
❸ help는 목적격보어로 to부정사나 동사원형을 취하는 동사이다. lose weight: 체중을 줄이다
❹ 긍정에 대한 동의는 too를 쓴다.

Check(√) True or False

(3) The boy wants the girl to lose some weight.   T ☐ F ☐

(4) The girl suggests an idea that will help the boy lose weight.   T ☐ F ☐

(5) The boy will walk his dog in order to lose his weight.   T ☐ F ☐

Listen and Speak 1 A-2

B: ❶Is something wrong? You don't look so good.

G: ❷I have a sore throat. I think it's because of the fine dust these days.

B: ❸Put some plants in your room. They take bad air in and produce fresh air.

G: Really? I'll get ❹a few plants right away.

❶ 주로 상대방이 좋지 않아 보여서 걱정이 되는 상황일 때 쓰는 말로 'What's the matter?', 'Is anything wrong with you?'와 같다.
❷ 병이 있다고 말할 때는 주로 동사 have를 사용하여 말한다.
❸ 명령문을 사용하여 조언하는 말을 할 수 있다.
❹ 셀 수 있는 명사를 수식하는 수량형용사이다.

Listen and Speak 2 A-2

B: ❶How are your tomatoes doing? Are they growing well?

G: No. I've gotten only a few tomatoes ❷so far. ❸What do you think I should do?

B: Where do you have the pot?

G: In the kitchen.

B: Well, tomato plants need about 7 hours of sunlight a day.

G: Oh, ❹I see. I'll move the pot over to the window.

❶ 'How is[are] ~ doing?'은 안부를 묻는 말이다.
❷ 현재완료와 함께 쓰여 '지금까지'라는 의미로 사용된다.
❸ 조언을 구하는 말로 'What should I do to ~?', 'What do you advise me to do?' 등으로 대체하여 쓸 수 있다.
❹ I see는 I understand라는 의미로 사용된다.

Communicate A

Anna: Suho, ❶is something wrong? You're very quiet today.

Suho: I'm just a bit tired. I slept very little last night.

Anna: Did you do something late last night?

Suho: Yes, I watched a movie on my phone until 2 a.m. That's what I often do these days.

Anna: Oh, ❷that's why you have red eyes. You should go to bed before midnight for your health.

Suho: I think my eyes are getting worse. What do you think I should do?

Anna: ❸Try eating lots of carrots and tomatoes. They're rich in vitamin A, so they'll keep your eyes healthy.

Suho: I see. Thank you, Anna.

❶ 'Is anything wrong with you?'라고 말해도 좋다.
❷ 'That's why ~.'는 결과를 이끄는 말이다.
❸ 'What about eating lots of carrots and tomatoes?'라고 말해도 좋다.

Progress Check 1

B: ❶Is something wrong?

G: I'm just a little tired. I've watched a movie on my phone ❷for two hours.

B: ❸That's why you have red eyes. Try putting a warm towel over your eyes.

G: O.K. Thanks.

❶ 'What's the matter?'라고 물을 수 있다.
❷ '~ 동안'이라는 의미로 쓰인다.
❸ 'That is the reason why ~.'로 풀어 쓸 수 있다.

Progress Check 2

G: What's wrong? You look worried.

B: Well, I broke my mom's favorite plate. ❶What do you think I should do?

G: ❷Tell her the truth. She will understand.

B: I hope you're right.

❶ 'What should I do?'라고 말해도 좋다.
❷ 'Why don't you tell her the truth?'라고 말할 수 있다.

● 다음 우리말과 일치하도록 빈칸에 알맞은 말을 쓰시오.

Listen & Speak 1 A-1

B: Bomi, do you have _____ _____?

G: Why? Is _____ _____?

B: I have _____. I think I ate _____ _____ for lunch.

G: Why don't you _____ _____ _____?

B: O.K. I'll give _____ _____ _____.

Listen & Speak 1 A-2

B: Is _____ _____? You don't look _____ _____.

G: I have _____ _____ _____. I think it's _____ _____ the fine dust these days.

B: _____ some plants in your room. They _____ bad air _____ and _____ fresh air.

G: Really? I'll _____ _____ _____ right away.

Listen & Speak 2 A-1

B: It's _____ _____ _____ _____ weight. What _____ _____ _____ I should do?

G: Well, why don't you _____ _____ _____ every day?

B: My dog would love _____, but would _____ _____ me _____ _____?

G: Sure. When you walk your dog, you're _____ _____, _____.

B: O.K. I'll _____ _____ _____.

Listen & Talk 2 A-2

B: _____ _____ your tomatoes _____? Are they _____ well?

G: No. I've _____ only _____ _____ tomatoes _____ _____. What do you think _____ _____ _____?

B: _____ do you have the pot?

G: _____ the kitchen.

B: Well, tomato plants _____ _____ 7 hours of sunlight _____ _____.

G: Oh, I see. I'll _____ the pot _____ to the window.

Communicate A

Anna: Suho, _____ _____ _____? You're very _____ today.

Suho: I'm just _____ _____ _____. I slept very _____ last night.

Anna: Did you do _____ _____ last night?

Suho: Yes, I watched a movie _____ my phone _____ 2 a.m. That's _____ _____ _____ _____ these days.

Anna: Oh, _____ _____ you have red eyes. You should go to bed _____ midnight for your health.

Suho: I think my eyes are _____ _____. What do you think _____ _____ _____?

Anna: Try _____ _____ _____ _____ and tomatoes. They're _____ _____ _____ A, so they'll _____ your eyes _____.

Suho: I _____. Thank you, Anna.

Progress Check 1

B: _____ something _____?

G: I'm just _____ _____ tired. I've _____ a movie on my phone _____ two hours.

B: That's _____ you have _____ _____. Try _____ a warm towel _____ your eyes.

G: O.K. Thanks.

Progress Check 2

G: What's _____? You look _____.

B: Well, I _____ my mom's favorite _____. What _____ _____ _____ I should do?

G: _____ her the truth. She will _____.

B: I _____ you're _____.

해석

Anna: 수호야, 무슨 일 있어? 오늘 굉장히 조용하네.

수호: 조금 피곤한 것뿐이야. 어젯밤에 정말 조금 잤거든.

Anna: 어젯밤 늦게까지 뭔가 했니?

수호: 응, 새벽 2시까지 휴대폰으로 영화를 봤어. 요즘 종종 하는 일이야.

Anna: 오, 그래서 눈이 충혈됐구나. 건강을 위해 자정 전에는 잠자리에 들어야 해.

수호: 눈이 점점 나빠지는 것 같아. 내가 뭘 해야 한다고 생각해?

Anna: 당근이랑 토마토를 많이 먹어 봐. 그것들은 비타민 A가 많아서, 네 눈을 건강하게 유지해 줄 거야.

수호: 알겠어. 고마워, Anna.

B: 무슨 문제 있어?

G: 조금 피곤한 것뿐이야. 휴대전화로 영화를 두 시간 동안 봤거든.

B: 그래서 눈이 충혈됐구나. 따뜻한 수건으로 눈을 덮어 봐.

G: 알겠어. 고마워.

G: 무슨 문제 있어? 걱정이 있는 것 같은데.

B: 그게, 어머니께서 가장 아끼시는 접시를 깨뜨렸어. 내가 뭘 해야 한다고 생각하니?

G: 솔직히 말씀 드려. 이해하실 거야.

B: 네 말이 맞길 바라.

Conversation 시험대비 기본평가

01 다음 대화의 빈칸에 알맞은 것은?

> **B:** _____ You don't look so good.
> **G:** I have a sore throat.

① How do you care your neck?
② Is there something interesting?
③ What are you doing?
④ What is the matter?
⑤ How long have you been here?

02 다음 대화의 밑줄 친 부분과 바꾸어 쓸 수 있는 것은?

> **B:** I lost my wallet that my father gave me. <u>What do you think I should do</u>?
> **G:** I think you should tell him the truth. He will understand you.

① What should I find?
② What did I do?
③ What do you suggest?
④ How can you help me?
⑤ What can you say to him?

[03~04] 다음 대화를 읽고 물음에 답하시오.

> **B:** Is something wrong?
> **G:** I'm just a little ___(A)___ . I've watched a movie on my phone for two hours.
> **B:** That's why you have red eyes. Try putting a warm towel over your eyes.
> **G:** O.K. Thanks.

03 빈칸 (A)에 들어갈 말로 가장 적절한 것은?

① boring
② upset
③ tired
④ excited
⑤ sleepy

04 How long has the girl watched a movie on her phone?

➡ _____

01 다음 대화의 밑줄 친 부분의 목적으로 가장 적절한 것은?

> **A:** I have a cold. <u>What do you think I should do?</u>
>
> **B:** Why don't you drink some hot honey tea?

① 안부 묻기 ② 길 묻기
③ 조언 구하기 ④ 제안에 응하기
⑤ 승낙하기

02 다음 짝지어진 대화 중 <u>어색한</u> 것은?

① A: I lied to my mom. What should I do?
   B: I think you should tell her the truth.
② A: Is something wrong?
   B: I forgot to bring my umbrella.
③ A: How have you been?
   B: Great. I have a sore throat.
④ A: What's wrong? You look upset.
   B: I can't find my bicycle.
⑤ A: How are you doing?
   B: Not bad. How are you?

[03~04] 다음 대화를 읽고 물음에 답하시오.

> **B:** Bomi, do you have some medicine?
> **G:** Why? Is something wrong?
> **B:** I have a stomachache. I think I ate too much for lunch.
> **G:** Why don't you go for a walk?
> **B:** O.K. (A)<u>I'll give it a try.</u>

03 다음 중 밑줄 친 (A)의 의미로 가장 적절한 것은?

① I will take the medicine.
② I will eat less next time.
③ I will try to exercise more often.
④ I will try walking.
⑤ I will go see a doctor.

04 서답형 Write the reason why the boy wants some medicine. Use the phrase below.

> It's because

➡ _____

[05~07] 다음 대화를 읽고 물음에 답하시오.

> **B:** It's so ①<u>hard</u> to lose weight. (A)<u>What do you think I should do?</u>
> **G:** Well, why don't you ②<u>walk</u> your dog every day?
> **B:** My dog would love it, but would it help me ③<u>losing</u> weight?
> **G:** Sure. When you walk your dog, you're actually ④<u>exercising</u>, ⑤<u>too</u>.
> **B:** O.K. I'll think about it.

05 다음 중 밑줄 친 (A)를 대신하여 쓸 수 있는 것은?

① What do you think I am doing?
② What can I do for you?
③ How come I should lose weight?
④ What do you advise me to do?
⑤ What do you think I am doing?

06 ①~⑤ 중 어법상 바르지 <u>않은</u> 것은?

①   ②   ③   ④   ⑤

07 위 대화를 읽고 답할 수 있는 것은?

① How does the girl think about the boy?
② What is the girl's suggestion for the boy's problem?
③ How long have they known each other?
④ Why does the boy want to lose weight?
⑤ How old is the boy's dog?

서답형

08 자연스러운 대화가 되도록 (A)~(D)를 바르게 나열하시오.

> (A) Well, I broke my mom's favorite plate. What do you think I should do?
> (B) I hope you're right.
> (C) What's wrong? You look worried.
> (D) Tell her the truth. She will understand.

➡ _____

서답형

09 다음 상황을 읽고 빈칸에 들어갈 말을 조건에 맞게 쓰시오.

> You fought with one of your friend, Mina, today. On your way home, you thought you were sorry to have blamed her. So you wanted some advice from your best friend, Mike. In this situation, what would you say to Mike?
> **You:** "Mike, _____ "
> (should / say sorry)

➡ _____

[10~11] 다음 대화를 읽고 물음에 답하시오.

> B: How are your tomatoes doing? Are they growing well?
> G: No. I've gotten only a few tomatoes so far. What do you think I should do?
> B: Where do you have the pot?
> G: In the kitchen.
> B: Well, tomato plants need about 7 hours of sunlight a day.
> G: Oh, I see. I'll move the pot over to the window.

서답형

10 Where does the girl have the tomato pot? Answer in English with a full sentence.

➡ _____

중요

11 위 대화의 내용과 일치하는 것은?

① The boy doesn't know if the girl is growing tomatoes.
② The girl has gotten lots of tomatoes.
③ The boy wants some tomatoes.
④ The boy gives the girl a tip about growing tomatoes.
⑤ The girl will put the pot in the kitchen.

[12~13] 다음 대화를 읽고 물음에 답하시오.

> Anna: Suho, is something wrong? You're very ①quiet today.
> Suho: I'm just a bit tired. I slept very ②little last night.
> Anna: Did you do something ③late last night?
> Suho: Yes, I watched a movie on my phone until 2 a.m. That's what I often do these days.
> Anna: Oh, that's why you have red eyes. You should go to bed ④before midnight for your health.
> Suho: I think my eyes are getting worse. What do you think I should do?
> Anna: Try eating lots of carrots and tomatoes. They're rich in vitamin A, so they'll keep your eyes ⑤unhealthy.
> Suho: I see. Thank you, Anna.

12 ①~⑤ 중 대화의 흐름상 어색한 것은?

①   ②   ③   ④   ⑤

서답형

13 What does Suho often do these days? Answer in English with a full sentence.

➡ _____

01 주어진 단어를 활용하여 다음 우리말을 영어로 쓰시오.

> A: I'm tired because of my neighbor. She keeps playing the piano at night. <u>내가 무엇을 해야 한다고 생각해?</u>
> (what / you / think / should)
> B: Why don't you ask her to stop playing the piano at night?

➡ _____

[02~04] 다음 대화를 읽고 물음에 답하시오.

> B: Is something wrong, Jane? You don't look so good.
> G: I ___(A)___ a sore throat. I think it's because of the fine dust these days.
> B: Put some plants in your room. They ___(B)___ bad air in and produce fresh air.
> G: Really? I'll ___(C)___ a few plants right away.

02 주어진 단어를 빈칸 (A)~(C)에 적절하게 쓰시오.

> take / have / get

➡ (A) _____ (B) _____ (C) _____

03 대화의 내용에 맞게 빈칸에 알맞은 말을 쓰시오.

> Jane thinks that _____ _____ makes her throat _____.

04 What is Jane likely to do after the conversation? Answer in English.

➡ _____

[05~06] 다음 대화를 읽고 물음에 답하시오.

> B: (A)<u>Is something wrong?</u>
> G: I'm just a little tired. I've watched a movie on my phone for two hours.
> B: That's why you have red eyes. Try putting a warm towel over your eyes.
> G: O.K. Thanks.

05 주어진 단어를 활용하여 밑줄 친 (A)와 같은 의미의 말을 4단어로 쓰시오.

> (what / wrong)

➡ _____

06 Write the reason why the girl is tired. Use the phrase 'It's because.'

➡ _____

➡ _____

07 자연스러운 대화가 되도록 (A)~(E)를 바르게 나열하시오.

> (A) I have a stomachache. I think I ate too much for lunch.
> (B) O.K. I'll give it a try.
> (C) Bomi, do you have some medicine?
> (D) Why don't you go for a walk?
> (E) Why? Is something wrong?

➡ _____

08 다음 상황을 읽고 빈칸에 알맞은 말을 쓰시오. 한 칸에 하나의 단어만 쓰시오.

> You meet your friend, Yumi, and find that she looks a little sad. You want to ask her if she is okay. In this situation, what do you say to her?
> You: Yumi, _____ _____ _____?
> You look sad.

Grammar

① 분사

> • Peter is a boy **throwing** a big ball. Peter는 큰 공을 던지는 소년이다.
> • I know the dog **barking** at Joseph. 나는 Joseph을 향해 짖는 개를 안다.

■ 현재분사는 '동사원형+-ing' 형태로 형용사처럼 명사를 앞 또는 뒤에서 꾸며준다. 일반적으로는 명사 앞에서, 다른 어구와 함께 구(phrase)를 이룰 때는 명사를 뒤에서 꾸민다.
  • **The crying baby** stopped kicking. 울고 있는 아기가 발차기를 멈췄다.
  • Did you see **the baby crying for the toy**? 장난감을 달라고 울고 있는 아기를 봤니?

■ 현재분사(-ing)는 능동/진행의 의미, 과거분사(p.p.)는 수동/완료의 의미를 갖는다.
  • The researchers are **searching** for the cause of storms. 연구진들은 폭풍우의 원인을 찾고 있는 중이다.
  • John saw the girl **dancing** on the stage. John은 무대에서 춤추고 있는 소녀를 봤다.
  • Watch out the **broken** pieces of glasses! 깨진 유리잔 조각들을 조심하세요!
  • The actors **invited** to the film festival showed up. 영화제에 초대된 배우들이 등장했다.

■ 명사를 뒤에서 꾸미는 분사구는 '주격 관계대명사+be동사'가 생략된 것으로 볼 수 있다.
  • The girl (**who was**) **wearing** Hanbok was Sophia. 한복을 입고 있는 그 소녀는 Sophia였다.
  • The students wanted to read the books (**which were**) **written** by O. Henry. 학생들은 O. Henry에 의해 쓰인 책들을 읽고 싶어했다.

■ 분사는 명사를 꾸며주는 한정 용법 외에, 주어나 목적어의 보충 설명을 하는 서술 용법이 있다. 이 경우, 분사가 주격 보어 또는 목적격 보어가 된다.
  • A gentleman stood **looking** at the picture. 한 신사가 그림을 보며 서 있었다.
  • The injured sheep lay **surrounded** by the wolves. 다친 양이 늑대들에게 둘러싸인 채로 누워 있었다.
  • He was sorry to keep me **waiting**. 그가 나를 기다리게 해서 미안해했다.
  • He heard his name **called**. 그는 그의 이름이 불리는 것을 들었다.
  • Susan had her dream house **built** in her hometown. Susan은 그녀의 고향에 자신의 꿈의 집이 건축되도록 했다.

핵심 Check

1. 다음 괄호 안에서 알맞은 단어를 고르시오.
  (1) A man (named / naming) Robert wanted to prove that tomatoes were safe to eat.
  (2) James had his arms (breaking / broken) while playing soccer.

② 동사 강조

> • I **do love** swimming in the lake. 나는 호수에서 수영하는 것을 정말 좋아한다.
> • James **does prefer** to eat spinach. James는 시금치 먹기를 정말 선호한다.

■ 문장에서 동사의 앞에 do를 써서 동사의 의미를 강조할 수 있다. 주어의 인칭과 시제에 맞춰 do/does/ did 등을 활용하며, really(정말)의 의미로 해석한다.

  • Popeye **did get** his superpower by eating spinach. Popeye는 시금치를 먹음으로써 그의 막강한 힘을 정말 얻었다.

  • Sam doesn't like horror movies, but he **does like** comedies. Sam은 공포영화를 좋아하지 않지만, 코미디는 정말 좋아한다.

■ Be로 시작하는 명령문도, Be 앞에 Do를 써서 강조할 수 있다.

  • Be nice to others! = **Do** be nice to others! 다른 사람들에게 정말 착하게 대하라!

■ do는 동사를 강조하는데 반해, 재귀대명사는 (대)명사를 강조한다.

  • Emma **did play** the piano. Emma가 피아노를 정말 연주했다.

  • Emma played the piano **herself**. = Emma **herself** played the piano. Emma가 직접 피아노를 연주했다.

■ It ~ that 강조구문에서는 명사 또는 부사(구/절)를 강조한다. 강조하려는 대상에 따라 that을 관계대명사 who(사람), which(사물)로, 또는 관계부사 when(시간), where(장소) 등으로 대체할 수 있다.

  • Clara broke the toy car at her cousin's house yesterday. Clara가 어제 사촌네 집에서 그 장난감 차를 부쉈다.

  → **It was** Clara **that[who]** broke the toy car at her cousin's house yesterday. 어제 사촌네 집에서 그 장난감 차를 부순 것은 바로 Clara였다.

  → **It was** the toy car **that[which]** Clara broke at her cousin's house yesterday. Clara가 어제 사촌네 집에서 부순 것은 바로 그 장난감 차였다.

  → **It was** yesterday **that[when]** Clara broke the toy car at her cousin's house. Clara가 사촌네 집에서 그 장난감 차를 부순 것은 바로 어제였다.

  → **It was** at her cousin's house **that[where]** Clara broke the toy car yesterday. 어제 Clara가 그 장난감 차를 부순 것은 바로 사촌네 집에서였다.

핵심 Check

2. 다음 괄호 안에서 알맞은 단어를 고르시오.

 (1) I (was / did) feel bad when I was passing by the smoking guys.

 (2) Carrots (does / do) contain a lot of vitamin A.

01 다음 문장에서 어법상 어색한 부분을 바르게 고쳐 쓰시오.

(1) In the future, carrots may actually be using in wars.

_____ ➡ _____

(2) I did called you the day before yesterday.

_____ ➡ _____

(3) Hannah is the one eats tomatoes right now.

_____ ➡ _____

(4) The manager received a letter writing in Latin.

_____ ➡ _____

02 다음 중 어법상 바르지 않은 것은?

① The villagers did build the castle about 100 years ago.
② Potatoes does help you in many ways.
③ Oliver does love what she cooks.
④ Patrick did come back home.
⑤ All of his family do like Anna's novel.

03 다음 대화의 밑줄 친 부분 중에서 어법상 잘못된 곳을 고르시오.

A: ①Aren't you ②tiring ③of eating spinach every day?
B: No, I'm not. I ④do ⑤feel healthy.

04 다음 우리말에 맞게 주어진 단어를 알맞게 배열하시오.

(1) 대부분의 미국인들은 토마토가 독성이 있다고 정말 생각했다. (did, were, poisonous, that, Americans, tomatoes, most, think)

➡ _____

(2) Lily가 찍은 사진들은 인상적이었다. (were, by, the, Lily, pictures, taken, impressive)

➡ _____

01 다음 괄호 안의 단어가 올바른 형태로 순서대로 짝지어진 것은?

> • The boy (pick) up the flower is my son.
> • The money (spend) for her tour in Europe was too much.
> • Some insects are (scare) of tomatoes.

① picking – spending – scaring
② picking – spent – scaring
③ picking – spent – scared
④ picked – spending – scared
⑤ picked – spent – scaring

 02 다음 빈칸에 공통으로 들어갈 말로 알맞은 것은?

> • Kate _____ like her doll.
> • Sophie always _____ the laundry right after she comes home.

① does   ② has   ③ do
④ have   ⑤ don't

서답형
03 다음 예시와 같이 두 문장을 한 문장으로 연결할 때, 빈칸에 알맞은 말을 넣으시오.

> • British pilots improved their night vision.
> • They ate carrots.
> → British pilots eating carrots improved their night vision.

(1) • There were many people.
   • They were watching the pet contest.
   → There _____ _____ _____
   _____ the pet contest.

(2) • The swimming pool is very large.
   • It was built by my grandfather.
   → The swimming pool _____
   _____ very large.

 04 밑줄 친 부분이 어법상 올바른 것은?

① The researcher did warned the people.
② Do be polite to the elderly!
③ The boy did changed his choice.
④ She does believed it is a dream.
⑤ My uncle does looks happy.

서답형
05 다음 문장에서 어법상 틀린 부분을 찾아 바르게 고쳐 쓰시오.

> He bought a shirt making in Vietnam.

_____ ➡ _____

06 다음 중 두 문장의 뜻이 같지 않은 것은?

① I do spend much time playing chess.
   → I really spend much time playing chess.
② Jenny did show me what she drew.
   → Jenny really showed me the picture that was drawn by her.
③ It was Ann that cooked me pizza.
   → It was Ann who cooked me pizza.
④ Sarah did break her leg.
   → Sarah really broke her leg.
⑤ He did find the missing kid in the amusement park.
   → He was able to find the missing kid in the amusement park.

 07 밑줄 친 부분의 쓰임이 다른 하나는?

① My dad hearing the news got disappointed.
② The kids tried locking the safe.
③ I want to raise a talking parrot.
④ The girl passing by them is Joan.
⑤ The barking wolf seemed like a puppy.

08 다음 우리말에 맞게 괄호 안에 주어진 단어를 알맞게 배열하시오.

> 꿀이 섞인 감자 주스가 당신의 피부를 부드럽게 만들어 준다.
> (honey, juice, potato, skin, with, soft, mixed, your, makes)

➡ _____

_____

09 다음 빈칸에 알맞은 말이 순서대로 바르게 짝지어진 것은?

> • Emily _____ love eating vegetables.
> • Peter and Mary _____ hope to be famous when they first made the group.

① did – does   ② do – did
③ does – did   ④ did – do
⑤ does – do

10 다음 밑줄 친 ⓐ, ⓑ를 어법상 알맞게 고친 것이 차례대로 짝지어진 것은?

> • She warned the little kid not to touch the ⓐburn fire.
> • The students ⓑsing by the tree were our school choir members.

① burning – sang   ② burning – singing
③ burnt – are singing   ④ burnt – being sung
⑤ burning – be singing

11 다음 빈칸에 들어갈 말로 어색한 것은?

> A: Scott, you don't eat spinach any longer, do you?
> B: No, but I _____ when I was watching Popeye on TV.

① used to eat it a lot   ② ate it a lot
③ did ate it a lot   ④ used to do
⑤ did eat it a lot

12 다음 중 어법상 어색한 것을 모두 고르면?

① The little girl eats tomatoes on the chair is Sally.
② Spinach is actually considered one of the ten healthiest foods on the planet.
③ The researcher developing new material from carrots was Jenny.
④ Olivia was lied to all of us.
⑤ The people her family meeting in New York were so kind and gentle.

13 다음 밑줄 친 부분 중 어법상 어색한 것은?

① She did hide the book under the desk.
② All the jury do think she is innocent.
③ The poor do need the public support.
④ She does learn design 11 years ago.
⑤ Tom did repair his car this morning.

14 다음 중 어법상 옳은 것은?

① He sat surrounding by his friends.
② The old woman sat next to Mr. Brown was the mayor of the city.
③ Spinach can be using in a surprising way in the near future.
④ There was no pizza leaving for Mary.
⑤ The road leading to the city hall was full of traffic.

15 다음 문장의 밑줄 친 부분을 강조하는 문장으로 가장 알맞은 것은?

> Robert <u>ate</u> a basket of tomatoes.

① Robert ate so a basket of tomatoes.
② Robert did ate a basket of tomatoes.
③ Robert ate only a basket of tomatoes.
④ Robert did eat a basket of tomatoes.
⑤ Robert eating a basket of tomatoes.

서답형

16 다음 각 문장에서 어법상 <u>어색한 부분</u>을 하나씩 찾아서 알맞게 고치시오.

(1) Bill bought a book writing in Greek.

_____ ➡ _____

(2) Kate likes the potato juice mixing with honey.

_____ ➡ _____

(3) The volunteers took care of the cry babies in the orphanage.

_____ ➡ _____

17 다음 중 각 밑줄 친 부분의 쓰임이 주어진 문장의 밑줄 친 <u>did</u>와 같은 것은?

> The Americans <u>did</u> believe that something poisonous was in tomatoes.

① Everyone admitted Tom <u>did</u> his best.
② I <u>did</u> not have much information.
③ He <u>did</u> his role as a photographer.
④ I don't like it, but he <u>does</u> like it.
⑤ Monica has lots of things to <u>do</u>.

18 다음 중 밑줄 친 부분의 쓰임이 <u>어색한 것</u>을 <u>모두</u> 고르면?

① The students thought the story had lots of <u>touched</u> scenes.
② The dancing class may be the most <u>interesting</u> one here.
③ It was the most <u>excited</u> day of his life.
④ They were so curious that they tried to open the <u>locked</u> safe.
⑤ The clock is something <u>shown</u> you the time of the day.

19 다음 중 어법상 옳은 문장은?

① Spinach do keep our eyes healthy.
② Tim finally did made a sandwich cookie.
③ Liz does love seeing her pets.
④ Michael does plays the violin.
⑤ Barbara did called you yesterday.

서답형

20 다음 〈보기〉에 주어진 동사를 한 번씩만 사용하여 어법에 맞게 분사 형태로 빈칸을 완성하시오.

> ┌ 보기 ┐
> know, cover, mean, name, use, make

> I'd like to introduce you to the snowboard (A)_____ from carrots. Carrots are well (B)_____ for having a lot of vitamin A. The Scottish researchers made a light and strong material (C)_____ carrots. The snowboard is so strong and light that it is (D)_____ Crosscarros, (E)_____ that carrots cross the steep mountain (F)_____ with snow.

중요

21 Which of the following has the same usage as the underlined part below?

> The twins don't enjoy most vegetables, but they <u>do</u> like potatoes.

① Mary folds her arms and so <u>do</u> I.
② I'm sure that she <u>did</u> do her work.
③ Matt teaches math, <u>doesn't</u> he?
④ The students are <u>doing</u> some research on exercise.
⑤ What she <u>did</u> was to fix the roof.

서답형

22 다음 괄호 안의 어휘들을 배열하여, 우리말을 영작할 때 5번째와 10번째 단어를 쓰시오.

> 이것은 해바라기의 특성을 이용한다는 아이디어로부터 발명된 배터리이다.
> (using / a battery / of / the idea / sunflowers / this / the characteristic / invented from / of / is).

➡ _____, _____

01 다음 각 문장을 밑줄 친 부분을 강조하는 문장으로 바꿔 쓰시오.

(1) Sofia <u>found</u> her missing cat.

➡ _____

(2) Gordon <u>knows</u> many K-pop songs.

➡ _____

(3) Grace <u>wrote</u> these essays last week.

➡ _____

02 다음 괄호 안의 단어들을 바르게 배열하여 문장을 완성하시오. (단, 동사를 어법상 알맞은 형태로 변형할 것.)

(1) The _____ is waiting for her boy friend. (stand / girl / the street / across)

(2) Do you know the music _____? (by / on / play / the band / the stage)

(3) Luna is the one _____.
(a / wear / shirt / red)

03 다음 대화의 빈칸을 채우되, 동사를 강조하는 'do'를 활용하시오.

(1) A: It's amazing. I can't believe David really built the huge tower.
B: Yeah, but he _____ _____ it.

(2) A: Don't you think she should stop running?
B: I _____ _____ so. I've been worried about her.

(3) A: Can you believe Evelyn wrote the classical music only at the age of 3?
B: She _____ _____ the music at the age of 3.

04 다음 문장에서 어법상 어색한 부분을 찾아 바르게 고쳐 다시 쓰시오.

(1) This is the thing placing on the wall.

➡ _____

(2) Sarah is the one wore glasses.

➡ _____

(3) Mary is erasing the scores writing on the board.

➡ _____

(4) I do love Susan, the girl drunk water.

➡ _____

(5) The news was really shocked.

➡ _____

05 다음 두 문장을 '분사'를 활용하여 한 문장으로 만들 때, 분사에 대한 조건에 맞게 빈칸에 적절한 단어를 넣으시오.

(1) Lily tried to play with the baby. The baby was crying. (명사 앞에서 수식)
→ Lily tried to play _____ _____ _____ _____.

(2) They watched the birds. The birds were flying southwards. (명사 뒤에서 수식)
→ They watched _____ _____ _____ _____.

(3) There is a taxi. It is illegally parked. (명사 앞에서 수식)
→ There is _____ _____ _____ _____.

06 다음 우리말에 맞게 빈칸을 채우되, 괄호 안의 어휘를 이용하시오.

> Unlike Sarah (A)_____(sit) on a chair, the other members of the band played their instruments (B)_____(stand) on the stage, with Joy's eyes (C)_____(close).
> (의자에 앉아 있는 Sarah와 달리, 다른 멤버들은 무대 위에 서서 그들의 악기를 연주했는데, Joy는 눈을 감고 있었다.)

07 다음 문장을 각각의 주어진 조건에 맞게 강조하는 문장으로 바꿔 쓰시오.

> Alex called you yesterday.

(1) Alex 강조. 재귀대명사 사용.

➡ _____

(2) you 강조. It ~ that 구문 사용.

➡ _____

(3) called 강조.

➡ _____

(4) yesterday 강조.

➡ _____

08 다음 괄호 안의 어휘를 배열하여 우리말에 맞게 빈칸을 채우시오.

> _____,
> (Ethan이 정말로 두통을 느꼈기 때문에), he went to the clinic for treatment. (feel, did, as, a, headache, Ethan)

09 다음 우리말에 맞게 영작할 때, 빈칸에 알맞은 단어를 〈보기〉에서 찾아, 어법에 맞게 활용하여 쓰시오.

> ┤ 보기 ├
> kill   call   hide   do

(1) Stella는 재즈 음악을 정말 좋아한다.
   → Stella _____ like Jazz music.

(2) 어떤 과학자들은 시금치의 특성을 이용해서 땅속에 숨겨진 폭탄을 찾았다.
   → Some scientists used the characteristic of spinach to find bombs _____ in the ground.

(3) 그 곰이 개를 정말 죽였다.
   → The bear did _____ the dog.

(4) 코끼리 귀라고 불리는 식물은 독성이 있는 식물들 중 하나이다.
   → A plant _____ elephant ear is one of the poisonous plants.

10 다음 그림을 보고, 괄호 안의 어휘를 배열하여 우리말에 맞게 빈칸을 채우시오.

> If you want to keep insects away from your room, _____ in a corner of your room.
> 당신이 만약 당신의 방에서 벌레들을 쫓아내고 싶다면, 으깬 토마토 한 컵을 당신의 방 구석에 놓아두시오.
> (crushed / tomatoes / a cup / place / of)

➡ _____

Hidden Stories about Plants

Popeye and the Great Spinach

Popeye is a world-famous cartoon character. He gets his super power
by eating spinach. When Popeye became popular in the 1930s in the
by+동명사: '~함으로써'   *'~할 때'(접속사)*

United States, a lot of children began to eat spinach. Crystal City in
begin은 목적어로 to부정사와 동명사를 모두 사용할 수 있다.

Texas, which is called the spinach capital of the world, even built
관계대명사의 계속적 용법: 관계대명사 앞에 콤마가 있는 경우. that(×). is called: 수동태 구문

a statue of Popeye. Although eating spinach will not give us super
= Though

powers, spinach does have a lot of nutrients. It is actually considered
조동사 does가 일반동사인 have를 강조   *'~라고 여겨진다'*

one of the ten healthiest foods on the planet.
one+of+the+최상급+복수 명사: '가장 ~한 … 중 하나'

   Spinach can be used in a surprising way. When it absorbs water,
조동사가 있는 수동태: 조동사+be동사+p.p.

spinach also absorbs many other things from the soil. Some scientists

have used this characteristic of spinach to find bombs hidden in the
to부정사의 부사적 용법(목적)   *bombs를 수식하는 과거분사로 앞에 '관계대명사+be동사'가 생략된 형태*

ground. They make special spinach plants with sensors on their leaves.
~이 있는

When these plants soak up traces from bombs, the sensors light up.

hide 숨기다 (hide–hid–hidden)

spinach 시금치

cartoon 만화

capital 수도

statue 조각상, 동상

although ~임에도 불구하고, 비록 ~
이지만

nutrient 영양소

consider 고려하다, 여기다

planet 행성, 세상

absorb 흡수하다, 빨아들이다

characteristic 특성, 특징

soak up 흡수하다, 빨아들이다

trace 흔적, 자취

확인문제

● 다음 문장이 본문의 내용과 일치하면 T, 일치하지 않으면 F를 쓰시오.

1 Popeye gets his super power by eating spinach. ☐

2 Crystal City in Texas, which is called the spinach center of the world, even built a
statue of Popeye. ☐

3 Spinach is actually considered one of the ten healthiest foods on the planet. ☐

4 When it absorbs water, spinach also absorbs many other things from the air. ☐

5 Some scientists make special spinach plants with sensors on their leaves. ☐

6 When these special spinach plants soak up water from soils, the sensors light up. ☐

Carrots in World War II

In 1940, the Royal Air Force defeated German fighters during World War II by using a radar system. The British government wanted to keep this technology a secret, so it published an article in the newspaper. It said that British pilots improved their night vision because they ate a lot of carrots. Everybody believed the story and began to eat a lot more carrots than before. Can we really improve night vision by eating lots of carrots? Not really, but carrots contain a lot of vitamin A, which does keep our eyes healthy.

In the future, carrots may actually be used in wars. Scottish researchers have discovered a way to turn carrots into a very strong and light material. It can even be used to make battleships. This new material has already been used to make snowboards and bicycles.

Tomatoes, the Scariest Vegetables

We all know that tomatoes are good for our health. Up until the 1800s, however, most Americans thought that tomatoes were poisonous. In 1820, a man named Robert Johnson wanted to prove that tomatoes were safe to eat. So, he ate a basket of tomatoes in front of many people watching him. They all expected him to die, but nothing happened to him. Ever since then, Americans have enjoyed eating tomatoes.

We are no longer afraid of tomatoes, but some insects are still scared of them. If you want to keep insects away from your room, place a bowl of crushed tomatoes in a corner of your room. Insects will not come near the tomatoes.

defeat 물리치다, 패배시키다
radar 레이더, 전파 탐지기
system 시스템, 체계, 장치
government 정부, 국가
keep a secret 비밀을 지키다
article 기사
pilot 비행사, 조종사
improve 개선하다, 향상시키다
vision 시력
contain 함유하다, 들어 있다
researcher 연구원, 조사원
snowboard 스노보드
poisonous 유독한, 독성의
insect 곤충, 벌레
crush 으스러뜨리다

확인문제

● 다음 문장이 본문의 내용과 일치하면 T, 일치하지 <u>않으면</u> F를 쓰시오.

1 In 1940, the Royal Air Force won against German fighters during World War II by using a radar system. ☐

2 British pilots improved their night vision because they ate a lot of carrots. ☐

3 Up until the 1800s, most Americans thought that tomatoes were safe. ☐

4 Some insects are still scared of tomatoes. ☐

5 If you place a bowl of crushed tomatoes in a corner of your room, insects will come near the tomatoes. ☐

● 우리말을 참고하여 빈칸에 알맞은 말을 쓰시오.

1 _____ **Stories about Plants**

2 **Popeye and the Great** _____

3 Popeye is a world-famous _____ _____.

4 He gets his super power _____ _____.

5 When Popeye _____ _____ in the 1930s in the United States, a lot of children began to eat spinach.

6 Crystal City in Texas, which is called _____ _____ _____ of the world, even built _____ _____ of Popeye.

7 _____ eating spinach will not give us super powers, spinach _____ _____ a lot of nutrients.

8 It is actually considered _____ _____ _____ _____ on the planet.

9 Spinach can be used _____ _____ _____ _____.

10 When it absorbs water, spinach _____ _____ many other things _____ the soil.

11 Some scientists have used this characteristic of spinach to find bombs _____ _____ _____ _____.

12 They make special spinach plants _____ _____ _____ _____ _____.

13 When these plants _____ _____ traces from bombs, the sensors _____ _____.

14 **Carrots in** _____ _____ _____

15 In 1940, the Royal Air Force _____ German fighters _____ World War II _____ _____ a radar system.

16 The British government wanted to _____ this technology a _____, so it published _____ _____ in the newspaper.

17 It said that British pilots _____ _____ _____ _____ because they ate a lot of carrots.

1 식물에 대한 숨겨진 이야기
2 Popeye와 위대한 시금치
3 Popeye는 세계적으로 유명한 만화 캐릭터다.
4 그는 시금치를 먹음으로써 초인적인 힘을 얻는다.
5 Popeye가 1930년대 미국에서 인기를 얻었을 때, 많은 어린이들이 시금치를 먹기 시작했다.
6 텍사스의 크리스털 시티는 세계의 시금치 수도라고 불리는데, 이곳에서는 Popeye의 동상을 세우기까지 했다.
7 비록 시금치를 먹는 것이 우리에게 초인적인 힘을 주지는 않지만, 시금치는 정말로 많은 영양분을 가지고 있다.
8 이것은 실제로 지구상에서 가장 건강한 식품 10개 중 하나로 여겨진다.
9 시금치는 놀라운 용도로 사용될 수 있다.
10 그것이 물을 흡수할 때, 시금치는 흙으로부터 다른 많은 것들도 흡수한다.
11 몇몇 과학자들은 시금치의 이 특성을 땅에 숨겨진 폭탄을 찾는 데 사용했다.
12 그들은 잎에 감지기가 있는 특별한 시금치를 만든다.
13 이 식물들이 폭탄의 흔적을 흡수하면, 감지기가 빛난다.
14 제2차 세계대전에서의 당근
15 1940년, 영국 공군은 제2차 세계 대전에서 레이더 시스템을 사용해 독일군을 패배시켰다.
16 영국 정부는 이 기술을 비밀로 하기를 원했기 때문에, 신문에 기사를 하나 냈다.
17 그것은 영국 비행사들이 당근을 많이 먹어 야간 시력이 좋아졌다는 내용이었다.

18 Everybody believed the story and began to eat a lot more carrots _____ _____.

19 Can we really improve night vision _____ _____ lots of carrots?

20 Not really, but carrots contain a lot of vitamin A, _____ _____ _____ our eyes healthy.

21 In the future, carrots _____ _____ _____ _____ in wars.

22 Scottish researchers have discovered a way to _____ carrots _____ a very strong and light material.

23 It _____ _____ _____ _____ to make battleships.

24 This new material _____ _____ _____ _____ to make snowboards and bicycles.

25 **Tomatoes, the _____ Vegetables**

26 We all know that tomatoes _____ _____ _____ our health.

27 _____ _____ the 1800s, however, most Americans thought that tomatoes were _____.

28 In 1820, a man _____ Robert Johnson wanted to prove that tomatoes were _____ _____ _____.

29 So, he ate _____ _____ _____ tomatoes in front of many people _____ him.

30 They all expected him to die, but nothing _____ _____ him.

31 Ever since then, Americans _____ _____ _____ tomatoes.

32 We are _____ _____ afraid of tomatoes, but some insects are still _____ _____ them.

33 If you want to _____ insects _____ _____ your room, _____ a bowl of _____ tomatoes in a corner of your room.

34 Insects will not _____ _____ the tomatoes.

18 모두가 그 이야기를 믿었고 전보다 훨씬 많은 당근을 먹기 시작했다.

19 우리는 정말 당근을 많이 먹어서 야간 시력을 높일 수 있을까?

20 실제로 그렇지는 않지만, 당근은 많은 비타민 A를 함유하는데, 그것은 정말로 우리 눈을 건강하게 유지해 준다.

21 미래에는, 당근이 실제로 전쟁에 이용될지도 모른다.

22 스코틀랜드의 연구원들은 당근을 매우 강하고 가벼운 물질로 바꾸는 방법을 발견했다.

23 그것은 심지어 전함을 만드는 데 사용될 수도 있다.

24 이 새로운 소재는 이미 스노보드와 자전거를 만드는 데 사용되었다.

25 토마토, 가장 무서운 채소

26 우리는 모두 토마토가 건강에 좋다는 것을 안다.

27 그러나, 1800년대까지 대부분의 미국인들은 토마토에 독성이 있다고 생각했다.

28 1820년에, Robert Johnson이라는 이름의 남자가 토마토가 먹기에 안전하다는 것을 증명하기를 원했다.

29 그래서, 그는 그를 지켜보는 많은 사람들 앞에서 한 바구니의 토마토를 먹었다.

30 그들은 모두 그가 죽을 것이라고 예상했으나 그에게는 아무 일도 일어나지 않았다.

31 그 이후로, 미국인들은 토마토를 먹는 것을 즐겼다.

32 우리는 더 이상 토마토를 두려워하지 않지만, 몇몇 곤충들은 여전히 그것을 무서워한다.

33 만약 곤충들이 방에 들어오지 않게 하고 싶다면, 으깬 토마토 한 그릇을 방구석에 놓아 두어라.

34 곤충들은 토마토 가까이 오지 않을 것이다.

● 우리말을 참고하여 본문을 영작하시오.

1 식물에 대한 숨겨진 이야기
➡ _____

2 Popeye와 위대한 시금치
➡ _____

3 Popeye는 세계적으로 유명한 만화 캐릭터다.
➡ _____

4 그는 시금치를 먹음으로써 초인적인 힘을 얻는다.
➡ _____

5 Popeye가 1930년대 미국에서 인기를 얻었을 때, 많은 어린이들이 시금치를 먹기 시작했다.
➡ _____

6 텍사스의 크리스털 시티는 세계의 시금치 수도라고 불리는데, 이곳에서는 Popeye의 동상을 세우기까지 했다.
➡ _____

7 비록 시금치를 먹는 것이 우리에게 초인적인 힘을 주지는 않지만, 시금치는 정말로 많은 영양분을 가지고 있다.
➡ _____

8 이것은 실제로 지구상에서 가장 건강한 식품 10개 중 하나로 여겨진다.
➡ _____

9 시금치는 놀라운 용도로 사용될 수 있다.
➡ _____

10 그것이 물을 흡수할 때, 시금치는 흙으로부터 다른 많은 것들도 흡수한다.
➡ _____

11 몇몇 과학자들은 시금치의 이 특성을 땅에 숨겨진 폭탄을 찾는 데 사용했다.
➡ _____

12 그들은 잎에 감지기가 있는 특별한 시금치를 만든다.
➡ _____

13 이 식물들이 폭탄의 흔적을 흡수하면, 감지기가 빛난다.
➡ _____

14 제2차 세계대전에서의 당근
➡ _____

15 1940년, 영국 공군은 제2차 세계 대전에서 레이더 시스템을 사용해 독일군을 패배시켰다.
➡ _____

16 영국 정부는 이 기술을 비밀로 하기를 원했기 때문에, 신문에 기사를 하나 냈다.
➡ _____

17 그것은 영국 비행사들이 당근을 많이 먹어 야간 시력이 좋아졌다는 내용이었다.

➡ _____

18 모두가 그 이야기를 믿었고 전보다 훨씬 많은 당근을 먹기 시작했다.

➡ _____

19 우리는 정말 당근을 많이 먹어서 야간 시력을 높일 수 있을까?

➡ _____

20 실제로 그렇지는 않지만, 당근은 많은 비타민 A를 함유하는데, 그것은 정말로 우리 눈을
건강하게 유지해 준다.

➡ _____

21 미래에는, 당근이 실제로 전쟁에 이용될지도 모른다.

➡ _____

22 스코틀랜드의 연구원들은 당근을 매우 강하고 가벼운 물질로 바꾸는 방법을 발견했다.

➡ _____

23 그것은 심지어 전함을 만드는 데 사용될 수도 있다.

➡ _____

24 이 새로운 소재는 이미 스노보드와 자전거를 만드는 데 사용되었다.

➡ _____

25 토마토, 가장 무서운 채소

➡ _____

26 우리는 모두 토마토가 건강에 좋다는 것을 안다.

➡ _____

27 그러나, 1800년대까지 대부분의 미국인들은 토마토에 독성이 있다고 생각했다.

➡ _____

28 1820년에, Robert Johnson이라는 이름의 남자가 토마토가 먹기에 안전하다는 것을 증명하기를 원했다.

➡ _____

29 그래서, 그는 그를 지켜보는 많은 사람들 앞에서 한 바구니의 토마토를 먹었다.

➡ _____

30 그들은 모두 그가 죽을 것이라고 예상했으나 그에게는 아무 일도 일어나지 않았다.

➡ _____

31 그 이후로, 미국인들은 토마토를 먹는 것을 즐겼다.

➡ _____

32 우리는 더 이상 토마토를 두려워하지 않지만, 몇몇 곤충들은 여전히 그것을 무서워한다.

➡ _____

33 만약 곤충들이 방에 들어오지 않게 하고 싶다면, 으깬 토마토 한 그릇을 방구석에 놓아 두어라.

➡ _____

_____

34 곤충들은 토마토 가까이 오지 않을 것이다.

➡ _____

[01~03] 다음 글을 읽고 물음에 답하시오.

Popeye is a world-famous cartoon ⓐ character. (①) He gets his super power by eating spinach. (②) When Popeye became popular in the 1930s in the United States, a lot of children began to eat spinach. (③) Crystal City in Texas, which is called the spinach capital of the world, even built a statue of Popeye. (④) It is actually considered one of the ten healthiest foods on the planet. (⑤)

01 위 글의 흐름으로 보아, 주어진 문장이 들어가기에 가장 적절한 곳은?

> Although eating spinach will not give us super powers, spinach does have a lot of nutrients.

①   ②   ③   ④   ⑤

02 위 글의 밑줄 친 ⓐcharacter와 같은 의미로 쓰인 것을 고르시오.

① She is my sister, but we have very different character.

② He was a minor character in the book, but everyone loved him.

③ This Chinese character means good luck.

④ The climate of this city plays a big role in the city's character.

⑤ He is a man of fine character.

03 According to the passage, which is NOT true?

① Popeye gets his super power by eating spinach.

② Many children began to eat spinach when Popeye became popular in the 1930s in the United States.

③ People call Crystal City in Texas the spinach capital of the world.

④ In fact, eating spinach will give us super powers.

⑤ Spinach is actually considered one of the ten healthiest foods on the earth.

[04~06] 다음 글을 읽고 물음에 답하시오.

Spinach can be used in a surprising way. When it absorbs water, spinach also absorbs many other things ____ⓐ____ the soil. Some scientists have used (A)this characteristic of spinach to find bombs hidden in the ground. They make special spinach plants ____ⓑ____ sensors on their leaves. (B)When these plants soak up traces from bombs, the sensors go out.

04 위 글의 빈칸 ⓐ와 ⓑ에 들어갈 전치사가 바르게 짝지어진 것은?

　　　ⓐ　　ⓑ　　　　　　ⓐ　　ⓑ
① from – with　　② on – to
③ on – from　　　④ from – at
⑤ to – with

서답형

05 위 글의 밑줄 친 (A)this characteristic이 가리키는 것을 우리말로 쓰시오.

➡ _____

_____

서답형

06 위 글의 밑줄 친 (B)에서 흐름상 어색한 부분을 찾아 고치시오.

_____ ➡ _____

[07~09] 다음 글을 읽고 물음에 답하시오.

In 1940, the Royal Air Force defeated German fighters during World War II by using a radar system. The British government wanted to keep this technology a secret, so (A)it published an article in the newspaper. It said that British pilots improved their night ___@___ because they ate a lot of carrots. Everybody believed the story and began to eat a lot more carrots than before. Can we really improve night ___ⓑ___ by eating lots of carrots? Not really, but carrots contain a lot of vitamin A, which does keep our eyes healthy.

07 위 글의 빈칸 @와 ⓑ에 공통으로 들어갈 알맞은 말을 고르시오.

① version ② sense of touch
③ hearing ④ vision
⑤ sense of smell

서답형

08 위 글의 밑줄 친 (A)it이 가리키는 것을 본문에서 찾아 쓰시오.

➡ _____

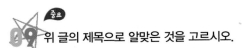

09 위 글의 제목으로 알맞은 것을 고르시오.

① Hidden Stories about Nature
② Carrots in World War II
③ How to Eat a Lot More Carrots
④ A Radar System of the Royal Air Force
⑤ Carrots, Good for the Night Vision

[10~12] 다음 글을 읽고 물음에 답하시오.

In the future, @당근이 실제로 전쟁에 이용될지도 모른다. Scottish researchers have discovered a way to turn carrots into a very strong and light material. It can even be used to make battleships. This new material ⓑhas already been used to make snowboards and bicycles.

서답형

10 위 글의 밑줄 친 @의 우리말에 맞게 주어진 어휘를 이용하여 7 단어로 영작하시오.

actually, used

➡ _____

11 위 글의 밑줄 친 ⓑ의 현재완료 용법과 같은 용법으로 쓰인 것을 모두 고르시오.

① How long has he been ill in bed?
② I have just finished my homework.
③ They have never seen such a horrible movie.
④ Has she met him yet?
⑤ I have lost my pen.

12 Which question CANNOT be answered after reading the passage?

① In the future, is it possible for carrots to be used in wars?
② What have Scottish researchers discovered?
③ How do Scottish researchers turn carrots into a very strong and light material?
④ Can the very strong and light material made from carrots be used to make battleships?
⑤ Has the very strong and light material made from carrots been used yet?

[13~15] 다음 글을 읽고 물음에 답하시오.

We all know that tomatoes are good for our health. Up until the 1800s, ____ⓐ____, most Americans thought that tomatoes were poisonous. In 1820, a man named Robert Johnson wanted to prove that tomatoes were safe to eat. So, he ate a basket of tomatoes in front of many people watching him. They all expected him to die, but nothing happened to him. Ever since then, Americans have enjoyed eating tomatoes.

We are no longer afraid of tomatoes, but some insects are still scared of them. If you want to keep insects away from your room, place a bowl of crushed tomatoes in a corner of your room. Insects will not come near the tomatoes.

13 위 글의 빈칸 ⓐ에 들어갈 알맞은 말을 고르시오.

① as a result   ② furthermore
③ that is   ④ for example
⑤ however

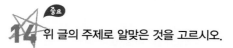

14 위 글의 주제로 알맞은 것을 고르시오.

① eating tomatoes to be healthy
② the spread of tomatoes in America
③ the myth and truth about tomatoes
④ the danger of eating poisonous tomatoes
⑤ how to keep insects away from the room

서답형

15 본문의 내용과 일치하도록 다음 빈칸 (A)와 (B)에 알맞은 단어를 쓰시오.

> If you place a bowl of (A)_____ _____ in a corner of your room,

you can keep insects away from your room. It's because some insects are still (B)_____ of tomatoes, they will not come near the tomatoes.

[16~18] 다음 글을 읽고 물음에 답하시오.

ⓐSpinach can be used in a surprising way. When it absorbs water, spinach also absorbs many other things from the soil. Some scientists have used this characteristic of spinach ⓑto find bombs hidden in the ground. They make special spinach plants with sensors on their leaves. When these plants ⓒsoak up traces from bombs, the sensors light up.

서답형

16 위 글의 밑줄 친 문장 ⓐ의 구체적인 용도에 해당하는 문장을 본문에서 찾아, 첫 단어와 마지막 단어를 쓰시오

➡ 첫 단어: _____, 마지막 단어: _____

17 위 글의 밑줄 친 ⓑto find와 to부정사의 용법이 다른 것을 모두 고르시오.

① I've worked hard to find bombs.
② But I don't know how to find bombs.
③ Is it easy to find bombs hidden in the ground?
④ Who is the best person to find bombs?
⑤ Let's start to find bombs together.

서답형

18 위 글의 밑줄 친 ⓒsoak up을 본문에 나오는 어휘를 사용하여 한 단어로 바꿔 쓰시오.

➡ _____

[19~21] 다음 글을 읽고 물음에 답하시오.

Popeye is a world-famous cartoon character. He gets his super power by eating spinach. When Popeye became popular in the 1930s in the United States, a lot of children began to eat spinach. Crystal City in Texas, which is (A)[calling / called] the spinach (B)[capital / capitol] of the world, even built a statue of Popeye. Although ⓐeating spinach will not give us super powers, spinach (C)[did / does] have a lot of nutrients. It is actually considered one of the ten healthiest foods on the planet.

서답형

19 위 글의 괄호 (A)~(C)에서 문맥이나 어법상 알맞은 낱말을 골라 쓰시오.

➡ (A) _____ (B) _____ (C) _____

20 아래 〈보기〉에서 위 글의 밑줄 친 ⓐeating과 문법적 쓰임이 같은 것의 개수를 고르시오.

━━┤ 보기 ├━━
① Eating spinach will keep you healthy.
② I saw her eating spinach.
③ He is fond of eating spinach.
④ Is eating spinach really good for your health?
⑤ When I met her, she was eating spinach.

① 1개　② 2개　③ 3개　④ 4개　⑤ 5개

서답형

21 How does Popeye get his super power? Answer in English in a full sentence. (6 words)

➡ _____

[22~24] 다음 글을 읽고 물음에 답하시오.

We all know that tomatoes are good for our health. Up until the 1800s, however, most Americans thought that tomatoes were poisonous. In 1820, a man named Robert Johnson wanted to prove that tomatoes were safe to eat. So, he ate a basket of tomatoes in front of many people watching him. They all expected him to die, but nothing happened to him. Ever since then, Americans have enjoyed eating tomatoes.

We are no longer afraid of tomatoes, but some insects are still scared of ⓐthem. If you want to keep insects away from your room, place a bowl of crushed tomatoes in a corner of your room. Insects will not come near the tomatoes.

서답형

22 위 글의 밑줄 친 ⓐthem이 가리키는 것을 본문에서 찾아 쓰시오.

서답형 ➡ _____

23 다음 문장에서 위 글의 내용과 다른 부분을 찾아서 고치시오.

In 1820, a man named Robert Johnson ate a basket of tomatoes in front of many people watching him and died against their expectations.

중요 _____ ➡ _____

24 위 글을 읽고 알 수 없는 것을 고르시오.

① Up until the 1800s, what did most Americans think about tomatoes?
② What did Robert Johnson want to prove?
③ Since when, have Americans enjoyed eating tomatoes?
④ What insects are scared of tomatoes?
⑤ If you place a bowl of crushed tomatoes in a corner of your room, what will happen?

[01~03] 다음 글을 읽고 물음에 답하시오.

Popeye is a world-famous cartoon character. He gets his super power by eating spinach. When Popeye became popular in the 1930s in the United States, a lot of children began to eat spinach. Crystal City in Texas, which is called the spinach capital of the world, even built a statue of Popeye. ⓐAs eating spinach will not give us super powers, spinach does have a lot of nutrients. ⓑIt actually considers one of the ten healthiest foods on the planet.

01 위 글의 밑줄 친 ⓐ에서 흐름상 어색한 부분을 찾아 고치시오.

_____ ➡ _____

02 위 글의 밑줄 친 ⓑ에서 어법상 틀린 부분을 찾아 고치시오.

_____ ➡ _____

03 본문의 내용과 일치하도록 다음 빈칸 (A)와 (B)에 알맞은 단어를 쓰시오.

Popeye, who gets his super power by eating spinach, is a world-famous (A)_____ _____. Thanks to Popeye, a lot of children in the United States began (B)_____ in the 1930s.

[04~06] 다음 글을 읽고 물음에 답하시오.

Spinach can ___ⓐ___ in a surprising way. When it absorbs water, spinach also absorbs many other things from the soil. Some scientists have used this characteristic of spinach to find bombs ___ⓑ___ in the ground. ⓒThey make special spinach plants with sensors on ⓓtheir leaves. When these plants soak up traces from bombs, the sensors light up.

04 위 글의 빈칸 ⓐ에 use를, ⓑ에 hide를 각각 알맞은 형태로 쓰시오.

➡ ⓐ _____ ⓑ _____

05 위 글의 밑줄 친 ⓒThey와 ⓓtheir가 가리키는 것을 본문에서 찾아 쓰시오.

➡ ⓒ _____ ⓓ _____

06 다음 빈칸 (A)와 (B)에 알맞은 단어를 넣어 땅에 숨겨진 폭탄을 찾는 데 시금치를 사용하는 방법을 완성하시오.

Spinach absorbs many other things in addition to water from the soil. When the special spinach plants with (A)_____ on their leaves soak up traces from bombs, the sensors light up and help people find (B)_____ under the ground.

[07~10] 다음 글을 읽고 물음에 답하시오.

In 1940, the Royal Air Force (A)[defeated / was defeated] German fighters (B)[during / while] ⓐWorld War II by using a radar system. The British government wanted to keep this technology a secret, so it published an article in the newspaper. ⓑIt said that British pilots improved their night vision because they ate a lot of carrots. Everybody believed the story and began to eat a lot more carrots than before. Can we really improve night vision by eating lots of carrots? Not really, but carrots contain a lot of vitamin A, which does keep our eyes (C)[healthy / healthily].

07 위 글의 괄호 (A)~(C)에서 문맥이나 어법상 알맞은 낱말을 골라 쓰시오.

➡ (A) _____ (B) _____ (C) _____

08 위 글의 밑줄 친 ⓐWorld War II를 읽는 법을 영어로 쓰시오.

➡ _____

09 위 글의 밑줄 친 ⓑIt이 가리키는 것을 본문에서 찾아 쓰시오.

➡ _____

10 위 글을 읽고, (1) 영국 정부가 신문기사로 당근의 효능에 관해 발표한 것과 (2) 당근의 실제 효능을 우리말로 쓰시오.

➡ (1) _____
_____

(2) _____
_____

[11~14] 다음 글을 읽고 물음에 답하시오.

We all know that tomatoes are good for our health. Up until the 1800s, however, most Americans thought that tomatoes were poisonous. In 1820, a man named Robert Johnson wanted to prove that tomatoes were safe to eat. So, he ate a basket of tomatoes in front of many people watching him. They all expected him to die, but nothing happened to him. ⓐ그 이후로, 미국인들은 토마토를 먹는 것을 즐겼다.

ⓑWe are no longer afraid of tomatoes, but some insects are still scared of them. ⓒIf you want to keep insects away from your room, place a bowl of crushing tomatoes in a corner of your room. Insects will not come near the tomatoes.

11 위 글의 밑줄 친 ⓐ의 우리말에 맞게 주어진 어휘를 이용하여 8 단어로 영작하시오.

Ever, then, have enjoyed

➡ _____

12 위 글의 밑줄 친 ⓑ를 다음과 같이 바꿔 쓸 때 빈칸에 들어갈 알맞은 말을 두 단어로 쓰시오.

➡ We are not afraid of tomatoes _____

_____,

13 위 글의 밑줄 친 ⓒ에서 어법상 틀린 부분을 찾아 고치시오.

_____ ➡ _____

14 Why did Robert Johnson eat a basket of tomatoes in front of many people watching him? Answer in English beginning with "Because". (11 words)

➡ _____
_____

Inventions from Plants

The Sunflower Battery is a good way to produce energy. It is a battery
to부정사의 형용사적 용법
invented from the idea of using the characteristic of sunflowers. Like
battery를 수식하는 과거분사(수동)   소유를 나타내는 of   전치사로 사용
sunflowers, it faces the sun during the day, so it produces more electricity than
= the Sunflower Battery   결과를 이끄는 접속사
other batteries.
other+복수 명사

구문해설 · way: 방법 · characteristic: 특성, 특징 · face: ~을 향하다
· produce: 만들다, 생산하다

해바라기 배터리는 에너지를 만드는 좋은 방법입니다. 그것은 해바라기의 특징을 이용한다는 생각에서 만들어진 배터리입니다. 해바라기처럼, 그것은 낮 동안에 태양을 향해서, 다른 배터리보다 더 많은 전기를 만들어 냅니다.

After You Read A Read and Match

1. Spinach

· the secret of Popeye's super power

· one of the ten healthiest foods on the planet
　　one of the+복수 명사: ~ 중의 하나
· used with sensors to find bombs hidden in the ground
　　to부정사의 부사적 용법(목적) 과거분사(수동)

2. Carrots

· used to make snowboards and bicycles
　　to부정사의 부사적 용법(목적)
· made into a very strong and light material
　　~으로(변화)
· containing a lot of vitamin A, which keeps our eyes healthy
　　= and it(계속적 용법의 관계대명사) keep+목적어+목적격보어(형용사) healthily(×)

3. Tomatoes

· good for keeping insects away
　　keep ~ away: ~을 가까이 오지 못하게 하다
· considered poisonous until the 1800s

구문해설 · spinach: 시금치 · snowboard: 스노보드 · contain: 함유하다, 들어 있다
· insect: 곤충, 벌레 · consider: 고려하다, 여기다

1. 시금치
· Popeye의 초인적인 힘의 비밀
· 지구상에서 가장 건강한 식품 10개 중 하나
· 땅에 숨겨진 폭탄을 찾기 위해 감지기와 함께 사용된다.

2. 당근
· 스노보드와 자전거를 만드는 데 사용된다.
· 매우 강하고 가벼운 물질이 된다.
· 많은 비타민 A를 함유하는데, 그것은 정말로 우리 눈을 건강하게 유지해 준다.

3. 토마토
· 곤충들이 가까이 오지 못하게 하는 데 좋다.
· 1800년대까지 독성이 있다고 여겨졌다.

Write

Potatoes are good for your health. They keep your heart healthy because they
　　　　　　　　　　　　　　　　　5형식 V +목적어+목적보어 종속접속사(이유)
lower blood pressure. They also solve your skin problems. Potato juice mixed
　　　　　　　　　　　　　　　　　　　　　　　　　　　　　　　　　과거분사
with honey makes your skin soft and clear. In addition, they help you lose
　　　　　　단수 동사에 유의 목적보어1 목적보어2 (병렬구조) to lose도 가능(help: 준사역동사)
weight. If you eat potatoes, you will stay full for a long time. Potatoes help
　　　　　　　　　　　　　　　　　　　　2형식 V+형용사(주격보어)
you stay healthy in many ways.

구문해설 · be good for: ~에 좋다 · keep+A+형용사: A를 ~한 상태로 유지시켜 주다 · lower: 낮추다
· blood pressure: 혈압 · in addition: 게다가 · stay full: 배부른 상태를 유지하다

감자는 당신의 건강에 좋다. 감자는 혈압을 낮춰주기 때문에 당신의 심장을 건강하게 지켜준다. 감자는 또한 당신의 피부 문제를 해결해 준다. 꿀을 넣은 감자 주스는 당신의 피부를 부드럽고 깨끗하게 만들어 준다. 게다가, 감자는 당신이 살을 빼도록 도와준다. 당신이 감자를 먹으면, 오랜 시간 배부른 상태를 유지할 것이다. 감자는 여러 가지 면에서 당신을 건강하게 지내도록 도와준다.

01 다음 중 단어의 관계가 <u>다른</u> 하나는?

① improve – get better
② absorb – soak up
③ contain – involve
④ consider – regard
⑤ defeat – yield

02 다음 중 주어진 단어를 풀이하는 말로 가장 적절한 것은?

nutrient

① someone who is asking questions at an interview
② an occasion when people sit down and eat, usually at a regular time
③ a chemical or food that provides what is needed for plants for animals to live and grow
④ all the different foods you use when you are cooking a particular dish
⑤ taste of a food or drink

03 주어진 단어를 활용하여 다음 우리말을 영어로 쓰시오.

(1) 그 마법사는 모자를 토끼로 바꾸었다.
(magician / turn)

➡ _____

(2) 내가 무엇을 하도록 조언하시겠어요?
(advise)

➡ _____

(3) 신선한 공기를 마시는 건 어때?
(why / you / some)

➡ _____

04 다음 빈칸에 공통으로 들어갈 말로 가장 적절한 것은?

• Yesterday the ship disappeared without _____.
• They could finally _____ him to an address in New York.

① happen
② email
③ trace
④ rule
⑤ notice

05 다음 중 주어진 단어의 밑줄 친 부분과 같은 의미로 쓰인 것은?

Crystal City in Texas is called the spinach <u>capital</u> of the world.

① English is written with a <u>capital</u> 'E'.
② A large amount of <u>capital</u> is invested in the company.
③ Paris is the fashion <u>capital</u> of the world.
④ The firm is having difficulty raising <u>capital</u>.
⑤ The cause of business failure is a lack of <u>capital</u>.

06 다음 우리말에 맞게 빈칸에 알맞은 말을 쓰시오.

(1) 그 감독과 배우 둘 다 정말 놀라운 사람들이야.
➡ Both _____ _____ and _____ _____ are really _____ people.

(2) 몇몇 방문객들은 그 개를 두려워했습니다.
➡ Some _____ _____ _____ the dog.

07 다음 대화의 빈칸에 들어갈 말로 적절하지 <u>않은</u> 것은?

> A: I forgot my promise with Sumi. I think she is really upset. _____
>
> B: Why don't you just say sorry to her? She will accept your apology.

① What do you think I should do?
② What do you suggest?
③ How I should keep the promise?
④ What's your advice?
⑤ What do you advise me to do?

[08~09] 다음 대화를 읽고 물음에 답하시오.

> B: Is ①<u>something wrong</u>? You don't look so ②<u>good</u>.
>
> G: I have a sore throat. I think ③<u>it's</u> because of the fine dust these days.
>
> B: Put ④<u>some plants</u> in your room. They take bad air in and produce fresh air.
>
> G: Really? I'll get ⑤<u>a little</u> plants right away.

08 ①~⑤ 중 어법상 바르지 <u>않은</u> 것을 찾아 바르게 고쳐 쓰시오.

_____ ➡ _____

09 다음 중 대화의 내용과 일치하는 것은?

① The boy doesn't care if something is wrong with the girl.
② The girl feels great because of the fresh air.
③ The boy thinks that the fine dust made the girl's throat sore.
④ The girl is going to get some plants after a long time.
⑤ The boy advises the girl to get some plants in her room.

[10~11] 다음 대화를 읽고 물음에 답하시오.

> B: How are your tomatoes doing? Are they growing well? (①)
>
> G: No. I've gotten only a few tomatoes so far. (②)
>
> B: Where do you have the pot? (③)
>
> G: In the kitchen.
>
> B: Well, tomato plants need about 7 hours of sunlight a day. (④)
>
> G: Oh, I see. I'll move the pot over to the window. (⑤)

10 ①~⑤ 중 주어진 문장이 들어가기에 가장 적절한 곳은?

> What do you think I should do?

①   ②   ③   ④   ⑤

11 대화의 내용에 맞게 빈칸에 알맞은 말을 여섯 단어로 쓰시오.

> For the pot to get enough sunlight, the girl will _____.

➡ _____

12 다음 대화의 밑줄 친 부분을 대신하여 쓸 수 있는 것은?

> B: Is something wrong?
>
> G: I'm just a little tired. I've watched a movie on my phone for two hours.
>
> B: That's why you have red eyes. Try putting a warm towel over your eyes.
>
> G: <u>O.K. Thanks.</u>

① Alright. Never mind.
② Okay, but I'm sorry.
③ I'll give it a try.
④ You should keep that in mind.
⑤ O.K. You're welcome.

Grammar

13 다음 중 어법상 올바른 문장은?

① A man naming Popeye is so strong.

② The teacher recommended vegetables growing by the farmers.

③ This is the material made out of carrots.

④ I love eating carrots contained a lot of vitamin A.

⑤ Those inviting to the party didn't show up.

14 다음 중 어법상 올바른 문장은?

① Vegetables does make you healthy.

② He does says she's crazy.

③ Jason is looks handsome on the stage.

④ Shelly did make a decision.

⑤ The Smiths do met them last year.

15 다음 빈칸에 알맞은 말이 바르게 짝지어진 것은?

- In the future, carrots may actually be _____ in wars.
- Some kinds of insects are still _____ of tomatoes.

① used – scared   ② using – scaring

③ using – scared   ④ used – scary

⑤ use – scaring

16 다음 우리말을 괄호 안의 단어를 활용하여 영작하고, 주어진 조건에 맞는 문장으로 바꾸시오.

Robert가 자신을 지켜보는 많은 사람들 앞에서 한 바구니의 토마토를 먹었다.

(1) 영작

= Robert _____

_____.

(tomatoes / many people / watch / eat / a basket of / him / in front of)

(2) '먹었다'를 강조, '관계대명사+be동사' 추가

= Robert _____

_____.

17 다음 밑줄 친 부분의 쓰임이 나머지와 다른 것은?

① Potatoes do help you in many ways.

② They do eat tomatoes every morning.

③ Angela does work for the company.

④ Maybe you can do some laundry once in a while.

⑤ Ron did play the superhero character.

18 다음 밑줄 친 부분의 쓰임이 나머지 셋과 다른 것은? (2개)

① Carrots containing a lot of vitamin A help keep you healthy.

② The researchers were busy developing the new material from carrots.

③ Many people watching 'Popeye' on TV liked to eat spinach.

④ People reading the article believed that carrots improved night vision.

⑤ Popeye gets his super power by eating spinach.

19 다음 그림을 보고 괄호 안의 단어를 활용해서 빈칸에 알맞게 채우시오.

(1)

➡ When I finished reading *The Little Prince*, it _____ (do) make me impressed.

(2)

➡ The most famous Egyptian pyramids are those _____ (find) at Giza, Egypt.

20 다음 문장들에서 우리말을 영어로 옮긴 것 중 어법상 어색한 것을 고르시오.

① 선생님은 팔짱을 낀 채로 학생들에게 얘기를 시작했다.
　→ The teacher began talking to the students with his arms folded.
② 그는 창문을 열어 놓은 채로 잠이 들었다.
　→ He fell asleep with the window open.
③ Scarlet은 다리를 꼰 채로 경찰관을 쳐다보았다.
　→ Scarlet looked at the police officer with her legs crossing.
④ 나는 셔츠가 완전히 젖은 채로 집에 왔다.
　→ I came home with my shirt all wet.
⑤ Elsa는 눈을 감은 채로 노래를 불렀다.
　→ Elsa sang with her eyes closed.

21 다음 중 각각의 (A)와 (B)에서 밑줄 친 부분의 쓰임이 서로 같은 것을 고르시오.

① (A) Frank <u>did</u> keep his promise.
　(B) They <u>did</u> something to correct it.
② (A) What should he <u>do</u> now?
　(B) Emma <u>does</u> believe what he says.
③ (A) Peter <u>does</u> eat a lot of spinach.
　(B) Susan knows that I <u>do</u> believe her.
④ (A) Everyone wonders how he <u>did</u> it.
　(B) <u>Do</u> be nice to others.
⑤ (A) <u>Do</u> you know when she will come?
　(B) People don't trust him even if he <u>does</u> good things.

22 다음 중 어법상 어색한 것을 모두 고르시오.

① The room does feel too cold.
② His uncle do likes playing with him.
③ Sandy did believe what you said.
④ Do be careful when you drive.
⑤ Mom did forced me to eat tomatoes.

23 다음 두 문장을 현재분사를 이용하여, 한 문장으로 만드시오.

• The man was Robert Johnson.
• He wanted to prove that tomatoes were safe to eat.

➡ The man _____
_____.

[24~26] 다음 글을 읽고 물음에 답하시오.

Popeye is a world-famous cartoon character. He gets his super power by eating spinach. When Popeye became popular in the 1930s in the United States, a lot of children began to eat spinach. Crystal City in Texas, which is called the spinach ⓐcapital of the world, even built a statue of Popeye. Although eating spinach will not give us super powers, spinach does have a lot of nutrients. ⓑ이것은 실제로 지구상에서 가장 건강한 식품 10개 중 하나로 여겨진다.

24 위 글의 밑줄 친 ⓐcapital과 같은 의미로 쓰인 것을 고르시오.

① We need capital investment.
② Please write in capital letters.
③ Cairo is the capital of Egypt.
④ He set up a business with a starting capital of £100,000.
⑤ He was sentenced to a capital punishment.

25 위 글의 밑줄 친 ⓑ의 우리말에 맞게 주어진 어휘를 이용하여 13 단어로 영작하시오.

> actually, consider, healthiest, planet

➡ _____

_____

26 본문의 내용과 일치하도록 다음 빈칸 (A)~(C)에 알맞은 단어를 쓰시오.

> We won't get super powers by eating (A)_____, but it really has lots of (B)_____. In fact, people consider it one of the ten (C)_____ foods on the planet.

[27~29] 다음 글을 읽고 물음에 답하시오.

In 1940, the Royal Air Force defeated German fighters during World War II by using a radar system. (①) The British government wanted to keep ⓐthis technology a secret, so it published an article in the newspaper. (②) Everybody believed the story and began to eat a lot more carrots than before. (③) Can we really improve night vision by eating lots of carrots? (④) Not really, but carrots contain a lot of vitamin A, which does keep our eyes healthy. (⑤)

27 위 글의 흐름으로 보아, 주어진 문장이 들어가기에 가장 적절한 곳은?

> It said that British pilots improved their night vision because they ate a lot of carrots.

①   ②   ③   ④   ⑤

28 위 글의 밑줄 친 ⓐthis technology가 가리키는 것을 본문에서 찾아 쓰시오.

➡ _____

29 According to the passage, which is NOT true?

① In 1940, German fighters were defeated by the Royal Air Force during World War II.
② The British government published an article in the newspaper, which said that British pilots improved their night vision by eating a lot of carrots.
③ Everybody believed the article and began to eat a lot more carrots than before.
④ We can really improve night vision by eating lots of carrots.
⑤ Vitamin A contained a lot in carrots does keep our eyes healthy.

01 출제율 95%

다음 중 단어의 관계가 나머지 넷과 <u>다른</u> 하나는?

① edit – editor
② teach – teacher
③ cook – cooker
④ sail – sailor
⑤ visit – visitor

02 출제율 100%

다음 중 밑줄 친 단어의 우리말 의미가 바르지 <u>않은</u> 것은?

① I <u>am afraid of</u> darkness. (~을 두려워하다)
② Why don't you <u>get some fresh air</u>? (신선한 공기를 마시다)
③ I think I <u>have a fever</u>. (열이 나다)
④ <u>In addition</u>, you should try harder. (게다가)
⑤ You should <u>keep away from</u> it. (~에 가까워지다)

03 출제율 90%

다음과 같이 풀이되는 단어로 가장 적절한 것은?

> a person in a book, play, film etc.

① actor
② director
③ character
④ founder
⑤ writer

04 출제율 95%

주어진 단어를 활용하여 다음 우리말을 아홉 단어로 이루어진 한 문장의 영어로 쓰시오

> 너는 여전히 너의 친구들과 연락하고 지내니?
> (keep / still)

➡ _____

05 출제율 100%

자연스러운 대화가 되도록 (A)~(D)를 바르게 나열하시오.

> (A) I have a sore throat. I think it's because of the fine dust these days.
> (B) Really? I'll get a few plants right away.
> (C) Put some plants in your room. They take bad air in and produce fresh air.
> (D) Is something wrong? You don't look so good.

➡ _____

[06~08] 다음 대화를 읽고 물음에 답하시오.

> G: What's wrong? You look worried.
> B: Well, I broke my mom's favorite plate.
>   (A)
> G: (B)Tell her the truth. She will understand.
> B: I hope you're right.

06 출제율 95%

다음 중 빈칸 (A)에 들어갈 말로 적절하지 <u>않은</u> 것은?

① What do you think I should do?
② What do you suggest?
③ What do you advise me to do?
④ What is your advise?
⑤ What can you do for me?

07 출제율 90%

주어진 단어를 활용하여 밑줄 친 (B)와 같은 의미의 문장을 쓰시오.

> what about

➡ _____

08 출제율 95%

Write the reason why the boy looks worried. Use the phrase 'It's because.'

➡ _____

09 다음 대화의 내용과 일치하는 것은?

> **B:** Bomi, do you have some medicine?
>
> **G:** Why? Is something wrong?
>
> **B:** I have a stomachache. I think I ate too much for lunch.
>
> **G:** Why don't you go for a walk?
>
> **B:** O.K. I'll give it a try.

① Bomi is suffering from a stomachache.

② There is a matter with Bomi.

③ Bomi will go for a walk.

④ Bomi wants to know why the boy needs some medicine.

⑤ Bomi doesn't give any advice to the boy.

10 다음 중 빈칸에 들어갈 말로 적절하지 <u>않은</u> 것은?

> **A:** I've found some money on the street. What do you think I should do?
>
> **B:** _____

① You should take it to the police station.

② How about taking it to the police station?

③ I suggest you should take it to the police station.

④ If I were you, I would take it to the police station.

⑤ Make sure taking it to the police station.

11 다음 중 밑줄 친 단어의 바로 앞에 '주격 관계대명사+be동사'가 생략되어 있다고 볼 수 <u>없는</u> 것을 <u>모두</u> 고르면?

① Spinach is the vegetable <u>considered</u> one of the 10 healthiest foods.

② What is the language <u>spoken</u> in Mali?

③ I'm <u>interested</u> in Mexican artworks.

④ Don't touch the baby bears <u>sleeping</u> with their mother.

⑤ Is there anyone who saw the <u>sleeping</u> beauty in the woods?

⑥ There are many school buses <u>parked</u> at the parking lot.

⑦ Jason's presentation was not impressive at all and even <u>boring</u>.

⑧ The cameras <u>made</u> in Taiwan are quite inexpensive and good in quality.

12 다음 중 어법상 어색한 문장을 <u>모두</u> 고르시오.

① You are make me happy.

② Carrots do contains vitamin A.

③ Sean did take good care of his dogs.

④ Munch did paint *The Scream*.

⑤ The kid did believe what the magician showed.

⑥ The citizens did understood what the mayor announced.

⑦ It were the books that he bought there.

13 다음 중 밑줄 친 부분의 용법이 나머지 넷과 <u>다른</u> 것은?

① She liked collecting the leaves <u>fallen</u> on the road.

② Some students went to see the works of Picasso <u>displayed</u> in the art museum.

③ Kelly was so proud of <u>being</u> the fan of BTS that she couldn't help crying.

④ My dad came home with a huge box <u>filled</u> with toys.

⑤ Do you know that pretty girl <u>smiling</u> at a lady?

14 다음 중 괄호 안의 단어를 분사로 바꾸어 빈칸에 넣을 때, 분사의 종류가 나머지 셋과 다른 두 개를 고르시오.

① Cathy likes to help _____ dogs. (abandon)
② The boys saw grey smoke _____ out of the chimney. (come)
③ Brandon must make himself _____ in Japanese. (understand)
④ She kept him _____ while she took some pictures. (wait)
⑤ Sofia didn't see the boy _____ at her at the meeting. (smile)

15 다음 두 문장을 접속사 Although로 시작하는 한 문장으로 고쳐 쓰되, 밑줄 친 부분을 강조하여 쓰시오.

• Eating spinach won't give us super powers.
• But spinach has a lot of nutrients.

➡ Although _____

_____ .

[16~18] 다음 글을 읽고 물음에 답하시오.

Popeye is a world-famous cartoon character. He gets his super power by eating spinach. When Popeye became popular in the 1930s in the United States, a lot of children began to eat spinach. Crystal City in Texas, which is called the spinach capital of the world, even built a statue of Popeye. @Although eating spinach will not give us super powers, spinach ⓑdoes have a lot of nutrients. It is actually considered one of the ten healthiest foods on the planet.

16 위 글의 밑줄 친 @를 3형식 문장으로 고치시오.

➡ _____

_____

17 위 글의 밑줄 친 ⓑdoes와 문법적 쓰임이 같은 것을 고르시오.

① She does not like fish.
② Not only does she speak Spanish, she's also good with computers.
③ Mom does the dishes.
④ What does he do in his free time?
⑤ He does look tired.

18 위 글을 읽고, (1) Popeye가 준 시금치의 이미지와 (2) 시금치에 관한 실제 사실을 우리말로 쓰시오.

➡ (1) Popeye가 준 시금치의 이미지: _____

_____

(2) 시금치에 관한 실제 사실: _____

_____

_____

[19~21] 다음 글을 읽고 물음에 답하시오.

In the future, carrots may actually be used in wars. Scottish researchers have discovered a way to turn carrots into a very strong and light material. @It can even be used to making battleships. ⓑThis new material has already been used to make snowboards and bicycles.

19 위 글의 밑줄 친 @에서 어법상 틀린 부분을 찾아 고치시오.

_____ ➡ _____

20 다음 빈칸 (A)와 (B)에 알맞은 단어를 넣어 위 글의 밑줄 친 ⓑ에 대한 소개를 완성하시오. 〈출제율 90%〉

> It is a very (A)_____ _____
> _____ material made from
> (B)_____ by Scottish researchers.

21 위 글의 주제로 알맞은 것을 고르시오. 〈출제율 100%〉

① the way to turn carrots into a very strong and light material

② the advantage of a very strong and light material

③ the uses of carrots in wars in the future

④ the products made from the same raw material

⑤ the material used to make snowboards and bicycles

[22~24] 다음 글을 읽고 물음에 답하시오.

We all know that tomatoes are good for our health. (①) Up until the 1800s, however, most Americans thought that tomatoes were poisonous. (②) In 1820, ⓐRobert Johnson이라는 이름의 남자가 토마토가 먹기에 안전하다는 것을 증명하기를 원했다. (③) So, he ate a basket of tomatoes in front of many people watching him. (④) Ever since then, Americans have enjoyed eating tomatoes. (⑤)

We are no longer afraid of tomatoes, but some insects are still scared of them. If you want to keep insects away from your room, place a bowl of crushed tomatoes in a corner of your room. Insects will not come near the tomatoes.

22 위 글의 흐름으로 보아, 주어진 문장이 들어가기에 가장 적절한 곳은? 〈출제율 95%〉

> They all expected him to die, but nothing happened to him.

①   ②   ③   ④   ⑤

23 위 글의 밑줄 친 ⓐ의 우리말에 맞게 주어진 어휘를 알맞게 배열하시오. 〈출제율 90%〉

> that / to eat / Robert Johnson / safe / tomatoes / a man / were / wanted / named / to prove

➡ _____
_____

24 According to the passage, which is NOT true? 〈출제율 100%〉

① All of us know that tomatoes are healthy food.

② Up until the 1800s, most Americans thought that it was safe to eat tomatoes.

③ Robert Johnson ate a basket of tomatoes while many people were watching him.

④ We are not afraid of tomatoes any more.

⑤ You can keep insects away from your room by placing a bowl of crushed tomatoes in a corner of your room.

[25~26] 다음 글을 읽고 물음에 답하시오.

Potatoes are good for your health. They keep your heart healthy because they lower blood pressure. They also solve your skin problems. Potato juice mixed with honey makes your skin soft and clear. ____ⓐ____, they help you lose weight. If you eat potatoes, you will stay full for a long time. ⓑPotatoes help you stay healthy in many ways.

25 위 글의 빈칸 ⓐ에 들어갈 알맞은 말을 고르시오. 〈출제율 95%〉

① In addition   ② Therefore   ③ However
④ By contrast   ⑤ For example

26 위 글의 밑줄 친 ⓑ의 내용을 본문에서 찾아 우리말로 쓰시오. (세 가지) 〈출제율 90%〉

➡ (1) _____
　 (2) _____
　 (3) _____

[01~02] 다음 대화를 읽고 물음에 답하시오.

> B: (A)몸무게를 줄이는 건 너무 어려워. What do you think I should do?
>
> G: Well, why don't you walk your dog every day?
>
> B: My dog would love it, but would it help me lose weight?
>
> G: Sure. When you walk your dog, you're actually exercising, too.
>
> B: O.K. I'll think about it.

01 주어진 단어를 활용하여 밑줄 친 우리말 (A)를 영어로 쓰시오.

> (it / so / hard)

➡ _____

02 대화의 내용에 맞게 빈칸에 알맞은 말을 쓰시오.

> The girl suggests that the boy walk his dog every day because she thinks it will help him _____ _____.

03 다음 상황을 읽고 빈칸에 알맞은 말을 쓰시오. 한 칸에 하나의 단어만 쓰시오.

> You come home from school and find that your mom is sitting on a chair. She looks like she is sick. You want to ask her if she is all right. What do you say to her?
>
> **You:** Mom, _____ _____ _____?

04 다음 중 밑줄 친 부분을 어법에 맞게 고치고, 고친 단어의 종류가 다른 두 개를 찾아, 그 이유를 설명하시오.

> ⓐ Spinach can be used in a surprise way.
> ⓑ They are waiting for the train leave at 7:00.
> ⓒ Popeye gets his power by eat spinach.
> ⓓ We saw a beautiful wall of a building cover with ivy.
> ⓔ She memorized a poem write by Ralph Waldo Emerson.
> ⓕ Since Robert's experiment, Americans have enjoyed eat tomatoes.

➡ ⓐ _____ ⓑ _____ ⓒ _____
　 ⓓ _____ ⓔ _____ ⓕ _____
　 이유: _____

05 다음 주어진 문장을 밑줄 친 부분을 강조하는 문장으로 바꾸어 쓰시오.

(1) British pilots ate a lot of carrots.

　➡ _____

(2) Place a bowl of crushed tomatoes in a corner of your room.

　➡ _____

(3) People in Hong Kong love freedom.

　➡ _____

06 다음 그림을 보고 괄호 안의 단어를 알맞게 배열하여 빈칸에 넣으시오. (동사는 어법에 맞게 변형 가능)

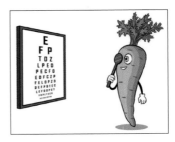

➡ Can we really improve night vision by eating lots of carrots? Not really, but carrots contain a lot of vitamin A, _____.

(keep, eyes, which, our, healthy, do)

[07~09] 다음 글을 읽고 물음에 답하시오.

We all know that tomatoes are good for our health. Up until the 1800s, however, most Americans thought that tomatoes were poisonous. In 1820, a man (A)[naming / named] Robert Johnson wanted to prove that tomatoes were safe to eat. So, he ate a basket of tomatoes in front of many people (B) [watching / watched] him. They all expected him ___ⓐ___, but nothing (C)[happened / was happened] to him. Ever since then, Americans have enjoyed eating tomatoes.

We are no longer afraid of tomatoes, but some insects are still scared of them. If you want to keep insects away from your room, place a bowl of crushed tomatoes in a corner of your room. Insects will not come near the tomatoes.

07 위 글의 빈칸 ⓐ에 die를 알맞은 형태로 쓰시오.

➡ _____

08 위 글의 괄호 (A)~(C)에서 어법상 알맞은 낱말을 골라 쓰시오.

➡ (A) _____ (B) _____ (C) _____

09 위 글을 읽고, (1) 1800년대까지 대부분의 미국인들의 토마토에 대한 생각과 (2) 1820년 이후의 미국인들의 토마토에 대한 태도를 우리말로 쓰시오.

➡ (1) 1800년대까지 대부분의 미국인들의 토마토에 대한 생각: _____

(2) 1820년 이후의 미국인들의 토마토에 대한 태도: _____

[10~11] 다음 글을 읽고 물음에 답하시오.

In 1940, the Royal Air Force defeated German fighters during World War II by using a radar system. ⓐ영국 정부는 이 기술을 비밀로 하기를 원했기 때문에, 신문에 기사를 하나 냈다. It said that British pilots improved their night vision because they ate a lot of carrots. Everybody believed ⓑthe story and began to eat a lot more carrots than before. Can we really improve night vision by eating lots of carrots? Not really, but carrots contain a lot of vitamin A, which does keep our eyes healthy.

10 위 글의 밑줄 친 ⓐ의 우리말에 맞게 주어진 어휘를 알맞게 배열하시오.

a secret / published / to keep / so / wanted / the British government / it / in the newspaper / this technology / an article / ,

➡ _____
_____

11 위 글의 밑줄 친 ⓑthe story가 가리키는 것을 본문에서 찾아 쓰시오.

➡ _____

01 다음 대화를 참고하여 빈칸에 알맞은 말을 쓰시오.

Brian: How are your tomatoes doing? Are they growing well?

Grace: No. I've gotten only a few tomatoes so far. What do you think I should do?

Brian: Where do you have the pot?

Grace: In the kitchen.

Brian: Well, tomato plants need about 7 hours of sunlight a day.

Grace: Oh, I see. I'll move the pot over to the window.

Brain wonders if Grace's tomatoes are _____. However, Grace says _____ so far. Grace wants Brain to give _____, so he asks her _____. Grace answers she has it _____. Brian tells her that _____, so Grace says that _____ _____.

02 다음 그림들을 보고, 괄호 안에 주어진 어휘들을 필요한 만큼 활용하여, 분사가 들어가는 문장을 영작하시오. (두 문장 모두 Unlike 로 시작하고 인칭과 시제 등에 유의하여 활용할 것.)

(boss, sleep, man, present the plan)

(I, my sister, read a book, sofa, clean, table, on)

(1) _____.

(2) _____.

03 다음 내용을 바탕으로 감자의 이로운 점을 설명하는 글을 쓰시오.

Main Idea
Potatoes are good for your health.
Supporting Detail 1
keep your heart healthy

• lower blood pressure
Supporting Detail 2
solve your skin problems
• make your skin soft and clear

Potatoes are good for (A)_____. They keep your heart healthy because they (B)_____. They also solve your (C)_____. Potato juice mixed with honey makes your skin (D)_____.

단원별 모의고사

01 다음 중 빈칸에 들어갈 말이 <u>다른</u> 하나는?

① I can't promise I can _____ it a secret.

② Kate, _____ away from the edge of the cliff.

③ After our summer class ends, let's _____ in touch!

④ We can _____ better use of our resources.

⑤ I told the driver to _____ the change.

02 다음 중 주어진 단어와 같은 관계가 <u>아닌</u> 것은?

library – librarian

① call – caller

② play – player

③ science – scientist

④ economic – economist

⑤ visit – visitor

03 다음 중 단어의 영영풀이가 바르지 <u>않은</u> 것은?

① hide: to cover something so that you cannot be seen clearly

② cartoon: funny drawing in a newspaper or magazine

③ carrot: a long pointed orange vegetable that grows under the ground

④ defeat: not to succeed in winning the battle

⑤ discover: to become aware of something that you didn't know about before

04 자연스러운 대화가 되도록 (A)~(E)를 바르게 나열하시오.

(A) Well, why don't you walk your dog every day?

(B) O.K. I'll think about it.

(C) It's so hard to lose weight. What do you think I should do?

(D) Sure. When you walk your dog, you're actually exercising, too.

(E) My dog would love it, but would it help me lose weight?

➡ _____

[05~06] 다음 대화를 읽고 물음에 답하시오.

B: _____ (A) _____ You don't look so good.

G: I have a sore throat. I think it's because of the fine dust these days.

B: Put some plants in your room. They take bad air in and produce fresh air.

G: Really? I'll get a few plants right away.

05 다음 중 빈칸 (A)에 들어갈 말로 적절하지 <u>않은</u> 것은?

① Is something wrong?

② Did anything go wrong?

③ What's the matter with you?

④ What did you do wrong?

⑤ Did something happen?

06 대화의 내용에 맞게 빈칸에 알맞은 말을 쓰시오.

The girl thinks that because there is _____ _____ these days, she has a sore throat. So the boy advises her to _____ _____ _____ in her room.

07 다음 대화 중 자연스럽지 <u>않은</u> 것은?

① A: What's wrong?

　B: I made a few mistakes in the math test.

② A: I have a headache. What do you think I should do?

　B: Why don't you go see a doctor?

③ A: Is something wrong?

　B: I can't sleep well these days. What should I do?

④ A: I lied to my friend, Sumi. Please give me advice.

　B: I think you should apologize to her.

⑤ A: I can't save any money. What do you suggest?

　B: How about buying more clothes?

08 다음 대화의 빈칸에 들어갈 말로 적절하지 <u>않은</u> 것은?

A: Is something wrong?

B: This problem is too hard to solve. What do you think I should do?

A: _____

① Why don't you ask the teacher for help?

② How about asking the teacher for help?

③ Make sure the teacher asks you for help.

④ I suggest you should ask the teacher for help.

⑤ You should ask the teacher for help.

09 다음 대화의 밑줄 친 우리말을 일곱 단어로 이루어진 한 문장의 영어로 쓰시오.

A: Is something wrong?

B: I am so nervous about tomorrow's contest. 내가 뭘 해야 한다고 생각해?

A: Why don't you relax and practice more?

➡ _____

[10~12] 다음 대화를 읽고 물음에 답하시오.

Anna: Suho, is something ①<u>wrong</u>? You're very quiet today.

Suho: I'm just a bit tired. I slept very little last night.

Anna: Did you do something ②<u>late</u> last night?

Suho: Yes, I watched a movie on my phone until 2 a.m. That's what I often do these days.

Anna: Oh, ③<u>that's because</u> you have red eyes. You should go to bed before midnight for your health.

Suho: I think my eyes are getting ④<u>worse</u>. What do you think I should do?

Anna: Try eating lots of carrots and tomatoes. They're rich in vitamin A, so they'll keep your eyes healthy.

Suho: ⑤<u>I see</u>. Thank you, Anna.

10 ①~⑤ 중 글의 흐름상 어색한 것은?

① ② ③ ④ ⑤

11 Write the reason why Anna advises Suho to try eating lots of carrots and tomatoes. Use the phrase 'It's because.'

➡ _____

_____

12 위 대화를 읽고 답할 수 <u>없는</u> 것은?

① Why is Suho very quiet today?

② Why did Suho sleep very little last night?

③ What does Suho often do these days?

④ What does Anna advise Suho to do for his health?

⑤ How long does Suho watch a movie on his phone?

13 다음 밑줄 친 부분 중 어법상 어색한 것을 고르시오.

① The new material <u>using</u> carrots can even be used to make battleships.

② Kevin felt <u>interested</u> in the healthy effects of spinach.

③ She likes the sound of <u>falling</u> rain.

④ Clocks are something <u>showing</u> you the time.

⑤ Olivia bought some vegetables <u>included</u> spinach, carrots, and tomatoes.

14 다음 중 주어진 문장의 밑줄 친 부분과 쓰임이 같은 것을 모두 고르시오.

> When it takes in water, spinach also <u>does</u> absorb many other things.

① <u>Do</u> we really improve night vision by eating a lot of carrots?

② She <u>doesn't</u> have any food to eat.

③ They <u>do</u> think it's even healthier to eat tomatoes every day.

④ <u>Do</u> not expect the man to help us.

⑤ Susan <u>did</u> the dishes by herself.

⑥ We all <u>do</u> know that tomatoes are good for our health.

⑦ I wonder how he <u>did</u> the trick.

15 괄호 안의 단어를 사용하여 어법에 맞게 주어진 문장의 빈칸을 쓸 때, 빈칸에 들어갈 말과 쓰임이 같지 <u>않은</u> 것을 고르시오.

> Scottish scientists turned carrots into a very strong and light material, which is already _____ (use) to make snowboards and bicycles.

① My father has invented a box _____ (design) to keep tomatoes fresh.

② She can't attend the meeting _____ (schedule) on Thursday.

③ Many people eat carrots _____ (contain) a lot of vitamin A.

④ Don't touch the tomato _____ (crush) to make insect repellent.

⑤ Sue gathered the dishes _____ (break) by her mistake.

16 우리말과 일치하도록 괄호 안의 어구를 바르게 배열하시오.

(1) 이 새로운 물질이 벌써 자전거를 만들기 위해 사용되어져 왔다.

(bicycles, material, been, has, to, new, this, used, make, already).

➡ _____

_____

(2) 어떤 과학자들은 땅 속에 숨겨진 폭탄을 찾기 위해 시금치의 이러한 특성을 이용해 왔다.

(this characteristic, bombs, to find, used, of, some scientists, have, spinach, in the ground, hidden).

➡ _____

_____

17 다음 중 밑줄 친 단어의 쓰임이 나머지 넷과 <u>다른</u> 것은?

① Crystal City in Texas <u>called</u> the spinach capital of the world is a small town.

② Vitamin A <u>contained</u> in carrots does keep our eyes healthy.

③ Some insects <u>scared</u> of tomatoes don't come near tomato crush.

④ Chinese do love eating <u>boiled</u> vegetables.

⑤ The female pop singer, IU, has <u>composed</u> a lot of good songs.

[18~19] 다음 글을 읽고 물음에 답하시오.

Popeye is a world-famous cartoon character. He gets his super power by eating spinach. When Popeye became popular in the 1930s in the United States, a lot of children began to eat spinach. Crystal City in Texas, which is called the spinach capital of the world, even built a statue of Popeye. Although eating spinach will not give us super powers, spinach does have a lot of nutrients. ⓐIt is actually considered one of the ten healthiest foods on the planet.

18 다음 문장에서 위 글의 내용과 다른 부분을 찾아서 고치시오.

> Popeye is a real person.

➡ _____   _____

19 위 글의 밑줄 친 ⓐIt이 가리키는 것을 본문에서 찾아 쓰시오.

➡ _____

[20~22] 다음 글을 읽고 물음에 답하시오.

In 1940, the Royal Air Force defeated German fighters during World War II by using a radar system. The British government wanted to keep this technology a secret, so it published an (A)article in the newspaper. It said that British pilots improved their night vision because they ate a lot of carrots. Everybody believed the story and began to eat a lot more carrots than before. Can we really improve night vision by eating lots of carrots? Not really, but carrots contain a lot of vitamin A, (B)which ⓐ____ our eyes healthy.

20 위 글의 빈칸 ⓐ에 keeps를 강조하는 형태로 바꿔 쓰시오.

➡ _____

21 위 글의 밑줄 친 (A)article과 같은 의미로 쓰인 것을 고르시오.

① We need an article of clothing.
② Have you seen that article about young fashion designers?
③ She didn't pay for the article she had bought.
④ According to the article 3, it is against the law.
⑤ This shampoo is a first class article.

22 위 글의 밑줄 친 (B)를 접속사를 사용하여 고치시오.

➡ _____

[23~25] 다음 글을 읽고 물음에 답하시오.

We all know that tomatoes are good for our health. Up until the ⓐ1800s, however, most Americans thought that tomatoes were poisonous. In ⓑ1820, a man named Robert Johnson wanted to prove that tomatoes were safe ⓒto eat. So, he ate a basket of tomatoes in front of many people watching him. They all expected him to die, but nothing happened to him. Ever since then, Americans have enjoyed eating tomatoes.

We are no longer afraid of tomatoes, but some insects are still scared of them. If you want to keep insects away from your room, place a bowl of crushed tomatoes in a corner of your room. Insects will not come near the tomatoes.

23 위 글의 밑줄 친 ⓐ1800s와 ⓑ1820을 읽는 법을 영어로 쓰시오.

➡ ⓐ _____   ⓑ _____

24 위 글의 밑줄 친 ⓒto eat과 to부정사의 용법이 다른 것을 모두 고르시오.

① It was safe to eat tomatoes.

② What is the best way to eat tomatoes?

③ I'm too young to eat tomatoes well.

④ Who chose to eat tomatoes?

⑤ Robert Johnson was brave enough to eat tomatoes.

25 위 글의 제목으로 알맞은 것을 고르시오.

① Tomatoes, Good for Our Health

② The Reason Americans Were Afraid of Tomatoes

③ Robert Johnson Liked Tomatoes Very Much

④ Tomatoes, the Scariest Vegetables

⑤ The Kind of Insects Which Are Scared of Tomatoes

[26~27] 다음 글을 읽고 물음에 답하시오.

We all know that tomatoes are good for our health. Up until the 1800s, however, most Americans thought that tomatoes were ____ⓐ____ . In 1820, a man named Robert Johnson wanted to prove that tomatoes were ____ⓑ____ to eat. So, he ate a basket of tomatoes in front of many people watching him. They all expected him to die, but nothing happened to him. Ever since then, Americans ⓒhave enjoyed eating tomatoes.

26 위 글의 빈칸 ⓐ와 ⓑ에 들어갈 알맞은 말을 고르시오.

① safe – harmless

② poisonous – safe

③ precious – harmful

④ harmless – precious

⑤ evil – poisonous

27 위 글의 밑줄 친 ⓒhave enjoyed와 현재완료의 용법이 다른 것을 모두 고르시오.

① I have studied English since the second grade of elementary school.

② They have lived in this house for 10 years.

③ She has never visited the National Museum of Korea.

④ His father has been dead for ten years.

⑤ I have watched the movie twice.

[28~29] 다음 글을 읽고 물음에 답하시오.

Garlic is good for your health. It keeps your heart healthy because it lowers blood pressure. It also helps you get over a cold. ⓐGarlic tea mixed with honey makes you get better faster. In addition, it helps you prevent future sickness. Eating garlic helps your body fight against bad viruses. Garlic helps you stay healthy in many ways.

28 How can garlic keep your heart healthy? Answer in English beginning with "By". (4 words)

➡ _____

29 위 글의 밑줄 친 문장 ⓐ에 생략된 단어들을 넣어 문장을 다시 쓰시오.

➡ _____

_____

MEMO

Lesson 4

This Is Korea

🎙 의사소통 기능

- 궁금한 것 묻고 답하기
  A: I wonder why he is running.
  B: I think he is late for school.

- 설명 요청하기
  A: Could you explain what this is?
  B: It's a traditional Korean hat. It's called a gat.

🎙 언어 형식

- '과거완료' had + 과거분사
  She kept laughing even after she **had been** in the water for over five hours.

- 간접의문문
  They didn't understand **why I wanted to take their pictures**.

Words & Expressions
교과서

Key Words

- **ad** [æd] 명 광고 (= advertisement)
- **attend** [əténd] 동 참석하다
- **audience** [ɔ́ːdiəns] 명 청중
- **audio guide** 음성 안내기
- **bakery** [béikəri] 명 빵집
- **beat** [biːt] 명 (북 등을 치는) 소리, (심장의) 고동
- **black-and-white** 형 (사진, TV 등) 흑백의
- **bookstore** [búkstɔr] 명 서점
- **breadwinner** [brédwinər] 명 생계를 책임지는 사람, 가장
- **breathe** [briːð] 동 호흡하다
- **bridge** [bridʒ] 명 교량, 다리
- **community** [kəmjúːnəti] 명 지역 공동체
- **complete** [kəmplíːt] 동 완성[완료]하다
- **continue** [kəntínjuː] 동 계속하다
- **copy machine** 복사기
- **destroy** [distrɔ́i] 동 파괴하다
- **device** [diváis] 명 기구
- **diver** [dáivər] 명 잠수부
- **environment** [inváiərənmənt] 명 환경
- **exhibition** [èksəbíʃən] 명 전시회, 박람회
- **female** [fíːmeil] 형 여성의
- **good harvest** 풍년
- **greenhouse** [gríːnhàus] 명 온실
- **harvest** [háːrvist] 동 수확하다
- **heritage** [héritidʒ] 명 유산
- **intangible** [intǽndʒəbl] 형 무형의, 만질 수 없는
- **jellyfish** [dʒélifiʃ] 명 해파리
- **marine** [məríːn] 형 해양의, 바다의
- **moved** [muːvd] 형 감동받은
- **nationwide** [néiʃənwàid] 형 전국적인
- **overseas** [óuvərsiz] 부 해외로, 해외에
- **overwork** [óuvərwərk] 동 과로하다
- **past** [pæst] 형 지나간 명 과거
- **path** [pæθ] 명 경로, 길
- **photographer** [fətágrəfər] 명 사진작가
- **press** [pres] 동 누르다 명 언론, 기자
- **promote** [prəmóut] 동 홍보하다, 촉진하다
- **realize** [ríːlàiz] 동 깨닫다, 인식하다
- **seafood** [síːfud] 명 해산물
- **several** [sévərəl] 형 몇몇의
- **suitable** [súːtəbl] 형 적합한, 적절한
- **sunshine** [sʌ́nʃain] 명 햇빛
- **tightly** [táitli] 부 단단히, 꽉
- **traditional** [trədíʃənl] 형 전통적인
- **trail** [treil] 명 좁은 길
- **underground** [ʌ́ndərgráund] 형 지하의
- **underwater** [ʌ́ndərwɔ́tər] 형 수중의, 물속에서
- **volcanic** [vɑlkǽnik] 형 화산의, 화산 작용에 의한
- **waterfall** [wɔ́tərfɔl] 명 폭포
- **wetsuit** [wétsuːt] 명 잠수용 고무옷, 잠수복
- **worldwide** [wɔ́rldwaid] 부 세계적으로

Key Expressions

- **a couple of** 두 서너 개의
- **a little bit** 조금, 약간
- **an intangible cultural treasure** 무형문화재
- **be good for** ~에 유익하다
- **be suitable for** ~에 적절하다
- **check ~ out** ~을 확인하다, ~을 조사하다
- **cheer up** 힘을 북돋아 주다, 격려하다
- **get into** ~에 들어가다
- **give (someone) a call** 전화를 걸다
- **give (someone) a hand** 거들어 주다, 돕다
- **give a presentation** 발표하다
- **give a talk** 강의하다, 연설하다
- **go on vacation** 휴가 가다
- **happen to** 우연히 ~하다
- **keep -ing** 계속해서 ~하다
- **make double-sided copies** 양면 복사를 하다
- **take a photo** 사진을 찍다
- **walk along** ~을 따라 걷다
- **Why don't we ~?** ~하는 것이 어때?
- **Why not?** 왜 안 되겠어?, 좋고말고.
- **wish for** ~을 기원하다
- **would like to** ~하고 싶다

Word Power

※ 서로 비슷한 뜻을 가진 어휘

- ad 광고(**advertisement**) : **commercial** 광고
- device 기구 : **tool** 도구
- moved 감동받은 : **touched** 감동받은
- several 몇몇의 : **a few** 몇몇의

- borrow 빌리다 : **rent** 임대하다
- environment 환경 : **surroundings** 환경
- path 경로, 길 : **trail** 좁은 길
- suitable 적합한, 적절한 : **proper** 적절한

※ 서로 반대되는 뜻을 가진 어휘

- borrow 빌리다 ↔ **lend** 빌려주다
- nationwide 전국적인 ↔ **local** 지역적인

- female 여성의 ↔ **male** 남성의
- suitable 적합한 ↔ **unsuitable** 부적절한

※ 동사 – 명사

- attend 참석하다 – **attendance** 참석
- continue 계속하다 – **continuity** 연속
- explain 설명하다 – **explanation** 설명
- realize 깨닫다 – **realization** 깨달음

- breathe 호흡하다 – **breath** 호흡
- destroy 파괴하다 – **destruction** 파괴
- promote 홍보하다 – **promotion** 홍보

※ 형용사 – 명사

- good 좋은 – **goodness** 선량함
- aware 알고 있는 – **awareness** 인식
- weak 약한 – **weakness** 약함
- polite 예의 바른 – **politeness** 예의 바름
- sad 슬픈 – **sadness** 슬픔

- ill 아픔 – **illness** 질병
- fair 공정한 – **fairness** 공정함
- kind 친절한 – **kindness** 친절
- happy 행복한 – **happiness** 행복
- dark 어두운 – **darkness** 어둠

English Dictionary

- **ad** 광고 (= **advertisement**)
  → a picture, set of words, or a short film, intended to persuade people to buy
  사람들이 사도록 설득하려고 의도된 사진, 어구, 또는 짧은 영상

- **beat** (북 등을 치는) 소리
  → one of a series of regular movements or hitting actions 일련의 규칙적인 움직임 또는 치는 동작 중의 하나

- **breadwinner** 생계를 책임지는 사람, 가장
  → the member of a family who earns the money to support the others 가족을 부양하려고 돈을 버는 가족 구성원

- **breathe** 호흡하다
  → to take air into your lungs and send it out again
  폐로 공기를 들여보내고 그것을 다시 내보내다

- **community** 지역 공동체
  → the people who live in the same area, town, etc.
  같은 지역이나 마을 등에 사는 사람들

- **heritage** 유산
  → the traditional beliefs, values, customs of a family, country, or society
  한 가족, 국가, 사회의 전통적인 믿음, 가치관, 관습

- **intangible** 무형의, 만질 수 없는
  → having value but not existing physically
  가치가 있지만 물리적으로 존재하지는 않는

- **overseas** 해외의
  → to or in a foreign country that is across the sea
  바다 건너 있는 외국으로 가거나 외국에 있는

01 다음 짝지어진 단어의 관계가 같도록 빈칸에 알맞은 말을 쓰시오.

> female : male = _____ : borrow

02 다음 영영풀이가 가리키는 것을 고르시오.

> having value but not existing physically

① underground ② traditional
③ volcanic ④ marine
⑤ intangible

03 다음 중 밑줄 친 부분의 뜻풀이가 바르지 <u>않은</u> 것은?

① All the <u>audience</u> stood up and gave the performer a big hand. (청중)
② We can't <u>breathe</u> in outer space. (호흡하다)
③ It is an important part of <u>community</u> life. (공동체)
④ She invited me to her photo <u>exhibition</u>. (전시회)
⑤ The trip was a great <u>experience</u>. (실험)

04 다음 우리말에 맞게 빈칸에 알맞은 말을 쓰시오. (철자가 주어진 경우, 그 철자로 시작하여 쓸 것.)

(1) 심해 잠수를 위해 잠수복을 가져와라.
  ➡ Bring a w_____ for deep sea diving.
(2) 그 영화는 전세계적으로 유명해졌다.
  ➡ The movie has become famous w_____.

(3) 그들은 지역 신문에 광고를 실었다.
  ➡ They put an _____ in the local paper.
(4) 우리는 강 위에 놓인 다리를 건넜다.
  ➡ We crossed the _____ over the river.

05 다음 문장의 빈칸에 들어갈 말을 〈보기〉에서 골라 알맞은 형태로 쓰시오.

> ┤ 보기 ├
> cheer up / wish for / get into / be good for / walk along

(1) Walking _____ your health.
(2) I _____ lots of interests for our new products.
(3) _____! You can do better next time.
(4) If you _____ the street, you can find the post office.
(5) It is hard to _____ the medical school.

06 다음 주어진 문장의 밑줄 친 press와 같은 의미로 쓰인 것은?

> Please <u>press</u> the start button.

① Jack blamed the <u>press</u> photographers for violating his privacy.
② Which switch should I <u>press</u> to turn it off?
③ Some people don't believe the <u>press</u> reports.
④ They are fighting for the freedom of the <u>press</u>.
⑤ The car accident in my town was reported in the <u>press</u>.

01 다음 짝지어진 단어의 관계가 같도록 빈칸에 알맞은 말을 쓰시오.

> thin : thick = future : _____

02 다음 우리말에 맞게 빈칸에 알맞은 말을 쓰시오. (철자가 주어진 경우, 그 철자로 시작하여 쓸 것.)

(1) 길은 단풍잎으로 덮여 있었다.
➡ The p_____ was covered with colorful leaves.

(2) 전 지역 공동체가 바이러스에 대해 걱정했다.
➡ The whole _____ was concerned about the virus.

(3) 그 밴드는 그들의 새로운 앨범을 홍보할 필요가 있다.
➡ The band needs to p_____ their new album.

(4) 해파리를 본 적이 있나요?
➡ Have you ever seen the _____?

03 다음 우리말과 일치하도록 주어진 단어를 모두 배열하여 완성하시오.

(1) 우리는 작년에 풍년이 들었다.
(last / harvest / had / we / a / good / year)
➡ _____

(2) 돈이 항상 행복을 가져다주지는 않는다.
(does / happiness / money / not / bring / always)
➡ _____

(3) 우리의 국가적 유산이 화재에 의해 파괴되었다.
(was / by / the / our / heritage / destroyed / fire / national)
➡ _____

04 다음 우리말을 주어진 단어를 이용하여 영작하시오.

(1) 우리는 한 시간 동안 길을 따라 걸었다. (along, for, street)
➡ _____
_____

(2) 이 책은 초등학생들에게 적합하다. (suitable, elementary)
➡ _____
_____

(3) 종이를 절약하기 위해 양면 복사를 하자. (let's, save)
➡ _____
_____

05 다음 문장의 빈칸에 들어갈 말을 〈보기〉에서 골라 쓰시오.

> ┤ 보기 ├
> realize / promote / underwater / volcanic / several

(1) This campaign will _____ the education for all ages.

(2) He didn't _____ that he was acting differently.

(3) I go hiking _____ times a month.

(4) The _____ photographer is diving into the sea.

(5) Dokdo was created from _____ activity.

Conversation

교과서

1 궁금한 것 묻고 답하기

> **A** I wonder why he is running. 왜 그가 달리고 있는지 궁금해.
> **B** I think he is late for school. 내 생각엔 그가 학교에 늦은 것 같아.

- 궁금증을 표현할 때 wonder(궁금하다), curious(궁금한, 호기심이 많은), want to know(알고 싶다) 등의 표현을 이용하여 'I wonder ~.'라고 말한다. 이때 어순은 'I wonder+의문사+주어+동사 ~.', 'I wonder+if/whether+주어+동사 ~.'이다. 또한 궁금한 내용을 'I want to know ~.', 'I don't know why ~.'로 표현할 수 있다.

- 'Can I ~?', 'Can/Could you ~?' 등과 같이 요구/요청을 나타내는 조동사 표현을 사용하여 'Can I ask you ~?' 또는 'Can you tell me ~?'와 같이 궁금한 점에 대하여 물어볼 수 있다. 그 외에 궁금증을 나타낼 때는 'Do you know ~?' 등을 사용할 수도 있다.

- 궁금함을 나타낼 때 'I wonder ~.' 대신에 쓸 수 있는 표현으로 'I'm curious ~.' 또는 'I want to know ~.' 등이 있다. 'I'm curious'와 명사구를 같이 쓸 때는 'I'm curious about+명사구'이고, 명사절과 함께 쓸 때는 'I'm curious if/whether ~.' 또는 'I'm curious 의문사+주어+동사'이다.

궁금한 것 묻고 답하기

- I'm wondering + if/whether 주어+동사/의문사절. ~인지 궁금하다.
- Can you tell me ~? ~에 대해 말해 줄 수 있니?
- Can I ask you + 의문사절? ~에 대하여 물어봐도 되니?
- I'm curious if/whether 주어+동사. ~가 궁금하다.
- I want to know 명사구/명사절. ~을 알고 싶다.
- I'd be very interested to ~. 나는 ~에 매우 관심이 많다.

핵심 Check

1. 밑줄 친 우리말을 괄호 안에 주어진 어휘를 이용하여 영작하시오.

   G: Wow, look at the bridge in this ad.

   <u>어디에서 찍은 사진인지 궁금하네.</u> (the photo, taken)

   B: That's Gwangandaegyo in Busan.

   G: How do you know that?

   B: I went there with my family last summer.

   ➡ _____

② 설명 요청하기

> **A** Could you explain what this is? 이게 무엇인지 설명해 줄 수 있니?
>
> **B** It's a traditional Korean hat. It's called a gat. 그것은 한국의 전통적인 모자야. 갓이라고 불러.

■ 상대방에게 궁금한 내용에 대한 설명을 요청할 때는 '설명하다, 말하다'의 의미를 가지는 동사 'explain', 'tell' 또는 'give information' 등의 표현을 사용하여 'Could/Can you explain 의문사절?', 'Could/Can you tell me more about ~?'라고 표현한다. Could 대신 Would, Can, Will 등을 사용할 수 있고, 'Do you mind if I ask you to explain ~?'이라고 말할 수도 있다.

■ 상대방의 말을 듣고 추가로 더 많이 설명해 달라고 할 때는 'Could/Can you tell me more about it?'이라고 한다. 좀 더 공손하게 표현하여 Can 대신에 Could나 Would를 사용할 수도 있다. tell 대신에 explain을 써서 'Could/Can you explain that more, please?'라고 할 수 있다.

■ 상대방이 말하는 의도를 모르거나 사용하는 단어의 뜻을 몰라서 설명을 요청할 때 쓰는 표현은 'What does that mean?(그것이 무슨 뜻입니까?)', 'What do you mean by that?(그것이 무슨 뜻이니?)' 등이다. 상대방의 말을 알아듣지 못했을 때는 'I'm not following you.(잘 알아듣지 못하겠습니다.)', 'I don't get it.(제대로 이해를 못하겠어요.)' 등의 표현을 사용하여 상대방이 다시 설명을 하도록 요청할 수도 있다.

설명 요청하기

- Could/Can you explain what this is? 이게 무엇인지 설명해 줄 수 있니?
- Could/Can you tell me more about it? 그것에 대해 좀 더 말해 줄 수 있니?
- I think I need some more information about it. 그것에 대해 정보가 더 필요한 것 같아.
- Could you give me more information? 좀 더 정보를 주시겠습니까?
- Could you be more specific? 좀 더 구체적으로 말해 주시겠습니까?
- What is the meaning of that exactly? 그게 정확하게 무슨 뜻입니까?

핵심 Check

2. 다음 대화를 자연스러운 순서로 배열하시오.

B: Excuse me, I'd like to use a copy machine.

(A) Sure. Press the button for double-sided copies, and then press the start button.

(B) Could you explain how to make double-sided copies?

(C) O.K. You can use this machine.

B: Thank you.

➡ ＿＿＿＿＿＿＿＿＿＿＿＿＿＿

Listen & Speak 1 A-2

B: Look over there. ❶I wonder why there are so many people waiting in line.

G: They're waiting to ❷get into the new bakery there.

B: Why? Is ❸it famous?

G: Yes. ❸It was on a TV program.

B: Really? We should try their bread then.

G: Sure.

B: 저기 좀 봐. 왜 저렇게 많은 사람들이 줄을 서서 기다리고 있는지 궁금하네.

G: 새로 생긴 제과점에 들어가려고 기다리고 있는 거야.

B: 왜? 유명한 곳이야?

G: 맞아. TV 프로그램에 나왔어.

B: 정말? 그럼 우리 저곳의 빵을 먹어 봐야겠다.

G: 그래.

❶ 궁금한 것을 묻는 표현으로 'I want to know why there are so many people waiting in line.' 등으로 바꾸어 쓸 수 있다.

❷ get into: ~에 들어가다

❸ It은 The new bakery를 가리킨다.

Check(√) True or False

(1) The boy wants to know why there are lots of people waiting in line.   T ☐ F ☐

(2) The new bakery became famous after it was on a TV program.   T ☐ F ☐

Communicate A

Jaden: Do you hear that? I wonder where that music is coming from.

Yuri: I think it's coming from over there. Do you want to go and ❶check it out?

Jaden: Yes, I love that strong beat. Is it ❷traditional Korean music?

Yuri: Yes, it's called nongak. It's a kind of ❸community band music.

Jaden: Nongak? ❹Could you explain a little bit more about it?

Yuri: It's traditionally used to ❺cheer up farmers and ❻wish for a good harvest.

Jaden: I see. Look! Some people are dancing to the rhythm.

Yuri: Yes, that's a big part of nongak. Dancing together completes the music.

Jaden: Let's join them.

Yuri: Sure. Why not?

Jaden: 저거 들리니? 저 음악이 어디서 오는 것인지 궁금하네.

유리: 저기서 나오는 것 같은데. 가서 확인해 볼래?

Jaden: 그래. 저 강한 비트가 마음에 들어. 이게 한국의 전통 음악이니?

유리: 맞아. 농악이라고 해. 공동체 악단 음악의 한 종류야.

Jaden: 농악? 그것에 대해 좀 더 설명해 줄래?

유리: 그건 전통적으로 농부들의 힘을 북돋아 주고 풍년을 기원하기 위해 사용되었어.

Jaden: 그렇구나. 봐! 몇몇 사람들이 리듬에 맞춰 춤추고 있어.

유리: 그래, 그게 농악의 큰 부분이야. 함께 춤추는 것이 음악을 완성하지.

Jaden: 저들과 함께 하자.

유리: 물론이야. 왜 안 되겠어?

❶ check (something) out: ~을 확인하다, 조사하다   ❷ traditional: 전통적인   ❸ community: 지역 공동체

❹ 상대방에게 궁금한 내용에 대한 설명을 요청할 때 쓰는 표현으로 'Could you tell me a little bit more about it?' 등으로 바꾸어 쓸 수 있다.

❺ cheer up: 격려하다   ❻ wish for: ~을 기원하다

Check(√) True or False

(3) Jaden and Yuri are listening to nongak.   T ☐ F ☐

(4) The strong beat is a big part of nongak.   T ☐ F ☐

Listen & Speak 1 A-1

G: Wow, look at the ❶bridge in this ❷ad. I wonder where the photo was taken.

B: That's Gwangandaegyo in Busan.

G: How do you know that?

B: I went ❸there with my family last summer.

❶ bridge: 다리
❷ ad(= advertisement): 광고
❸ there는 Gwangandaegyo in Busan을 가리킨다.

Listen & Speak 2 A-1

W: Excuse me, ❶I'd like to ❷borrow ❸an audio guide.

M: Here you are.

W: ❹Could you explain how to use ❺it?

M: Sure. Press this button, and it'll tell you what to do.

❶ would like to ~: ~하고 싶다
❷ borrow: 빌리다
❸ audio guide: 음성 안내기
❹ 'Could you tell me how to use it?' 등으로 바꾸어 표현할 수 있다.
❺ it은 the audio guide를 가리킨다.

Listen & Speak 2 A-2

B: Are you going somewhere this summer?

G: I'm going to Jejudo to ❶walk along the Jeju Olle Trail.

B: The Jeju Olle Trail? Could you explain what ❷that is?

G: It's a long hiking ❸path around Jejudo.

B: Oh, I see. I hope you enjoy your trip!

❶ walk along: ~을 따라 걷다
❷ that은 the Jeju Olle Trail을 가리킨다.
❸ path: 길

Progress Check 1

W: Look over there. ❶I wonder why there are so many cars on the road.

M: Lots of people are ❷going on vacation this weekend.

W: Really? Then, ❸why don't we go somewhere, too?

M: O.K.

❶ 궁금한 것을 묻는 표현으로 'Could you tell me why there are so many cars on the road?'로 바꾸어 표현할 수 있다.
❷ go on vacation: 휴가를 가다
❸ why don't we ~? = how about ~? = what about ~? = ~하는 게 어때?

Progress Check 2

B: Excuse me, I'd like to use a ❶copy machine.

W: O.K. You can use ❷this machine.

B: Could you explain how to ❸make double-sided copies?

W: Sure. ❹Press the button for double-sided copies, and then press the start button.

B: Thank you.

❶ copy machine: 복사기
❷ this machine은 복사기를 가리킨다.
❸ make double-sided copies: 양면 복사를 하다
❹ press: 누르다

● 다음 우리말과 일치하도록 빈칸에 알맞은 말을 쓰시오.

Listen & Speak 1 A-1

G: Wow, look at the _____ in this _____. I wonder _____ _____ _____ _____ _____.

B: That's Gwangandaegyo in Busan.

G: _____ do you know that?

B: I went there _____ my family _____ _____.

Listen & Speak 1 A-2

B: Look over there. _____ _____ _____ there are so many people _____ _____ _____.

G: They're waiting to _____ _____ the new bakery there.

B: Why? Is it _____?

G: Yes. It was _____ a TV program.

B: Really? We should _____ their bread then.

G: Sure.

Listen & Speak 2 A-1

W: Excuse me, _____ _____ _____ _____ an audio guide.

M: Here you are.

W: Could you _____ _____ _____ _____ _____?

M: Sure. _____ this button, and it'll tell you _____ _____ _____.

Listen & Speak 2 A-2

B: Are you going _____ this summer?

G: I'm going to Jejudo to _____ _____ the Jeju Olle Trail.

B: The Jeju Olle Trail? _____ _____ _____ what that is?

G: It's a _____ _____ _____ around Jejudo.

B: Oh, I see. I hope you _____ _____ _____!

Communicate A

Jaden: Do you hear that? _____ _____ _____ that music is coming from.

Yuri: I think it's coming from over there. Do you want to go and _____ _____ _____?

Jaden: Yes, I love that _____ _____. Is it _____ Korean music?

Yuri: Yes, it's called nongak. It's a kind of _____ band music.

Jaden: Nongak? _____ _____ _____ a little bit more about it?

Yuri: It's _____ used to _____ _____ farmers and wish for a _____ _____.

Jaden: I see. Look! Some people are dancing to the _____.

Yuri: Yes, that's a big part of nongak. Dancing together _____ the music.

Jaden: Let's join them.

Yuri: Sure. _____ _____?

Progress Check 1

W: Look over there. _____ _____ _____ _____ _____ _____ _____ _____ on the road.

M: Lots of people are _____ _____ _____ this weekend.

W: Really? Then, _____ _____ _____ go somewhere, too?

M: O.K.

Progress Check 2

B: Excuse me, I'd like to use a _____ _____.

W: O.K. You can use this machine.

B: Could you explain _____ _____ _____ _____ _____?

W: Sure. _____ the button for double-sided copies, and then _____ the start button.

B: Thank you.

[01~02] 다음 대화를 읽고 물음에 답하시오.

> G: Wow, look at the bridge in this ad. (A)I wonder where was the photo taken.
>
> B: That's Gwangandaegyo in Busan.
>
> G: (B)그걸 어떻게 아니?
>
> B: I went there with my family last summer.

01 위 대화의 밑줄 친 (A)를 어법상 바르게 고치시오.

➡ _____

02 위 대화의 밑줄 친 우리말 (B)를 5 단어로 영작하시오.

➡ _____

[03~04] 다음 대화를 읽고 물음에 답하시오.

> Tom: Are you going somewhere this summer?
>
> Jane: I'm going to Jejudo to walk along the Jeju Olle Trail.
>
> Tom: The Jeju Olle Trail? (A)Could you explain what that is? (tell)
>
> Jane: It's a long hiking path around Jejudo.
>
> Tom: Oh, I see. I hope you enjoy your trip!

03 위 대화의 밑줄 친 (A)와 의미가 같도록 주어진 단어를 사용하여 바꿔 쓰시오.

➡ _____

04 위 대화의 내용과 일치하지 <u>않는</u> 것은?

① Jane은 이번 여름에 제주도에 갈 예정이다.
② Jane은 제주도에서 올레길을 걸을 것이다.
③ 올레길은 제주도 둘레에 있는 긴 하이킹 코스이다.
④ Tom은 Jane이 즐거운 여행을 하길 바란다.
⑤ Tom은 이미 올레길에 대해 잘 알고 있다.

서답형

01 다음 대화가 자연스럽게 이어지도록 순서대로 배열하시오.

> Look over there. I wonder why there are so many people waiting in line.

> (A) Sure.
> (B) Yes. It was on a TV program.
> (C) Why? Is it famous?
> (D) Really? We should try their bread then.
> (E) They're waiting to get into the new bakery there.

➡ _____

중요

02 다음 대화의 빈칸 (A)에 들어갈 말로 적절하지 <u>않은</u> 것은?

> W: Excuse me, I'd like to borrow an audio guide.
> M: Here you are.
> W: _____(A)_____
> M: Sure. Press this button, and it'll tell you what to do.

① Could you explain how to use it?
② Can you tell me how to use it?
③ Could you give me more information about how to use it?
④ Could you be more specific about how to use it?
⑤ What do you mean by that?

[03~04] 다음 대화를 읽고 물음에 답하시오.

> G: Wow, ⓐ<u>look</u> at the bridge in this ad. I wonder where the photo ⓑ<u>took</u>.
> B: That's Gwangandaegyo ⓒ<u>in</u> Busan.
> G: How do you know ⓓ<u>that</u>?
> B: I went ⓔ<u>there</u> with my family last summer.

서답형

03 위 대화의 밑줄 친 ⓐ~ⓔ 중 어법상 <u>틀린</u> 것을 찾아 바르게 고치시오.

➡ _____

중요

04 위 대화의 내용과 일치하지 <u>않는</u> 것은?

① The girl and the boy are watching the ad.
② There is a bridge in the ad.
③ The girl wants to know where the photo of the bridge was taken.
④ The boy visited Busan with his family last summer.
⑤ The girl wants to take a photo of the bridge.

[05~06] 다음 대화를 읽고 물음에 답하시오.

> Brian: Look over there. I wonder why there are so many people (A)[waited / waiting] in line.
> Sujin: They're waiting to (B)[get into / get out] the new bakery there.
> Brian: Why? Is it famous?
> Sujin: Yes. It was (C)[on / off] a TV program.
> Brian: Really? We should try their bread then.
> Sujin: Sure.

05 위 대화의 (A)~(C)에 들어갈 말로 바르게 짝지어진 것은?

	(A)	(B)	(C)
①	waited	get into	on
②	waited	get out	off
③	waiting	get out	on
④	waiting	get out	off
⑤	waiting	get into	on

06 위 대화의 내용과 일치하지 <u>않는</u> 것은?

① Brian은 왜 많은 사람들이 줄을 서서 기다리고 있는지 궁금하다.

② 새로 생긴 제과점에 들어가려고 많은 사람들이 줄을 서 있다.

③ 새로 생긴 제과점이 TV 프로그램에 나왔다.

④ Brian은 새로 생긴 제과점의 빵을 먹어 보고 싶다.

⑤ Brian과 수진은 함께 제과점 앞에서 줄을 서서 기다리고 있었다.

서답형

07 다음 대화가 자연스럽게 이어지도록 순서대로 배열하시오.

(A) Thank you.
(B) O.K. You can use this machine.
(C) Excuse me, I'd like to use a copy machine.
(D) Could you explain how to make double-sided copies?
(E) Sure. Press the button for double-sided copies, and then press the start button.

➡ _____

[08~09] 다음 대화를 읽고 물음에 답하시오.

Jaden: Do you hear that? (a)<u>I wonder where that music is coming from.</u>

Yuri: I think it's coming from over there. Do you want to go and check it out?

Jaden: Yes, I love that strong beat. Is it traditional Korean music?

Yuri: Yes, it's called nongak. It's a kind of community band music.

Jaden: Nongak? Could you explain a little bit more about it?

Yuri: It's traditionally used to cheer up farmers and wish for a good harvest.

Jaden: I see. Look! Some people are dancing to the rhythm.

Yuri: Yes, that's a big part of nongak. (b)<u>함께 춤추는 것이 음악을 완성하지</u>. (together)

Jaden: Let's join them.

Yuri: Sure. Why not?

08 위 대화의 밑줄 친 (a)와 바꾸어 쓸 수 있는 것을 고르시오.

① I don't know where that music is coming from.

② I'm sure where that music is coming from.

③ It's not certain where that music is coming from.

④ I want to know where that music is coming from.

⑤ I've been told where that music is coming from.

09 위 대화의 밑줄 친 (b)를 주어진 단어를 사용하여 5 단어로 영작하시오.

➡ _____

10 다음 짝지어진 대화가 <u>어색한</u> 것은?

① A: Look at the boy. I wonder why he is running.
   B: I think he is late for school.

② A: Look at her. I wonder why she looks surprised.
   B: I think she saw a celebrity.

③ A: Could you explain what this is?
   B: It's a traditional Korean hairpin. It's called a binyeo.

④ A: Can you tell me how to use this machine?
   B: Sure. Press this button first.

⑤ A: I want to know where the photo was taken.
   B: Thank you for your great efforts.

[01~02] 다음 대화를 읽고 물음에 답하시오.

> W: Excuse me, I'd like to borrow an audio guide.
> M: Here you are.
> W: _____
> M: Sure. Press this button, and it'll tell you what to do.

01 위 대화의 빈칸에 들어갈 말을 주어진 단어를 배열하여 영작하시오.

> you / how / it / could / to / explain / use

➡ _____

02 What does the woman get to know after pressing the button?

➡ _____

03 다음 대화의 내용과 일치하도록 빈칸을 완성하시오.

> Brian: Look over there. I wonder why there are so many people waiting in line.
> Sujin: They're waiting to get into the new bakery there.
> Brian: Why? Is it famous?
> Sujin: Yes. It was on a TV program.
> Brian: Really? We should try their bread then.
> Sujin: Sure.

> Brian and Sujin saw many people (A) _____ in front of (B) _____. People wanted to (C) _____ there. The new bakery was so popular because (D) _____. Brian and Sujin wanted to try its bread together.

[04~05] 다음 대화를 읽고 물음에 답하시오.

> Jaden: Do you hear that? I wonder where that music is coming from.
> Yuri: I think it's coming from over there. Do you want to go and check it out?
> Jaden: Yes, I love that strong beat. Is it traditional Korean music?
> Yuri: Yes, it's called nongak. It's a kind of community band music.
> Jaden: Nongak? Could you explain a little bit more about it?
> Yuri: It's traditionally used to cheer up farmers and wish for a good harvest.
> Jaden: I see. Look! Some people are dancing to the rhythm.
> Yuri: Yes, that's a big part of nongak. Dancing together completes the music.
> Jaden: Let's join them.
> Yuri: Sure. Why not?

04 위 대화를 읽고 빈칸에 알맞은 말을 써 넣으시오.

> **VISIT Korea**
> About Korea | **Culture** | Food | Travel | More
>
> Nongak …
> • is a community ___(1)___ music
> • has ___(2)___ beats
> • cheers up ___(3)___
> • wishes for a good ___(4)___

➡ (1) _____ (2) _____ (3) _____
(4) _____

05 What are Jaden and Yuri going to do after the conversation?

➡ _____
_____

Grammar

① '과거완료' had + 과거분사

- Until then, I **had** only **seen** black-and-white photos of haenyeo.
  그때까지, 나는 흑백 사진 속의 해녀만 보았다.
- She kept laughing even after she **had been** in the water for over five hours.
  그녀는 다섯 시간이 넘도록 물속에 있은 후에도 계속 웃었다.

■ 과거완료시제는 'had+과거분사' 형태로 표현하며, 과거의 어느 시점을 기준으로 그 이전에 일어난 동작이나 상태를 나타낸다.
  - Somi went shopping at the local market after she **had gone** swimming at Hyeopjae Beach.
    소미는 협재 해변으로 수영하러 간 후, 지역 시장으로 쇼핑하러 갔다.

■ 과거의 특정 시점을 기준으로 그 이전에 일어난 동작의 완료, 경험, 계속, 결과를 나타낸다.
  - (1) 완료: '막 ~했었다'는 의미로 과거 이전에 시작된 동작이 과거의 어느 시점에 완료된 일을 나타낸다. 보통 already, yet 등의 부사와 함께 쓰인다.
    - When I arrived, the class **had** already **begun**. 내가 도착했을 때, 수업이 벌써 시작됐다.
  - (2) 경험: '~한 적이 있었다'는 의미로 과거 이전부터 과거의 어느 시점까지의 경험을 나타낸다. 보통 never, ever, once, twice, before 등의 부사(구)와 함께 쓰인다.
    - Barbara recognized the suspect immediately, for she **had met** him online before.
      Barbara는 그 용의자를 즉시 알아봤는데, 전에 온라인상에서 그를 만난 적이 있었기 때문이었다.
  - (3) 결과: '(과거 이전에) ~해서, 그 결과 …했다'는 의미로 과거 이전의 동작이 과거의 어느 시점의 결과에 영향을 미치는 것을 나타낸다.
    - He **had gone** to work when I called. 내가 전화했을 때, 그는 (이미) 출근했다.
  - (4) 계속: '계속 ~하고 있었다'는 의미로 과거 이전부터 과거의 어느 시점까지 계속되는 동작이나 상태를 나타낸다. 보통 since, for 등과 함께 쓰인다.
    - Tiffany **had waited** for her brother for 2 years when he returned.
      그녀의 오빠가 돌아왔을 때, Tiffany는 오빠를 2년 동안이나 기다렸었다.

■ 부정문은 'had+not[never]+과거분사', 의문문은 'Had+주어+과거분사 ~?', 과거 어느 시점을 기준으로 전부터 진행 중인 동작을 강조할 때는 과거완료진행형 'had+been+V-ing'을 쓴다.
  - She **had never won** an Academy Award by then. 그녀는 그 때까지 아카데미상을 탄 적이 없었다.
  - **Had they met** the director before? 그들이 전에 감독을 만난 적이 있었나요?
  - I **had been watching** a movie until you came to see me. 당신이 나를 보러올 때까지 나는 영화를 보고 있었다.

핵심 Check

1. 괄호 안에서 알맞은 말을 고르시오.
   (1) My family (has / had) lived in Seoul before we moved to Busan.
   (2) Suji had never seen wild animals until she (visits / visited) the zoo.

② 간접의문문

- They didn't understand **why I wanted to take their pictures.**
  그들은 내가 왜 그들의 사진을 찍으려고 하는지 이해하지 못했다.

- Please tell us **what you're planning to do in the future.**
  앞으로 계획하고 있는 것에 대해 말씀해 주세요.

■ 간접의문문은 의문문이 다른 문장의 일부가 된 형태로 '의문사+주어+동사' 형태로 쓰며, 이때 의문사가 접속사 역할을 한다.

  • I want to know. + Where is he from?

  → I want to know **where he is from.** 나는 그가 어디에서 왔는지 알고 싶다.

  • I wonder. + Why did she leave so early?

  → I wonder **why she left so early.** 나는 그녀가 왜 그렇게 빨리 떠났는지 궁금하다.

■ 의문문의 '동사+주어'의 어순이, 간접의문문에서 '주어+동사'의 어순이 되지만, 의문사가 주어인 의문문은 어순의 변화가 생길 수 없다.

  • My teacher will tell us. + Who called the police?

  → My teacher will tell us **who called the police.**
    나의 선생님은 누가 경찰에게 전화를 했는지 우리에게 말해 줄 것이다.

■ 의문사가 없는 경우, **if** 또는 **whether**가 '~인지 (아닌지)'라는 의미의 명사절을 이끈다.

  • I don't know. + Does she like me?

  → I don't know **if[whether] she likes me.** 나는 그녀가 나를 좋아하는지 알지 못한다.

  • Tell us. + Is the lady married or not?

  → Tell us **if[whether] the lady is married or not.** 그 숙녀분이 결혼했는지 안 했는지를 우리에게 말해 주시오.

■ 생각이나 추측, 상상, 믿음 등을 나타내는 동사들(think, believe, guess, suppose, imagine)이 쓰인 문장에서 의문사가 이끄는 간접의문문이 목적어가 될 때, 간접의문문의 의문사를 문장 맨 앞으로 보낸다. 이 경우, 의문사가 문두로 가도, 어순은 '주어+동사'이다.

  • Do you believe? + What does he have in his bag?

  → **What** do you believe **he has in his bag?** 당신은 그의 가방 속에 그가 무엇을 가지고 있다고 생각합니까?

  • Do you think? + Who is going to marry you?

  → **Who** do you think **is going to marry you?** 당신은 누가 당신과 결혼할 것이라고 생각합니까?

핵심 Check

2. 다음 문장에서 어법상 **틀린** 부분을 찾아 바르게 고쳐 쓰시오.

(1) I wonder when will she make us the cookie. ➡ _____

(2) Nobody knows why was Sarah so upset. ➡ _____

01 다음 빈칸에 들어갈 말로 알맞은 것은?

> Parker was sure he _____ his laptop on the table last night, but he couldn't find it.

① put ② puts ③ has put
④ to put ⑤ had put

02 다음 두 문장을 한 문장으로 바꿔 쓸 때, 빈칸에 들어갈 말로 가장 적절한 것은?

> • Does Andy know?
> • Is that bus going to the airport?
> → Does Andy know _____ that bus is going to the airport?

① where ② but ③ if ④ how ⑤ so

03 다음 밑줄 친 부분 중 어법상 옳은 것을 고르시오.

① The old man had lived in the town for 40 years until now.
② The plane has already taken off when I reached the airport.
③ The police had found his wallet that was left under the desk.
④ She opened the box that Miles had sent a week before.
⑤ Nora has gone to London before her husband came back.

04 다음 두 문장을 간접의문문을 이용하여 한 문장으로 만들 때, 빈칸에 알맞은 말을 써 넣으시오.

(1) The reporter asked.
  How did she become interested in taking photos?
  ➡ The reporter _____ _____ _____ _____ _____ in taking photos.

(2) Could you tell us?
  What is so special about haenyeo?
  ➡ Could you _____ _____ _____ _____ _____ _____ about haenyeo?

01 밑줄 친 부분이 어법상 어색한 것은?

① After all the animals <u>had left</u> the burning woods, she felt relieved.

② The violinist <u>played</u> such a beautiful song that the audience gave her an endless applause that night.

③ Lucy asked the man how to fix the phone that <u>has broken</u> down.

④ The professor <u>had</u> just <u>left</u> the hall when the politician appeared.

⑤ Caroline ate the cookies that her grandma <u>had made</u> for her.

[02~03] 다음 우리말을 어법상 알맞게 영작한 것을 고르시오.

02

> 그게 무엇인지 설명해 주시겠어요?

① Could you explain that what it is?

② Could you explain that what that is?

③ Could you explain what is that?

④ Could you explain that what is that?

⑤ Could you explain what that is?

03

> 왜 저렇게 많은 사람들이 줄을 서서 기다리고 있는지 궁금하다.

① I wonder why so many people there waiting in line.

② I wonder why are there so many people waiting in line.

③ I wonder why do so many people are waiting in line.

④ I wonder why there are so many people waiting in line.

⑤ I wonder why there are so many people are waiting in line.

[04~05] 다음 중 어법상 옳은 것을 고르시오.

04 ① Jinsu had read the article about the history of Jeju for the last 3 years.

② William lived in New York before he had moved to San Francisco.

③ Kevin required that Minsu had completed the report.

④ He lost the watch which he had bought the day before.

⑤ I am hungry since I had not eaten anything so far.

05 ① Could you tell us more about what so special is about haenyeo?

② Does Julie know which subject do I like?

③ Do you imagine how old she is?

④ Tell me what is your favorite food.

⑤ Do you want to ask your English teacher what the sentence means?

서답형

06 다음 문장에서 어법상 어색한 단어 한 개를 찾아서 고치시오.

> It had been raining since Miranda went to Spain to learn tango.

_____ ➡ _____

07 다음 두 문장을 의미가 같도록 한 문장으로 바꿔 쓸 때 적절하지 <u>않은</u> 것은?

① I'd like to know. + When did Louise apply for the scholarship?
→ I'd like to know when Louise applied for the scholarship.

② May I ask you? + How much are the souvenir photos?
→ May I ask you how much the souvenir photos are?

③ David asked Emma. + Why was she angry with him?
→ David asked Emma why she was angry with him.

④ Could you tell us? + What did Frank buy at the mall?
→ Could you tell us what Frank bought at the mall?

⑤ Susan is wondering. + Who took away her kids' toys?
→ Susan is wondering who her kids' toys took away.

08 다음 중 밑줄 친 과거완료의 용법이 〈보기〉와 같은 것은?

┌─ 보기 ─┐

He <u>had</u> already <u>found</u> out the secret of the mystery cube when I asked him.

① Tiffany <u>had lived</u> in Busan for 7 months before she moved to Daegu.

② Anna <u>had</u> never <u>been</u> fat by the time she started learning swimming.

③ My cousin <u>had been</u> sick in bed for a week when I visited him.

④ I didn't know how long he <u>had waited</u> for me at the gate the other day.

⑤ Jordan <u>had</u> not <u>finished</u> the work when everyone was about to go out.

09 다음 중 밑줄 친 부분의 쓰임이 〈보기〉와 같은 것은?

┌─ 보기 ─┐

Chanho should not miss such a good opportunity <u>if</u> he wants to win the game.

① Does anybody know <u>if</u> the handsome guy over there has a girlfriend?

② I'm sure the company will succeed <u>if</u> it expands their market in Asia.

③ All of us were not sure <u>if</u> Peter's answer was right or wrong.

④ Taste the food to determine <u>if</u> more salt is required.

⑤ Sarah wondered <u>if</u> Ted would come to the party without the invitation.

10 다음 두 문장을 한 문장으로 만들 때 가장 적절한 것은?

• Do you think?
• Why did the haenyeo look happy?

① Do you think why did the haenyeo look happy?

② Do you think why the haenyeo looked happy?

③ Why do you think did the haenyeo look happy?

④ Why do you think the haenyeo looked happy?

⑤ Why do you think the haenyeo did looked happy?

[11~12] 다음 중 어법상 옳은 문장은?

11
① Cecilia had lost the necklace which I bought for her.

② You can't see the snowman anymore as it had melted this morning.

③ When we were about to leave home, my uncle had already arrived.

④ The passengers have been seated before the plane took off.

⑤ William has never seen the wallaby until he visited Australia.

12 중요
① Do you think where Clara first met her husband?

② Could you please tell us what did your action mean?

③ I wonder whether did anyone see the boy walking along the beach.

④ Do you know how the writer of these books old is?

⑤ Let me know what they are drinking.

서답형
[13~14] 우리말과 일치하도록 괄호 안에 주어진 어구를 바르게 배열하시오.

13
기자는 많은 고객들이 돈가스를 먹으려고 줄을 서서 상당한 시간을 보냈다고 말했다. (돈가스: pork cutlet)

→ The reporter said that (lining up, time, had spent, in order to, quite a long, many, eat, customers, pork cutlet).

➡ The reporter said that _____

_____

_____ .

14
당신은 그 절들이 왜 유명하다고 생각합니까? (the temples, you, famous, why, are, do, think)?

➡ _____

서답형
15 다음 그림을 보고 자연스러운 문장이 되도록 괄호 안에 주어진 어구를 바르게 배열하여 빈칸을 완성하시오.

(1)

➡ Jiho _____

_____ . (fly, could, asked, people, in the sky, his sister, why, not)

(2)

➡ Pooh _____

_____ . (a hive, told, touched, he, that morning, his friend, had, that)

01 다음 우리말과 일치하도록 괄호 안에 주어진 어구를 바르게 배열하여 문장을 완성하시오.

(1) 그 기업은 몇몇 프랑스인들이 전에 훔쳐갔었던 한국의 많은 보물들을 수집했다.

➡ The company _____

_____.

(before, French, stolen, collected, many, that, had, Korean treasures, some)

(2) 수민이는 어떻게 자신이 해녀를 전 세계적으로 홍보할 수 있을지 궁금하다.

➡ Sumin _____

_____. (the haenyeo, wonders, can, worldwide, promote, how, she)

(3) Jim이 출장에서 돌아왔을 때, 그는 누군가가 자신의 집에 침입했었던 것을 발견했다.

➡ When Jim came back from a business trip, _____

_____. (his house, found, broken, he, someone, into, had)

(4) 그 사진 작가가 어디에서 이 사진들을 찍었는지 추측할 수 있습니까?

➡ _____

these pictures? (guess, took, can, the photographer, where, you)

02 다음 〈보기〉와 같이 간접의문문을 활용하여 빈칸을 채우시오.

┌─ 보기 ├─
When does the post office close?
→ Do you know when the post office closes?
└────────

(1) How could they get to the meeting on time?

➡ Do you know _____

_____?

(2) Which boy did the girl next to Jane choose at the blind date?

➡ Can you tell me _____

_____?

(3) Hasn't Shrek learned German yet?

➡ Do you know _____

_____?

(4) Where did Alex find the baby tiger?

➡ Let her figure out _____

_____.

(5) How old does the new employee look?

➡ How old do you think _____

_____?

03 다음 사진을 참고하여 우리말에 맞게, 괄호 안에 주어진 어구를 활용하되, 과거완료시제를 써서 빈칸을 채우시오.

그 날까지 나는 흑백 사진들 속의 아주 지친 모습의 해녀만 봤었다. (who, haenyeo, photos, only see, black-and-white photos)

➡ Until the day, I _____

_____

looked very tired.

04 다음 문장에서 어법상 어색한 것을 바르게 고쳐 다시 쓰시오.

(1) Can you tell me where was the magician when he disappeared?

➡ _____

_____

(2) Does the young student know how the hotel is far?

➡ _____

_____

(3) Do you know could I take pictures of haenyeo?

➡ _____

_____

(4) They didn't understand why did the girl want to take their pictures.

➡ _____

_____

(5) Tell me what did Zin Kim promise the haenyeo.

➡ _____

_____

(6) I wonder why is Jejudo not suitable for farming.

➡ _____

_____

05 주어진 우리말을 〈조건〉에 맞게 영작하시오.

┌─ 조건 ┐

1. 부정 의미의 과거완료시제를 쓸 것.
2. The haenyeo를 포함, 총 18 단어로 쓸 것.
3. 숫자도 영어로 쓸 것..
4. the photographer, think, her picture, pretty, until, that, she, take 등을 활용할 것.
5. ago를 가장 마지막 단어로 할 것.

┌────────────────────────────┐
│ 그 사진작가가 12년 전에 그녀의 사진을 찍을 때 │
│ 까지, 그 해녀는 자신이 예쁘다고 생각하지 않았 │
│ 었다. │
└────────────────────────────┘

➡ _____

_____

_____

06 괄호 안에 주어진 어휘를 활용하여 글자 수대로 다음 우리말을 영작하시오.

(1) Tom은 해녀들이 어떤 호흡장치도 없이 어떻게 물속에 그렇게나 오래 머무를 수 있는지 궁금했다. (how, stay, wonder, so long, without, breathing devices, haenyeo, for, any, could, 16 단어)

➡ _____

_____

(2) 그들은 너무 많은 해양 생물을 채취하는 것이 바다를 어떻게 파괴할 수 있는지 연구하고 있다. (how, can, are, study, marine life, destroy, catching, too much, the ocean, 13 단어)

➡ _____

_____

(3) 마녀는 거울에게 세상에서 가장 아름다운 여자가 누구인지 물었다. (who, woman, the witch, in the world, beautiful, was, ask, the mirror, 14 단어)

➡ _____

_____

(4) 엄마 염소는 아기들이 늑대에게 언제 문을 열어 준 것인지 몰랐다. (when, to, the door, the mother goat, open, not know, the wolf, the babies, 15 단어)

➡ _____

_____

Reading

Haenyeo, Female Divers of Korea

For the past several years, the underwater photographer Zin Kim has promoted the culture of Jeju haenyeo worldwide. Haenyeo are Korean female divers who harvest seafood without any breathing devices. Their culture made UNESCO's Intangible Cultural Heritage list in 2016. At her studio last week, Zin Kim was interviewed about her experience of taking pictures of haenyeo.

Q. How did you become interested in taking photos of haenyeo?

One day, I happened to take pictures of a haenyeo. I was surprised to find that she was enjoying her job. Until then, I had only seen black-and-white photos of haenyeo who looked very tired. However, she kept laughing even after she had been in the water for over five hours. I realized then that I should take pictures of haenyeo.

Q. You take beautiful pictures of them, but isn't it difficult to take pictures of haenyeo?

At first, they didn't understand why I wanted to take their pictures. They didn't think they looked pretty in their wetsuits. So, I said to them, "You're very special. I want to show your culture to the world." They opened up to me then. Of course, I also promised them that I would make them look beautiful in my pictures.

---

female 여성의, 암컷의

past 지나간

several 몇몇의

underwater 수중의, 물속에서

photographer 사진작가

promote 홍보하다, 촉진하다

worldwide 세계적으로

breathe 호흡하다

intangible 무형의, 만질 수 없는

heritage 유산

experience 경험

happen to 우연히 ~하다

black-and-white (사진. TV 등) 흑백의

realize 깨닫다, 인식하다

wetsuit 잠수용 고무 옷

확인문제

● 다음 문장이 본문의 내용과 일치하면 T, 일치하지 않으면 F를 쓰시오.

1 Zin Kim is the underwater photographer. ☐

2 Haenyeo are Korean female divers who harvest seafood with breathing devices. ☐

3 At first, haenyeo understood why Zin Kim wanted to take their pictures. ☐

4 Haenyeo didn't think they looked pretty in their wetsuits. ☐

5 Zin Kim wants to show the culture of Korea to the world. ☐

Q. Could you tell us more about haenyeo? What's so special about them?

I can tell you three things. First, haenyeo are a symbol of strong women. Jejudo, <u>which</u> is a volcanic island, is not suitable for farming,
계속적 용법의 관계대명사. which가 Jejudo를 받아서 그에 대한 추가 설명을 덧붙이고 있다.
so many haenyeo have become the breadwinners for their families.

Second, haenyeo form their own communities and help each other. For example, <u>more-experienced</u> haenyeo train <u>less-experienced</u> haenyeo.
more(부사)+experienced(형용사)가 haenyeo를 꾸며 주고 있음.   less(부사)+experienced(형용사)가 haenyeo를 꾸며 주고 있음.
Third, because they stay in the water without any breathing devices, haenyeo can't catch a lot of seafood. This <u>is good for</u> the underwater
be good for: ~에 좋다
environment. <u>Catching too much marine life at one time in one place can destroy the ocean.</u>
동명사 주어   = It can destroy the ocean to catch too much marine life at one time in one place.

Q. Lastly, please tell us what you're planning to do in the future.
'What are you planning to do ~?'라는 의문문이 tell의 직접목적어로 쓰여 간접의문문이 된 형태
I once <u>attended</u> an overseas exhibition with <u>a couple of</u> haenyeo
attended at(×)   2~3명[개]
<u>to give</u> a talk about their lives. When I finished my talk, one of the
to부정사의 부사적 용법(목적)
haenyeo held <u>my</u> hand tightly. She said to me, "Thank you so much.
= me by the
I've <u>never known</u> in my whole life that I was <u>such a special person</u>."
경험 용법   such+a+형용사+명사
She was crying with happiness. Everyone in the audience was deeply
<u>moved</u>. I can never forget that moment, so I'll continue <u>to take</u> pictures
= touched   = taking
of haenyeo. I want to tell more beautiful stories about them to many
tell은 to를 사용하여 3형식으로 바꿀 수 있다.
more people in the world.

확인문제

- 다음 문장이 본문의 내용과 일치하면 T, 일치하지 <u>않으면</u> F를 쓰시오.

1 Many haenyeo have become the breadwinners for their families. ☐

2 Haenyeo can catch a lot of seafood at one time. ☐

3 Catching too much marine life at one time in one place can destroy the ocean. ☐

4 A couple of haenyeo attendeded an overseas exhibition and gave a talk about their lives. ☐

5 One of the haenyeo said that she had never known in her whole life that she was such a special person. ☐

volcanic 화산의, 화산 작용에 의한
suitable 적합한, 적절한
breadwinner 생계를 책임지는 사람, 가장
experienced 경험이 있는
marine 해양의, 바다의
once 한 번, 한때, 옛날
attend 참석하다
overseas 해외의
exhibition 전시회, 박람회
give a talk 강의하다, 연설하다
tightly 단단히, 꽉
audience 청중

● 우리말을 참고하여 빈칸에 알맞은 말을 쓰시오.

1 Haenyeo, _____ _____ of Korea

2 For the past several years, the _____ _____ Zin Kim _____ _____ the culture of Jeju haenyeo worldwide.

3 Haenyeo are Korean female divers who harvest seafood _____ _____ _____ _____.

4 Their culture _____ _____ _____ _____ in 2016.

5 At her studio last week, Zin Kim _____ _____ about her experience of taking pictures of haenyeo.

6 Q. How did you _____ _____ _____ taking photos of haenyeo?

7 One day, I _____ _____ take pictures of a haenyeo.

8 I _____ _____ _____ _____ that she was enjoying her job.

9 Until then, I had only seen black-and-white photos of haenyeo who _____ _____ _____.

10 However, she _____ _____ even after she had been in the water for over five hours.

11 I realized then that I _____ _____ pictures of haenyeo.

12 Q. You take beautiful pictures of them, but _____ _____ _____ to take pictures of haenyeo?

13 At first, they didn't understand _____ _____ _____ to take their pictures.

14 They didn't think they looked pretty _____ _____ _____.

15 So, I said to them, "You're _____ _____.

16 I want to _____ your culture _____ the world."

17 They _____ _____ to me then.

18 Of course, I also promised them that I would _____ _____ look _____ in my pictures.

1 해녀, 한국의 여성 잠수부

2 지난 몇 년 동안, 수중 사진작가 Zin Kim은 제주 해녀 문화를 전 세계에 홍보해 왔다.

3 해녀는 어떤 호흡 장치도 사용하지 않고 해산물을 채취하는 한국의 여성 잠수부들이다.

4 그들의 문화는 2016년에 유네스코 무형문화유산에 등재되었다.

5 지난주 그녀의 작업실에서, Zin Kim과 해녀의 사진을 찍는 그녀의 경험에 대해 인터뷰를 했다.

6 Q. 어떻게 해녀의 사진을 찍는 것에 관심을 가지게 되었나요?

7 어느 날, 저는 우연히 한 해녀의 사진을 찍게 되었어요.

8 저는 그녀가 자신의 일을 즐겁게 하는 것을 보고 놀랐습니다.

9 그때까지, 저는 흑백 사진 속의 아주 지친 모습의 해녀만 봐 왔죠.

10 하지만, 그녀는 다섯 시간이 넘도록 물속에 있은 후에도 계속 웃었어요.

11 저는 그때 해녀의 사진을 찍어야겠다고 깨달았어요.

12 Q. 작가님은 아름다운 해녀 사진들을 찍으시는데, 그들의 사진을 찍는 것이 어렵진 않으신가요?

13 처음에, 그들은 제가 왜 자신들의 사진을 찍으려고 하는지 이해하지 못했어요.

14 그들은 잠수복을 입은 자신들의 모습이 예뻐 보인다고 생각하지 않았으니까요.

15 그래서, 제가 그들에게 말했죠. "여러분들은 아주 특별해요.

16 저는 여러분의 문화를 세계에 알리고 싶어요."

17 그들은 그때 제게 마음을 열었어요.

18 물론, 저 또한 그들에게 제 사진 속에서 그들을 아름답게 보이도록 하겠다고 약속했지요.

19 Q. Could you tell us _____ _____ haenyeo?

20 What's _____ _____ about them?

21 I _____ _____ _____ three things.

22 First, haenyeo are a symbol of _____ _____.

23 Jejudo, which is a volcanic island, _____ _____ _____ _____ farming, so many haenyeo have become _____ _____ _____ their families.

24 Second, haenyeo _____ their own communities and help _____ _____.

25 For example, _____ haenyeo train _____ haenyeo.

26 Third, because they stay in the water _____ any breathing devices, haenyeo _____ _____ a lot of seafood.

27 This _____ _____ _____ the underwater environment.

28 Catching too much marine life _____ _____ _____ _____ _____ _____ can destroy the ocean.

29 Q. Lastly, please tell us what you're _____ _____ _____ in the future.

30 I once _____ an overseas exhibition with a couple of haenyeo to _____ _____ _____ about their lives.

31 When I finished my talk, one of the haenyeo _____ _____ tightly.

32 She said to me, "Thank you _____ _____.

33 I've never known in my whole life that I was _____ _____ _____ _____."

34 She was crying _____ _____.

35 Everyone in the audience _____ _____ _____.

36 I _____ _____ _____ that moment, so I'll continue to take pictures of haenyeo.

37 I want to tell _____ _____ _____ _____ _____ to many more people in the world.

19 Q. 해녀에 대해서 더 말씀해 주시겠어요?

20 그들은 무엇이 그렇게 특별한가요?

21 세 가지를 말씀 드릴게요.

22 첫 번째로, 해녀들은 강인한 여성의 상징이에요.

23 제주도는 화산섬이고, 이는 농사에 적합하지 않아서 많은 해녀들이 가족들의 생계비를 버는 가장이 되어 왔어요.

24 둘째로, 해녀들은 그들 자신의 공동체를 조직하고 서로 도와요.

25 예를 들어, 경험이 더 많은 해녀들이 경험이 적은 해녀들을 훈련시키지요.

26 세 번째로, 어떤 호흡 장치도 사용하지 않고 물속에 머물기 때문에, 해녀는 많은 해산물을 채취할 수가 없어요.

27 이것은 수중 환경에 좋은 것이지요.

28 한 번에 한 장소에서 너무 많은 해양생물을 채취하는 것은 바다를 파괴할 수 있으니까요.

29 Q. 마지막으로, 앞으로 계획하고 있는 것에 대해 말씀해 주세요.

30 예전에 두 명의 해녀들과 함께 그들의 삶에 대해 이야기하기 위해 해외에서 열리는 박람회에 참가한 적이 있어요.

31 제가 연설을 마쳤을 때, 해녀 중 한 분이 제 손을 꼭 잡았어요.

32 그분이 말했죠. "너무 고마워.

33 내 평생 내가 이렇게 특별한 사람이라는 걸 미처 알지 못했어."

34 그녀는 행복해서 울고 있었어요.

35 청중들 모두가 깊은 감동을 받았어요.

36 전 그 순간을 절대 잊을 수가 없기 때문에 해녀의 사진을 계속해서 찍을 거예요.

37 저는 그들에 대한 더 많은 아름다운 이야기들을 세계의 더 많은 사람들에게 알려 주고 싶어요.

● 우리말을 참고하여 본문을 영작하시오.

1 ▶ 해녀, 한국의 여성 잠수부

➡ _____

2 ▶ 지난 몇 년 동안, 수중 사진작가 Zin Kim은 제주 해녀 문화를 전 세계에 홍보해 왔다.

➡ _____
_____

3 ▶ 해녀는 어떤 호흡 장치도 사용하지 않고 해산물을 채취하는 한국의 여성 잠수부들이다.

➡ _____

4 ▶ 그들의 문화는 2016년에 유네스코 무형문화유산에 등재되었다.

➡ _____

5 ▶ 지난주 그녀의 작업실에서, Zin Kim과 해녀의 사진을 찍는 그녀의 경험에 대해 인터뷰를 했다.

➡ _____

6 ▶ Q. 어떻게 해녀의 사진을 찍는 것에 관심을 가지게 되었나요?

➡ _____

7 ▶ 어느 날, 저는 우연히 한 해녀의 사진을 찍게 되었어요.

➡ _____

8 ▶ 저는 그녀가 자신의 일을 즐겁게 하는 것을 보고 놀랐습니다.

➡ _____

9 ▶ 그때까지, 저는 흑백 사진 속의 아주 지친 모습의 해녀만 봐 왔죠.

➡ _____

10 ▶ 하지만, 그녀는 다섯 시간이 넘도록 물속에 있은 후에도 계속 웃었어요.

➡ _____

11 ▶ 저는 그때 해녀의 사진을 찍어야겠다고 깨달았어요.

➡ _____

12 ▶ Q. 작가님은 아름다운 해녀 사진들을 찍으시는데, 그들의 사진을 찍는 것이 어렵진 않으신가요?

➡ _____

13 ▶ 처음에, 그들은 제가 왜 자신들의 사진을 찍으려고 하는지 이해하지 못했어요.

➡ _____

14 ▶ 그들은 잠수복을 입은 자신들의 모습이 예뻐 보인다고 생각하지 않았으니까요.

➡ _____

15 ▶ 그래서, 제가 그들에게 말했죠, "여러분들은 아주 특별해요.

➡ _____

16 ▶ 저는 여러분의 문화를 세계에 알리고 싶어요."

➡ _____

17 ▶ 그들은 그때 제게 마음을 열었어요.

➡ _____

18 ▶ 물론, 저 또한 그들에게 제 사진 속에서 그들을 아름답게 보이도록 하겠다고 약속했지요.

➡ _____

19 ▶ Q. 해녀에 대해서 더 말씀해 주시겠어요?

➡ _____

20 그들은 무엇이 그렇게 특별한가요?

➡ _____

21 세 가지를 말씀 드릴게요.

➡ _____

22 첫 번째로, 해녀들은 강인한 여성의 상징이에요.

➡ _____

23 제주도는 화산섬이고, 이는 농사에 적합하지 않아서 많은 해녀들이 가족들의 생계비를 버는 가장이 되어 왔어요.

➡ _____

_____

24 둘째로, 해녀들은 그들 자신의 공동체를 조직하고 서로 도와요.

➡ _____

25 예를 들어, 경험이 더 많은 해녀들이 경험이 적은 해녀들을 훈련시키지요.

➡ _____

26 세 번째로, 어떤 호흡 장치도 사용하지 않고 물속에 머물기 때문에, 해녀는 많은 해산물을 채취할 수가 없어요.

➡ _____

_____

27 이것은 수중 환경에 좋은 것이지요.

➡ _____

28 한 번에 한 장소에서 너무 많은 해양생물을 채취하는 것은 바다를 파괴할 수 있으니까요.

➡ _____

29 Q. 마지막으로, 앞으로 계획하고 있는 것에 대해 말씀해 주세요.

➡ _____

30 예전에 두 명의 해녀들과 함께 그들의 삶에 대해 이야기하기 위해 해외에서 열리는 박람회에 참가한 적이 있어요.

➡ _____

_____

31 제가 연설을 마쳤을 때, 해녀 중 한 분이 제 손을 꼭 잡았어요.

➡ _____

32 그분이 말했죠, "너무 고마워.

➡ _____

33 내 평생 내가 이렇게 특별한 사람이라는 걸 미처 알지 못했어."

➡ _____

34 그녀는 행복해서 울고 있었어요.

➡ _____

35 청중들 모두가 깊은 감동을 받았어요.

➡ _____

36 전 그 순간을 절대 잊을 수가 없기 때문에 해녀의 사진을 계속해서 찍을 거예요.

➡ _____

37 저는 그들에 대한 더 많은 아름다운 이야기들을 세계의 더 많은 사람들에게 알려 주고 싶어요.

➡ _____

[01~03] 다음 글을 읽고 물음에 답하시오.

For the past several years, the underwater photographer Zin Kim has promoted the culture of Jeju haenyeo worldwide. Haenyeo are Korean female divers ___ⓐ___ harvest seafood without any breathing devices. Their culture ⓑmade UNESCO's Intangible Cultural Heritage list in 2016. At her studio last week, Zin Kim was interviewed about her experience of taking pictures of haenyeo.

01 위 글의 빈칸 ⓐ에 들어갈 알맞은 말을 <u>모두</u> 고르시오.

① which   ② who   ③ what
④ that   ⑤ whom

02 위 글의 밑줄 친 ⓑmade와 같은 의미로 쓰인 것을 고르시오.

① She made her own clothes.
② He always made me laugh.
③ She made him her assistant.
④ They made me repeat the whole story.
⑤ Jones made a professor in five years.

03 중요
According to the passage, which is NOT true?

① Zin Kim is an underwater photographer.
② Zin Kim has promoted the culture of Jeju haenyeo worldwide for the past several years.
③ Haenyeo are Korean female divers.
④ Haenyeo harvest seafood with the help of breathing devices.
⑤ Haenyeo's culture has been UNESCO's Intangible Cultural Heritage since 2016.

[04~06] 다음 글을 읽고 물음에 답하시오.

Q. _____ⓐ_____
One day, I happened to take pictures of a haenyeo. I was surprised to find that she was enjoying her job. Until then, I had only seen black-and-white photos of haenyeo who looked very tired. However, she kept ___ⓑ___ even after she ⓒhad been in the water for over five hours. I realized then that I should take pictures of haenyeo.

04 중요
위 글의 빈칸 ⓐ에 들어갈 알맞은 질문을 고르시오.

① Could you tell us more about haenyeo?
② What's so special about haenyeo?
③ How did you become interested in taking photos of haenyeo?
④ What do you want to do in the future?
⑤ Is it difficult to take pictures of haenyeo?

서답형
05 위 글의 빈칸 ⓑ에 laugh를 알맞은 형태로 쓰시오.

➡ _____

06 아래 〈보기〉에서 위 글의 밑줄 친 ⓒhad been과 과거완료의 용법이 <u>다른</u> 것의 개수를 고르시오.

┌─ 보기 ─┐
① I had just finished my homework when she came.
② He had lived there for ten years when his father died.
③ I found that I had lost my wallet on the subway.
④ The train had already left when he got to the station.
⑤ They had never met a student like him before.
└─────┘

① 1개   ② 2개   ③ 3개   ④ 4개   ⑤ 5개

[07~09] 다음 글을 읽고 물음에 답하시오.

Q. **You take beautiful pictures of them, but isn't it difficult to take pictures of haenyeo?**

(①) At first, ⓐ그들은 제가 왜 자신들의 사진을 찍으려고 하는지 이해하지 못했어요. (②) They didn't think they looked pretty in their wetsuits. (③) So, I said to them, "You're very special. (④) I want to show your culture to the world." (⑤) Of course, I also promised them that I would make them look beautiful in my pictures.

07 위 글의 흐름으로 보아, 주어진 문장이 들어가기에 가장 적절한 곳은?

They opened up to me then.

①   ②   ③   ④   ⑤

08 위 글의 제목으로 알맞은 것을 고르시오.

① Why Do You Want to Take Pictures of Haenyeo?

② Wow! Haenyeo Let Me Show Their Culture through Pictures!

③ Why Is It Important to Show Haenyeo's Culture?

④ Are You Interested in Taking Pictures of Haenyeo?

⑤ How Can You Make Haenyeo Look Beautiful in Your Pictures?

09 위 글의 밑줄 친 ⓐ의 우리말에 맞게 주어진 어휘를 이용하여 10 단어로 영작하시오.

why, their pictures

➡ _____

_____

[10~13] 다음 글을 읽고 물음에 답하시오.

Q. **Lastly, please tell us what you're planning to do in the future.**

I once (A)[attended / attended to] an overseas exhibition with a couple of haenyeo to give a talk about their lives. When I finished my talk, one of the haenyeo held my hand tightly. She said to me, "Thank you so much. ⓐI've never known in my whole life that I was (B)[so / such] a special person." She was crying with happiness. Everyone in the audience was deeply moved. I can never forget that moment, (C)[as / so] I'll continue to take pictures of haenyeo. I want to tell more beautiful stories about them to many more people in the world.   <I: Zin Kim>

서답형

10 위 글의 괄호 (A)~(C)에서 문맥이나 어법상 알맞은 낱말을 골라 쓰시오.

➡ (A) _____ (B) _____ (C) _____

11 위 글의 분위기로 가장 알맞은 것을 고르시오.

① confusing   ② interesting

③ depressing   ④ boring

⑤ touching

12 Which question CANNOT be answered after reading the passage?

① With whom did Zin Kim attend an overseas exhibition?

② Why did Zin Kim attend an overseas exhibition?

③ When Zin Kim finished her talk, what did one of the haenyeo tell her?

④ How long has Zin Kim taken pictures of haenyeo?

⑤ What does Zin Kim want to tell to many more people in the world?

13 위 글의 밑줄 친 ⓐ의 현재완료와 용법이 같은 것을 모두 고르시오.

① I have just bought my watch.

② I have been to England twice.

③ Have you ever seen a panda?

④ Have you finished it yet?

⑤ Alice has lived in New York since January.

[14~17] 다음 글을 읽고 물음에 답하시오.

Q. Could you tell us more about haenyeo? What's so special about them?

I can tell you three things. First, haenyeo are a symbol of strong women. (A)Jejudo, that is a volcanic island, is not suitable for farming, so many haenyeo have become the ____ⓐ____ for their families. Second, haenyeo form their own communities and help each other. For example, more-experienced haenyeo train less-experienced haenyeo. Third, because they stay in the water without any breathing devices, haenyeo can't catch a lot of seafood. (B)This is good for the underwater environment. Catching too much marine life at one time in one place can destroy the ocean.

14 주어진 영영풀이를 참고하여 빈칸 ⓐ에 철자 b로 시작하는 단어를 쓰시오.

the people who earn the money that the family need for essential things

➡ _____

15 위 글의 밑줄 친 (A)에서 어법상 틀린 부분을 찾아 고치시오.

_____ ➡ _____

16 위 글의 밑줄 친 (B)This가 가리키는 것을 본문에서 찾아 쓰시오.

➡ _____

_____

17 위 글의 주제로 알맞은 것을 고르시오.

① haenyeo as the subject of pictures

② what is special about haenyeo

③ haenyeo as a symbol of strong women

④ the hard lives of the breadwinners

⑤ the way haenyeo form their own communities

[18~21] 다음 글을 읽고 물음에 답하시오.

Q. ①You take beautiful pictures of them, but isn't it difficult to take pictures of haenyeo?

At first, ②they didn't understand why I wanted to take ③their pictures. They didn't think they looked pretty ____ⓐ____ their wetsuits. So, I said to ④them, "⑤You're very special. I want to show your culture ____ⓑ____ the world." They opened up to me then. Of course, ⓒI also promised them that I would make them looking beautiful in my pictures.

<I: Zin Kim>

18 위 글의 빈칸 ⓐ와 ⓑ에 들어갈 전치사가 바르게 짝지어진 것은?

	ⓐ	ⓑ		ⓐ	ⓑ
①	for	from	②	in	by
③	in	to	④	on	to
⑤	for	by			

19 밑줄 친 ①~⑤ 중에서 가리키는 대상이 나머지 넷과 <u>다른</u> 것은?

①   ②   ③   ④   ⑤

[서답형]

20 위 글의 밑줄 친 ©에서 어법상 <u>틀린</u> 부분을 찾아 고치시오.

_____ ➡ _____

[중요]

21 자신들의 사진을 찍는 것에 대한 해녀들의 심경 변화로 가장 알맞은 것을 고르시오.

① hopeful → nervous
② delighted → upset
③ bored → agreeing
④ puzzled → consenting
⑤ confused → disappointed

[22~25] 다음 글을 읽고 물음에 답하시오.

Q. Could you tell us more about haenyeo? What's so special about them?

 I can tell you three things. First, haenyeo are a symbol of strong women. (A)Jejudo, which is a volcanic island, is suitable for farming, so many haenyeo have become the breadwinners for their families. Second, haenyeo form their own communities and help each other. ____ⓐ____, more-experienced haenyeo train less-experienced haenyeo. Third, because they stay in the water without any (B)breathing devices, haenyeo can't catch a lot of seafood. This is good for the underwater environment. (C)Catching too much marine life at one time in one place can destroy the ocean.

22 위 글의 빈칸 ⓐ에 들어갈 알맞은 말을 고르시오.

① Therefore   ② However
③ For example   ④ Moreover
⑤ As a result

[서답형]

23 위 글의 밑줄 친 (A)에서 흐름상 어색한 부분을 찾아 고치시오.

_____ ➡ _____

[중요]

24 위 글의 밑줄 친 (B)breathing과 문법적 쓰임이 <u>다른</u> 것을 <u>모두</u> 고르시오.

① He is a <u>walking</u> dictionary.
② Where is my <u>sleeping</u> bag?
③ She is in the <u>waiting</u> room.
④ If you want to smoke, you need to go to a <u>smoking</u> room in the lobby.
⑤ Look at the <u>dancing</u> girl over there.

[서답형]

25 위 글의 밑줄 친 (C)를 다음과 같이 바꿔 쓸 때 빈칸에 들어갈 알맞은 말을 두 단어로 쓰시오.

➡ It can destroy the ocean _____ too much marine life at one time in one place.

[01~03] 다음 글을 읽고 물음에 답하시오.

> **Q. How did you become interested in taking photos of haenyeo?**
> ⓐOne day, I happened to take pictures of a haenyeo. I was surprised to find that she was enjoying her job. ⓑUntil then, I have only seen black-and-white photos of haenyeo who looked very tired. However, she kept laughing even after she had been in the water for over five hours. I realized then that I should take pictures of haenyeo. <I: Zin Kim>

01 위 글의 밑줄 친 ⓐ를 다음과 같이 바꿔 쓸 때 빈칸에 들어갈 알맞은 말을 두 단어로 쓰시오.

➡ One day, I took pictures of a haenyeo _____ (또는 _____).

02 위 글의 밑줄 친 ⓑ에서 어법상 틀린 부분을 찾아 고치시오.

_____ ➡ _____

03 다음 빈칸 (A)와 (B)에 알맞은 단어를 넣어 Zin Kim이 해녀의 사진을 찍는 것에 관심을 가지게 된 계기를 완성하시오.

> When Zin Kim happened to take pictures of a haenyeo, she was (A)_____ her job and kept (B)_____ even after she had been in the water for over five hours. Zin Kim was surprised at that and decided to take pictures of haenyeo.

[04~06] 다음 글을 읽고 물음에 답하시오.

> (A)[During / For] the past several years, the underwater photographer Zin Kim has promoted the culture of Jeju haenyeo worldwide. Haenyeo are Korean female divers who harvest seafood without (B)[any / no] breathing devices. ⓐTheir culture made UNESCO's (C)[Tangible / Intangible] Cultural Heritage list in ⓑ2016. At her studio last week, Zin Kim was interviewed about her experience of taking pictures of haenyeo.

04 위 글의 괄호 (A)~(C)에서 문맥이나 어법상 알맞은 낱말을 골라 쓰시오.

➡ (A) _____ (B) _____ (C) _____

05 위 글의 밑줄 친 ⓐTheir가 가리키는 것을 본문에서 찾아 쓰시오.

➡ _____

06 위 글의 밑줄 친 ⓑ2016을 영어로 읽는 법을 쓰시오.

➡ _____

[07~09] 다음 글을 읽고 물음에 답하시오.

> **Q. Could you tell us more about haenyeo? What's so special about them?**
> I can tell you three things. First, haenyeo are a symbol of strong women. Jejudo, which is a volcanic island, is not suitable for farming, so many haenyeo have become the breadwinners for their families. Second, haenyeo form their own communities and

help each other. For example, more-experienced haenyeo train less-experienced haenyeo. Third, because they stay in the water without any breathing devices, haenyeo can't catch a lot of seafood. This is good for the underwater environment. Catching too much ____ⓐ____ life at one time in one place can destroy the ocean.

07 주어진 영영풀이를 참고하여 빈칸 ⓐ에 철자 m으로 시작하는 단어를 쓰시오.

> relating to the sea or to the animals and plants that live in the sea

➡ _____

08 Why is the way haenyeo catch seafood good for the underwater environment? Fill in the blanks (A) and (B) with suitable words.

> Because they stay in the water without any (A)_____ _____, haenyeo (B)_____ _____ a lot of seafood.

09 해녀에 대한 특별한 점 3가지를 우리말로 쓰시오.

➡ (1) _____
　 (2) _____
　 (3) _____
　 　 _____

[10~13] 다음 글을 읽고 물음에 답하시오.

> **Q. Lastly, please tell us ____ⓐ____.**
> I once attended an overseas exhibition with a couple of haenyeo to give a talk about their lives. When I finished my talk, ⓑone of the haenyeo held my hand tightly. She

said to me, "Thank you so much. I've never known in my whole life that I was such a special person." She was crying with happiness. Everyone in the audience was deeply ⓒmoved. I can never forget that moment, so I'll continue to take pictures of haenyeo. I want to tell more beautiful stories about them to many more people in the world.
　　　　　　　　　　　　　<I: Zin Kim>

10 다음 주어진 의문문을 위 글의 빈칸 ⓐ에 알맞은 순서로 배열하여 쓰시오.

> What are you planning to do in the future?

➡ _____

11 위 글의 밑줄 친 ⓑ를 다음과 같이 바꿔 쓸 때 빈칸에 들어갈 알맞은 단어를 쓰시오.

➡ one of the haenyeo held _____ by the hand tightly

12 위 글의 밑줄 친 ⓒmoved와 바꿔 쓸 수 있는 말을 쓰시오.

➡ _____

13 위 글의 내용과 일치하도록 다음 빈칸 (A)와 (B)에 알맞은 단어를 쓰시오.

> Zin Kim will continue to (A)_____ _____ of haenyeo as she can never forget the moment when one of the haenyeo thanked her. She wants to tell (B)_____ _____ _____ about haenyeo to many more people in the world.

해석

Communicate – B Talk and Play

A: I wonder what these are.
간접의문문 어순으로 '의문사+주어+동사'의 순서로 이어진다.
B: They're called songpyeon.

A: Could you explain more about them?
= songpyeon
B: They're traditional Korean rice cakes.

구문해설 · traditional: 전통적인

A: 나는 이것들이 무엇인지 궁금해.

B: 그것들은 송편이라고 불려.

A: 이것에 대해 좀 더 설명해 줄래?

B: 그것들은 전통적인 한국 떡이야.

After You Read A

A Photographer Who Loves Haenyeo

Zin Kim, an underwater photographer, has promoted the culture of Jeju
현재완료(계속적 용법)
haenyeo worldwide. She decided to take pictures of them when she met a
= take their pictures
haenyeo who was enjoying her job. It was not easy taking their pictures at
관계대명사(주격)   가주어   진주어(동명사)
first. However, when she told them that she wanted to show their culture to the
접속사(명사절)
world, the haenyeo finally opened their minds. At an overseas exhibition, she
부사(동사 수식)   →its(×) 주의 haenyeo는 복수(a haenyeo는 단수)
gave a talk about the lives of haenyeo. After her speech, one of the haenyeo
one of the 복수명사+단수동사
was crying with happiness. Zin Kim said that she would continue to take
시제 일치(will과거)
pictures of haenyeo.

구문해설 · underwater: 수중의, 물속의 · promote: 홍보하다, 촉진하다 · overseas: 해외의
· exhibition: 전시회

해녀를 사랑하는 사진작가

수중 사진작가 김진은 전 세계에 제주의 해녀 문화를 홍보해 왔다. 그녀는 자신의 일을 즐기고 있었던 한 해녀를 만났을 때, 그들의 사진을 찍기로 결심했다. 처음에는 그들의 사진을 찍는 것이 쉽지 않았다. 그러나, 그녀가 세상 사람들에게 그들의 문화를 보여주고 싶다고 그들에게 말했을 때, 마침내 해녀들은 마음을 열었다. 한 해외 전시회에서 그녀는 해녀들의 삶에 대해 강연했다. 그녀의 연설이 끝나자 해녀들 중 한 사람은 기쁨의 눈물을 흘렸다. 김진은 앞으로도 해녀들의 사진 찍는 일을 계속할 것이라고 말했다.

Write

Kim Minho is a barista. He makes coffee drinks for a living. He became a
for a living: 밥벌이로, 생계 수단으로
barista after he had found out about his passion for coffee. His favorite part of
바리스타가 되기 전에 발견한 것이므로, 과거완료시제를 사용
his job is decorating coffee with hot milk and watching his customers enjoying
동명사 보어   동명사 보어   지각동사 whatching의
목적격보어로 쓰인 현재분사
it. He is planning to open his own coffee shop.
opening(×)

구문해설 · barista: 바리스타, 커피 내리는 사람 · find out: 발견하다, 찾다 · passion: 열정, 흥미
· decorate: 장식하다, 꾸미다 · customer: 손님

김민호는 바리스타이다. 그의 직업은 커피 음료를 만드는 것이다. 그는 커피에 대한 그의 열정을 발견한 후에 바리스타가 되었다. 그의 직업에서 그가 가장 좋아하는 부분은 뜨거운 우유로 커피를 장식하고 그의 손님들이 그것을 즐기는 것을 보는 것이다. 그는 자신의 커피점을 열 계획이다.

Words & Expressions

01 다음 짝지어진 단어의 관계가 같도록 빈칸에 알맞은 말을 쓰시오.

> dark : darkness = happy : _____

02 다음 영영풀이가 가리키는 것을 고르시오.

> the member of a family who earns the money to support the others

① baker
② breadwinner
③ diver
④ audience
⑤ presenter

03 다음 중 밑줄 친 부분의 뜻풀이가 바르지 <u>않은</u> 것은?

① Could you <u>explain</u> more about it? (설명하다)
② There are a lot of <u>female</u> teachers in Korea. (여성의)
③ I'm planning an <u>overseas</u> trip. (해외의)
④ I have been on a trip for the <u>past</u> few days. (지나간)
⑤ She is walking along the <u>path</u>. (신뢰)

04 다음 우리말에 맞게 빈칸에 알맞은 말을 쓰시오.

(1) 너는 어디로 휴가를 가고 싶니?
 ➡ Where do you want to _____?
(2) 제가 두 서너 개의 질문을 하겠습니다.
 ➡ I'm going to ask _____ questions.
(3) 이 음악은 군인들을 격려하기 위해 만들어졌다.
 ➡ This music was made to _____ soldiers.

(4) 질문이 있다면 제게 전화주세요.
 ➡ _____ me _____ if you have any questions.

05 다음 문장의 빈칸에 들어갈 말을 〈보기〉에서 골라 쓰시오.

> ┤ 보기 ├
> heritage / greenhouse / device / breathe / overwork

(1) Her _____ and stress caused her to be ill.
(2) In winter, farmers grow vegetables in their _____.
(3) Cotton clothing allows your skin to _____.
(4) They tried to invent a _____ to measure brain activity during sleep.
(5) We should protect our national _____.

Conversation

[06~07] 다음 대화를 읽고 물음에 답하시오.

> Jack: Excuse me, I'd like to use a copy machine.
> Sue: O.K. You can use this machine.
> Jack: Could you explain how to make double-sided copies?
> Sue: Sure. Press the button for double-sided copies, and then press the start button.
> Jack: Thank you.

06 What does Jack want to make?
 ➡ _____

07 What will Jack do before pressing the start button?
 ➡ _____

[08~09] 다음 대화를 읽고 물음에 답하시오.

Tom: Are you going somewhere this summer?
(A)
Jane: I'm going to Jejudo to walk along the Jeju Olle Trail. (B)
Tom: The Jeju Olle Trail? (C)
Jane: It's a long hiking path around Jejudo. (D)
Tom: Oh, I see. I hope you enjoy your trip! (E)

08 위 대화의 (A)~(E) 중 주어진 문장이 들어가기에 가장 적절한 곳은?

> Could you explain what that is?

① (A) ② (B) ③ (C) ④ (D) ⑤ (E)

09 위 대화를 읽고 대답할 수 없는 것은?

① Where is Jane going to visit this summer?
② What is the Jeju Olle Trail?
③ Why does Jane want to visit Jejudo?
④ What does Tom hope for Jane?
⑤ What does Tom want to do in Jejudo?

[10~12] 다음 대화를 읽고 물음에 답하시오.

Jaden: Do you hear that? I wonder where that music is coming from.
Yuri: I think it's coming from over there. Do you want to go and ⓐcheck out it?
Jaden: Yes, I love ⓑthat strong beat. Is it traditional Korean music?
Yuri: Yes, it's ⓒcalled nongak. It's a kind of community band music.
Jaden: Nongak? Could you explain a little bit more about it?
Yuri: It's traditionally used to cheer up farmers and ⓓwish for a good harvest.

Jaden: I see. Look! Some people are dancing to the rhythm.
Yuri: Yes, that's a big part of nongak. Dancing together ⓔcompletes the music.
Jaden: Let's join them.
Yuri: Sure. Why not?

10 위 대화의 밑줄 친 ⓐ~ⓔ 중 어법상 어색한 것을 찾아 바르게 고치시오.

➡ _____

11 위 대화에서 다음 주어진 영영풀이가 가리키는 말을 찾아 쓰시오.

> one of a series of regular movements or hitting actions

➡ _____

12 위 대화의 내용과 일치하지 <u>않는</u> 것은?

① Jaden은 들려오는 음악의 강한 비트가 마음에 든다.
② Jaden과 유리는 농악을 듣고 있다.
③ 농악은 공동체 악단 음악의 한 종류이다.
④ 농악은 전통적으로 농부들의 힘을 북돋아 주고 풍년을 기원하기 위해 사용되었다.
⑤ 리듬은 농악의 큰 부분으로서 음악을 완성한다.

13 다음 대화를 참고하여 주어진 빈칸에 적절한 단어를 쓰시오.

Philip: Sam, have you ever eaten cheese fondue made with Swiss style?
Sam: Yes, two times.
Philip: When did you first eat it?
Sam: Before I graduated from the college.

➡ Sam _____ _____ cheese fondue before he graduated from the college.

[14~15] 다음 중 어법상 어색한 문장을 모두 고르시오.

14 ① The people can't even guess where are the monsters from.
② The participants don't understand why the speaker is interested in.
③ Mom doesn't know whether Jamie and Esther are coming.
④ When do you think the researcher will complete the project?
⑤ There's no one knowing when the car accident happened.

15 ① I wonder why she didn't choose me as her colleague.
② Do you know who made these yummy cookies and drinks?
③ Would you tell me when did he leave the office?
④ Do you think when Tracy will come back for her original position?
⑤ Do you have any idea how long it will take to get to the wedding?

16 다음 그림을 보고 괄호 안의 단어를 배열하여 빈칸을 알맞게 채우시오.

(1)

어느 대학

➡ Junho is _____
_____. (which, go, thinking, should, he, to, about, university)

(2)

➡ Ye-eun is _____
_____. (when, stop, will, the, wondering, rain)

17 다음 괄호 안에서 어법상 알맞은 것을 고르시오.

(1) Sven dropped the carrot that Olaf (had pulled / has pulled) out of the field in the snow.
(2) Last week, we learned that Kennedy (had been killed / was killed) by gunshot in 1963.
(3) The rock band (has already gone / had already gone) to New York before their fans got informed of the news.
(4) Some film lovers around the world said that they (have been / had been) learning Korean to watch *Parasite* without subtitles.
(5) An invitation was sent to the girl after the prince (had seen / has seen) her dancing on the street.
(6) I wonder when the angels (had appeared / appeared / has appeared) to the nuns.

18 다음 쇼핑몰의 안내 페이지와 〈보기〉의 질문을 참고하여 알맞은 내용을 골라 빈칸에 간접의문을 써 넣으시오.

> **Fresh Daddy Grocery**
> • Open Hours: 10a.m. ~ 8p.m.
> • Address: 123 Ilsan, Goyang
> • Nearby Station: Daewha (line 3)
> • Contact: mngr@freshdaddy.co.kr

> ┌─ 보기 ─┐
> • Is there any subway station near the store?
> • What time does the store open?
> • How can we contact the store manager?
> • Where is the store located?

(1) Do you know _____?
   → The store opens at 10 a.m.
(2) Can you tell me _____
   _____?
   → By e-mail. mngr@freshdaddy.co.kr.
(3) Tell me _____.
   → Fresh Daddy Grocery is at 123 Ilsan, Goyang.
(4) Do you know _____
   _____?
   → Yes, the nearest subway station from the store is Daewha on line 3.

19 다음 각 문장의 밑줄 친 부분이 과거완료시제의 용법 중 어떤 것에 해당하는지 〈보기〉에서 찾아 기호를 쓰시오.

> ┌─ 보기 ─┐
> ⓐ 완료 ⓑ 경험 ⓒ 결과 ⓓ 계속

(1) I had never seen the desert until I went to Sahara last year. (_____)
(2) As soon as she came back to her desk, she felt something had gone from her drawer. (_____)

(3) Before the boss came up, Jessica had finished her report. (_____)
(4) The lady couldn't notice the old man since she had lost her sight. (_____)
(5) By the time the teacher found something strange, Michael had already completed his reading. (_____)
(6) Jacob had lived in Daejeon for 4 years by last year. (_____)
(7) Bong had won several awards before winning the Academy Award. (_____)
(8) The girl had stayed in the dormitory until her parents came to visit her. (_____)

20 다음 그림과 스케줄 표를 보고 과거완료시제를 활용하여, 빈칸에 알맞은 말을 써 넣으시오.

> **Today's Schedule**
> • Vanessa – clean the windows and wash the dishes
> • Sally – give the dog some food and water the plant

(1) When Mom came home, she found
   _____
   _____.
(2) When Mom came home, she found
   _____
   _____.

21 다음 우리말에 맞도록 괄호 안에 주어진 어휘를 알맞게 배열하시오.

(1) 수진이는 왜 자신이 다른 나라에 가서 요리법을 배워야 하는지 이해할 수 없었다. (had to, in, how, why, to cook, she, learn, another country)

➡ Sujin couldn't understand _____ _____.

(2) 비행기에 남은 좌석이 있는지 확인해 주시겠어요? (seats, there, the plane, left, any, on, are, if)

➡ Could you check _____ _____?

Reading

[22~24] 다음 글을 읽고 물음에 답하시오.

Q. Could you tell us more about haenyeo? What's so special about them?

I can tell you three things. First, haenyeo are a symbol of strong women. Jejudo, which is a volcanic island, is not suitable ⓐ___ farming, so many haenyeo have become the breadwinners ⓑ___ their families. Second, haenyeo form their own communities and help each other. For example, more-experienced haenyeo train less-experienced haenyeo. Third, because they stay in the water without any breathing devices, haenyeo can't catch a lot of seafood. This is good for the underwater environment. ⓒCatching too much marine life at one time in one place can destroy the ocean.

22 위 글의 빈칸 ⓐ와 ⓑ에 공통으로 들어갈 알맞은 전치사를 고르시오.

① to   ② on   ③ for
④ in   ⑤ at

---

23 위 글의 밑줄 친 ⓒCatching과 문법적 쓰임이 같은 것을 모두 고르시오.

① Our cat is good at catching mice.
② Do you know the man catching fish?
③ I think I'm catching a cold.
④ My hobby is catching the fish.
⑤ I saw a woman catching a butterfly.

24 According to the passage, which is NOT true?

① Haenyeo are a symbol of strong women.
② Jejudo is a volcanic island.
③ Haenyeo form their own communities.
④ Haenyeo stay in the water with no breathing devices.
⑤ Haenyeo can catch a lot of seafood at one time.

[25~26] 다음 글을 읽고 물음에 답하시오.

Q. Lastly, please tell us what you're planning to do in the future.

I once attended an overseas exhibition with a couple of haenyeo to give a talk about their lives. When I finished my talk, one of the haenyeo held my hand tightly. She said to me, "Thank you so much. I've never known in my whole life that I was such a special person." She was crying with happiness. Everyone in the audience was deeply ⓐmoved. I can never forget that moment, so I'll continue to take pictures of haenyeo. I want to tell more beautiful stories about them to many more people in the world.   <I: Zin Kim>.

25 위 글의 밑줄 친 ⓐmoved와 같은 의미로 쓰인 것을 고르시오.

① He moved towards the window.
② The sight moved me to tears.
③ We moved to the country last week.
④ The ship moved before the wind.
⑤ I moved that a vote should be taken on this.

26 위 글의 주제로 알맞은 것을 고르시오.

① an overseas exhibition Zin Kim attended
② giving a talk about haenyeo's lives
③ Zin Kim's plan in the future
④ the happiness of one of the haenyeo
⑤ beautiful stories about haenyeo

27 위 글의 빈칸 ⓐ에 들어갈 알맞은 말을 고르시오.

① That is
② Moreover
③ Thus
④ For example
⑤ However

28 위 글의 종류로 알맞은 것을 고르시오.

① review
② book report
③ diary
④ article
⑤ autobiography

29 Which question CANNOT be answered after reading the passage?

① What does Zin Kim do?
② How did Zin Kim take pictures of haenyeo?
③ When did Zin Kim decide to take pictures of haenyeo?
④ Was it easy to take pictures of haenyeo at first?
⑤ What did Zin Kim want to show to the world?

[27~29] 다음 글을 읽고 물음에 답하시오.

A Photographer Who Loves Haenyeo

Zin Kim, an underwater photographer, has promoted the culture of Jeju haenyeo worldwide. She decided to take pictures of them when she met a haenyeo who was enjoying her job.

It was not easy taking their pictures at first. _____ⓐ_____, when she told them that she wanted to show their culture to the world, the haenyeo finally opened their minds.

At an overseas exhibition, she gave a talk about the lives of haenyeo. After her speech, one of the haenyeo was crying with happiness. Zin Kim said that she would continue to take pictures of haenyeo.

01 다음 문장의 빈칸에 공통으로 들어갈 말을 고르시오. 출제율 95%

> • The manager will _____ a presentation on the new items.
> • Can you _____ me your hand?
> • I usually _____ a call to my grandmother every week.

① give ② take ③ keep
④ like ⑤ check

02 다음 대화가 자연스럽게 이어지도록 순서대로 배열하시오. 출제율 90%

> (A) Really? Then, why don't we go somewhere, too?
> (B) O.K.
> (C) Lots of people are going on vacation this weekend.
> (D) Look over there. I wonder why there are so many cars on the road.

➡ _____

[03~04] 다음 대화를 읽고 물음에 답하시오.

> Jaden: Do you hear that? I wonder where that music is coming from.
> Yuri: (A) I think it's coming from over there. Do you want to go and check it out?
> Jaden: Yes, I love that strong beat. Is it traditional Korean music?
> Yuri: (B) It's a kind of community band music.
> Jaden: Nongak? Could you explain a little bit more about it?
> Yuri: (C) It's traditionally used to cheer up farmers and wish for a good harvest.
> Jaden: (D) I see. Look! Some people are dancing to the rhythm.

> Yuri: Yes, that's a big part of nongak. Dancing together completes the music.
> Jaden: (E) Let's join them.
> Yuri: Sure. Why not?

03 위 대화의 (A)~(E) 중 주어진 문장이 들어가기에 적절한 곳은? 출제율 95%

> Yes, it's called nongak.

① (A) ② (B) ③ (C) ④ (D) ⑤ (E)

04 위 대화를 읽고 대답할 수 없는 것은? 출제율 100%

① Where is the strong beat coming from?
② What is nongak?
③ What are some people doing to the rhythm?
④ What is a big part of nongak?
⑤ What kind of dancing can complete the music?

[05~06] 다음 대화를 읽고 물음에 답하시오.

> W: Excuse me, I'd like to borrow an audio guide.
> M: Here you are.
> W: Could you explain how to use it?
> M: Sure. Press this button, and it'll tell you what to do.

05 What does the woman want to do? 출제율 90%

➡ _____

06 What should the woman do to use the audio guide? 출제율 90%

➡ _____

[07~08] 다음 대화를 읽고 물음에 답하시오.

Emma: Look over there. (A)도로에 왜 저렇게 차가 많은지 궁금하네요.

Mike: Lots of people are going on vacation this weekend.

Emma: Really? Then, (B)why don't we go somewhere, too? (how)

Mike: O.K.

07 위 대화의 밑줄 친 (A)의 우리말을 〈보기〉에 주어진 단어들을 모두 배열하여 영작하시오.

┌ 보기 ┐
there / wonder / on / I / the / cars / so / are / road / why /many
└─────┘

➡ _____

08 위 대화의 밑줄 친 (B)와 의도가 같도록 주어진 단어를 사용하여 다시 쓰시오.

➡ _____

09 다음 대화가 자연스럽게 이어지도록 순서대로 배열하시오.

(A) How do you know that?
(B) That's Gwangandaegyo in Busan.
(C) I went there with my family last summer.
(D) Wow, look at the bridge in this ad. I wonder where the photo was taken.

➡ _____

[10~11] 다음 대화를 읽고 물음에 답하시오.

Jack: Excuse me, I'd like to use a copy machine.

Sue: O.K. You can use this machine.

Jack: 어떻게 양면 복사를 하는지 설명해 주실 수 있나요?

Sue: Sure. Press the button for double-sided copies, and then press the start button.

Jack: Thank you.

10 위 대화의 밑줄 친 우리말을 〈보기〉에 주어진 단어를 알맞게 배열하여 영작하시오.

┌ 보기 ┐
how / you / copies / explain / could / make / double-sided / to
└─────┘

➡ _____

_____

11 위 대화의 내용과 일치하지 <u>않는</u> 것은?

① Jack wants to use a copy machine.
② Jack wants to make double-sided copies.
③ Sue knows how to make double-sided copies.
④ Jack should press the two buttons to make double-sided copies.
⑤ Jack should press the start button at first.

12 다음 우리말을 바르게 영작한 것은?

당신은 Paul이 무슨 음악을 듣고 있다고 생각합니까?

① What music do you suppose Paul is listening to?
② What do you suppose music is Paul listening to?
③ Do you suppose what music is Paul listening to?
④ Is what music you suppose Paul listening to?
⑤ What music do you suppose is Paul listening to?

13 〈보기〉와 같이 과거완료시제를 이용하여, 두 문장을 괄호 안에 주어진 접속사로 시작하는 한 문장으로 만드시오.

> ┤ 보기 ├
>
> All the Korean film fans shouted for joy. Bong won the Academy Awards. (because)
> → Because Bong had won the Academy Awards, all the Korean film fans shouted for joy.

(1) Susan promised her teacher not to throw away used batteries. She learned the importance of recycling. (after)

➡ _____

_____

(2) Sunwoo lay in his room all day long. He sprained his ankle during the basketball game. (before)

➡ _____

_____

14 다음 빈칸에 들어가기에 어색한 문장을 모두 골라 번호를 쓰고 알맞게 고쳐 다시 쓰시오.

> Do you know _____ ?

ⓐ when does the shopping mall close

ⓑ where the nearest subway station is

ⓒ what kind of movie was she watching

ⓓ what does she usually do on Sundays

ⓔ how many toys there are in the room

ⓕ what time does the show begin

➡ _____

_____

_____

15 다음 중 어법상 올바른 문장을 <u>모두</u> 고르면? (정답 2개)

① His family happened to know that Brian has worked hard only to be taken to hospital the day before.

② The first half of the match already started when we had arrived at the stadium.

③ Most Asians felt proud that Director Bong has won the grand prize at the Cannes Film Festival for the film.

④ Marty returned the umbrella which she had borrowed from the restaurant.

⑤ The flower looked much fresher than before because it had rained the day before.

16 다음 그림을 보고, 내용에 맞게 〈보기〉에서 알맞은 단어를 각각 선택하여 어법에 맞게 빈칸에 채워 넣으시오.

> ┤ 보기 ├
>
> • already / much / often / how → 1회씩 사용
> • gain / eat / weigh → 1회씩 사용, 어형변화 가능
> • had / he → 2회씩 사용

> The bulldog wanted to know _____
> _____ _____ _____ . He was
> surprised to find that _____ _____
> _____ _____ weight before he
> stood on the scale. He regretted that he
> _____ _____ _____ some snacks
> before going to bed.

17 출제율 90%

다음 우리말과 그 영작이 바르게 짝지어지지 <u>않은</u> 것은?

① 네가 몇 시에 올 것인지 궁금하다.
→ I wonder what time you will come.

② 누가 그 강아지를 내게 줬는지 말해줘.
→ Tell me who gave me the puppy.

③ 그녀가 무슨 드레스를 입었는지 기억이 안 난다.
→ I can't remember what dress she put on.

④ 그녀가 몇 살이라고 짐작하니?
→ Do you guess how old she is?

⑤ 수민이가 왜 날 싫어하는지 몰라.
→ I don't know why Sumin hates me.

[18~20] 다음 글을 읽고 물음에 답하시오.

> **Q. How did you become interested in taking photos of haenyeo?**
>
> One day, I happened to take pictures of a haenyeo. I was surprised to find that she was enjoying her job. Until then, I had only seen black-and-white photos of haenyeo who looked very tired. ___ⓐ___, she kept laughing even after she had been in the water for over five hours. I realized then that I should take pictures of haenyeo. <I: Zin Kim>

18 출제율 95%

위 글의 빈칸 ⓐ에 들어갈 알맞은 말을 고르시오.

① In addition   ② For example
③ That is   ④ However
⑤ Therefore

19 출제율 100%

위 글의 주제로 알맞은 것을 고르시오.

① how to take pictures of haenyeo
② the hard lives of haenyeo
③ the reason Zin Kim became interested in taking photos of haenyeo
④ the difficulty of taking pictures of haenyeo
⑤ the most beautiful picture that has ever been taken

20 출제율 90%

Until she happened to take pictures of a haenyeo, what kind of photos of haenyeo had Zin Kim only seen? Answer in English in a full sentence.

➡ _____

_____

[21~22] 다음 글을 읽고 물음에 답하시오.

> **Q. You take beautiful pictures of them, but isn't ⓐit difficult to take pictures of haenyeo?**
>
> At first, they didn't understand why I wanted to take their pictures. They didn't think they looked pretty in their wetsuits. So, I said to them, "You're very special. I want to show your culture to the world." They opened up to me then. Of course, I also promised them that I would make them look beautiful in my pictures. <I: Zin Kim>

21 출제율 95%

위 글의 밑줄 친 ⓐit과 문법적 쓰임이 같은 것을 고르시오.

① I make <u>it</u> a rule to eat breakfast.
② <u>It</u> is 2 miles from here to the airport.
③ <u>It</u> is I that am to blame.
④ Did you see <u>it</u>?
⑤ <u>It</u> is important for you to have a dream.

22 According to the passage, which is NOT true?

① Zin Kim takes beautiful pictures of haenyeo.

② From the beginning, Zin Kim had no difficulty in taking pictures of haenyeo.

③ Haenyeo didn't think they looked pretty in their wetsuits.

④ Zin Kim wanted to show haenyeo's culture to the world.

⑤ Zin Kim promised haenyeo that she would make them look beautiful in her pictures.

[23~25] 다음 글을 읽고 물음에 답하시오.

Q. ⓐ**Lastly, please tell us what you're planning to do in the future.**

I once attended an overseas exhibition with a couple of haenyeo ⓑto give a talk about their lives. (①) She said to me, "Thank you so much. (②) I've never known in my whole life that I was such a special person." (③) She was crying with happiness. (④) Everyone in the audience was deeply moved. (⑤) I can never forget that moment, so I'll continue to take pictures of haenyeo. I want to tell more beautiful stories about them to many more people in the world.

23 위 글의 흐름으로 보아, 주어진 문장이 들어가기에 가장 적절한 곳은?

When I finished my talk, one of the haenyeo held my hand tightly.

①   ②   ③   ④   ⑤

24 위 글의 밑줄 친 ⓐLastly와 바꿔 쓸 수 있는 말을 고르시오.

① Eventually   ② Immediately

③ Extremely   ④ Finally

⑤ At last

25 위 글의 밑줄 친 ⓑto give와 to부정사의 용법이 다른 것의 개수를 고르시오.

┤ 보기 ├

① She went there to give a talk about it.

② It's your turn to give a talk about it.

③ He is wise enough to give a talk about it.

④ I felt proud to give a talk about it.

⑤ It was exciting to give a talk about it.

① 1개   ② 2개   ③ 3개   ④ 4개   ⑤ 5개

[26~28] 다음 글을 읽고 물음에 답하시오.

Kim Minho is a barista. He makes coffee drinks ___ⓐ___ a living. He became a barista after he had found out about his passion ___ⓑ___ coffee. His favorite part of his job is decorating coffee with hot milk and watching his customers enjoying it. He is planning to open his own coffee shop.

26 위 글의 빈칸 ⓐ와 ⓑ에 공통으로 들어갈 알맞은 전치사를 쓰시오.

➡ _____

27 주어진 영영풀이에 해당하는 단어를 본문에서 찾아 쓰시오.

a person who makes and serves coffee in a coffee bar

➡ _____

28 What's Kim Minho's favorite part of his job? Answer in English beginning with "It's".

➡ _____

_____

[01~03] 다음 대화를 읽고 물음에 답하시오.

> Brian: Look over there. I wonder why there are so many people waiting in line.
> Sujin: They're waiting to get into the new bakery there.
> Brian: Why? Is it famous?
> Sujin: Yes. It was on a TV program.
> Brian: Really? We should try their bread then.
> Sujin: Sure.

01 Why are so many people waiting in line?

➡ _____

02 Why is the new bakery famous? (7 words)

➡ _____

03 What does Brian want to try?

➡ _____

[04~05] 다음 중에서 틀린 문장을 찾아 번호를 쓰고, 바르게 고쳐 문장을 다시 쓰시오.

04 ① The film director had been tired because he spoke in front of so many people.
② The mechanic told her that someone had touched the tires of her car.
③ Emilia found out that she had lost her smartphone.
④ Julie decided to marry Jake as she had liked him for a long time.
⑤ The accounting manager said he had already completed his financial report.

➡ _____
_____

05 ① The president wants to know what his secretary bought a week ago.
② I have no idea why the super hero is blamed for the accident.
③ Could you tell us if the injured soldier will come tomorrow morning?
④ Do you think where the police officer caught the thief?
⑤ Does Michael know how you could escape from the prison?

➡ _____
_____

06 〈보기〉처럼 괄호 안에 주어진 접속사와 과거완료시제를 이용하여 두 문장을 한 문장으로 쓰시오.

> ┤ 보기 ├
> James was too full to eat more. He ate all three meals by himself. (Because로 시작)
> → Because James had eaten all three meals by himself, he was too full to eat more.

(1) Mary fought off a strange man's attack. She learned taekwondo before. (Because로 시작)

➡ _____
_____
_____

(2) Kevin never thought of quitting drinking. He saw a video of himself being a heavy drinker. (Until로 시작)

➡ _____
_____
_____

[07~09] 다음 글을 읽고 물음에 답하시오.

Q. You take beautiful pictures of them, but isn't it difficult to take pictures of haenyeo?

At first, they didn't understand why I wanted to take their pictures. ⓐThey didn't think they looked prettily in their wetsuits. So, I said to them, "You're very special. I want to show your culture to the world." They opened up to me then. Of course, I also promised them that ⓑ내 사진 속에서 그들을 아름답게 보이도록 하겠다. <I: Zin Kim>

07 위 글의 밑줄 친 ⓐ에서 어법상 틀린 부분을 찾아 고치시오.

_____ ➡ _____

08 위 글의 밑줄 친 ⓑ의 우리말에 맞게 주어진 어휘를 알맞게 배열하시오.

> them / pictures / beautiful / make / I / in / would / my / look

➡ _____

09 Why did Zin Kim want to take pictures of haenyeo? Fill in the blanks (A) and (B) with suitable words.

> Because haenyeo are (A)_____ _____ and she wanted to (B)_____ _____ _____ to the world.

[10~12] 다음 글을 읽고 물음에 답하시오.

Q. Could you tell us more about haenyeo? What's so special about them?

I can tell you three things. First, haenyeo are a symbol of strong women. Jejudo, which is a volcanic island, is not suitable for farming, so many haenyeo have become the breadwinners for their families. Second, haenyeo form their own communities and help each other. For example, more-experienced haenyeo train less-experienced haenyeo. Third, because they stay in the water (A)[with / without] any breathing devices, haenyeo can't catch a lot of seafood. This is good (B)[at / for] the underwater environment. Catching too much marine life at one time in one place can (C)[destroy / protect] the ocean.

10 위 글의 괄호 (A)~(C)에서 문맥상 알맞은 낱말을 골라 쓰시오.

➡ (A) _____ (B) _____ (C) _____

11 다음 빈칸 (A)와 (B)에 알맞은 단어를 넣어 해녀들이 그들 자신의 공동체를 조직하고 서로 돕는 한 예를 완성하시오.

> (A)_____ haenyeo are trained by (B)_____ haenyeo.

12 Why is it impossible for haenyeo to catch a lot of seafood at one time? Answer in English beginning with "Because".

➡ _____

_____

창의사고력 서술형 문제

01 다음 대화를 읽고 대화의 내용과 일치하도록 Jaden의 일기를 완성하시오.

> **Jaden:** Do you hear that? I wonder where that music is coming from.
>
> **Yuri:** I think it's coming from over there. Do you want to go and check it out?
>
> **Jaden:** Yes, I love that strong beat. Is it traditional Korean music?
>
> **Yuri:** Yes, it's called nongak. It's a kind of community band music.
>
> **Jaden:** Nongak? Could you explain a little bit more about it?
>
> **Yuri:** It's traditionally used to cheer up farmers and wish for a good harvest.
>
> **Jaden:** I see. Look! Some people are dancing to the rhythm.
>
> **Yuri:** Yes, that's a big part of nongak. Dancing together completes the music.
>
> **Jaden:** Let's join them.
>
> **Yuri:** Sure. Why not?

> Walking down the street, I heard music with a (A)_____. I wanted to know (B)_____. Yuri and I found that it was traditional Korean music, called (C)_____. Yuri explained that it's a kind of (D)_____ and traditionally used to (E)_____. It was impressive for me that some people were dancing to the rhythm because dancing was a big part of nongak. Yuri and I joined them and completed the music together.

02 다음 그림을 보고, 그림의 상황에 맞게 〈보기〉와 같이 간접의문문을 사용하여 어법에 맞게 자유롭게 영작하시오.

> **보기**
>
> Do you know when you should feed the puppy?
> Tell me if you checked our mailbox.

(1) _____

(2) _____

(3) _____

단원별 모의고사

01 다음 영영풀이가 가리키는 것을 고르시오.

> a picture, set of words, or a short film, intended to persuade people to buy

① advertisement　② audio guide
③ jellyfish　④ beat
⑤ sunshine

02 다음 주어진 문장의 밑줄 친 beat와 같은 의미로 쓰인 것은?

> This type of music has a strong beat.

① I like the steady beat of the drums.
② He beat me at chess.
③ Hailstones beat against the window.
④ My mother beat dust out of the carpet.
⑤ I heard the sound of beating the door.

03 다음 우리말에 맞게 주어진 단어를 활용하여 영작하시오.

(1) 나는 사진작가가 되고 싶다. (photo)
　➡ _____

(2) 그녀는 가장 적절한 후보였다. (suit)
　➡ _____

(3) 그는 내 손을 꽉 잡았다. (hold, tight)
　➡ _____

(4) 나는 소설을 빌리고 싶습니다. (like)
　➡ _____

[04~05] 다음 대화를 읽고 물음에 답하시오.

> G: Wow, look at the bridge in this ad.
> _____
> B: That's Gwangandaegyo in Busan.
> G: How do you know that?
> B: I went there with my family last summer.

04 위 대화의 빈칸에 들어갈 말로 적절하지 <u>않은</u> 것은?

① I wonder where the photo was taken.
② Can you tell me where the photo was taken?
③ Can I ask you where the photo was taken?
④ I want to know where the photo was taken.
⑤ I'm sure where the photo was taken.

05 Where did the boy visit last summer?

➡ _____
_____

[06~07] 다음 대화를 읽고 물음에 답하시오.

> Brian: Look over there. _____
> Sujin: They're waiting to get into the new bakery there.
> Brian: Why? Is it famous?
> Sujin: Yes. It was on a TV program.
> Brian: Really? We should try their bread then.
> Sujin: Sure.

06 위 대화의 빈칸에 들어갈 말을 〈보기〉에 주어진 단어들을 배열하여 완성하시오.

> ┤ 보기 ├
> many / in / why / are / wonder / so / I /
> people / waiting / line / there

➡ _____
_____

07 위 대화를 읽고 대답할 수 <u>없는</u> 것은?

① What is Brian wondering?
② Why are many people waiting in line?
③ Why is the new bakery famous?
④ What does Brian want to try?
⑤ When was the new bakery on the TV program?

08 다음 대화가 자연스럽게 이어지도록 순서대로 배열하시오.

> (A) It's a long hiking path around Jejudo.
> (B) Oh, I see. I hope you enjoy your trip!
> (C) Are you going somewhere this summer?
> (D) I'm going to Jejudo to walk along the Jeju Olle Trail.
> (E) The Jeju Olle Trail? Could you explain what that is?

➡ _____

[09~10] 다음 대화를 읽고 물음에 답하시오.

Emma: Look over there. I wonder why there are so many cars on the road.
Mike: Lots of people are going on vacation this weekend.
Emma: Really? Then, why don't we go somewhere, too?
Mike: O.K.

09 Why are so many cars on the road?

➡ _____
_____

10 What did Emma suggest to Mike?

➡ _____

11 다음 짝지어진 대화가 어색한 것은?

① A: I'm wondering why he got upset.
　 B: I think he had a fight with his brother.
② A: Can you tell me what they are?
　 B: They're called songpyeon.
③ A: Could you tell me about them?
　 B: They're traditional Korea rice cakes.
④ A: Would you give me more information?
　 B: Sure. Let's take a look at this book together.
⑤ A: I'm curious why she looks so sad.
　 B: I'm not following you.

12 다음 주어진 우리말을 영작한 것으로 옳은 것은?

> 이것이 무엇인지 설명해 주시겠어요?

① Can you explain what is this?
② Could you explain what this is?
③ Could you explain that what this is?
④ What could you explain this is?
⑤ What could you explain is this?

13 다음 두 문장을 한 문장으로 만들 때 빈칸에 들어갈 말로 가장 알맞은 것은?

> • He was infected by the virus.
> • He stayed at the center of the disease for 3 months.
> → He was infected by the virus because
> _____

① he might stay at the center of the disease for 3 months.
② had he stayed at the center of the disease for 3 months.
③ he has stayed at the center of the disease for 3 months.
④ he had stayed at the center of the disease for 3 months.
⑤ he could have stayed at the center of the disease for 3 months.

14 다음 중 밑줄 친 부분의 쓰임이 나머지 넷과 다른 것은?

① Mr. Baker doesn't know where the post office is located.

② Mina asked me what time the bank would close.

③ I wonder when my girlfriend will come to France.

④ The executives of the company don't understand why the facility is required.

⑤ Let everybody know about the man who won the Oscars yesterday.

15 다음 그림을 보고, 주어진 단어들을 알맞게 배열하여 영작하되, 과거완료시제를 반드시 포함하시오. (동사를 변형)

(the woman, put, the fish, really, if)

➡ James wondered _____

_____ in the fish-shaped bun.

16 다음에 등장하는 사람과 직업에 대한 안내문을 읽고 괄호 안에 주어진 어휘를 알맞게 배열하여 빈칸 (A)와 (B)를 채우시오.

Yori became a content creator (A)_____

_____(gotten, she, after, views, had, 20,000) on her first video clip on WeTube. Her favorite part of her job is (B)_____

_____(about, what, sharing, special, Korean food, is) with many people around the world.

[17~18] 다음 글을 읽고 물음에 답하시오.

Q. How did you become interested in taking photos of haenyeo?

One day, I happened to take pictures of a haenyeo. I was surprised ⓐto find that she was enjoying her job. Until then, I had only seen black-and-white photos of haenyeo who looked very tired. However, she kept laughing even after she had been in the water for over five hours. I realized then that I should take pictures of haenyeo. <I: Zin Kim>

17 위 글의 밑줄 친 ⓐto find와 to부정사의 용법이 같은 것을 모두 고르시오.

① She was too tired to find it.

② Do you know how to find it?

③ I was eager to find it.

④ Tell me the way to find it.

⑤ Is it difficult to find it?

18 According to the passage, which is NOT true?

① Zin Kim happened to take pictures of a haenyeo.

② The haenyeo was enjoying her job.

③ Before Zin Kim took pictures of a haenyeo, she had seen many colorful photos of haenyeo.

④ The haenyeo Zin Kim took pictures of kept laughing even after she had been in the water for over five hours.

⑤ At that time, Zin Kim realized that she should take pictures of haenyeo.

[19~21] 다음 글을 읽고 물음에 답하시오.

> **Q. Could you tell us more about haenyeo?**
> _____ⓐ_____
>
> I can tell you three things. First, haenyeo are a symbol of strong women. Jejudo, which is a volcanic island, is not suitable for farming, so ⓑ많은 해녀들이 가족들의 생계비를 버는 가장이 되어 왔어요. (①) Second, haenyeo form their own communities and help each other. (②) For example, more-experienced haenyeo train less-experienced haenyeo. (③) Third, because they stay in the water without any breathing devices, haenyeo can't catch a lot of seafood. (④) Catching too much marine life at one time in one place can destroy the ocean. (⑤)

19 위 글의 빈칸 ⓐ에 들어갈 알맞은 질문을 고르시오.

① What's so special about them?
② How did you become interested in taking photos of them?
③ Isn't it difficult to take their pictures?
④ What's the secret of holding their breath?
⑤ What are you planning to do in the future?

20 위 글의 흐름으로 보아, 주어진 문장이 들어가기에 가장 적절한 곳은?

> This is good for the underwater environment.

①　　　②　　　③　　　④　　　⑤

21 위 글의 밑줄 친 ⓑ의 우리말에 맞게 9 단어로 영작하시오.
➡ _____
_____

[22~24] 다음 글을 읽고 물음에 답하시오.

> Yori is a content creator about traditional Korean food. She posts her video clips about making and eating Korean food. She became a content creator after she had gotten ⓐ20,000 views on her first video clip on WeTube. Her favorite part of her job is sharing ⓑwhat is special about Korean food with many people around the world. She is planning to write a cookbook on Korean food.

22 위 글의 밑줄 친 ⓐ를 영어로 읽는 법을 쓰시오.

➡ _____

23 위 글의 밑줄 친 ⓑwhat과 바꿔 쓸 수 있는 말을 세 단어로 쓰시오.

➡ _____

24 위 글을 읽고 답할 수 없는 질문을 고르시오.

① What does Yori do?
② How did Yori become a content creator?
③ When did Yori get 20,000 views on her first video clip on WeTube?
④ What is Yori's favorite part of her job?
⑤ What is Yori planning to do in the future?

Lesson 5

A Journey into Your Mind

Words & Expressions

Key Words

- **actually** [ǽktʃuəli] 분 실제로
- **anxious** [ǽŋkʃəs] 형 불안해하는
- **apart** [əpɑ́ːrt] 분 (거리·공간·시간상으로) 떨어져
- **behavior** [bihéivjər] 명 행동
- **bored** [bɔːrd] 형 지루해하는
- **carefully** [kɛ́ərfəli] 분 조심스럽게
- **chew** [tʃuː] 동 (음식을) 씹다
- **competition** [kɑ̀mpətíʃən] 명 경쟁, 대회
- **confident** [kɑ́nfədənt] 형 자신감 있는
- **convenient** [kənvíːnjənt] 형 편리한
- **decide** [disáid] 동 결심하다
- **enemy** [énəmi] 명 적
- **famously** [féiməsli] 분 유명하게
- **graduate** [grǽdʒuət] 동 졸업하다
- **guess** [ges] 동 추측하다
- **helpless** [hélplis] 형 무력한
- **hip** [hip] 명 엉덩이, 허리께
- **instead** [instéd] 분 대신에
- **judge** [dʒʌdʒ] 동 판단하다
- **lend** [lend] 동 빌려주다
- **lucky** [lʌ́ki] 형 행운인, 운이 좋은
- **Mexican** [méksikən] 형 멕시코 출신의, 멕시코의
- **mind** [maind] 명 마음, 정신
- **nervous** [nɔ́ːrvəs] 형 불안해하는
- **place** [pleis] 동 놓다, 두다
- **political** [pəlítikəl] 형 정치적인
- **practice** [prǽktis] 동 연습하다
- **prepare** [pripɛ́ər] 동 준비하다
- **presentation** [prɛ̀zəntéiʃən] 명 발표
- **professional** [prəféʃənl] 형 전문적인
- **psychologist** [saikɑ́lədʒist] 명 심리학자
- **psychology** [saikɑ́lədʒi] 명 심리학
- **rare** [rɛər] 형 드문, 희귀한
- **relax** [rilǽks] 동 휴식을 취하다
- **relay** [ríːlei] 명 이어달리기
- **relieved** [rilíːvd] 형 안도하는
- **rival** [ráivəl] 명 경쟁자
- **seafood** [síːfud] 명 해산물, 해물
- **solution** [səlúːʃən] 명 해결책
- **Sports Day** 운동회
- **stranger** [stréindʒər] 명 낯선 사람
- **stressful** [strésfəl] 형 스트레스가 많은
- **study** [stʌ́di] 명 과목, 연구
- **supporter** [səpɔ́ːrtər] 명 지원자
- **unique** [juːníːk] 형 독특한

Key Expressions

- **according to** ~에 따르면
- **be good at** ~을 잘하다
- **be worried about** ~을 걱정하다
- **by oneself** 혼자서
- **chances are that** 아마 ~일 것이다
- **clear one's mind** 마음을 가다듬다, 마음을 맑게 하다
- **come over** (장소에) 들르다
- **come up with** (해답 등을) 찾아내다, 내놓다
- **do ~ a favor** ~에게 호의를 베풀다
- **get off** 내리다
- **get up** 일어나다
- **have no idea** 알지 못하다
- **I can't wait!** 너무 기다려져!
- **in front of** ~의 앞에
- **make a presentation** 발표하다
- **make a reservation** 예약하다
- **not ~ anymore** 더 이상 ~가 아닌
- **not ~ at all** 결코 ~가 아닌
- **not only A but also B** A뿐만 아니라 B도 또한
- **put too much pressure on** ~에게 너무 많은 부담을 주다
- **Shall we ~?** ~할까요?
- **stand tall** 당당해 보이다, 우뚝 서다
- **with one's feet apart** 양발을 벌린 채로
- **stop by** ~에 들르다
- **strangely enough** 매우 이상하게도
- **turn A into B** A를 B로 바꾸다
- **What if ~?** ~하면 어쩌지?
- **Why don't you ~?** ~하지 않겠니?
- **Why not?** 좋죠!

Word Power

※ 서로 비슷한 뜻을 가진 어휘

- □ **actually** 실제로 : **really** 실제로
- □ **carefully** 조심스럽게 : **attentively** 주의 깊게
- □ **guess** 추측하다 : **suppose** 추측하다
- □ **lucky** 운이 좋은 : **fortunate** 운 좋은

- □ **anxious** 불안해하는 : **nervous** 불안해하는
- □ **confident** 자신감 있는 : **convinced** 확신하는
- □ **helpless** 무력한 : **powerless** 힘없는
- □ **place** 놓다, 두다 : **put** 두다

※ 서로 반대되는 뜻을 가진 어휘

- □ **carefully** 조심스럽게 ↔ **carelessly** 부주의하게
- □ **convenient** 편리한 ↔ **inconvenient** 불편한
- □ **lend** 빌려주다 ↔ **borrow** 빌리다
- □ **rare** 드문, 희귀한 ↔ **common** 흔한

- □ **certain** 확실한 ↔ **uncertain** 불확실한
- □ **enemy** 적 ↔ **friend** 친구
- □ **lucky** 운이 좋은 ↔ **unlucky** 운이 나쁜

※ 명사 – 형용사

- □ **beauty** 아름다움 – **beautiful** 아름다운
- □ **care** 보살핌, 조심 – **careful** 조심스러운
- □ **thought** 생각 – **thoughtful** 신중한
- □ **hope** 희망 – **hopeful** 희망찬
- □ **person** 사람 – **personal** 개인적인
- □ **nation** 국가 – **national** 국가적인

- □ **color** 색 – **colorful** 다채로운
- □ **success** 성공 – **successful** 성공적인
- □ **power** 힘 – **powerful** 힘 있는
- □ **stress** 스트레스 – **stressful** 스트레스가 많은
- □ **option** 선택 – **optional** 선택적인
- □ **tradition** 전통 – **traditional** 전통적인

※ Word Partner (collocations)

- □ **come back** 돌아오다
- □ **come over** (장소에) 들르다
- □ **come to a decision** 결정을 내리다
- □ **come to an end** 끝내다

- □ **come first** 최우선이다
- □ **come prepared** 준비해 오다
- □ **come to an agreement** 합의에 이르다
- □ **come up with** 생각해 내다

English Dictionary

- □ **bake** 굽다
  → to cook something using dry heat, in an oven
  오븐에서 열을 이용해서 어떤 것을 요리하다

- □ **chew** (음식을) 씹다
  → to bite food several times before swallowing it
  삼키기 전에 음식을 몇 번 물다

- □ **convenient** 편리한
  → useful to you because it saves you time
  시간을 덜어주기 때문에 쓸모가 있는

- □ **enemy** 적
  → someone who hates you and wants to harm you
  당신을 싫어하며 당신에게 해를 끼치고 싶어 하는 사람

- □ **graduate** 졸업하다
  → to complete your education at a college, school, etc.
  대학이나 학교 등에서 교육을 끝내다

- □ **presentation** 발표
  → an event at which you describe or explain a new product or idea
  새로운 상품이나 생각을 묘사하거나 설명하는 행사

- □ **psychology** 심리학
  → the study of the mind and how it influences people's behavior
  사람의 마음과 그것이 행동에 영향을 미치는 방식을 연구하는 학문

01 다음 짝지어진 단어의 관계가 같도록 빈칸에 알맞은 말을 주어진 철자로 시작하여 쓰시오.

carefully : carelessly = common : r_____

02 다음 영영풀이가 가리키는 것을 고르시오.

the study of the mind and how it influences people's behavior

① politics
② psychology
③ psychologist
④ presentation
⑤ solution

03 다음 중 밑줄 친 부분의 뜻풀이가 바르지 <u>않은</u> 것은?

① He decided to retire because of the political scandals. (정치적인)
② Wild flowers are becoming rare. (드문, 귀한)
③ You should not judge a man by his appearance. (판단하다)
④ She was in a relaxed and confident mood. (편안한)
⑤ The man is responsible for a very professional job. (전문적인)

04 다음 주어진 문장의 밑줄 친 judge와 같은 의미로 쓰인 것은?

Don't judge a book by its cover.

① Chris was asked to judge the singing competition.
② He was brought before the judge.

③ It's difficult to judge how long the journey will take.
④ Mr. White will judge this case.
⑤ We can't judge whether what you're doing well or not.

05 다음 문장에 공통으로 들어갈 말을 고르시오.

• When will you _____ back?
• My twin sister tried to _____ up with a unique idea.
• We would love to have you _____ over and celebrate with us.

① go
② get
③ lend
④ decide
⑤ come

서답형
06 다음 우리말에 맞게 빈칸에 알맞은 말을 쓰시오.

(1) 당신은 그것들을 적어도 1미터는 떨어뜨려 놓아야 합니다.
➡ You should place them at least one meter _____.

(2) 아이들은 그들의 잘한 행동에 대해 사탕을 받았다.
➡ Children were given sweets for their good _____.

(3) Jack은 양 허리께에 손을 대고 서 있다.
➡ Jack is standing with his hands on his _____.

(4) 대부분의 별들은 사람의 시야에 보이지 않는다.
➡ Most stars are _____ to human sight.

01 다음 짝지어진 단어의 관계가 같도록 빈칸에 알맞은 말을 쓰시오.

> person : personal = care : _____

02 다음 우리말에 맞게 빈칸에 알맞은 말을 쓰시오.

(1) 아마 그는 회의에 늦을 것이다.

➡ _____ _____ _____ he will be late for the meeting.

(2) 매우 이상하게도, 나는 전혀 불안하지 않다.

➡ _____ _____, I don't feel nervous at all.

(3) 항상 당당해 보이고 리더가 되어라.

➡ Always _____ _____ and be a leader.

(4) 나는 혼자서 이 모든 것을 할 수 없다.

➡ I can't do it all _____ _____.

03 다음 우리말을 주어진 단어를 이용하여 영작하시오.

(1) 나는 전문적인 심리학자가 되고 싶다. (become)

➡ _____

(2) 아이들은 쉽게 지루해한다. (get, bored)

➡ _____

(3) 내 개는 종종 내 신발을 씹는다. (shoes)

➡ _____

(4) 네 자신을 믿어라, 그리고 자신감을 가져라. (be, in)

➡ _____

04 다음 문장의 빈칸에 들어갈 말을 〈보기〉에서 골라 쓰시오.

> ─┤ 보기 ├─
> rivals / seat / judge / loudly / law

(1) Do not _____ a book by its cover.

(2) People say it is Murphy's _____ when something goes wrong.

(3) When I am happy, I sing _____.

(4) The two teams have been _____ since the first match.

(5) You don't have to sit in your _____.

05 우리말과 일치하도록 주어진 단어를 모두 배열하여 영작하시오.

(1) 그의 그림 실력은 거의 전문가적이다. (skills / professional / are / his / almost / drawing)

➡ _____
_____

(2) 그녀가 예약하는 걸 잊어버리면 어떡하죠? (she / make / a / if / what / reservation / to / forgets)

➡ _____
_____

(3) 나는 마음을 가다듬기 위해 산책하기로 결심했다. (to / a / to / my / I / take / mind / decided / walk / clear)

➡ _____
_____

(4) 두 발을 벌리고 서서 손바닥은 위로 향하게 하라. (upwards / stand / feet / your / your / facing / apart / hands / with / and)

➡ _____
_____

Condersation

Conversation

① 걱정하기

• I'm worried about Sports Day. 난 운동회가 걱정돼.

■ 걱정이 된다는 것을 나타내는 표현은 'I'm worried ~(나는 ~가 걱정돼.)' 또는 'I'm concerned ~(나는 ~가 걱정돼.)'라고 한다. 걱정을 나타내는 nervous 또는 문제를 나타내는 trouble을 써서 'I'm nervous about ~', 'I'm in trouble ~'이라고 할 수도 있다.

■ 걱정이 되는 것이 두려움이나 무서움을 포함하고 있을 때는 scared, frightened, terrified 등을 써서 'I'm scared ~', 'I'm frightened ~', 'I'm terrified ~' 등으로 나타내기도 한다. 이 말에 공감할 때는 'Me, too.(나도 그래.)'라고 한다.

■ 걱정이 되는 내용을 덧붙일 때는 전치사 about나 접속사 that을 써서 'I'm worried about ~' 또는 'I'm worried that ~'이라고 한다. about 뒤에는 명사나 동명사를 쓰고 that 뒤에는 주어, 동사가 있는 절을 쓴다.

걱정하기

• I'm worried about 명사 / that 주어+동사 ~.	나는 ~가 걱정돼.
• I'm concerned about ~.	나는 ~가 걱정이야.
• I'm afraid that ~ .	나는 ~가 걱정돼.
• I'm nervous about ~.	나는 ~가 불안해.
• I'm anxious about ~.	나는 ~가 걱정이야.

핵심 Check

1. 다음 밑줄 친 (A)의 우리말과 일치하도록 주어진 어휘를 포함하여 영어로 쓰시오.

    G: What happened to your shoes? Aren't they new?

    B: Yes, but my dog chewed them. He does it all the time. (A)난 그가 걱정돼. (worried, him)

    G: He was probably bored. Why don't you play with him more often?

    B: O.K, I will. I hope he will stop chewing my shoes.

    ➡ _____

② 의무 부인하기

> • You don't have to clean the classroom. 너는 교실을 청소할 필요가 없어.

- '~해야 한다'는 뜻의 의무를 나타내는 표현은 'You have to+동사원형(~해야 한다)', 'You must+동사원형(~해야 한다)', 'You should/ought to+동사원형(~해야 한다)', 'You need to+동사원형(~할 필요가 있다)' 등이다.

- 의무를 나타내는 'have to'를 부정하여 'don't/doesn't have to+동사원형'이 되면 의무를 부인하여 '~할 필요가 없다'는 뜻으로 'don't need to+동사원형'과 비슷한 의미가 된다. 'There is no need to+동사원형'도 '~할 필요가 없다.'는 의미로 의무를 부인하는 표현이다. must, should는 긍정 표현일 때는 의무를 나타내지만, 'must not', 'should not'처럼 부정이 되면 '~해서는 안 된다'는 의미의 금지를 나타내는 표현이 된다.

- 그 외에 의무를 나타내는 표현으로 'be supposed to+동사원형(~해야 한다, ~하기로 되어 있다)'가 있고, 'have to'를 강조하여 'have got to+동사원형(~해야 한다)'이 있다. 'be not supposed to'는 '~해서는 안 된다'는 의미의 금지 표현이다.

의무 부인하기

- You don't have to ~.   ~할 필요가 없다.
- You don't need to ~.   ~할 필요가 없다.
- There's no need to ~.   ~할 필요가 없다.

핵심 Check

2. 다음 대화의 밑줄 친 (A)의 우리말에 해당하는 적절한 표현을 쓰시오.

A: I'm going to the school library. Do I have to bring my student ID?

B: (A)아니, 그럴 필요 없어.

➡ _____ / _____

3. 다음 대화를 자연스러운 순서로 배열하시오.

M: Shall we have seafood spaghetti for dinner?

(A) You don't have to do that. We already have what we need.

(B) Oh, I see. Then, I'll be back home by 6 to help you cook.

(C) Sure. I'll stop by the store on the way home.

➡ _____

Listen and Speak 1 A-1

G: What happened to your shoes? Aren't ❶they new?

B: Yes, but my dog chewed them. ❷He does it all the time. ❸I'm worried about ❷him.

G: He was probably ❹bored. ❺Why don't you play with him more often?

B: O.K., I will. I hope he will ❻stop chewing my shoes.

G: 신발이 왜 그래? 새것 아니었어?

B: 맞는데, 내 개가 씹어 버렸어. 항상 그렇게 해. 그 개가 걱정돼.

G: 아마 심심했었을 거야. 개와 더 자주 놀아 주는 게 어때?

B: 알겠어, 그럴게. 그 개가 내 신발 씹는 걸 그만두면 좋겠네.

❶ they는 your shoes를 가리킨다.   ❷ He와 him은 my dog을 가리킨다.

❸ 걱정이 된다는 것을 나타내는 표현으로 'I'm concerned about him.' 또는 'I'm anxious about him.'으로 바꾸어 표현할 수 있다.

❹ bored: 지루해하는

❺ 'Why don't you ~?'는 무언가를 제안하는 표현으로 'How about ~?' 또는 'What about ~?' 등으로 바꾸어 표현할 수 있다.

❻ stop+ing: ~하던 것을 멈추다, stop+to부정사: ~하기 위해 멈추다

Check(√) True or False

(1) The boy's dog chewed his new shoes.   T ☐ F ☐

(2) The boy is going to play with his dog if his dog stops chewing his shoes.   T ☐ F ☐

Communicate A

Yuri: Hi, Jaden. Sports Day is next Friday. ❶I can't wait!

Jaden: Really? I'm actually worried about ❷it.

Yuri: Why? ❸Aren't you good at sports?

Jaden: Yes, I am, but I'm worried about the 800-meter relay.

Yuri: What do you mean?

Jaden: I'm the last runner. ❹What if our team loses because of me?

Yuri: I think you're ❺putting too much pressure on yourself.

Jaden: Really? Don't you think I should practice every day?

Yuri: No, you don't have to do that. It's just a school race. It's not about winning or losing.

Jaden: I guess you're right, Yuri. I'm lucky to have a friend like you.

유리: 안녕, Jaden. 운동회가 다음 주 금요일이야. 너무 기다려져!

Jaden: 정말? 난 사실 걱정돼.

유리: 왜? 너 운동 잘하지 않아?

Jaden: 응, 그렇긴 하지만, 800미터 릴레이가 걱정돼.

유리: 무슨 뜻이니?

Jaden: 내가 마지막 주자거든. 나 때문에 우리 팀이 지면 어쩌지?

유리: 넌 네 스스로에게 너무 많은 압박을 주고 있는 것 같아.

Jaden: 그래? 내가 매일 연습해야 한다고 생각하지 않니?

유리: 아니, 그럴 필요 없어. 그냥 학교 경기일 뿐인걸. 이기고 지고에 관한 게 아냐.

Jaden: 네 말이 맞는 것 같다, 유리야. 너 같은 친구를 둬서 다행이야.

❶ 'I can't wait!'은 '너무 기다려져!'라고 기대감을 나타내는 표현으로 'I'm looking forward to it.' 등으로 바꾸어 표현할 수 있다.

❷ it은 'Sports Day'를 가리킨다.   ❸ be good at ~: ~을 잘하다

❹ What if ~?: '~하면 어쩌지?'라는 의미를 나타낸다.   ❺ put too much pressure on: ~에게 너무 많은 부담을 주다

Check(√) True or False

(3) Jaden is going to take part in the 800-meter relay as the last runner.   T ☐ F ☐

(4) Yuri focuses on the importance of winning at the race.   T ☐ F ☐

Listen and Speak 1 A-2

B: You look a bit ❶nervous.

G: I'm worried about my swimming ❷ competition this Saturday.

B: Don't worry. You're ❸such a good swimmer. Just relax and enjoy yourself!

G: Thanks. I feel much better now.

❶ nervous: 긴장된
❷ competition: 대회
❸ such a(n)+형용사+명사

 Listen and Speak 2 A-1

B: Mom, what time are we going to ❶Grandma's place tomorrow morning?

W: About 8 a.m. I'm going to ❷bake cookies for ❸her before we go.

B: Then, should I ❹get up early to help you?

W: ❺You don't have to. Your dad will help me.

B: O.K, then. Good night, Mom!

❶ place: 주택, 집
❷ bake: 굽다
❸ her는 Grandma를 가리킨다.
❹ get up: 일어나다
❺ 의무를 부인하는 표현으로 'You don't need to.'로 바꾸어 표현할 수 있다.

Listen and Speak 2 A-2

W: Shall we try that new Mexican restaurant tomorrow?

M: ❶Why not? I'll call the restaurant to ❷make a reservation for us.

W: You don't have to call them. You can ❸do it online.

M: Oh, I see. How ❹convenient!

❶ 'Why not?'은 '좋죠!'라는 동의의 표현이다.
❷ make a reservation: 예약하다
❸ do it = make a reservation
❹ convenient: 편리한

 Progress Check 1

B: You look ❶a bit nervous.

G: Well, I'm worried about my ❷presentation in history class.

B: Don't worry. ❸You've prepared ❹a lot. You'll ❺do a great job.

G: Thanks. I feel much better now.

❶ a bit: 조금
❷ presentation: 발표
❸ have p.p. 형태로 현재완료 시제를 나타낸다. prepare: 준비하다
❹ a lot: 많이
❺ do a great job: 잘하다

 Progress Check 2

M: ❶Shall we have ❷seafood spaghetti for dinner?

W: Sure. I'll ❸stop by the store ❹on the way home.

M: You don't have to ❺do that. We already have what we need.

W: Oh, I see. Then, I'll ❻be back home by 6 to help you cook.

❶ Shall we ~?: 우리 ~할까요?
❷ seafood: 해산물
❸ stop by: ~에 들르다 (= drop by)
❹ on the way home: 집에 가는 길에
❺ do that = stop by the store
❻ be back home: 집에 돌아오다

● 다음 우리말과 일치하도록 빈칸에 알맞은 말을 쓰시오.

Listen & Speak 1 A-1

G: What _____ _____ your shoes? Aren't they new?

B: Yes, but my dog _____ them. He does it _____ _____ _____. I'm _____ _____ him.

G: He was probably _____. _____ _____ _____ play with him more often?

B: O.K., I will. I _____ he will stop _____ my shoes.

G: 신발이 왜 그래? 새것 아니었어?

B: 맞는데, 내 개가 씹어 버렸어. 항상 그렇게 해. 그 개가 걱정돼.

G: 아마 심심했었을 거야. 개와 더 자주 놀아 주는 게 어때?

B: 알겠어, 그렇게. 그 개가 내 신발 씹는 걸 그만두면 좋겠네.

Listen & Speak 1 A-2

B: You look a bit _____.

G: I'm worried about my _____ _____ this Saturday.

B: Don't _____. You're such a good swimmer. Just _____ and _____ yourself!

G: Thanks. I feel much _____ now.

B: 너 좀 긴장한 것 같아 보이는데.

G: 이번 토요일에 있는 수영 대회가 걱정돼.

B: 걱정 마. 너는 수영을 아주 잘 하잖아. 그냥 긴장을 풀고 즐겨!

G: 고마워. 기분이 훨씬 괜찮아졌어.

Listen & Speak 2 A-1

B: Mom, _____ _____ are we going to Grandma's place tomorrow morning?

W: About 8 a.m. I'm going to _____ _____ for her before we go.

B: Then, should I _____ _____ early to help you?

W: You _____ _____ _____. Your dad will help me.

B: O.K, then. Good night, Mom!

B: 엄마, 우리 내일 아침 몇 시에 할머니 댁에 가나요?

W: 8시쯤에. 가기 전에 할머니를 위해 쿠키를 구울 거란다.

B: 그럼, 제가 일찍 일어나서 도와드릴까요?

W: 그럴 필요 없단다. 아빠가 도와주실 거야.

B: 알겠어요, 그럼. 안녕히 주무세요, 엄마!

Listen & Speak 2 A-2

W: _____ _____ _____ that new Mexican restaurant tomorrow?

M: _____ not? I'll call the restaurant to _____ _____ _____ for us.

W: You _____ _____ _____ call them. You can do it _____.

M: Oh, I see. How _____!

W: 우리 내일 새로 생긴 멕시코 레스토랑에 가 볼까요?

M: 좋죠! 레스토랑에 전화해서 예약해 둘게요.

W: 전화할 필요 없어요. 온라인으로 할 수 있거든요.

M: 오, 그렇군요. 정말 편리하네요!

Communicate A

Yuri: Hi, Jaden. Sports Day is next Friday. I can't _____!

Jaden: Really? I'm actually _____ about it.

Yuri: Why? Aren't you _____ _____ sports?

Jaden: Yes, I am, but I'm worried about the 800-meter _____.

Yuri: _____ do you _____?

Jaden: I'm the _____ _____. _____ _____ our team loses because of me?

Yuri: I think you're _____ _____ _____ _____ yourself.

Jaden: Really? Don't you think I should _____ every day?

Yuri: No, you _____ _____ _____ _____ that. It's just a school race. It's not about _____ or _____.

Jaden: I guess you're _____, Yuri. I'm _____ to have a friend like you.

Progress Check 1

B: You look a bit _____.

G: Well, I'm worried about my _____ in _____ class.

B: Don't worry. You've _____ a lot. You'll _____ a great _____.

G: Thanks. I _____ _____ _____ now.

Progress Check 2

M: Shall we have _____ _____ for dinner?

W: Sure. I'll _____ _____ the store _____ _____ _____ home.

M: _____ _____ _____ _____ _____ do that. We already have _____ we need.

W: Oh, I see. Then, I'll be _____ home by 6 to _____ you _____.

Conversation 시험대비 기본평가

[01~02] 다음 대화를 읽고 물음에 답하시오.

Jane: What ⓐhappened to your shoes? Aren't they new?

Brian: Yes, but my dog ⓑchewed them. He does it all the time. I'm ⓒ worried about him.

Jane: He was probably ⓓbored. Why don't you play with him more often?

Brian: O.K., I will. I hope he will stop ⓔto chew my shoes

01 위 대화의 ⓐ~ⓔ중 어색한 것을 찾아 바르게 고치시오.

➡ _____

02 위 대화의 내용과 일치하지 <u>않는</u> 것은?

① Brian의 새 신발이 망가졌다.

② Brian의 개가 Brian의 신발을 처음으로 씹었다.

③ Brian은 그의 개가 걱정이 된다.

④ Jane은 Brian에게 개와 더 자주 놀아줄 것을 제안했다.

⑤ Brian은 그의 개가 신발을 씹는 걸 그만 두길 바란다.

[03~04] 다음 대화를 읽고 물음에 답하시오.

B: You look a bit nervous.

G: I'm worried about my swimming competition this Saturday.

B: Don't worry. You're such a good swimmer. Just relax and enjoy yourself!

G: Thanks. I feel much better now.

03 What's the matter with the girl?

➡ _____

04 What does the boy advise the girl to do?

➡ _____

[01~03] 다음 대화를 읽고 물음에 답하시오.

Jane: What happened to your shoes? Aren't they new?

Brian: Yes, but my dog chewed them. He does it all the time. (A)I'm worried about him.

Jane: He was probably bored. (B)Why don't you play with him more often? (about, how)

Brian: O.K., I will. I hope he will stop chewing my shoes.

01 위 대화의 밑줄 친 (A)와 바꾸어 쓸 수 있는 것을 <u>모두</u> 고르시오.

① I'm anxious about him.
② I'm fond of him.
③ I'm concerned about him.
④ I'm tired of him.
⑤ I'm glad to see him.

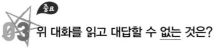

02 위 대화의 밑줄 친 (B)와 의미가 같도록 주어진 단어를 사용하여 다시 쓰시오.

➡ _____

03 위 대화를 읽고 대답할 수 <u>없는</u> 것은?

① What's the problem with Brian's shoes?
② Who chewed Brian's shoes?
③ What is Brian worried about?
④ What does Jane suggest to Brian?
⑤ When did Brian buy his shoes?

[04~05] 다음 대화를 읽고 물음에 답하시오.

B: You look a bit __(A)__ .

G: I'm worried about my swimming competition this Saturday.

B: Don't worry. You're such a good swimmer. Just relax and enjoy yourself!

G: Thanks. I feel much better now.

04 위 대화의 빈칸 (A)에 들어갈 말로 적절한 것은?

① satisfied   ② excited
③ happy   ④ pleased
⑤ nervous

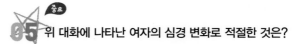

05 위 대화에 나타난 여자의 심경 변화로 적절한 것은?

① worried → relieved
② nervous → disappointed
③ worried → lonely
④ nervous → lonely
⑤ disappointed → worried

06 다음 대화가 자연스럽게 이어지도록 순서대로 배열하시오.

(A) O.K, then. Good night, Mom!
(B) Then, should I get up early to help you?
(C) About 8 a.m. I'm going to bake cookies for her before we go.
(D) You don't have to. Your dad will help me.
(E) Mom, what time are we going to Grandma's place tomorrow morning?

➡ _____

[07~08] 다음 대화를 읽고 물음에 답하시오.

> Emily: Shall we try that new Mexican restaurant tomorrow?
>
> Tom: Why not? I'll call the restaurant to make a reservation for us.
>
> Emily: You don't have to call them. You can do it online.
>
> Tom: Oh, I see. How convenient!

서답형

07 What does Emily suggest doing?

➡ _____

_____

서답형

08 Why doesn't Tom need to call the restaurant to make a reservation? (6 words)

➡ _____

[09~10] 다음 대화를 읽고 물음에 답하시오.

> Yuri: Hi, Jaden. Sports Day is next Friday. I can't wait!
>
> Jaden: Really? I'm actually worried about it.
>
> Yuri: Why? Aren't you good at sports?
>
> Jaden: Yes, I am, but I'm (A)[concerned / concerning] about the 800-meter relay.
>
> Yuri: What do you mean?
>
> Jaden: I'm the last runner. What if our team loses (B)[because / because of] me?
>
> Yuri: I think you're putting too much pressure on (C)[you / yourself].
>
> Jaden: Really? Don't you think I should practice every day?
>
> Yuri: No, you don't have to do that. It's just a school race. It's not about winning or losing.
>
> Jaden: I guess you're right, Yuri. I'm lucky to have a friend like you.

09 위 대화의 (A)~(C)에 들어갈 말이 바르게 짝지어진 것은?

	(A)	(B)	(C)
①	concerned	because	you
②	concerned	because of	yourself
③	concerned	because of	you
④	concerning	because of	yourself
⑤	concerning	because	you

10 위 대화를 읽고 대답할 수 <u>없는</u> 것은?

① When is Sports Day?
② What is Jaden worried about?
③ How has Jaden's feeling changed?
④ Should Jaden practice for the 800-meter relay every day?
⑤ Who is the first runner of the 800-meter relay?

11 다음 짝지어진 대화가 <u>어색한</u> 것은?

① A: I'm worried about Sports Day. I'm not good at sports.
  B: I know how you feel, but try to enjoy it.
② A: I'm concerned about my brother. He gets angry so often these days.
  B: How about trying to calm him down?
③ A: I'm worried about my English speaking test.
  B: Don't worry. You've prepared a lot. You can make it.
④ A: I'm anxious about my future.
  B: You're such a good student! Everything will be fine.
⑤ A: I'm nervous about my presentation in English class.
  B: I feel much better now. Thanks a lot.

01 다음 대화가 자연스럽게 이어지도록 순서대로 배열하시오.

(A) Thanks. I feel much better now.

(B) You look a bit nervous.

(C) Don't worry. You've prepared a lot. You'll do a great job.

(D) Well, I'm worried about my presentation in history class.

➡ _____

[02~04] 다음 대화를 읽고 물음에 답하시오.

Jack: Mom, what time are we going to Grandma's place tomorrow morning?

Mom: About 8 a.m. I'm going to bake cookies for her before we go.

Jack: Then, should I get up early to help you?

Mom: You don't have to. Your dad will help me.

Jack: O.K, then. Good night, Mom!

중요
02 What is Jack going to do tomorrow?

➡ _____

03 What is Jack's mom going to do before she visits Jack's grandma's place?

➡ _____

중요
04 Why doesn't Jack's mom need his help tomorrow morning?

➡ _____

05 다음 대화의 내용과 일치하도록 Jaden의 일기를 완성하시오.

Yuri: Hi, Jaden. Sports Day is next Friday. I can't wait!

Jaden: Really? I'm actually worried about it.

Yuri: Why? Aren't you good at sports?

Jaden: Yes, I am, but I'm worried about the 800-meter relay.

Yuri: What do you mean?

Jaden: I'm the last runner. What if our team loses because of me?

Yuri: I think you're putting too much pressure on yourself.

Jaden: Really? Don't you think I should practice every day?

Yuri: No, you don't have to do that. It's just a school race. It's not about winning or losing.

Jaden: I guess you're right, Yuri. I'm lucky to have a friend like you.

Mon, June 15th, 2020

Today, I was so concerned about Sports Day. I was chosen as the (A)_____ of the 800-meter relay. All my classmates believed that I can do it very well. But I felt so burdened. I was worried that (B)_____. I talked about it to Yuri and she said that I was putting too (C)_____ on myself. Actually, I was thinking whether (D)_____ every day or not. Yuri advised me not to do so, because it's just a school race, not about (E)_____ . I was encouraged by her a lot. I really appreciated her today.

Grammar

① 분사구문

> • **Feeling** nervous, Jisu was carefully studying her notes in her chair.
> 지수는 긴장이 되어, 의자에 앉아 자신의 필기를 열심히 들여다보고 있었다.

■ 종속접속사가 이끄는 부사절을 분사를 이용하여 간략한 부사구로 바꾼 것이다.

  • **While I was walking** on the street, I saw my teacher.

   = **Walking** on the street, I saw my teacher. 거리를 걷고 있었을 때, 나는 선생님을 봤다.

■ 부사구와 주절의 관계에 따라 양보, 동시동작, 이유, 시간, 조건 등의 의미로 쓰인다.

  (1) 양보: **Although he is** over 90, the businessman runs faster than the young.

   = **Being** over 90, the businessman runs faster than the young.
   비록 그 사업가는 90세가 넘었지만, 젊은 사람들보다 빨리 뛴다.

  (2) 동시동작(부대상황): **While she sat** on the bed, she watched TV.

   = **Sitting** on the bed, she watched TV. 침대에 앉아서 그녀는 TV를 시청했다.

  (3) 이유: **As he was** tired, Harry went to bed early.

   = **Being tired**, Harry went to bed early. 피곤했기 때문에, Harry는 일찍 잠자리에 들었다.

  (4) 시간: **When she doesn't work**, she enjoys the board games.

   = **Not working**, she enjoys the board games. 일하지 않을 때, 그녀는 보드게임을 즐긴다.

  (5) 조건: **If you take** a taxi, you'll get to the party on time.

   = **Taking** a taxi, you'll get to the party on time. 택시를 타면, 파티에 제 시간에 도착할 거야.

■ 종속절의 시제가 주절보다 앞선 경우, 완료분사구문을 사용한다.

  • **As she had done** it before, Susan knew how to fix the copy machine.

   = **Having done** it before, Susan knew how to fix the copy machine.

■ 주절과 종속절의 주어가 다를 경우, 분사구문의 주어를 남겨 두는 것을 독립분사구문이라고 하며, 일반인이 주어일 경우에는 생략 가능하다. (비인칭 독립분사구문)

  (1) 독립분사구문: **As it was** cloudy, we couldn't go on a field trip.

   = **It being** cloudy, we couldn't go on a field trip. 날이 흐려서, 소풍을 갈 수 없었다.

  (2) 비인칭 독립분사구문: **generally speaking**(일반적으로 말해), **considering**(~를 고려하면)

  (3) with+목적어+분사: Mom fell asleep **with the TV turned on**. (TV를 켠 채로)

핵심 Check

1. 다음 괄호 안에서 알맞은 말을 고르시오.

  (1) (Feeling / Felt) worried, Jake drove to the subway station to pick her up.

  (2) With night (come / coming) on, it got colder and colder.

② 상관접속사 not only ~ but also ...

• His rival became **not only** a political supporter **but also** a good friend.
그의 경쟁자는 정치적 지원자 뿐만 아니라 좋은 친구가 되었다.

■ 상관접속사 'not only A but also B'는 'A뿐만 아니라 B도 또한'이라는 뜻이며, 'B as well as A'로 바꿀 수 있다. 접속사이므로 A와 B 자리에 명사뿐만 아니라 동사, 형용사, 준동사 등 어떤 것이든 올 수 있으며, A에 동사가 오면 B에도 동사가 와야 한다.

• My mom is **not only** a good cook **but also** a great painter.

= My mom is a great painter as well as a good cook. 우리 어머니는 훌륭한 요리사일 뿐만 아니라 대단한 화가이기도 하다.

■ 상관접속사의 종류와 주어로 쓰일 때의 수 일치

(1) Not only A but also B(= B as well as A): A뿐만 아니라 B도 또한 (B에 일치)

• **Not only** they **but also** she **wants** the job. 그들뿐만 아니라 그녀도 그 일을 원한다.

= She **as well as** they **wants** the job.

(2) Not A but B: A가 아니라 B (B에 일치)

• **Not** they **but** she **wants** the job. 그들이 아니라 그녀가 그 일을 원한다.

(3) Both A and B: A와 B 둘 다 (복수 주어)

• **Both** they **and** she **want** the job. 그들과 그녀 모두 다 그 일을 원한다.

(4) Either A or B: A 또는 B 둘 중 하나 (동사와 가까운 주어에 일치)

• **Either** they **or** she **wants** the job. 그들 또는 그녀 둘 중 하나는 그 일을 원한다.

(5) Neither A nor B: A도 B도 아닌 (동사와 가까운 주어에 일치)

• **Neither** they **nor** she **wants** the job. 그들도 그녀도 그 일을 원하지 않는다.

■ Not only가 주어가 아닌 동사를 받을 경우 문두에 오면 도치가 일어난다.

• **Not only** is he wise, **but also** he is kind. 그는 현명할 뿐만 아니라 친절하다.

• **Not only** could she read the book, **but also** she could memorize it.
그녀는 그 책을 읽을 수 있었을 뿐만 아니라 그 책을 외울 수도 있었다.

■ not only ~ but also에서 only 대신 just, simply 등을 쓸 수 있고, also는 생략해서 쓰기도 한다.

• The fairy was **not just** wise **but** beautiful. 그 요정은 지혜로울 뿐만 아니라 아름다웠다.

핵심 Check

2. 다음 문장에서 어법상 틀린 부분을 찾아 바르게 고쳐 쓰시오.

(1) Andy not only plays but also teach the guitar. ➡ _____

(2) Not only you but also he are responsible for the problem. ➡ _____

01 다음 빈칸에 들어갈 말로 알맞은 것은?

> Mina is not only a good listener but also _____.

① sings well   ② beautiful   ③ has a sense of humor

④ poor at hearing   ⑤ a great leader

02 다음 부사절을 분사구문으로 바꿔 쓸 때, 빈칸에 들어갈 말로 가장 적절한 것은?

> As he wanted to make his dad feel better, Harry smiled brightly at him.
>
> → _____ to make his dad feel better, Harry smiled brightly at him.

① He wanting   ② As he wanting   ③ Wanting

④ Having wanted   ⑤ Being wanting

03 다음 중 어법상 옳지 <u>않은</u> 것을 고르시오.

① She is both generous and intelligent.

② Frank's friends not only sing well but also paint well.

③ He is interested either in soccer or in hockey.

④ Kevin not only writes well but also dancing well.

⑤ Nora has not only the dolls but also their house.

04 다음 분사구문을 접속사가 이끄는 부사절로 만들 때, 빈칸에 알맞은 말을 써 넣으시오.

(1) Listening to music, John cleaned his room.

➡ While _____ _____ _____ _____, John cleaned his room.

(2) Feeling lonely, she called her mother in New York.

➡ As _____ _____ _____, she called her mother in New York.

(3) Being small and weak, Ron has enough courage to complete the difficult mission before him.

➡ _____ _____ _____ _____ _____ _____, Ron has enough courage to complete the difficult mission before him.

01 다음 중 어법상 어색한 것은?

① Not only your friends but also my uncle have those problems.

② The violinist not only played a beautiful song but also gave a great influence on young kids.

③ Lucy has lived not only in France but also in Egypt.

④ Not only the professor but also the student is working on the project.

⑤ Caroline ate not only the cookies but also the jams that her mother made.

[02~03] 다음 우리말을 알맞게 영작한 것을 고르시오.

02

> 그는 눈을 감은 채로 걷고 있었다.

① He was walking his eyes closing.

② He was closing his eyes and walking.

③ He walked and closed his eyes.

④ He was walking closed his eyes with.

⑤ He was walking with his eyes closed.

03

> 많은 사람들을 괴롭혔는데도 불구하고, Tom은 부자로 잘 살았다.

① Even though he having bullied many people, Tom lived well off.

② Although he bullying many people, Tom lived well off.

③ Having bullied many people, Tom living well off.

④ Though having bullied many people, Tom lived well off.

⑤ He had bullied many people, though Tom lived well off.

[04~05] 다음 중 어법상 옳은 것을 고르시오.

04 ① Both Jinsu and his sister is reading the article about the history of Jeju.

② Not only William but also Bentley have lived in New York since last year.

③ Kevin bought Minsu not only the laptop but also a bag.

④ I don't have neither a pen nor a pencil.

⑤ Not only I am hungry but also can't move a little.

05 ① Not only Mary but also Chris speak Spanish well.

② Not only the students but also the teacher know who the girl is.

③ Not only he but also you is wrong.

④ Tell me not only what you like but also she likes to go.

⑤ Elizabeth not only teaches swimming but also sells a lot of swim suits.

서답형

06 다음 문장에서 어법상 어색한 단어 한 개를 찾아서 고치시오.

> Exhausting after the hard work, Paula laid herself down on the bed on coming home.

_____ ➡ _____

07 다음 두 문장을 의미가 같도록 한 문장으로 바꿔 쓸 때 적절하지 <u>않은</u> 것은?

① Tom likes the book. + Jimmy likes the book, too.
→ Not only Tom but also Jimmy likes the book.

② Cory listens to the radio program. + Sean listens to the radio program, too.
→ Both Cory and Sean listens to the radio program.

③ One of the two students, Martha or Sue, may have the answer sheet.
→ Either Martha or Sue may have the answer sheet.

④ Kim doesn't know the way home. Her cousins don't know the way home, either.
→ Neither Kim nor her cousins know the way home.

⑤ Sharon could solve the quiz. + Sharon could pass the exam as well.
→ Sharon could not only solve the quiz but also pass the exam.

08 다음 중 밑줄 친 분사구문의 용법이 〈보기〉와 같은 것은?

> ┤ 보기 ├
> <u>Born</u> in America, Sam isn't good at speaking English.

① <u>Living</u> in Busan for over 10 years, Rena can't understand the conversation between Busan citizens.

② <u>Finishing</u> her homework, Anna went outside to meet her boyfriend.

③ <u>Having</u> nothing special to do, I just called Robert.

④ <u>Not knowing</u> how long she waited for me, I was surprised at her cold hands.

⑤ <u>Turning</u> left at first corner, you can find the post office.

09 다음 〈보기〉의 문장과 가장 가까운 뜻을 가진 문장을 고르시오.

> ┤ 보기 ├
> Not only Josh but also Mina doesn't like smoking as well as drinking.

① Both Josh and Mina don't like smoking but drinking.

② Neither Josh nor Mina likes both smoking and drinking.

③ Either Josh or Mina doesn't like smoking nor drinking.

④ Neither Josh nor Mina doesn't like smoking but also drinking.

⑤ Both Josh and Mina hate not smoking but drinking.

10 다음 주어진 분사구문을 접속사를 이용한 부사절로 만들 때 가장 적절한 것은?

> The disease having come from China, Chinese government blames Korea.

① Since the disease comes from China, Chinese government blames Korea.

② Although the disease comes from China, Chinese government blames Korea.

③ If the disease came from China, Chinese government blames Korea.

④ Though the disease came from China, Chinese government blames Korea.

⑤ While the disease comes from China, Chinese government blames Korea.

[11~12] 다음 중 어법상 옳은 문장은?

11
① Cecilia had lost not only the necklace and also the rings.
② You can not only see the snowman but also likes the colder weather in winter.
③ My uncle not only arrived earlier but also prepared our dinner.
④ Not only the passengers were surprised but also irritated.
⑤ William likes only the pen but also the notebooks.

12 중요
① Both Clara or her husband watched the movie *Parasite*.
② Can either you nor the doctor please explain us what worsens the situation?
③ Not only I but also David wonder whether the speaker is telling the truth.
④ I think either you or your mom know how the problem was solved.
⑤ Eliza loves not only Raynold but also me.

서답형
[13~14] 우리말과 일치하도록 괄호 안에 주어진 단어들을 바르게 배열하시오.

13
아주 오래 전에 나무와 마른 풀로 지어졌기 때문에, 그 집은 항상 화재의 위험에 노출되어 있다.
→ (wood, grass, having, and, built, of, been, dry) so long ago, the house is always exposed to the danger of fire.

➡ _____

14
또 다시 회의에 늦고 싶지 않았기 때문에, 그녀는 지하철역으로 최대한 빨리 뛰었다.
(be, for, not, the meeting, to, wanting, late) again, she ran to the subway station as fast as she could.

➡ _____

서답형
15 다음 그림을 보고 자연스러운 문장이 되도록 괄호 안에 주어진 단어를 바르게 배열하여 빈칸을 완성하시오.

(1)

➡ After _____
_____, (tall, Wonder Woman, for, a few, standing, minutes, like), Jisu didn't feel nervous anymore.

(2)

➡ Jenny was _____
_____ a splash on the street. (for, by, school, only, not, but, late, hit, also)

01 다음 우리말과 일치하도록 괄호 안에 주어진 단어들을 바르게 배열하여 문장을 완성하시오.

(1) 마음을 정리하고 싶기 때문에, Kobe는 혼자 하루 여행을 떠나기로 결정했다. (his, to, wanting, mind, clear)

➡ _____, Kobe decided to take a day trip by himself.

(2) 당신은 자신에 대한 확신이 생길 뿐만 아니라, 다른 사람이 보기에도 자신감에 차 보일 것이다. (look, feel, only, about, confident, sure, not, also, yourself, but)

➡ You will _____
_____ to other people.

(3) 경쟁자를 친구로 만들고 싶다면, 경쟁자에게 부탁을 하라. (into, a rival, turn, wanting, a friend, to)

➡ _____,
ask your rival to do you a favor.

02 다음 〈보기〉에 있는 접속사를 한 번씩만 사용하여, 각 밑줄 친 분사구문을 부사절로 바꾸시오. (단, 진행형 표현은 쓸 수 없다.)

┌─── 보기 ───┐
while   because   when   if   though
└───────────┘

(1) Graduating from high school next year, Tammy wants to become a professional farmer.

➡ _____
_____

(2) Being sick all day long, I could complete the difficult project.

➡ _____
_____

(3) Having a problem that you cannot share with your family or friends, try talking to a stranger.

➡ _____
_____

(4) Listening to the radio, Henry cleaned his guitars.

➡ _____

(5) Not having to worry about being judged, we often tell strangers about our problems.

➡ _____

03 다음 글을 읽고, 질문에 답하시오.

The hardest time in my life was my first grade in middle school. When my family moved to another city, I had to go to a new school. (A)As I didn't have any friends at school, I felt sad and lonely. One day, I asked one of my classmates to show me her notes. (B)(she, help, become, good friend) From this experience, I have learned that asking for help is a good way to make friends.

(1) 밑줄 친 (A)를 접속사가 없는 분사구문으로 바꾸되 'no'를 사용하시오.

➡ _____

(2) (B)의 괄호 속에 밑줄 친 단어들과 not only ~ but also를 활용해, 문맥에 맞게 영작하시오. (시제에 주의할 것)

➡ _____

_____

(3) 위에 나온 단어들을 활용하여, 다음 우리말을 7 단어의 분사구문으로 영작하시오.
'도움을 청하면, 당신은 친구를 사귈 수 있다.'

➡ _____

⭐중요
04 주어진 어구를 이용하여 〈조건〉에 맞게 영작하시오.

┤ 조건 ├
1. 'not only A but also B'를 사용할 것.
2. 주어진 단어를 활용하되, 괄호 안의 글자 수 조건에 맞출 것.

(1) Minju's mom, good doctor, great cook (13 단어)

➡ _____

_____

(2) Harry, speak Spanish, dance well (9 단어)

➡ _____

_____

(3) Seohyun, beautiful, very kind (9 단어)

➡ _____

_____

(4) Frank, his parents, nice (9 단어)

➡ _____

_____

05 다음 문장에서 어법상 어색한 단어를 하나씩만 찾아 바르게 고치시오.

(1) Not only does she believe that she has to get a perfect score on every test but also she study without sleeping.

➡ _____ ➡ _____

(2) Both my cat and your puppy is sick now.

_____ ➡ _____

(3) Either Ms. Brown or her sons is responsible for the problem.

_____ ➡ _____

(4) The new job she got lately was not only difficult but also too stress.

_____ ➡ _____

(5) I wonder why not only Jejudo but also the islands in the south coast is crowded with visitors these days.

_____ ➡ _____

🏠고난이도
06 다음 그림을 보고 괄호 안의 단어를 배열하여 빈칸을 알맞게 채우시오.

(1)

➡ The reason I recommend this restaurant is

_____

_____. (food, only, healthy, its, not, that, also, is, but, delicious)

(2)

➡ _____

to the local governor. (the farmer, donated, picked, huge, carrot, having, it, a)

Psychology Answers Your Questions

Do you think you have a unique problem? <u>Chances are that</u> many
아마 ~일 것이다. ~할 가능성이 충분하다
other people have the same problem. Psychology is the study of the
human mind and behavior, so <u>it</u> can <u>help you find</u> a solution <u>to</u> your
= psychology   ~가 …하는 것을 도와주다   ~에 대한
problem.

How do I become less nervous?

It was five minutes before Jisu's big presentation in front of the
whole class. <u>Feeling</u> nervous, Jisu was carefully studying her notes in
분사구문(= Because she was feeling)
her chair. Then, her teacher <u>came over</u> and told her <u>to stand</u> tall like
~에 오다, (집에) 들르다   told의 목적격보어
Wonder Woman. After standing tall for a few minutes, Jisu did not feel
nervous anymore. <u>In fact,</u> she was confident that she would make a
앞 문장에 나온 내용에 대해서 자세한 내용을 덧붙이거나 내용을 강조할 때 사용
great presentation. <u>According to</u> Amy Cuddy, <u>a famous psychologist,</u>
according to+명사(구): ~에 따르면   Amy Cuddy와 동격
we can become more confident just <u>by standing</u> tall for two minutes
by+동명사: ~함으로써
before stressful events. Our bodies change our minds, and our minds
can change our behavior. Do you want to feel confident? Stand
<u>with your feet apart</u>, and place your hands on your hips. You will
양발을 벌리고
<u>not only</u> feel sure about yourself <u>but also</u> look confident to other people.
not only A but also: A뿐만 아니라 B도(A와 B에는 문법적으로 동등한 형태의 표현을 쓰며, B를 강조함)

psychology 심리학

unique 유일무이한, 독특한

chances are that 아마 ~일 것이다

mind 마음, 정신

behavior 행동

solution 해법, 해결책

stand tall 당당해 보이다, 우뚝 서다

confident 자신감 있는

apart (거리·공간·시간상으로) 떨어져

hip 엉덩이, 허리께

확인문제

● 다음 문장이 본문의 내용과 일치하면 T, 일치하지 <u>않으면</u> F를 쓰시오.

1 Only you have a unique problem. ☐

2 Psychology is the study of the human mind and behavior. ☐

3 After standing tall like Wonder Woman, Jisu felt confident. ☐

4 Our minds can't change our behavior. ☐

Who can help me feel better?

When he graduates from high school next year, Taeho wants to become a professional farmer. However, he has never told anyone
역접의 연결어(앞과 뒤에 상반되는 말이 나옴.)
about it. He is worried that his parents or his friends will not understand. Wanting to clear his mind, Taeho decided to take a day
분사구문(이유. = Because he wanted)
trip on a train by himself. On the train, he told a complete stranger
혼자서
sitting beside him about his problem. He had no idea why he did it.
a complete stranger를 수식하는 현재분사구   *간접의문문(의문사+주어+동사)*
However, he felt much better when he got off the train. Strangely
비교급 강조(= even. a lot. far. still)   *정말 이상하게도*
enough, we often tell strangers about our problems just like Taeho. That is because we do not have to worry about being judged or seeing them again. If you have a problem that you cannot share with your family or friends, try talking to a stranger. You will feel much better.
try -ing: ~해 보다   *= far. even*

How do I turn a rival into a friend?

Benjamin Franklin once had a political rival who did not like him
not at all: 전혀 ~가 아닌
at all. Franklin wanted to become friends with him, so he came up with a plan. His rival had a rare book. Franklin asked his rival to lend him
ask+목적어+목적격보어(to부정사)
the book for a few days. When Franklin returned the book, he thanked him deeply. Since that day, his rival became not only a political
('매우'의 의미로) 깊이, 철저하게 (cf. deep: (깊이가) 깊이, 깊게)
supporter but also a good friend. Franklin famously said, "Enemies
A뿐만 아니라 B도(여기서 A와 B에는 모두 문법적으로 동등한 형태인 명사구가 쓰였음)
who do you one favor will want to do more." If you want to turn a rival
turn A into B: A를 B로 바꾸다
into a friend, don't do your rival a favor. Instead, ask your rival to do you a favor.

graduate 졸업하다
professional 전문적인, 직업의
clear one's mind 마음을 가다듬다. 마음을 맑게 하다
by oneself 혼자
judge 판단하다
political 정치와 관련된, 정치적인
rival 경쟁자, 경쟁 상대
come up with (해답 등을) 찾아내다. 내놓다
rare 드문, 희귀한, 살짝 익힌
do ~ a favor ~에게 호의를 베풀다

📎 **확인문제**

● 다음 문장이 본문의 내용과 일치하면 T, 일치하지 <u>않으면</u> F를 쓰시오.

1 Taeho has never told anyone about what he wants to be. ☐

2 Taeho told his friends about his future hope. ☐

3 Franklin borrowed a rare book from his rival. ☐

4 Franklin's rival remained his political rival. ☐

● 우리말을 참고하여 빈칸에 알맞은 말을 쓰시오.

1 _____ Answers Your Questions

2 Do you think you have a _____ problem?

3 _____ _____ that many other people have the same problem.

4 Psychology is the study of the _____ _____ and _____, _____ it can help you _____ a solution _____ your problem.

5 How do I _____ _____ nervous?

6 It was five minutes before Jisu's _____ in front of the _____ _____.

7 _____ nervous, Jisu was _____ _____ her notes in her chair.

8 Then, her teacher _____ _____ and told her _____ _____ _____ like Wonder Woman.

9 After _____ _____ for a few minutes, Jisu did _____ feel nervous _____.

10 _____ _____, she was _____ _____ she would _____ a great presentation.

11 According to Amy Cuddy, a famous psychologist, we can _____ more confident just _____ _____ _____ for two minutes before _____ _____.

12 Our _____ change our _____, and our _____ can change our _____.

13 Do you want to _____ _____?

14 Stand with your feet _____, and _____ your hands _____ your hips.

15 You will _____ _____ _____ _____ about yourself _____ _____ _____ to other people.

16 Who can help me _____ better?

17 When he _____ _____ high school next year, Taeho wants to become a _____ farmer.

18 _____, he _____ _____ _____ anyone about it.

1 심리학이 당신의 물음에 답하다
2 여러분은 당신만의 유일무이한 고민을 가지고 있다고 생각하는 가?
3 아마 많은 다른 사람들이 여러 분과 똑같은 고민을 가지고 있을 것이다.
4 심리학은 인간의 마음과 행동에 관한 연구이며, 따라서 여러분이 문제에 대한 해결책을 찾는 데 도움을 줄 수 있다.
5 어떻게 하면 긴장을 덜 할 수 있나요?
6 지수가 반 전체 앞에서 발표를 하기 5분 전이었다.
7 지수는 긴장이 되어, 의자에 앉아 자신의 필기를 열심히 들여다보고 있었다.
8 그때 선생님이 다가와서는 원더 우먼처럼 꼿꼿이 서 있어 보라고 말했다.
9 그렇게 몇 분을 우뚝 선 후에, 지수는 더 이상 긴장되지 않았다.
10 사실, 그녀는 발표를 멋지게 할 수 있을 것이라는 자신감이 생겼다.
11 유명한 심리학자인 Amy Cuddy에 의하면, 우리는 스트레스를 받는 상황 이전에 2분 정도 꼿꼿이 서 있는 것만으로도 자신 감이 더 생길 수 있다고 한다.
12 우리의 몸은 마음을 바꾸고, 마음은 우리의 행동을 바꿀 수 있다.
13 자신감이 생기기를 원하는가?
14 양발을 벌리고, 허리께에 손을 올려 보아라.
15 자신에 대한 확신이 생길 뿐만 아니라 다른 사람이 보기에도 자신감에 차 보인다.
16 누가 내 기분을 낫게 해 줄 수 있나요?
17 내년에 고등학교를 졸업한 이후에 태호는 전문적인 농부가 되고 싶어 한다.
18 하지만, 누구에게도 그것에 대해 한 번도 말하지 않았다.

19 He is _____ _____ his parents or his friends _____ _____ _____.

20 _____ to _____ _____ _____, Taeho decided _____ _____ a day trip on a train _____ _____.

21 On the train, he told a _____ stranger _____ beside him about his problem.

22 He had no idea _____ _____ _____.

23 _____, he _____ _____ _____ when he got off the train.

24 _____ _____, we often tell strangers about our problems just like Taeho.

25 That is _____ we do not have to worry about _____ _____ or _____ them again.

26 If you have a problem _____ you cannot _____ _____ your family or friends, try _____ to a stranger.

27 You will _____ _____ better.

28 How do I _____ a _____ _____ a friend?

29 Benjamin Franklin once had a political rival _____ did _____ like him _____ _____.

30 Franklin wanted to _____ _____ _____ him, so he _____ _____ _____ a plan.

31 His rival had a _____ book.

32 Franklin asked his rival _____ _____ him the book for _____ _____ _____.

33 When Franklin returned the book, he thanked him _____.

34 _____ that day, his rival became _____ _____ a political supporter _____ _____ a good friend.

35 Franklin famously said, "Enemies _____ _____ _____ _____ _____ will want to do more."

36 If you want to _____ a rival _____ a friend, don't _____ _____ _____ _____.

37 _____, ask your rival _____ _____ you a favor.

---

19 그는 부모님이나 친구들이 이해하지 못할까 걱정이 된다.

20 마음을 정리하기 위해서, 태호는 혼자 하루 기차 여행을 떠나기로 결심했다.

21 기차에서, 그는 옆에 앉은 전혀 모르는 사람에게 자신의 고민에 대해서 말했다.

22 그는 자신이 왜 그랬는지 알 수 없었다.

23 그러나, 기차에서 내릴 때 기분이 훨씬 좋아졌다.

24 정말 이상하게도, 우리는 태호처럼 우리의 문제에 대해 낯선 사람에게 말할 때가 있다.

25 그것은 우리가 평가받거나 그 사람을 다시 볼 것이라는 걱정을 할 필요가 없기 때문이다.

26 만약 가족이나 친구들과도 나눌 수 없는 고민이 있다면, 낯선 이에게 말해 보아라.

27 기분이 훨씬 나아질 것이다.

28 라이벌을 어떻게 친구로 만들 수 있을까요?

29 Benjamin Franklin에게는 한때 그를 전혀 좋아하지 않는 정치적 경쟁자가 있었다.

30 Franklin은 그와 친구가 되고 싶어서, 계획을 세웠다.

31 그의 경쟁자는 희귀한 책을 가지고 있었다.

32 Franklin은 그의 정적에게 그 책을 며칠 동안 빌려달라고 부탁했다.

33 Franklin이 그 책을 돌려줄 때, 그는 그에게 진심으로 감사를 표했다.

34 그날 이후로, 그의 경쟁자는 정치적인 후원자뿐만 아니라 좋은 친구가 되었다.

35 Franklin은 "당신을 한 번 도운 적은 더 돕고 싶어 하게 된다."라는 유명한 말을 했다.

36 여러분이 경쟁자를 친구로 만들고 싶다면, 경쟁자의 부탁을 들어주지 마라.

37 대신, 경쟁자에게 부탁을 해 보아라.

● 우리말을 참고하여 본문을 영작하시오.

1 심리학이 당신의 물음에 답하다

➡ _____

2 여러분은 당신만의 유일무이한 고민을 가지고 있다고 생각하는가?

➡ _____

3 아마 많은 다른 사람들이 여러분과 똑같은 고민을 가지고 있을 것이다.

➡ _____

4 심리학은 인간의 마음과 행동에 관한 연구이며, 따라서 여러분이 문제에 대한 해결책을 찾는 데 도움을 줄 수 있다.

➡ _____

_____

5 어떻게 하면 긴장을 덜 할 수 있나요?

➡ _____

6 지수가 반 전체 앞에서 발표를 하기 5분 전이었다.

➡ _____

7 지수는 긴장이 되어, 의자에 앉아 자신의 필기를 열심히 들여다보고 있었다.

➡ _____

8 그때 선생님이 다가와서는 원더우먼처럼 꼿꼿이 서 있어 보라고 말했다.

➡ _____

9 그렇게 몇 분을 우뚝 선 후에, 지수는 더 이상 긴장되지 않았다.

➡ _____

10 사실, 그녀는 발표를 멋있게 할 수 있을 것이라는 자신감이 생겼다.

11 유명한 심리학자인 Amy Cuddy에 의하면, 우리는 스트레스를 받는 상황 이전에 2분 정도 꼿꼿이 서 있는 것만으로도 자신감이 더 생길 수 있다고 한다.

➡ _____

12 우리의 몸은 마음을 바꾸고, 마음은 우리의 행동을 바꿀 수 있다.

➡ _____

13 자신감이 생기기를 원하는가?

➡ _____

14 양발을 벌리고, 허리께에 손을 올려 보아라.

➡ _____

15 자신에 대한 확신이 생길 뿐만 아니라 다른 사람이 보기에도 자신감에 차 보인다.

➡ _____

16 누가 내 기분을 낫게 해 줄 수 있나요?

➡ _____

17 내년에 고등학교를 졸업한 이후에 태호는 전문적인 농부가 되고 싶어 한다.

➡ _____

18 하지만, 누구에게도 그것에 대해 한 번도 말하지 않았다.
➡ _____

19 그는 부모님이나 친구들이 이해하지 못할까 걱정이 된다.
➡ _____

20 마음을 정리하기 위해서, 태호는 혼자 하루 기차 여행을 떠나기로 결심했다.
➡ _____

21 기차에서, 그는 옆에 앉은 전혀 모르는 사람에게 자신의 고민에 대해서 말했다.
➡ _____

22 그는 자신이 왜 그랬는지 알 수 없었다.
➡ _____

23 그러나, 기차에서 내릴 때 기분이 훨씬 좋아졌다.
➡ _____

24 정말 이상하게도, 우리는 태호처럼 우리의 문제에 대해 낯선 사람에게 말할 때가 있다.
➡ _____

25 그것은 우리가 평가받거나 그 사람을 다시 볼 것이라는 걱정을 할 필요가 없기 때문이다.
➡ _____

26 만약 가족이나 친구들과도 나눌 수 없는 고민이 있다면, 낯선 이에게 말해 보아라.
➡ _____

27 기분이 훨씬 나아질 것이다.
➡ _____

28 라이벌을 어떻게 친구로 만들 수 있을까요?
➡ _____

29 Benjamin Franklin에게는 한때 그를 전혀 좋아하지 않는 정치적 경쟁자가 있었다.
➡ _____

30 Franklin은 그와 친구가 되고 싶어서, 계획을 세웠다.
➡ _____

31 그의 경쟁자는 희귀한 책을 가지고 있었다.
➡ _____

32 Franklin은 그의 정적에게 그 책을 며칠 동안 빌려달라고 부탁했다.
➡ _____

33 Franklin이 그 책을 돌려줄 때, 그는 그에게 진심으로 감사를 표했다.
➡ _____

34 그날 이후로, 그의 경쟁자는 정치적인 후원자뿐만 아니라 좋은 친구가 되었다.
➡ _____

35 Franklin은 "당신을 한 번 도운 적은 더 돕고 싶어 하게 된다."라는 유명한 말을 했다.
➡ _____

36 여러분이 경쟁자를 친구로 만들고 싶다면, 경쟁자의 부탁을 들어주지 마라.
➡ _____

37 대신, 경쟁자에게 부탁을 해 보아라.
➡ _____

[01~03] 다음 글을 읽고 물음에 답하시오.

Do you think you have a ⓐunique problem? Chances are that many other people have the same problem. Psychology is the study of the human mind and behavior, so it can help you find a solution to your problem.

(A)

It was five minutes before Jisu's big presentation in front of the whole class. Feeling ⓑnervous, Jisu was carefully studying her notes in her chair. Then, her teacher came over and told her to stand tall like Wonder Woman. After standing tall for a few minutes, Jisu did not feel nervous anymore. In fact, she was confident that she would make a great presentation. According to Amy Cuddy, a famous ⓒpsychology, we can become more confident just by standing tall for two minutes before stressful events. Our bodies change our minds, and our minds can change our behavior. Do you want to feel confident? Stand with your feet ⓓapart, and place your hands on your hips. You will not only feel sure about yourself but also look ⓔconfident to other people.

01 위 글의 빈칸 (A)에 들어갈 알맞은 말을 고르시오.

① Why do we become nervous?
② How do I become less nervous?
③ How do I turn a rival into a friend?
④ How do we feel better?
⑤ Who can help me feel better?

02 위 글의 밑줄 친 ⓐ~ⓔ 중 잘못 쓰인 것을 고르시오.

① ⓐ ② ⓑ ③ ⓒ ④ ⓓ ⑤ ⓔ

03 According to the passage, which is NOT true?

① Many people probably have the same problem as we do.
② Psychology can help us find a solution to our problem.
③ Jisu was going to make a big presentation in front of the whole class.
④ Jisu's teacher asked her to stand still for a few minutes.
⑤ Our bodies change our minds, and our minds can change our behavior.

[04~06] 다음 글을 읽고 물음에 답하시오.

How do I turn a rival into a friend?
  Benjamin Franklin once had a political rival who did not like ①him at all. Franklin wanted to become friends with ②him, so ③he came up with a plan. His rival had a rare book. Franklin asked his rival to lend ④him the book for a few days. When Franklin returned the book, he thanked him deeply. Since that day, ⑤his rival became not only a political supporter but also a good friend. Franklin famously said, "Enemies ___ⓐ___ do you one favor will want to do more." If you want to turn a rival into a friend, don't do your rival a favor. Instead, ask your rival ___ⓑ___ you a favor.

04 위 글의 빈칸 ⓐ에 들어갈 알맞은 말을 모두 고르시오.

① that   ② what   ③ which
④ whose   ⑤ who

05 빈칸 ⓑ에 do를 알맞은 형태로 쓰시오.

➡ _____

06 위 글의 밑줄 친 ①~⑤ 중에서 가리키는 대상이 다른 것을 고르시오.

① ② ③ ④ ⑤

[07~09] 다음 글을 읽고 물음에 답하시오.

Who can help me feel better?

When he graduates from high school next year, Taeho wants to become a professional farmer. (①) He is worried that his parents or his friends will not understand. (②) Wanting to clear his mind, Taeho decided to take a day trip on a train ___ⓐ___ . (③) On the train, he told a complete stranger sitting beside him about his problem. (④) He had no idea why he did it. (⑤) However, he felt much better when he got off the train. Strangely enough, we often tell strangers about our problems just like Taeho. ⓑThat is why we do not have to worry about being judged or seeing them again. If you have a problem that you cannot share with your family or friends, try talking to a stranger. You will feel much better.

07 위 글의 흐름으로 보아, 주어진 문장이 들어가기에 가장 적절한 곳은?

> However, he has never told anyone about it.

① ② ③ ④ ⑤

서답형

08 위 글의 빈칸 ⓐ에 'alone'과 같은 뜻의 말을 두 단어로 어법에 맞게 쓰시오.

➡ _____

서답형

09 위 글의 밑줄 친 ⓑ에서 어색한 것을 찾아 바르게 고쳐 쓰시오.

_____ ➡ _____

[10~13] 다음 글을 읽고 물음에 답하시오.

Do you think you have a unique problem? ___ⓐ___ are that many other people have the same problem. Psychology is the study of the human mind and behavior, so it can help you find a solution to your problem.

How do I become (A)[less / more] nervous?

It was five minutes before Jisu's big presentation in front of the whole class. ⓑFeeling nervous, Jisu was carefully studying her notes in her chair. Then, her teacher came over and told her to stand tall like Wonder Woman. After standing tall for a few minutes, Jisu did not feel nervous anymore. In fact, she was confident that she would make a great presentation. According to Amy Cuddy, a famous psychologist, we can become more (B)[nervous / confident] just by standing tall for two minutes before stressful events. Our bodies change our minds, and our minds can change our behavior. Do you want to feel confident? Stand with your feet (C)[apart / together], and place your hands on your hips. You will not only feel sure about yourself but also look confident to other people.

10 위 글의 괄호 (A)~(C)에서 문맥이나 어법상 알맞은 낱말을 골라 쓰시오.

➡ (A) _____ (B) _____ (C) _____

11 위 글의 빈칸 ⓐ에 알맞은 말을 쓰시오.

➡ _____

12 위 글의 밑줄 친 ⓑFeeling과 쓰임이 같은 것을 고르시오.

① I watched Kate singing on the stage.

② He was enjoying himself at the camp.

③ When young, Lindsey was good at playing the piano.

④ Drinking water is good for your health.

⑤ Returning the book, Franklin thanked him deeply.

13 Which question CANNOT be answered after reading the passage?

① What is Amy Cuddy?

② How can we become less nervous?

③ What is the advice of Jisu's teacher?

④ Why do our bodies change our minds?

⑤ How long did Jisu stand tall?

[14~16] 다음 글을 읽고 물음에 답하시오.

(A)

Benjamin Franklin once had a political rival who did not like him at all. Franklin wanted to become friends with him, so he came up with a plan. His rival had a rare book. Franklin asked his rival to lend him the book for _____ⓐ_____ days. When Franklin returned the book, he thanked him deeply. Since that day, ⓑhis rival became not only a political supporter but also a good friend. Franklin famously said, "Enemies who do you one favor will want to do more." If you want to turn a rival into a friend, don't do your rival a favor. Instead, ask your rival to do you a favor.

14 위 글의 빈칸 (A)에 들어갈 말로 적절한 것은?

① How did Benjamin approach his political rival?

② How do I turn a rival into a friend?

③ Why do we need to turn a rival into a friend?

④ Don't ask your rival to do you a favor.

⑤ Why did Benjamin need to borrow the book?

15 위 글의 빈칸 ⓐ에 들어갈 말로 알맞은 것은?

① little   ② a little   ③ a lot

④ few   ⑤ a few

서답형

16 위 글의 밑줄 친 ⓑ를 'as well as'를 이용하여 바꿔 쓰시오.

➡ _____

_____

[17~20] 다음 글을 읽고 물음에 답하시오.

Who can help me feel better?

When he graduates from high school next year, Taeho wants to become a _____ⓐ_____ farmer. However, he has never told anyone about it. He is worried that his parents or his friends will not understand. Wanting to clear his mind, Taeho decided to take a day trip on a train by himself. On the train, he told a complete stranger sitting beside him about his problem. He had no idea why he did it. _____ⓑ_____, he felt much better when he got off the train. Strangely enough, we often tell strangers about our problems just like Taeho. That is because we do not have to worry about being judged or seeing them again. If you have a problem that you cannot share with your family or friends, try talking to a stranger. You will feel (A)much better.

서답형

17 주어진 영영풀이의 빈칸에 해당하는 말을 빈칸 ⓐ에 철자 p 로 시작하여 쓰시오.

> _____ people have jobs that require advanced education or training

➡ _____

18 빈칸 ⓑ에 들어갈 알맞은 말을 고르시오.

① Moreover　　② For example
③ Therefore　　④ However
⑤ In addition

19 위 글의 밑줄 친 (A)much와 바꿔 쓸 수 없는 말을 고르시오.

① very　　② a lot
③ even　　④ still
⑤ far

중요

20 Which question CANNOT be answered after reading the passage?

① What does Taeho want to become when he graduates from high school next year?
② To whom has Taeho told about his wish?
③ Why did Taeho tell a complete stranger sitting beside him about his problem?
④ Why did Taeho decide to take a day trip on a train by himself?
⑤ How can we feel better when we have a problem?

[21~23] 다음 글을 읽고 물음에 답하시오.

How do I become 　ⓐ　 nervous?

It was five minutes before Jisu's big presentation in front of the whole class. Feeling nervous, Jisu was carefully studying her notes in her chair. Then, her teacher came over and told her to stand tall like Wonder Woman. (A)After standing tall for a few minutes, Jisu did not feel nervous no more. In fact, she was confident that she would make a great presentation. According to Amy Cuddy, a famous psychologist, we can become more confident just by (B)standing tall for two minutes before stressful events. Our bodies change our minds, and our minds can change our behavior. Do you want to feel confident? Stand with your feet apart, and place your hands on your hips. You will not only feel sure about yourself but also look confident to other people.

21 위 글의 빈칸 ⓐ에 들어갈 알맞은 말을 고르시오.

① few　　② little　　③ less
④ more　　⑤ very

서답형

22 위 글의 밑줄 친 (A)에서 흐름상 어색한 부분을 찾아 고치시오.

_____ ➡ _____

23 위 글의 밑줄 친 (B)standing과 문법적 쓰임이 다른 것을 모두 고르시오.

① He was standing by the gate.
② Standing on my hands was difficult.
③ Her punishment was standing silently.
④ She looked so miserable, standing there in the rain.
⑤ Standing under the sun was terrible.

[01~03] 다음 글을 읽고 물음에 답하시오.

(A)Who can help me feel better?

When he graduates from high school next year, Taeho wants to become a professional farmer. However, he has never told anyone about it. He is worried that his parents or his friends will not understand. Wanting to clear his mind, Taeho decided to take a day trip on a train by himself. On the train, he told a complete stranger sitting beside him about his problem. He had no idea why he did it. However, he felt much better when he got off the train. ⓐ정말 이상하게도, we often tell strangers about our problems just like Taeho. (B)That is because we do not have to worry about being judged or seeing them again. If you have a problem that you cannot share with your family or friends, try talking to a stranger. You will feel much better.

01 위 글의 밑줄 친 (A)의 답이 될 수 있는 것을 본문에서 찾아 세 단어를 쓰시오.

➡ _____

02 밑줄 친 ⓐ의 우리말에 맞게 enough를 이용하여 두 단어를 쓰시오.

➡ _____

03 위 글의 밑줄 친 (B)That이 가리키는 것을 본문에서 찾아 쓰시오.

➡ _____

_____

[04~06] 다음 글을 읽고 물음에 답하시오.

Do you think you have a unique problem? Chances are that many other people have the same problem. Psychology is the study of the human mind and behavior, so it can help you find a solution to your problem.

How do I become less nervous?

It was five minutes before Jisu's big presentation in front of the whole class. ⓐ Feeling nervous, Jisu was carefully studying her notes in her chair. Then, her teacher came over and told her to stand tall like Wonder Woman. After standing tall for a few minutes, Jisu did not feel nervous anymore. In fact, she was confident that she would make a great presentation. According to Amy Cuddy, a famous psychologist, we can become more confident just by standing tall for two minutes before stressful events. Our bodies change our minds, and our minds can change our behavior. Do you want to feel confident? Stand with your feet apart, and place your hands on your hips. You will not only feel sure about yourself but also look confident to other people.

04 Why can psychology help us find a solution to our problem?

➡ _____

_____

05 How can we get to be more confident?

➡ _____

_____

06 위 글의 밑줄 친 ⓐFeeling을 부사절로 고쳐 쓰시오.

➡ _____

[07~09] 다음 글을 읽고 물음에 답하시오.

How do I turn a rival into a friend?

Benjamin Franklin once had a political rival who did not like him at all. Franklin wanted to become friends ___ⓐ___ him, so he came up ___ⓐ___ a plan. His rival had a rare book. Franklin asked his rival to lend him the book for a few days. ⓑWhen Franklin returned the book, he thanked him deep. Since that day, ⓒ his rival became not only a political supporter but also a good friend. Franklin famously said, "Enemies who do you one favor will want to do more." If you want to turn a rival into a friend, don't do your rival a favor. Instead, ask your rival to do you a favor.

07 위 글의 빈칸 ⓐ에 공통으로 들어갈 전치사를 쓰시오.

➡ _____

08 위 글의 밑줄 친 ⓑ에서 어색한 부분을 찾아 고치시오.

_____ ➡ _____

09 위 글의 밑줄 친 ⓒ를 'as well as'를 이용하여 바꿔 쓰시오.

➡ _____

_____

[10~13] 다음 글을 읽고 물음에 답하시오.

Who can help me feel better?

When he graduates from high school next year, Taeho wants to become a professional farmer. However, he has never told anyone about ⓐit. He is worried that his parents or his friends will not understand. (A)[Wanting / Wanted] to clear his mind, Taeho decided to take a day trip on a train by himself. On the train, he told a complete stranger (B)[sat / sitting] beside him about his problem. ⓑ그는 자신이 왜 그랬는지 알 수 없었다. However, he felt much better when he got off the train. Strangely enough, we often tell strangers about our problems just like Taeho. That is because we do not have to worry about (C) [being judged / judging] or seeing them again. If you have a problem that you cannot share with your family or friends, try talking to a stranger. You will feel much better.

10 위 글의 괄호 (A)~(C)에서 문맥이나 어법상 알맞은 낱말을 고르시오.

➡ (A) _____ (B) _____ (C) _____

11 위 글의 밑줄 친 ⓐit이 가리키는 것을 본문에서 찾아 쓰시오.

➡ _____

12 위 글의 밑줄 친 ⓑ의 우리말을 주어진 어휘를 이용하여 영작하시오. (no, idea, it)

➡ _____

13 위 글의 내용과 일치하도록 다음 빈칸 (A)와 (B)에 알맞은 단어를 쓰시오.

Taeho wants to become a professional farmer, but he is worried that his parents or his friends will not understand. While taking a day trip on a train by himself, he told (A)_____ _____ _____ about his problem. He didn't know why he did it. But he felt (B)_____ _____ when he got off the train.

해석

Listen & Speak 2 – B Think and Talk

A: What don't I have to do on Stress-Free Day?

B: You don't have to clean the classroom.
 = You don't need to

C: You don't have to come to school by 8:30.

구문해설 • stress-free: 스트레스가 없는

A: 스트레스가 없는 날에 무엇을 할 필요가 없을까?

B: 너는 교실 청소를 할 필요가 없어.

C: 너는 8:30분까지 학교에 올 필요가 없어.

Link

How confident do you feel about yourself? Wanting to find the answer
                                                   분사구문(= As[Because] we wanted)
to this question, we created a test about confidence. Thirty students took the
[행위·동작·작용의 대상] ~에 대하여   시험[검사]을 치르다
test. The average score was nine. Eighteen students scored above the average
                                                                   [초과] ~ 이상인[으로]
score. Thus, sixty percent of the students felt quite confident about themselves.
결과를 이끄는 연결어   them(×)

구문해설 • confident: 자신감이 있는 • confidence: 자신감 • average: 평균; 평균의

당신은 스스로에 대해 얼마나 확신이 있나요? 질문에 대한 답을 찾고 싶어, 우리는 자신감에 대한 검사지를 만들었습니다. 30명의 학생들이 검사를 했습니다. 평균적인 점수는 9점이었습니다. 18명의 학생들이 평균 점수를 넘었습니다. 따라서, 학생들의 60%가 그들 스스로에 대해 꽤 자신감을 갖고 있습니다.

Write

The hardest time in my life

The hardest time in my life was when my grandmother passed away five years
최상급   the time when: ~할 때
ago. When I was younger, she took care of me most of the time. Not having
       비교 대상 없는 비교급(자기 자신)   = As[Because] I didn't have her around의 분사구문
her around, I felt sad and lonely. One day, I found my grandmother's diary.
                지각동사+형용사
She not only wrote a lot about her memories but also wished that I would lead
(= Not only did she write ~. but also she wished)   병렬 구조   will의 과거형(시제 일치)
a happy life. From this experience, I have learned that I should try to be happy
              부사구   현재완료
just as she wished.
be 형용사 just as(접속사) S+wished: S가 원했던 것처럼 ~하다

구문해설 • pass away: 죽다 • have ~ around: ~가 곁에 있다 • just as: ~가 …한 것과 같이

내 삶에서 가장 힘들었던 순간

내 삶에서 가장 힘들었던 순간은 5년 전 할머니께서 돌아가셨을 때였다. 내가 더 어렸을 때, 그녀는 대부분의 시간 동안 나를 돌봐주셨다. 그녀가 곁에 없어서, 나는 슬프고 외로웠다. 어느 날, 나는 할머니의 일기장을 발견했다. 그녀는 그녀의 기억에 대해 많이 적었을 뿐만 아니라, 내가 행복한 삶을 살기를 바랐다. 이 경험을 통해, 나는 그녀가 원했던 것처럼 행복해지려고 노력해야 한다는 것을 배웠다.

Words & Expressions

01 다음 짝지어진 단어의 관계가 같도록 빈칸에 알맞은 말을 쓰시오.

> tradition : traditional = success : _____

02 다음 영영풀이가 가리키는 것을 고르시오.

> to complete your education at a college, school, etc.

① graduate   ② judge
③ guess   ④ decide
⑤ prepare

03 다음 중 밑줄 친 부분의 뜻풀이가 바르지 <u>않은</u> 것은?

① I want to be a specialist in child <u>psychology</u>. (심리학)
② We blamed his bad <u>behavior</u>. (행동)
③ Do you have a better <u>solution</u>? (해결책)
④ He drew a <u>unique</u> picture on the wall. (독특한)
⑤ The two houses stand 500 meters <u>apart</u>. (가까이)

04 다음 우리말에 맞게 빈칸에 알맞은 말을 쓰시오. (철자가 주어진 것은 그 철자로 시작할 것.)

(1) 그녀는 아마 며칠 후에 떠날 것이다.
➡ She will p_____ leave in a few days.

(2) 너는 그 문제에 대해 좀 전문적인 조언을 얻을 필요가 있다.
➡ You need to get some _____ advice about that problem.

(3) 나는 사람의 마음에 관심이 있어서, 대학에서 심리학을 공부할 것이다.
➡ I am interested in the human mind, so I will study _____ in college.

(4) 그녀는 희귀한 병을 가졌다.
➡ She has a r_____ disease.

05 다음 문장의 빈칸에 들어갈 말을 〈보기〉에서 골라 쓰시오.

> ┌── 보기 ──┐
> chances are that / get off / stop by /
> stand tall / make a presentation

(1) Are you going to _____ at the meeting?
(2) Could you _____ the store for some bread on the way home?
(3) Go out into the real world and _____, my students!
(4) _____ our team will win the championship.
(5) We need to _____ at the next station.

06 다음 문장에 공통으로 들어갈 말을 고르시오.

> • I can't handle this project _____ myself.
> • Would you stop _____ my office and do me a favor?
> • I'll be back home _____ 6 to help you.

① by   ② with
③ from   ④ to
⑤ of

Conversation

[07~09] 다음 대화를 읽고 물음에 답하시오.

Minsu: Shall we have seafood spaghetti ⓐfor dinner?

Emma: Sure. I'll (A)stop by the store ⓑon the way home.

Minsu: You don't have ⓒto do that. We already have ⓓwhat we need.

Emma: Oh, I see. Then, I'll be back home by 6 to ⓔhelp you cooking.

07 위 대화의 밑줄 친 ⓐ~ⓔ 중 어법상 틀린 것을 찾아 바르게 고치시오.

➡ _____ ➡ _____

08 위 대화의 밑줄 친 (A)와 바꾸어 쓸 수 있는 것은?

① drop
② chew
③ get
④ decide
⑤ judge

09 위 대화의 내용과 일치하지 않는 것은?

① 민수는 Emma에게 저녁에 해산물 스파게티 먹을 것을 제안했다.
② Emma는 집에 오는 길에 가게에 들를 것이다.
③ 민수는 이미 스파게티에 필요한 것을 갖고 있다.
④ Emma는 6시까지 집에 돌아올 것이다.
⑤ Emma는 민수가 요리하는 것을 도울 것이다.

[10~11] 다음 대화를 읽고 물음에 답하시오.

B: You look a bit nervous.
G: Well, _____ (A)
B: Don't worry. You've prepared a lot. You'll do a great job.
G: Thanks. I feel much better now.

10 위 대화의 빈칸 (A)에 들어갈 말을 주어진 단어를 모두 배열하여 영작하시오.

┌─ 보기 ┐
history class / about / in / presentation / worried / I'm / my
└──────────┘

➡ _____

11 위 대화의 내용과 일치하지 않는 것은?

① 소녀는 약간 긴장되어 보인다.
② 소녀는 역사 시간에 할 발표를 걱정한다.
③ 소녀는 발표 준비를 많이 했다.
④ 소녀는 소년 덕분에 기분이 훨씬 나아졌다.
⑤ 소년은 소녀의 발표를 칭찬하였다.

12 다음 대화가 자연스럽게 이어지도록 순서대로 배열하시오.

(A) Oh, I see. How convenient!
(B) You don't have to call them. You can do it online.
(C) Shall we try that new Mexican restaurant tomorrow?
(D) Why not? I'll call the restaurant to make a reservation for us.

➡ _____

[13~14] 다음 대화를 읽고 물음에 답하시오.

Jane: What happened to your shoes? Aren't they new?

Brian: Yes, but my dog chewed them. He does it all the time. I'm worried about him.

Jane: He was probably bored. Why don't you play with him more often?

Brian: O.K., I will. I hope he will stop chewing my shoes.

13 What happened to Brian's shoes?

➡ _____

14 What does Jane advise Brian to do?

➡ _____

Grammar

15 다음 문장의 밑줄 친 분사구문을 부사절로 바르게 바꾼 것은?

> <u>Living alone in this big apartment</u>, I rarely feel lonely.

① Because I live in this big apartment,
② While I'm living in this big apartment,
③ If I live in this big apartment,
④ Though I live in this big apartment,
⑤ Unless I live in this big apartment,

16 다음 그림을 보고 괄호 안의 단어를 배열하여 빈칸을 알맞게 채우시오. (단, 단어 배열은 그림의 왼쪽에서 오른쪽임.)

(1)

➡ _____
on the spider web. (in, the honeybee, are, the ladybug, both, and, trouble)

(2)

➡ Jiho has decided _____

_____. (to go, nor, to get, college, neither, to, a job)

17 다음 중 어법상 어색한 문장을 모두 고르시오.

① Not only can people guess the story but they also know the ending.
② Both the participants or the researchers were satisfied with the result.
③ Either Jamie and Esther is coming today.
④ I can't even imagine not only when but also where the event will happen.
⑤ Neither Thomas nor his team members were present at the meeting.

18 다음 괄호 안에서 어법상 알맞은 것을 고르시오.

(1) Not only Sammy but also Olga (like / likes) the soup so much.
(2) Maria required that the dance teams should practice not only singing but also (to dance / dancing).
(3) Either Kennedy (or / nor) Jason should complete the assignment by tomorrow.
(4) Either the recording engineers or the music director (is / are) going to direct the song production.
(5) Not the angels but the devil (appear / appears) before the sad soul.

19 다음 문장의 밑줄 친 부사절을 분사구문으로 알맞게 바꾼 것을 고르시오.

> As she doesn't have anyone around to encourage her, Joanne felt even more lonely.

① As she having not anyone around to encourage her,

② There being someone around to encourage her,

③ Having not anyone around to encourage her,

④ As having not anyone around to encourage her,

⑤ Not having anyone around to encourage her,

20 다음 밑줄 친 부분 중 어법상 어색한 것을 고르시오.

① Not having money, Robert couldn't buy the birthday present for his wife.

② Raining all day, the club members stayed at home and watched their video clips.

③ Being tired, Sonya went to bed early.

④ Finding the book he had lost, I called him to come over to my place.

⑤ Frankly speaking, the prime minster of Japan seemed like an idiot.

Reading

[21~22] 다음 글을 읽고 물음에 답하시오.

Do you think you have a unique problem? Chances are that many other people have the same problem. Psychology is the study of the human mind and behavior, so it can help you find a solution ⓐ your problem.

How do I become less nervous?

It was five minutes before Jisu's big presentation in front of the whole class. Feeling nervous, Jisu was carefully studying her notes in her chair. Then, her teacher came over and told her ⓑ stand tall like Wonder Woman. After standing tall for a few minutes, Jisu did not feel nervous anymore. ⓒ , she was confident that she would make a great presentation.

21 위 글의 빈칸 ⓐ와 ⓑ에 공통으로 들어갈 알맞은 전치사를 고르시오.

① to ② on ③ for

④ in ⑤ at

22 위 글의 빈칸 ⓒ에 알맞은 것을 고르시오.

① For example ② However

③ In addition ④ In fact

⑤ Thus

[23~25] 다음 글을 읽고 물음에 답하시오.

Who can help me feel better?

When he graduates from high school next year, Taeho wants to become a professional farmer. However, he has never told anyone about it. He is worried that his parents or his friends will not understand. ⓐWanting to clear his mind, Taeho decided to take a day trip on a train by himself. On the train, he told a complete stranger sitting beside him about his problem. He had no idea why he did it. However, he felt much better when he got off the train. Strangely enough, we often tell strangers about our problems just like Taeho. That is because we do not have to worry about being judged or seeing them again. If you have a problem that you cannot share with your family or friends, try talking to a stranger. You will feel much better.

23 위 글의 주제로 알맞은 것을 고르시오.

① how to meet a complete stranger
② how to feel better when we have a problem
③ how to clear our mind
④ why Taeho wants to be a professional farmer
⑤ why we tell a teacher about our problem

24 밑줄 친 ⓐ를 부사절로 알맞게 고친 것을 고르시오.

① As he wants to clear his mind
② Because he wanted to clear his mind
③ Though he wanted to clear his mind
④ If he wanted to clear his mind
⑤ After he wanted to clear his mind

25 According to the passage, which is NOT true?

① Taeho wants to become a professional farmer after graduation from high school.
② Taeho has never told anyone about becoming a professional farmer.
③ When we have a problem that we cannot share with our family or friends, we will feel much better by trying talking to a stranger.
④ Taeho took a day trip on a train by himself as he wanted to clear his mind.
⑤ Taeho knew why he told a complete stranger about his problem.

[26~29] 다음 글을 읽고 물음에 답하시오.

How do I turn a rival into a friend?

Benjamin Franklin once had a political rival who did not like him at all. (①) Franklin wanted to become friends with him, so he came up with a plan. (②) His rival had a rare book. (③) When Franklin returned the book, he thanked him deeply. (④) Since that day, his rival became not only a political supporter but also a good friend. (⑤) Franklin famously said, "Enemies who do you one favor will want to do more." If you want to turn a rival into a friend, don't do your rival a favor. _____ ⓐ _____ , ask your rival to do you a favor.

26 위 글의 빈칸 ⓐ에 들어갈 말로 알맞은 것을 고르시오.

① However   ② For instance
③ Nonetheless   ④ In fact
⑤ Instead

27 위 글의 흐름으로 보아, 주어진 문장이 들어가기에 가장 적절한 곳은?

> Franklin asked his rival to lend him the book for a few days.

①   ②   ③   ④   ⑤

28 위 글에 나타난 Franklin에 대한 설명으로 가장 적절한 것을 고르시오.

① wicked   ② honest   ③ wise
④ timid   ⑤ evil

29 What did Franklin's political rival do for Franklin? Answer in English with 7 words.

➡ _____

01 다음 영영풀이가 가리키는 것을 고르시오. *출제율 90%*

> someone who hates you and wants to harm you

① stranger　　② supporter
③ psychologist　　④ rival
⑤ enemy

02 다음 우리말을 주어진 단어를 이용하여 영작하시오. *출제율 95%*

(1) 네 자신에게 너무 많은 부담을 주지 마라. (pressure, too, on)

➡ _____

(2) 두 발을 벌리고 서라. (with, feet)

➡ _____

(3) 내가 식당에 전화해서 예약할게요. (make, restaurant)

➡ _____

[03~05] 다음 대화를 읽고 물음에 답하시오.

Minsu: Shall we have seafood spaghetti for dinner?
Emma: Sure. I'll stop by the store on the way home.
Minsu: You don't have to do that. We already have what we need.
Emma: Oh, I see. Then, I'll be back home by 6 to help you cook.

03 What is Minsu going to cook for dinner? *출제율 90%*

➡ _____
_____

04 Why doesn't Emma have to stop by the store? *출제율 95%*

➡ _____
_____

05 By when will Emma be back home to help Minsu? *출제율 90%*

➡ _____

06 다음 대화가 자연스럽게 이어지도록 순서대로 배열하시오. *출제율 95%*

> (A) He was probably bored. Why don't you play with him more often?
> (B) O.K., I will. I hope he will stop chewing my shoes.
> (C) What happened to your shoes? Aren't they new?
> (D) Yes, but my dog chewed them. He does it all the time. I'm worried about him.

➡ _____

[07~08] 다음 대화를 읽고 물음에 답하시오.

Jack: Mom, what time are we going to Grandma's place tomorrow morning?
Mom: About 8 a.m. I'm going to bake cookies for her before we go.
Jack: Then, should I get up early to help you?
Mom: (A)그럴 필요 없단다. (have) Your dad will help me.
Jack: O.K, then. Good night, Mom!

07 위 대화의 밑줄 친 (A)의 우리말을 주어진 단어를 사용하여 영작하시오. (4 words) *출제율 90%*

➡ _____

08 위 대화의 내용과 일치하지 <u>않는</u> 것은?

① Jack is supposed to visit his grandma with her mother.
② Jack is going to his grandma's place about 8 a.m. tomorrow morning.
③ Jack doesn't need to help his mom tomorrow morning.
④ Jack's mom is planning to bake cookies for Jack's grandma at night.
⑤ Jack's father is going to help Jack's mom to bake cookies.

[09~10] 다음 대화를 읽고 물음에 답하시오.

Yuri: Hi, Jaden. Sports Day is next Friday. I can't wait!

Jaden: Really? I'm actually worried about it.

Yuri: Why? Aren't you good at sports?

Jaden: (A) Yes, I am, but I'm worried about the 800-meter relay.

Yuri: What do you mean?

Jaden: (B) I'm the last runner. What if our team loses because of me?

Yuri: (C) I think you're putting too much pressure on yourself.

Jaden: (D) Really? Don't you think I should practice every day?

Yuri: (E) It's just a school race. It's not about winning or losing.

Jaden: I guess you're right, Yuri. I'm lucky to have a friend like you.

09 위 대화의 (A)~(E) 중 주어진 문장이 들어가기에 적절한 곳은?

> No, you don't have to do that.

① (A) ② (B) ③ (C) ④ (D) ⑤ (E)

10 위 대화의 내용과 일치하지 <u>않는</u> 것은?

① 운동회가 다음 주 금요일이다.
② Jaden은 운동을 잘하지만 800미터 릴레이가 걱정된다.
③ Jaden은 자신 때문에 팀이 질까봐 걱정한다.
④ 유리는 Jaden이 스스로에게 너무 많은 압박을 주고 있는 것 같다고 생각한다.
⑤ 유리는 이기거나 지는 것이 중요한 경기는 아니지만, Jaden이 매일 연습해야 한다고 생각한다.

11 다음 대화의 내용과 일치하지 <u>않는</u> 것은?

B: You look a bit nervous.
G: I'm worried about my swimming competition this Saturday.
B: Don't worry. You're such a good swimmer. Just relax and enjoy yourself!
G: Thanks. I feel much better now.

① 소녀는 긴장한 것 같아 보인다.
② 소녀는 다음 주 토요일에 있는 수영대회를 걱정하고 있다.
③ 소녀는 수영을 아주 잘한다.
④ 소년은 소녀에게 긴장을 풀고 즐기라고 하였다.
⑤ 소녀는 소년의 격려 덕분에 기분이 훨씬 괜찮아졌다.

12 다음 중 어법상 올바른 문장을 <u>모두</u> 고르면?

① Opened the drawer, he took out a letter.
② There being no bus service, we had to walk all the way home.
③ Worked hard to finish the project in time, Chris was taken to hospital.
④ Knowing not what to do, she asked him for help.
⑤ Director Bong winning the great awards, the fans in Korea felt proud of his films.

[13~14] 다음 중 빈칸에 들어갈 수 <u>없는</u> 말을 고르시오.

출제율 100%

13

The princess Elsa in the castle was not only _____ but also generous.

① beautiful　　② friendly　　③ lovely
④ truly　　　　⑤ wise

출제율 95%

14

My grandmother not only wrote a lot about her memories on her family and friends but also _____.

① wished that I would lead a happy life
② was sure that her children would be happy
③ was satisfied with a quiet life
④ proud of her family members
⑤ wanted to be remembered by us

출제율 95%

15 다음 각 문장의 부사절을 알맞은 분사구문으로 전환하시오.

(1) When we use green energy vehicles, we can reduce a good amount of CO_2 in the air.

➡ _____, we can reduce a good amount of CO_2 in the air.

(2) Because Anne didn't come back, her husband waited for three hours.

➡ _____, her husband waited for three hours.

(3) As Shane had not been invited to the final match, he stayed at home all day long.

➡ _____, Shane stayed at home all day long.

출제율 95%

16 다음 중 우리말과 그 영작이 바르게 짝지어지지 <u>않은</u> 것은?

① Ben은 영어뿐만 아니라 중국어도 말할 수 있다.
　→ Ben can speak not only English but also Chinese.
② 그 배우는 드라마뿐만 아니라 영화도 찍고 있다.
　→ The actor is filming not only a drama but also a movie.
③ 아이들뿐만 아니라 그들의 엄마도 펭수를 좋아한다.
　→ Not only the kids but also their mom like Pengsu.
④ BTS는 한국에서뿐만 아니라 일본에서도 콘서트를 열 것이다.
　→ BTS will hold a concert not only in Korea but also in Japan.
⑤ 불고기는 맛있을 뿐만 아니라 영양가도 있다.
　→ Bulgogi is not only delicious but also nutritious.

[17~18] 다음 글을 읽고 물음에 답하시오.

How confident do you feel about yourself? (A)Wanting to find the answer to this question, we created a test about confidence. Thirty students took the test. The average score was nine. Eighteen students scored above the average score. Thus, ⓐ percent of the students felt quite confident about themselves.

출제율 90%

17 위 글의 빈칸 ⓐ에 들어갈 알맞은 말을 영어로 쓰시오.

➡ _____

18 위 글의 밑줄 친 (A)를 부사절로 고쳐 쓰시오.

➡ _____

_____

[19~20] 다음 글을 읽고 물음에 답하시오.

Do you think you have a _____ ⓐ _____ problem? (A)아마 많은 다른 사람들이 여러분과 똑같은 고민을 가지고 있을 것이다. Psychology is the study of the human mind and behavior, so it can help you find a solution to your problem.

19 주어진 영영풀이에 해당하는 단어를 빈칸 ⓐ에 써 넣으시오.

being the only one of its kind

➡ _____

20 위 글의 밑줄 친 (A)의 우리말에 맞게 chances를 이용하여 10 단어로 영작하시오.

➡ _____

_____

[21~23] 다음 글을 읽고 물음에 답하시오.

How do I become less nervous?

It was five minutes before Jisu's big presentation in front of the whole class. (①) Feeling nervous, Jisu was carefully studying her notes in her chair. (②) Then, her teacher came over and told her to stand tall like Wonder Woman. (③) In fact, she was confident that she would make a great presentation. (④) According to Amy Cuddy,

a famous psychologist, we can become more confident just by standing tall for two minutes before stressful events. (⑤) Our bodies change our minds, and our minds can change our behavior. Do you want to feel confident? Stand with your feet apart, and place your hands on your hips. ⓐYou will not only feel sure about yourself but also look confident to other people.

21 위 글의 흐름으로 보아, 주어진 문장이 들어가기에 가장 적절한 곳은?

After standing tall for a few minutes, Jisu did not feel nervous anymore.

①   ②   ③   ④   ⑤

22 What did Jisu's teacher advise Jisu to do?

➡ _____

_____

23 위 글의 밑줄 친 ⓐ와 그 뜻이 다른 것을 고르시오.

① You will not only feel sure about yourself but look confident to other people.

② You will not simply feel sure about yourself but look confident to other people.

③ You will not just feel sure about yourself but also look confident to other people.

④ You will not merely feel sure about yourself but also look confident to other people.

⑤ You will not feel sure about yourself but look confident to other people.

[01~03] 다음 대화를 읽고 물음에 답하시오.

> Yuri: Hi, Jaden. Sports Day is next Friday. I can't wait!
>
> Jaden: Really? I'm actually worried about it.
>
> Yuri: Why? Aren't you good at sports?
>
> Jaden: Yes, I am, but I'm worried about the 800-meter relay.
>
> Yuri: What do you mean?
>
> Jaden: I'm the last runner. What if our team loses because of me?
>
> Yuri: I think you're putting too much pressure on yourself.
>
> Jaden: Really? Don't you think I should practice every day?
>
> Yuri: No, you don't have to do that. It's just a school race. It's not about winning or losing.
>
> Jaden: I guess you're right, Yuri. I'm lucky to have a friend like you.

01 What is Yuri looking forward to?

➡ _____

02 As the last runner of the 800-meter relay, what is Jaden worried about?

➡ _____

_____

03 Why does Yuri think Jaden doesn't have to practice every day?

➡ _____

_____

04 다음 우리말에 맞도록 괄호 안에 주어진 어휘를 알맞게 배열하시오.

(1) Bob과 Tom이 길을 걷고 있었을 때, 그들은 Julie가 노래 부르는 것을 봤다. (down, street, walking, the)

➡ _____, Bob and Tom saw Julie singing.

(2) 비록 Jane은 아버지의 뜻을 알지 못했지만, 그가 말한 대로 하기로 결심했다. (what, not, meant, knowing, her father)

➡ _____, Jane decided to do as he told.

(3) 그 비행기에 남은 좌석이 있다면, 나는 오늘 저녁에 LA로 갈 것이다. (seats, there, the plane, left, any, on, being)

➡ _____, I will go to L.A. this evening.

(4) 마음을 정리하고 싶었기 때문에, Karen은 회사를 그만두겠다고 사장에게 말했다. (clear, wanting, mind, to, her)

➡ _____, Karen told the boss that she'd quit the company.

05 다음 그림을 보고, 내용에 맞게 〈보기〉에서 알맞은 단어를 각각 선택하여, 어법에 맞게 대화의 빈칸에 채워 넣으시오.

┌─ 보기 ┐
• not / but / both / only / either / neither / also / nor / and
• 반드시 한 번씩만 사용할 것.
• 빈칸의 위치에 따라 대·소문자 구분할 것.

Jina: You know when Mom's birthday is?

Jihun: Sure. It's in November, isn't it?

Jina: Yeah, on which day?

Jihun: It probably falls on before or after the cookie stick *Pepero* day. So, it's _____ 10th, or 12th?

Jina: _____ 10th _____ 12th is right. It's 18th, just a week after *Pepero* day. _____ _____ Dad _____ _____ you don't care about Mom.

Jihun: Sorry for that. Instead, what should _____ Dad _____ I do?

[06~08] 다음 글을 읽고 물음에 답하시오.

The hardest time in my life

  The hardest time in my life was when my grandmother passed away five years ago. When I was younger, she took care of me most of the time. @Not having her around, I felt sad and lonely. One day, I found my grandmother's diary. ⓑShe not only wrote a lot about her memories but also wished that I would lead a happy life. From this experience, I have learned that I should try to be happy just as she wished.

06 위 글의 밑줄 친 @를 부사절로 고쳐 쓰시오.

➡ _____

07 위 글의 밑줄 친 ⓑ를 not only로 시작하여 바꿔 쓰시오.

➡ _____

08 위 글의 필자가 할머니의 일기장을 통해 얻은 교훈을 우리말에 쓰시오.

➡ _____

_____

[09~11] 다음 대화를 읽고 물음에 답하시오.

A: Who ate the cookies?

B: (*Touching his* __@__) I don't know. Maybe the dog ate them.

A: I can tell that you're (A)[lying / laying] because you're touching your __@__ .

C: This is an example of the Pinocchio Effect. People experience the Pinocchio Effect when they tell a lie. (B)[Not only they / Not only do they] feel (C)[even if / as if] their nose is getting hotter, but also the temperature around their eyes (D)[raises / rises].

09 위 글의 빈칸 @에 공통으로 들어갈 알맞은 말을 쓰시오.

➡ _____

10 Why do people touch their nose when they tell a lie? Fill in the blanks (A) and (B) with suitable words.

> Because they feel as if not only their nose is (A)_____ _____, but also the temperature around their eyes (B)_____.

11 위 글의 괄호 (A)~(D)에서 문맥상 알맞은 낱말을 골라 쓰시오.

➡ (A) _____ (B) _____
  (C) _____ (D) _____

01 다음 대화를 읽고 대화의 내용과 일치하도록 빈칸을 완성하시오.

> Jack: Mom, what time are we going to Grandma's place tomorrow morning?
>
> Mom: About 8 a.m. I'm going to bake cookies for her before we go.
>
> Jack: Then, should I get up early to help you?
>
> Mom: You don't have to. Your dad will help me.
>
> Jack: O.K, then. Good night, Mom!

> I'm looking forward to visiting (A)_____ tomorrow. We're going to leave about 8 a.m tomorrow. My mom is planning to (B)_____ for my grandma. (C)_____ is going to help her early in the morning. I can't wait to see my grandma!

02 다음 내용을 바탕으로 다른 사람에게 공감과 조언을 하는 편지의 빈칸을 알맞게 채우시오.

Situation	Feelings
• have just moved to a new school • have nobody to talk to • ask one of my classmates to show me her notes • Asking for help	• lonely • feel like crying • showed me her notes, started to talk about herself • help you make new friends

> To someone who (A)_____,
> I understand how (B)_____ you might be feeling now. I had to go to a new school like you because my whole family moved to Gunsan, a small city in Korea. (C)_____, I felt like crying on the first day at my new school. However, a small thing made the situation better. I asked one of my classmates to show me her notes. Then, she not only (D)_____. That was how she became my new friend. Asking for help sometimes (E)_____. I wish you all the best.

단원별 모의고사

01 다음 우리말에 맞게 빈칸을 완성하시오. (철자가 주어진 것은 그 철자로 시작할 것.)

(1) 그녀는 판매를 올리기 위한 새로운 아이디어를 떠올렸다.
➡ S h e _____ _____ _____ a new idea for increasing sales.

(2) 그는 저녁을 먹으러 우리집에 들렀다.
➡ He c_____ _____ to my house for dinner.

(3) 내가 돌아왔을 때, 이미 모두가 가버렸다.
➡ When I _____ _____, everybody was already gone.

02 다음 문장의 빈칸에 들어갈 말을 〈보기〉에서 골라 쓰시오.

┌─── 보기 ───┐
competition / text message / prepare / mind / anxious / unique
└──────────┘

(1) He sent a _____ to his dad.
(2) You don't have to be _____ about the exam.
(3) Everyone's fingerprint is _____.
(4) While I cook the pasta, would you _____ the sauce?
(5) I went for a walk to clear my _____.
(6) I'm worried about my swimming _____.

03 우리말과 일치하도록 주어진 단어를 배열하여 영작하시오.

(1) 당신은 정치적인 사안에 관심이 있나요?
(the / in / you / are / issue / interested / political)
➡ _____
_____

(2) 당신은 매일 연설 준비를 할 필요가 없어요.
(every day / prepare / you / your / don't / to / speech / have)
➡ _____
_____

(3) 나는 우리의 발표가 전혀 걱정되지 않아.
(worried / about / at / our / all / I'm / presentation / not)
➡ _____
_____

04 다음 짝지어진 대화가 어색한 것은?

① A: What don't I have to do on Stress-Free Day?
  B: You don't have to clean the classroom.

② A: I'm worried about my grade on the science test.
  B: You don't have to be good at every subject.

③ A: I'm concerned about my weight. I think I'm too fat.
  B: You don't need to worry about your weight. You look great.

④ A: I'm afraid that I'll make a mistake on my math test.
  B: You don't have to worry too much.

⑤ A: I'm worried about my family. We don't talk to each other much these days.
  B: You look a bit nervous. You don't need to talk to each other.

[05~06] 다음 대화를 읽고 물음에 답하시오.

> B: You look a bit nervous.
> G: Well, I'm worried about my presentation in history class.
> B: Don't worry. You've prepared a lot. You'll do a great job.
> G: Thanks. I feel much better now.

05 What is the girl concerned about?

➡ _____

_____

06 Why does the boy think the girl will do a great job?

➡ _____

07 다음 대화를 읽고 대답할 수 <u>없는</u> 것은?

> Jack: Mom, what time are we going to Grandma's place tomorrow morning?
> Mom: About 8 a.m. I'm going to bake cookies for her before we go.
> Jack: Then, should I get up early to help you?
> Mom: You don't have to. Your dad will help me.
> Jack: O.K, then. Good night, Mom!

① What is Jack going to do with his mom?
② What is Jack's mom going to do for his grandma?
③ Who will help Jack's mom in the morning?
④ When are Jack and his mom going to his grandma's place tomorrow?
⑤ What time is Jack's mom going to get up to bake cookies?

[08~09] 다음 대화를 읽고 물음에 답하시오.

> Emily: Shall we try that new Mexican restaurant tomorrow?
> Tom: Why not? I'll call the restaurant to _____(A)_____ for us.
> Emily: You don't have to call them. You can do it online.
> Tom: Oh, I see. How convenient!

08 위 대화의 빈칸 (A)에 '예약하다'를 3 단어로 쓰시오.

➡ _____

09 위 대화의 내용과 일치하지 <u>않는</u> 것은?

① Emily는 Tom에게 내일 새로 생긴 멕시코 레스토랑에 가자고 제안한다.
② Tom은 멕시코 레스토랑에 가는 것이 별로 마음에 들지 않는다.
③ Tom은 레스토랑에 전화로 예약할 필요가 없다.
④ 레스토랑 예약은 온라인으로 할 수 있다.
⑤ Tom은 온라인 예약이 편리하다고 생각한다.

10 다음 대화가 자연스럽게 이어지도록 순서대로 배열하시오.

> (A) Thanks. I feel much better now.
> (B) You look a bit nervous.
> (C) I'm worried about my swimming competition this Saturday.
> (D) Don't worry. You're such a good swimmer. Just relax and enjoy yourself!

➡ _____

11 다음 대화의 (A)~(C)에 들어갈 말이 바르게 짝지어진 것은?

> Jane: What happened to your shoes? Aren't they new?
>
> Brian: Yes, but my dog chewed them. He does it all the time. I'm (A)[worrying / worried] about him.
>
> Jane: He was probably (B)[boring / bored]. Why don't you play with him more often?
>
> Brian: O.K., I will. I hope he will stop (C)[to chew / chewing] my shoes.

	(A)	(B)	(C)
①	worrying	boring	to chew
②	worrying	bored	chewing
③	worried	bored	to chew
④	worried	bored	chewing
⑤	worried	boring	to chew

12 다음 대화와 일치하도록 빈칸을 완성하시오.

> B: You look a bit nervous.
>
> G: I'm worried about my swimming competition this Saturday.
>
> B: Don't worry. You're such a good swimmer. Just relax and enjoy yourself!
>
> G: Thanks. I feel much better now.

> The girl looked (A)_____. She was so worried because of (B)_____. It'll be held on (C)_____. The boy already knew she is a good swimmer, so he encouraged her, by saying (D)"_____". Thanks to the boy, the girl felt relieved.

[13~14] 다음 주어진 우리말을 영작한 것으로 옳은 것은?

13

> 지수는 자신에 대한 확신을 느꼈을 뿐만 아니라, 타인들에게도 자신감에 차 보였다.

① Jisu felt not only sure about herself but looked also confident to other people.

② Not only Jisu felt sure about herself but also other people looked confident.

③ Jisu not only felt sure about herself but looked confident to other people.

④ Not only did feel Jisu sure about herself but she also looked confident to other people.

⑤ Jisu not only felt sure about herself but also looked confidently to other people.

14

> Franklin은 기타를 연주할 수 있을 뿐만 아니라, 피아노 조율도 할 수 있다.

① Franklin can play not only the guitar, but also tune the piano.

② Franklin not only can play the guitar, but also can he tune the piano.

③ Not only can Franklin play the guitar, does he also tune the piano.

④ Not only can Franklin play the guitar, but he can tune the piano.

⑤ Not Franklin only can play the guitar, but can he also tune the piano.

15 다음 각 문장의 밑줄 친 분사구문을 부사절로 바꿀 때 어법상 어색한 것은?

① Visiting Vladivostok, she could learn the Russian dance.

→ When she visited Vladivostok,

② Seen from the high sky, the city seems to be made of the lego bricks.

→ If it is seen from the high sky,

③ There being nothing to eat, the mice moved to another city.

→ Since there was nothing to eat,

④ It being cold but fine, we went on a picnic.

→ Though it was cold but fine,

⑤ Completing the final review, Roberto went out for a walk with his pets.

→ After he completed the final review,

16 다음 그림을 보고, 주어진 단어들을 알맞게 배열하여 빈칸을 채우시오.

(Sam, Minju, are, joining, and, in, both, interested, a club)

➡ _____

_____ and doing volunteer work.

17 다음 각 문장의 밑줄 친 부사절을 분사구문으로 바꾼 것 중 옳은 것은?

① While Babe was watching TV, his pet puppies fell asleep.

→ Watching TV,

② Because she went to bed earlier last night, Reon woke up at dawn.

→ She going to bed earlier last night,

③ If you cut the wrong wire, the box will explode.

→ Cutting the wrong wire,

④ If it is fine tomorrow, we will go fishing in the sea.

→ Being fine tomorrow,

⑤ When it is seen from a spaceship, the Earth is blue.

→ Seen from a spaceship,

[18~19] 다음 중에서 틀린 문장을 찾아 기호를 쓰고, 바르게 고쳐 문장을 다시 쓰시오.

18 ① Finding the smartphone she had lost, Emilia cried out with joy.

② Someone having touched the tires of her car, Clara didn't use it that morning.

③ Seeing its master, the dog wagged its tail.

④ Julie having seen him before, she decided to make friends with Charles.

⑤ Speaking in front of many people for a long time, the director felt quite tired.

➡ _____

_____

19 ① Do both Michael and his employees know how the company survived?

② Can either you or your partner explain to me what's happening in this building?

③ Not only you but also they warned us of the danger of the viruses.

④ Not only can he fly the drones, but he also makes some drones himself.

⑤ Neither the president nor his secretaries wants to know the basic causes of the problem.

➡ _____

_____

[20~22] 다음 글을 읽고 물음에 답하시오.

①The hardest time in my life was my first grade in middle school. When my family moved to Gunsan, I had to go to a new school. ②Had no friends at school, I felt sad and lonely. One day, I asked one of my ③ classmate to show me her notes. She not only helped me but also ④became a good friend. From this experience, I have learned that _____ⓐ_____ is a good way ⑤to make friends.

20 위 글의 밑줄 친 ①~⑤에서 어법상 어색한 것을 두 개 골라 바르게 고치고 그 이유를 밝히시오.

➡ _____

이유: _____

_____

21 위 글의 빈칸 ⓐ에 알맞은 것을 고르시오.

① asking for help
② keeping silent
③ inquiring questions
④ moving to a new school
⑤ showing notes

22 According to the passage, which is NOT true?

① The writer had to go to a new school when her family moved to Gunsan.
② The writer's hardest time in her life was her first grade in middle school.
③ The writer had some friends at the new school.
④ One of the writer's classmates not only helped her but also became a good friend.
⑤ The writer learned a good way to make friends.

[23~25] 다음 글을 읽고 물음에 답하시오.

_____ⓐ_____

①When he graduates from high school next year, Taeho wants to become a professional farmer. ②Having no friends, he has never told anyone about it. ③He is worried that his parents or his friends will not understand. ④ Wanting to clear his mind, Taeho decided to take a day trip on a train by himself. ⑤On the train, he told a complete stranger sitting beside him about his problem. He had no idea why he did it. However, he felt much better when he got off the train. Strangely enough, we often tell strangers about our problems just like Taeho. That is because we do not have to worry about being judged or seeing them again. If you have a problem that you cannot share with your family or friends, try talking to a stranger. You will feel much better.

23 위 글의 빈칸 ⓐ에 알맞은 것을 고르시오.

① How do I become less nervous?
② Who can help me feel better?
③ Why has Taeho never told anyone about his problem?
④ How do I turn a rival into a friend?
⑤ How does psychology answer our questions?

24 Why did Taeho take a day trip on a train by himself?

➡ _____

_____

25 위 글의 ①~⑤ 중에서 흐름상 어색한 것을 고르시오.

①   ②   ③   ④   ⑤

MEMO

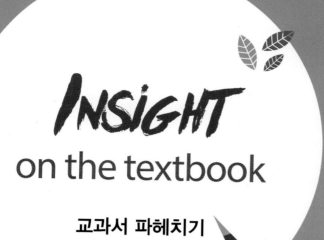

INSIGHT
on the textbook

교과서 파헤치기

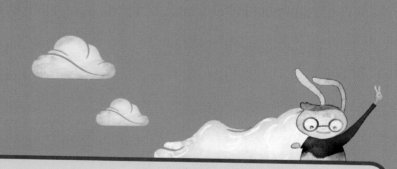

※ 다음 영어를 우리말로 쓰시오.

01	prove	
02	absorb	
03	publish	
04	bloom	
05	capital	
06	secret	
07	actually	
08	solve	
09	discover	
10	soak	
11	erase	
12	expect	
13	spinach	
14	face	
15	defeat	
16	character	
17	statue	
18	article	
19	battleship	
20	government	
21	bean	

22	hidden	
23	consider	
24	happen	
25	hide	
26	characteristic	
27	improve	
28	lower	
29	contain	
30	nutrient	
31	world-famous	
32	crush	
33	trace	
34	poisonous	
35	lose weight	
36	soak up	
37	keep ~ away from …	
38	turn A into B	
39	no longer	
40	be scared of	
41	give it a try	
42	keep a secret	
43	in addition	

※ 다음 우리말을 영어로 쓰시오.

01 흡수하다

02 기사, 논문

03 전함

04 꽃을 피우다

05 수도

06 등장인물

07 기대하다

08 고려하다, 여기다

09 물리치다, 패배시키다

10 특성, 특장; 특징적인

11 으스러뜨리다

12 유독한, 독성의

13 포함하다, 담고 있다

14 숨다, 숨기다

15 출판하다

16 조각상, 동상

17 개선하다, 향상시키다

18 낮추다

19 사실, 진실

20 흔적; 추적하다

21 시금치

22 물질, 재료

23 숨겨진

24 영양소, 영양분

25 증명하다

26 세계적으로 유명한

27 담그다, 적시다

28 행성

29 시력

30 비밀

31 해결하다

32 만화

33 연구원, 조사원

34 정부, 국가

35 포만감을 가지다

36 게다가

37 ~에 유익하다

38 살을 빼다

39 비밀을 지키다

40 더 이상 ~가 아닌

41 흡수하다, 빨아들이다

42 시도해 보다

43 약을 먹다

※ 다음 영영풀이에 알맞은 단어를 <보기>에서 골라 쓴 후, 우리말 뜻을 쓰시오.

1 _____ : a person in a book, play, film, etc.: _____

2 _____ : a funny drawing in a newspaper or magazine: _____

3 _____ : to cover something so that it cannot be seen clearly: _____

4 _____ : to use facts, evidence, etc. to show that something is true: _____

5 _____ : a small creature such as a fly or ant, that has six legs: _____

6 _____ : to prepare and produce a book, magazine, etc. for sale: _____

7 _____ : to put something in a liquid for a period of time: _____

8 _____ : a long pointed orange vegetable that grows under the ground: _____

9 _____ : a plant with dark green leaves that are eaten as a vegetable: _____

10 _____ : the largest type of ship used in war, with very big guns and heavy armour: _____

11 _____ : a fact that is known by only a small number of people, and is not told to anyone else: _____

12 _____ : a chemical or food that provides what is needed for plants or animals to live and grow: _____

13 _____ : an image of a person or animal that is made in solid material such as stone or metal: _____

14 _____ : a seed that is eaten as a vegetable and that comes from any one of many different kinds of climbing plants: _____

15 _____ : something such as a mark or an object which shows that someone or something was in a particular place: _____

16 _____ : a board like a wide ski that is used for sliding down hills of snow while standing: _____

보기			
snowboard	secret	battleship	hide
statue	bean	insect	character
trace	nutrient	prove	carrot
publish	spinach	soak	cartoon

Step1

※ 다음 우리말과 일치하도록 빈칸에 알맞은 말을 쓰시오.

해석

Listen & Speak 1 A-1

B: Bomi, do you have _____ _____?

G: Why? Is _____ _____?

B: I have _____ _____. I think I ate _____ _____ for lunch.

G: _____ _____ you _____ _____ _____ _____ _____ _____?

B: O.K. I'll give _____ _____ _____.

B: 보미야, 약 좀 있니?
G: 왜? 무슨 문제 있어?
B: 배가 아파. 점심을 너무 많이 먹었나 봐.
G: 산책을 좀 하는 게 어때?
B: 알겠어. 한번 해 볼게.

Listen & Speak 1 A-2

B: Is _____ _____? You don't _____ _____ _____ _____.

G: I have _____ _____ _____. I think it's _____ _____ the fine dust _____ _____.

B: _____ some plants in your room. They _____ bad air _____ and _____ _____ _____ _____.

G: Really? I'll _____ _____ _____ _____ _____ right away.

B: 어디 안 좋아? 안색이 나빠 보이는데.
G: 목이 아파. 최근의 미세먼지 때문인 것 같아.
B: 방에 식물을 좀 놓아 봐. 나쁜 공기를 흡수하고 신선한 공기를 만들어 내.
G: 정말? 당장 식물을 몇 그루 가져와야겠어.

Listen & Speak 2 A-1

B: It's _____ _____ _____ _____ _____ _____. What _____ _____ _____ I should do?

G: Well, why don't you _____ _____ _____ every day?

B: My dog would love _____, but would _____ _____ me _____ _____?

G: Sure. _____ you _____ your dog, you're _____ _____, _____.

B: O.K. I'll _____ _____ _____.

B: 몸무게를 줄이는 건 너무 어려워. 내가 뭘 해야 한다고 생각해?
G: 글쎄, 매일 너의 개를 산책시키는 건 어때?
B: 우리 개는 좋아하겠지만, 그게 살을 빼는 데 도움이 될까?
G: 물론이지. 네가 개를 산책시키면, 사실은 너도 운동하는 거잖아.
B: 좋아. 생각해 볼게.

Listen & Speak 2 A-2

B: _____ _____ your tomatoes _____? Are they _____ well?

G: No. I've _____ only _____ _____ tomatoes _____ _____. What do you think _____ _____ _____?

B: _____ do you have the pot?

G: _____ the kitchen.

B: Well, tomato plants _____ _____ 7 hours of sunlight _____ _____.

G: Oh, I see. I'll _____ the pot _____ to the window.

B: 네 토마토들 어떠니? 잘 자라고 있어?
G: 아니. 지금까지 토마토 몇 개밖에 못 얻었어. 내가 뭘 해야 한다고 생각하니?
B: 화분을 어디에 두는데?
G: 부엌에.
B: 음, 토마토는 하루에 7시간 정도 햇빛을 받아야 해.
G: 오, 그렇구나. 화분을 창문 쪽으로 옮겨야겠다.

Communicate A

Anna: Suho, _____ _____ _____? You're very _____ today.

Suho: I'm just _____ _____ _____. I slept very _____ last night.

Anna: Did you do _____ _____ last night?

Suho: Yes, I watched a movie _____ my phone _____ 2 a.m. That's _____ _____ _____ _____ _____ _____.

Anna: Oh, _____ _____ you have red eyes. You should go to bed _____ _____ for your health.

Suho: I think my eyes are _____ _____. What do you think _____ _____ _____?

Anna: Try _____ _____ _____ _____ and tomatoes. They're _____ _____ _____ A, so they'll _____ your eyes _____.

Suho: I _____. Thank you, Anna.

Anna: 수호야, 무슨 일 있어? 오늘 굉장히 조용하네.

수호: 조금 피곤한 것뿐이야. 어젯밤에 정말 조금 잤거든.

Anna: 어젯밤 늦게까지 뭔가 했니?

수호: 응, 새벽 2시까지 휴대폰으로 영화를 봤어. 요즘 종종 하는 일이야.

Anna: 오, 그래서 눈이 충혈됐구나. 건강을 위해 자정 전에는 잠자리에 들어야 해.

수호: 눈이 점점 나빠지는 것 같아. 내가 뭘 해야 한다고 생각해?

Anna: 당근이랑 토마토를 많이 먹어 봐. 그것들은 비타민 A가 많아서, 네 눈을 건강하게 유지해 줄 거야.

수호: 알겠어. 고마워, Anna.

Progress Check 1

B: _____ something _____?

G: I'm just _____ _____ _____. I've _____ a movie on my phone _____ _____ _____.

B: That's _____ you have _____ _____. Try _____ a warm towel _____ your eyes.

G: O.K. Thanks.

B: 무슨 문제 있어?

G: 조금 피곤한 것뿐이야. 휴대전화로 영화를 두 시간 동안 봤거든.

B: 그래서 눈이 충혈됐구나. 따뜻한 수건으로 눈을 덮어 봐.

G: 알겠어. 고마워.

Progress Check 2

G: What's _____? You _____ _____.

B: Well, I _____ my mom's favorite _____. What _____ _____ _____ I should do?

G: _____ her the _____. She will _____.

B: I _____ you're _____.

G: 무슨 문제 있어? 걱정이 있는 것 같은데.

B: 그게, 어머니께서 가장 아끼시는 접시를 깨뜨렸어. 내가 뭘 해야 한다고 생각하니?

G: 솔직히 말씀 드려. 이해하실 거야.

B: 네 말이 맞길 바라.

※ 다음 우리말에 맞도록 대화를 영어로 쓰시오.

Listen & Speak 1 A-1

B: _____

G: _____

B: _____

G: _____

B: _____

B: 보미야, 약 좀 있니?
G: 왜? 무슨 문제 있어?
B: 배가 아파. 점심을 너무 많이 먹었나 봐.
G: 산책을 좀 하는 게 어때?
B: 알겠어. 한번 해 볼게.

Listen & Speak 1 A-2

B: _____

G: _____

B: _____

G: _____

B: 어디 안 좋아? 안색이 나빠 보이는데.
G: 목이 아파. 최근의 미세먼지 때문인 것 같아.
B: 방에 식물을 좀 놓아 봐. 나쁜 공기를 흡수하고 신선한 공기를 만들어 내.
G: 정말? 당장 식물을 몇 그루 가져와야 겠어.

Listen & Speak 2 A-1

B: _____

G: _____

B: _____

G: _____

B: _____

B: 몸무게를 줄이는 건 너무 어려워. 내가 뭘 해야 한다고 생각해?
G: 글쎄, 매일 너의 개를 산책시키는 건 어때?
B: 우리 개는 좋아하겠지만, 그게 살을 빼는 데 도움이 될까?
G: 물론이지. 네가 개를 산책시키면, 사실은 너도 운동하는 거잖아.
B: 좋아. 생각해 볼게.

Listen & Speak 2 A-2

B: _____

G: _____

B: _____

G: _____

B: _____

G: _____

B: 네 토마토들 어떠니? 잘 자라고 있어?
G: 아니. 지금까지 토마토 몇 개밖에 못 얻었어. 내가 뭘 해야 한다고 생각하니?
B: 화분을 어디에 두는데?
G: 부엌에.
B: 음, 토마토는 하루에 7시간 정도 햇빛을 받아야 해.
G: 오, 그렇구나. 화분을 창문 쪽으로 옮겨야겠다.

Communicate A

Anna: _____

Suho: _____

Anna: _____

Suho: _____

_____

Anna: _____

_____

Suho: _____

Anna: _____

_____

Suho: _____

Progress Check 1

B: _____

G: _____

B: _____

G: _____

Progress Check 2

G: _____

B: _____

G: _____

B: _____

Anna: 수호야, 무슨 일 있어? 오늘 굉장히 조용하네.

수호: 조금 피곤한 것뿐이야. 어젯밤에 정말 조금 잤거든.

Anna: 어젯밤 늦게까지 뭔가 했니?

수호: 응, 새벽 2시까지 휴대폰으로 영화를 봤어. 요즘 종종 하는 일이야.

Anna: 오, 그래서 눈이 충혈됐구나. 건강을 위해 자정 전에는 잠자리에 들어야 해.

수호: 눈이 점점 나빠지는 것 같아. 내가 뭘 해야 한다고 생각해?

Anna: 당근이랑 토마토를 많이 먹어 봐. 그것들은 비타민 A가 많아서, 네 눈을 건강하게 유지해 줄 거야.

수호: 알겠어. 고마워, Anna.

B: 무슨 문제 있어?

G: 조금 피곤한 것뿐이야. 휴대전화로 영화를 두 시간 동안 봤거든.

B: 그래서 눈이 충혈됐구나. 따뜻한 수건으로 눈을 덮어 봐.

G: 알겠어. 고마워.

G: 무슨 문제 있어? 걱정이 있는 것 같은데.

B: 그게, 어머니께서 가장 아끼시는 접시를 깨뜨렸어. 내가 뭘 해야 한다고 생각하니?

G: 솔직히 말씀 드려. 이해하실 거야.

B: 네 말이 맞길 바라.

※ 다음 우리말과 일치하도록 빈칸에 알맞은 것을 골라 쓰시오.

1 _____ **Stories about** _____
A. Plants   B. Hidden

2 **Popeye and the** _____
A. Great   B. Spinach

3 Popeye is a _____ _____ _____ .
A. character   B. cartoon   C. world-famous

4 He _____ his super power _____ _____ _____ .
A. eating   B. by   C. gets   D. spinach

5 _____ Popeye _____ _____ in the 1930s in the United States, a _____ of children began to eat spinach.
A. popular   B. lot   C. became   D. when

6 Crystal City in Texas, which is _____ the spinach _____ of the world, even _____ a _____ of Popeye.
A. built   B. called   C. statue   D. capital

7 _____ eating spinach will not give us super _____ , _____ does have a lot of _____ .
A. spinach   B. although   C. nutrients   D. powers

8 It is actually _____ one of the ten _____ _____ on the _____ .
A. healthiest   B. planet   C. considered   D. foods

9 Spinach can be _____ in a _____ _____ .
A. surprising   B. used   C. way

10 _____ it absorbs water, spinach also _____ many _____ things from the _____ .
A. absorbs   B. soil   C. other   D. when

11 Some scientists have used this _____ of spinach to find _____ in the _____ .
A. characteristic   B. ground   C. bombs   D. hidden

12 They make special spinach plants _____ _____ their _____ .
A. ensors   B. leaves   C. on   D. with

13 When these plants _____ up traces from _____ , the sensors _____ _____ .
A. light   B. bombs   C. up   D. soak

14 **Carrots in** _____ _____ _____
A. War   B. World   C. II

15 In 1940, the Royal Air Force _____ German fighters _____ World War II _____ a radar system.
A. by   B. defeated   C. using   D. during

16 The British government wanted to _____ this technology a _____ , so it _____ an _____ in the newspaper.
A. secret   B. keep   C. published   D. article

17 It _____ that British pilots _____ their night _____ because they _____ a lot of carrots.
A. vision   B. said   C. ate   D. improved

1 식물에 대한 숨겨진 이야기

2 Popeye와 위대한 시금치

3 Popeye는 세계적으로 유명한 만화 캐릭터다.

4 그는 시금치를 먹음으로써 초인적인 힘을 얻는다.

5 Popeye가 1930년대 미국에서 인기를 얻었을 때, 많은 어린이들이 시금치를 먹기 시작했다.

6 텍사스의 크리스털 시티는 세계의 시금치 수도라고 불리는데, 이곳에서는 Popeye의 동상을 세우기까지 했다.

7 비록 시금치를 먹는 것이 우리에게 초인적인 힘을 주지는 않지만, 시금치는 정말로 많은 영양분을 가지고 있다.

8 이것은 실제로 지구상에서 가장 건강한 식품 10개 중 하나로 여겨진다.

9 시금치는 놀라운 용도로 사용될 수 있다.

10 그것이 물을 흡수할 때, 시금치는 흙으로부터 다른 많은 것들도 흡수한다.

11 몇몇 과학자들은 시금치의 이 특성을 땅에 숨겨진 폭탄을 찾는 데 사용했다.

12 그들은 잎에 감지기가 있는 특별한 시금치를 만든다.

13 이 식물들이 폭탄의 흔적을 흡수하면, 감지기가 빛난다.

14 제2차 세계대전에서의 당근

15 1940년, 영국 공군은 제2차 세계 대전에서 레이더 시스템을 사용해 독일군을 패배시켰다.

16 영국 정부는 이 기술을 비밀로 하기를 원했기 때문에, 신문에 기사를 하나 냈다.

17 그것은 영국 비행사들이 당근을 많이 먹어 야간 시력이 좋아졌다는 내용이었다.

18 Everybody _____ the story and began to eat a _____ more carrots _____ _____.
   A. than   B. lot   C. before   D. believed

19 Can we really _____ night vision _____ _____ lots of _____?
   A. improve   B. eating   C. by   D. carrots

20 Not really, but carrots _____ a lot of _____ A, which does _____ our eyes _____.
   A. vitamin   B. healthy   C. contain   D. keep

21 In the _____, carrots _____ actually be _____ in _____.
   A. used   B. future   C. wars   D. may

22 Scottish researchers have _____ a way to _____ carrots _____ a very strong and _____ material.
   A. turn   B. discovered   C. light   D. into

23 It can _____ _____ _____ to make _____.
   A. be   B. battleships   C. used   D. even

24 This new material _____ _____ _____ _____ to make snowboards and bicycles.
   A. been   B. has   C. used   D. already

25 **Tomatoes, the** _____ _____
   A. Vegetables   B. Scariest

26 We all know that tomatoes _____ _____ _____ our _____.
   A. good   B. health   C. are   D. for

27 _____ _____ the 1800s, _____, most Americans thought that tomatoes were _____.
   A. until   B. poisonous   C. up   D. however

28 In 1820, a man _____ Robert Johnson wanted to _____ that tomatoes were _____ to _____.
   A. prove   B. eat   C. named   D. safe

29 So, he _____ a _____ of tomatoes in _____ of many people _____ him.
   A. front   B. basket   C. watching   D. ate

30 They all _____ him to die, but _____ _____ _____ him.
   A. nothing   B. expected   C. to   D. happened

31 Ever _____ then, Americans _____ _____ _____ tomatoes.
   A. enjoyed   B. since   C. eating   D. have

32 We are _____ _____ afraid of tomatoes, but some insects are still _____ _____ them.
   A. scared   B. no   C. of   D. longer

33 If you want to _____ insects _____ from your room, _____ a bowl of _____ tomatoes in a corner of your room.
   A. away   B. crushed   C. keep   D. place

34 _____ will not _____ _____ the tomatoes.
   A. come   B. insects   C. near

18 모두가 그 이야기를 믿었고 전보다 훨씬 많은 당근을 먹기 시작했다.

19 우리는 정말 당근을 많이 먹어서 야간 시력을 높일 수 있을까?

20 실제로 그렇지는 않지만, 당근은 많은 비타민 A를 함유하는데, 그것은 정말로 우리 눈을 건강하게 유지해 준다.

21 미래에는, 당근이 실제로 전쟁에 이용될지도 모른다.

22 스코틀랜드의 연구원들은 당근을 매우 강하고 가벼운 물질로 바꾸는 방법을 발견했다.

23 그것은 심지어 전함을 만드는 데 사용될 수도 있다.

24 이 새로운 소재는 이미 스노보드와 자전거를 만드는 데 사용되었다.

25 토마토, 가장 무서운 채소

26 우리는 모두 토마토가 건강에 좋다는 것을 안다.

27 그러나, 1800년대까지 대부분의 미국인들은 토마토에 독성이 있다고 생각했다.

28 1820년에, Robert Johnson이라는 이름의 남자가 토마토가 먹기에 안전하다는 것을 증명하기를 원했다.

29 그래서, 그는 그를 지켜보는 많은 사람들 앞에서 한 바구니의 토마토를 먹었다.

30 그들은 모두 그가 죽을 것이라고 예상했으나 그에게는 아무 일도 일어나지 않았다.

31 그 이후로, 미국인들은 토마토를 먹는 것을 즐겼다.

32 우리는 더 이상 토마토를 두려워하지 않지만, 몇몇 곤충들은 여전히 그것을 무서워한다.

33 만약 곤충들이 방에 들어오지 않게 하고 싶다면, 으깬 토마토 한 그릇을 방구석에 놓아 두어라.

34 곤충들은 토마토 가까이 오지 않을 것이다.

※ 다음 우리말과 일치하도록 빈칸에 알맞은 것을 골라 쓰시오.

1 _____ Stories about _____

2 **Popeye and the Great** _____

3 Popeye is a _____ _____ _____ .

4 He gets his super power _____ _____ _____ .

5 When Popeye _____ _____ in the 1930s in the United States, _____ _____ _____ children began to eat spinach.

6 Crystal City in Texas, _____ is called _____ _____ _____ of the world, even built _____ _____ of Popeye.

7 _____ _____ spinach will not give us super powers, spinach _____ _____ a lot of _____ .

8 It is actually considered _____ _____ _____ _____ _____ _____ on the planet.

9 Spinach can be used _____ _____ _____ _____ .

10 _____ it _____ water, spinach _____ _____ many other things _____ the soil.

11 Some scientists have used this characteristic of spinach _____ _____ bombs _____ _____ _____ _____ .

12 They make special spinach plants _____ _____ _____ _____ _____ .

13 When these plants _____ _____ _____ from bombs, the sensors _____ _____ .

14 **Carrots in** _____ _____ _____

15 In 1940, the Royal Air Force _____ German fighters _____ World War II _____ _____ a radar system.

16 The British government wanted to _____ this technology a _____ , so it _____ _____ _____ in the newspaper.

17 It said that British pilots _____ _____ _____ _____ they ate a lot of carrots.

1 식물에 대한 숨겨진 이야기

2 Popeye와 위대한 시금치

3 Popeye는 세계적으로 유명한 만화 캐릭터다.

4 그는 시금치를 먹음으로써 초인적인 힘을 얻는다.

5 Popeye가 1930년대 미국에서 인기를 얻었을 때, 많은 어린이들이 시금치를 먹기 시작했다.

6 텍사스의 크리스털 시티는 세계의 시금치 수도라고 불리는데, 이곳에서는 Popeye의 동상을 세우기까지 했다.

7 비록 시금치를 먹는 것이 우리에게 초인적인 힘을 주지는 않지만, 시금치는 정말로 많은 영양분을 가지고 있다.

8 이것은 실제로 지구상에서 가장 건강한 식품 10개 중 하나로 여겨진다.

9 시금치는 놀라운 용도로 사용될 수 있다.

10 그것이 물을 흡수할 때, 시금치는 흙으로부터 다른 많은 것들도 흡수한다.

11 몇몇 과학자들은 시금치의 이 특성을 땅에 숨겨진 폭탄을 찾는 데 사용했다.

12 그들은 잎에 감지기가 있는 특별한 시금치를 만든다.

13 이 식물들이 폭탄의 흔적을 흡수하면, 감지기가 빛난다.

14 제2차 세계대전에서의 당근

15 1940년, 영국 공군은 제2차 세계 대전에서 레이더 시스템을 사용해 독일군을 패배시켰다.

16 영국 정부는 이 기술을 비밀로 하기를 원했기 때문에, 신문에 기사를 하나 냈다.

17 그것은 영국 비행사들이 당근을 많이 먹어 야간 시력이 좋아졌다는 내용이었다.

18 Everybody believed the story and began to eat _____ _____ more carrots _____ _____.

19 Can we really _____ night vision _____ _____ lots of carrots?

20 Not really, but carrots contain a lot of vitamin A, _____ _____ _____ our eyes _____.

21 In the future, carrots _____ _____ _____ _____ in wars.

22 Scottish researchers have discovered a way to _____ carrots _____ a very strong and _____ _____.

23 It _____ _____ _____ _____ to make battleships.

24 This new material _____ _____ _____ _____ to make snowboards and bicycles.

25 **Tomatoes, the _____ Vegetables**

26 We all know that tomatoes _____ _____ _____ our health.

27 _____ _____ the 1800s, _____, most Americans thought that tomatoes were _____.

28 In 1820, a man _____ Robert Johnson wanted _____ _____ that tomatoes were _____ _____ _____.

29 So, he ate _____ _____ _____ tomatoes _____ _____ many people _____ him.

30 They all expected him to die, but nothing _____ _____ him.

31 Ever _____ then, Americans _____ _____ _____ tomatoes.

32 We are _____ _____ afraid of tomatoes, but some insects are still _____ _____ them.

33 If you want to _____ insects _____ _____ your room, _____ a bowl of _____ tomatoes in a corner of your room.

34 Insects will not _____ _____ the tomatoes.

18 모두가 그 이야기를 믿었고 전보다 훨씬 많은 당근을 먹기 시작했다.

19 우리는 정말 당근을 많이 먹어서 야간 시력을 높일 수 있을까?

20 실제로 그렇지는 않지만, 당근은 많은 비타민 A를 함유하는데, 그것은 정말로 우리 눈을 건강하게 유지해 준다.

21 미래에는, 당근이 실제로 전쟁에 이용될지도 모른다.

22 스코틀랜드의 연구원들은 당근을 매우 강하고 가벼운 물질로 바꾸는 방법을 발견했다.

23 그것은 심지어 전함을 만드는 데 사용될 수도 있다.

24 이 새로운 소재는 이미 스노보드와 자전거를 만드는 데 사용되었다.

25 토마토, 가장 무서운 채소

26 우리는 모두 토마토가 건강에 좋다는 것을 안다.

27 그러나, 1800년대까지 대부분의 미국인들은 토마토에 독성이 있다고 생각했다.

28 1820년에, Robert Johnson이라는 이름의 남자가 토마토가 먹기에 안전하다는 것을 증명하기를 원했다.

29 그래서, 그는 그를 지켜보는 많은 사람들 앞에서 한 바구니의 토마토를 먹었다.

30 그들은 모두 그가 죽을 것이라고 예상했으나 그에게는 아무 일도 일어나지 않았다.

31 그 이후로, 미국인들은 토마토를 먹는 것을 즐겼다.

32 우리는 더 이상 토마토를 두려워하지 않지만, 몇몇 곤충들은 여전히 그것을 무서워한다.

33 만약 곤충들이 방에 들어오지 않게 하고 싶다면, 으깬 토마토 한 그릇을 방구석에 놓아 두어라.

34 곤충들은 토마토 가까이 오지 않을 것이다.

※ 다음 문장을 우리말로 쓰시오.

1 ▸ Hidden Stories about Plants
➡ _____

2 ▸ Popeye and the Great Spinach
➡ _____

3 ▸ Popeye is a world-famous cartoon character.
➡ _____

4 ▸ He gets his super power by eating spinach.
➡ _____

5 ▸ When Popeye became popular in the 1930s in the United States, a lot of children began to eat spinach.
➡ _____

6 ▸ Crystal City in Texas, which is called the spinach capital of the world, even built a statue of Popeye.
➡ _____

7 ▸ Although eating spinach will not give us super powers, spinach does have a lot of nutrients.
➡ _____

8 ▸ It is actually considered one of the ten healthiest foods on the planet.
➡ _____

9 ▸ Spinach can be used in a surprising way.
➡ _____

10 ▸ When it absorbs water, spinach also absorbs many other things from the soil.
➡ _____

11 ▸ Some scientists have used this characteristic of spinach to find bombs hidden in the ground.
➡ _____

12 ▸ They make special spinach plants with sensors on their leaves.
➡ _____

13 ▸ When these plants soak up traces from bombs, the sensors light up.
➡ _____

14 ▸ Carrots in World War II
➡ _____

15 ▸ In 1940, the Royal Air Force defeated German fighters during World War II by using a radar system.
➡ _____

16 ▸ The British government wanted to keep this technology a secret, so it published an article in the newspaper.
➡ _____

17 It said that British pilots improved their night vision because they ate a lot of carrots.

➡ _____

18 Everybody believed the story and began to eat a lot more carrots than before.

➡ _____

19 Can we really improve night vision by eating lots of carrots?

➡ _____

20 Not really, but carrots contain a lot of vitamin A, which does keep our eyes healthy.

➡ _____

21 In the future, carrots may actually be used in wars.

➡ _____

22 Scottish researchers have discovered a way to turn carrots into a very strong and light material.

➡ _____

23 It can even be used to make battleships.

➡ _____

24 This new material has already been used to make snowboards and bicycles.

➡ _____

25 Tomatoes, the Scariest Vegetables

➡ _____

26 We all know that tomatoes are good for our health.

➡ _____

27 Up until the 1800s, however, most Americans thought that tomatoes were poisonous.

➡ _____

28 In 1820, a man named Robert Johnson wanted to prove that tomatoes were safe to eat.

➡ _____

29 So, he ate a basket of tomatoes in front of many people watching him.

➡ _____

30 They all expected him to die, but nothing happened to him.

➡ _____

31 Ever since then, Americans have enjoyed eating tomatoes.

➡ _____

32 We are no longer afraid of tomatoes, but some insects are still scared of them.

➡ _____

33 If you want to keep insects away from your room, place a bowl of crushed tomatoes in a corner of your room.

➡ _____

34 Insects will not come near the tomatoes.

➡ _____

※ 다음 괄호 안의 단어들을 우리말에 맞도록 바르게 배열하시오.

1 (Stories / Hidden / Plants / about)
➡ _____

2 (and / Popeye / the / Spinach / Great)
➡ _____

3 (is / Popeye / a / cartoon / world-famous / character.)
➡ _____

4 (gets / he / his / power / super / eating / by / spinach.)
➡ _____

5 (Popeye / when / popular / became / the / in / 1930s / the / in / States, / United / lot / a / of / began / children / eat / to / spinach.)
➡ _____

6 (City / Crystal / Texas, / in / is / which / the / called / spinach / of / capital / world, / the / bulit / even / statue / a / Popeye. / of)
➡ _____

7 (eating / although / will / spinach / give / not / super / us / powers, / does / spinach / have / lot / a / nutrients. / of)
➡ _____

8 (is / it / considered / actually / of / one / the / healthiest / ten / on / foods / planet. / the)
➡ _____

9 (can / spinach / be / used / a / in / way. / surprising)
➡ _____

10 (it / when / water, / absorbs / also / spinach / many / absorbs / things / other / the / from / soil.)
➡ _____

11 (scientists / some / used / have / characteristic / this / spinach / of / find / to / hidden / bombs / the / in / ground.)
➡ _____

12 (make / they / spinach / special / with / plants / on / sensors / leaves. / their)
➡ _____

13 (these / when / soak / plants / traces / up / bombs, / from / sensors / the / up. / light)
➡ _____

14 (in / Carrots / War / World / II)
➡ _____

15 (1940, / in / Royal / the / Force / Air / German / defeated / during / fighters / War / World / by / II / using / radar / system. / a)
➡ _____

16 (British / the / wanted / government / keep / to / this / a / technology / secret, / it / so / an / published / article / the / in / newspaper.)
➡ _____

17 (said / it / British / that / improved / pilots / night / their / because / vision / ate / they / lot / a / carrots. / of)
➡ _____

1 식물에 대한 숨겨진 이야기

2 Popeye와 위대한 시금치

3 Popeye는 세계적으로 유명한 만화 캐릭터다.

4 그는 시금치를 먹음으로써 초인적인 힘을 얻는다.

5 Popeye가 1930년대 미국에서 인기를 얻었을 때, 많은 어린이들이 시금치를 먹기 시작했다.

6 텍사스의 크리스털 시티는 세계의 시금치 수도라고 불리는데, 이곳에서는 Popeye의 동상을 세우기까지 했다.

7 비록 시금치를 먹는 것이 우리에게 초인적인 힘을 주지는 않지만, 시금치는 정말로 많은 영양분을 가지고 있다.

8 이것은 실제로 지구상에서 가장 건강한 식품 10개 중 하나로 여겨진다.

9 시금치는 놀라운 용도로 사용될 수 있다.

10 그것이 물을 흡수할 때, 시금치는 흙으로부터 다른 많은 것들도 흡수한다.

11 몇몇 과학자들은 시금치의 이 특성을 땅에 숨겨진 폭탄을 찾는 데 사용했다.

12 그들은 잎에 감지기가 있는 특별한 시금치를 만든다.

13 이 식물들이 폭탄의 흔적을 흡수하면, 감지기가 빛난다.

14 제2차 세계대전에서의 당근

15 1940년, 영국 공군은 제2차 세계 대전에서 레이더 시스템을 사용해 독일군을 패배시켰다.

16 영국 정부는 이 기술을 비밀로 하기를 원했기 때문에, 신문에 기사를 하나 냈다.

17 그것은 영국 비행사들이 당근을 많이 먹어 야간 시력이 좋아졌다는 내용이었다.

18 (believed / everybody / story / the / and / to / began / eat / lot / a / carrots / more / before. / than)

➡ _____

19 (we / can / improve / really / vision / night / eating / by / of / carrots? / lots)

➡ _____

20 (really, / not / carrots / but / a / contain / of / lot / A, / vitamin / does / which / our / keep / healthy. / eyes)

➡ _____

21 (the / in / future, / may / carrots / be / actually / used / be / wars. / in)

➡ _____

22 (researchers / Scottish / discovered / have / way / a / turn / to / into / carrots / very / a / strong / and / material. / light)

➡ _____

23 (can / it / be / even / to / used / battleships. / make)

➡ _____

24 (new / this / has / material / been / already / to / used / make / and / snowboards / bycycles.)

➡ _____

25 (the / Tomatoes, / Vegetables / Scariest)

➡ _____

26 (all / we / that / know / are / tomatoes / good / our / for / health.)

➡ _____

27 (until / up / 1800s, / the / most / however, / thought / Americans / that / were / tomatoes / poisonous.)

➡ _____

28 (1820, / in / man / a / named / Johnson / Robert / to / wanted / that / prove / tomatoes / safe / were / eat. / to)

➡ _____

29 (he / so, / ate / of / basket / a / tomatoes / front / in / many / of / watching / people / him.)

➡ _____

30 (all / they / him / expected / die, / to / nothing / but / to / happened / him.)

➡ _____

31 (since / ever / then, / have / Americans / eating / enjoyed / tomatoes.)

➡ _____

32 (are / we / longer / no / of / afraid / tomatoes, / some / but / are / insects / still / of / scared / them.)

➡ _____

33 (you / if / to / want / insects / keep / from / away / room, / your / a / place / of / bowl / tomatoes / crushed / a / in / of / corner / room. / your)

➡ _____

34 (will / insects / come / not / the / near / tomatoes.)

➡ _____

---

18 모두가 그 이야기를 믿었고 전보다 훨씬 많은 당근을 먹기 시작했다.

19 우리는 정말 당근을 많이 먹어서 야간 시력을 높일 수 있을까?

20 실제로 그렇지는 않지만, 당근은 많은 비타민 A를 함유하는데, 그것은 정말로 우리 눈을 건강하게 유지해 준다.

21 미래에는, 당근이 실제로 전쟁에 이용될지도 모른다.

22 스코틀랜드의 연구원들은 당근을 매우 강하고 가벼운 물질로 바꾸는 방법을 발견했다.

23 그것은 심지어 전함을 만드는 데 사용될 수도 있다.

24 이 새로운 소재는 이미 스노보드와 자전거를 만드는 데 사용되었다.

25 토마토, 가장 무서운 채소

26 우리는 모두 토마토가 건강에 좋다는 것을 안다.

27 그러나, 1800년대까지 대부분의 미국인들은 토마토에 독성이 있다고 생각했다.

28 1820년에, Robert Johnson이라는 이름의 남자가 토마토가 먹기에 안전하다는 것을 증명하기를 원했다.

29 그래서, 그는 그를 지켜보는 많은 사람들 앞에서 한 바구니의 토마토를 먹었다.

30 그들은 모두 그가 죽을 것이라고 예상했으나 그에게는 아무 일도 일어나지 않았다.

31 그 이후로, 미국인들은 토마토를 먹는 것을 즐겼다.

32 우리는 더 이상 토마토를 두려워하지 않지만, 몇몇 곤충들은 여전히 그것을 무서워한다.

33 만약 곤충들이 방에 들어오지 않게 하고 싶다면, 으깬 토마토 한 그릇을 방구석에 놓아 두어라.

34 곤충들은 토마토 가까이 오지 않을 것이다.

※ 다음 우리말을 영어로 쓰시오.

1 식물에 대한 숨겨진 이야기

➡ _____

2 Popeye와 위대한 시금치

➡ _____

3 Popeye는 세계적으로 유명한 만화 캐릭터다.

➡ _____

4 그는 시금치를 먹음으로써 초인적인 힘을 얻는다.

➡ _____

5 Popeye가 1930년대 미국에서 인기를 얻었을 때, 많은 어린이들이 시금치를 먹기 시작했다.

➡ _____

6 텍사스의 크리스털 시티는 세계의 시금치 수도라고 불리는데, 이곳에서는 Popeye의 동상을 세우기까지 했다.

➡ _____

_____

7 비록 시금치를 먹는 것이 우리에게 초인적인 힘을 주지는 않지만, 시금치는 정말로 많은 영양분을 가지고 있다.

➡ _____

_____

8 이것은 실제로 지구상에서 가장 건강한 식품 10개 중 하나로 여겨진다.

➡ _____

9 시금치는 놀라운 용도로 사용될 수 있다.

➡ _____

10 그것이 물을 흡수할 때, 시금치는 흙으로부터 다른 많은 것들도 흡수한다.

➡ _____

11 몇몇 과학자들은 시금치의 이 특성을 땅에 숨겨진 폭탄을 찾는 데 사용했다.

➡ _____

12 그들은 잎에 감지기가 있는 특별한 시금치를 만든다.

➡ _____

13 이 식물들이 폭탄의 흔적을 흡수하면, 감지기가 빛난다.

➡ _____

14 제2차 세계대전에서의 당근

➡ _____

15 1940년, 영국 공군은 제2차 세계 대전에서 레이더 시스템을 사용해 독일군을 패배시켰다.

➡ _____

16 영국 정부는 이 기술을 비밀로 하기를 원했기 때문에, 신문에 기사를 하나 냈다.

➡ _____

17 그것은 영국 비행사들이 당근을 많이 먹어 야간 시력이 좋아졌다는 내용이었다.
➡ _____

18 모두가 그 이야기를 믿었고 전보다 훨씬 많은 당근을 먹기 시작했다.
➡ _____

19 우리는 정말 당근을 많이 먹어서 야간 시력을 높일 수 있을까?
➡ _____

20 실제로 그렇지는 않지만, 당근은 많은 비타민 A를 함유하는데, 그것은 정말로 우리 눈을 건강하게 유지해 준다.
➡ _____

21 미래에는, 당근이 실제로 전쟁에 이용될지도 모른다.
➡ _____

22 스코틀랜드의 연구원들은 당근을 매우 강하고 가벼운 물질로 바꾸는 방법을 발견했다.
➡ _____

23 그것은 심지어 전함을 만드는 데 사용될 수도 있다.
➡ _____

24 이 새로운 소재는 이미 스노보드와 자전거를 만드는 데 사용되었다.
➡ _____

25 토마토, 가장 무서운 채소
➡ _____

26 우리는 모두 토마토가 건강에 좋다는 것을 안다.
➡ _____

27 그러나, 1800년대까지 대부분의 미국인들은 토마토에 독성이 있다고 생각했다.
➡ _____

28 1820년에, Robert Johnson이라는 이름의 남자가 토마토가 먹기에 안전하다는 것을 증명하기를 원했다.
➡ _____

29 그래서, 그는 그를 지켜보는 많은 사람들 앞에서 한 바구니의 토마토를 먹었다.
➡ _____

30 그들은 모두 그가 죽을 것이라고 예상했으나 그에게는 아무 일도 일어나지 않았다.
➡ _____

31 그 이후로, 미국인들은 토마토를 먹는 것을 즐겼다.
➡ _____

32 우리는 더 이상 토마토를 두려워하지 않지만, 몇몇 곤충들은 여전히 그것을 무서워한다.
➡ _____

33 만약 곤충들이 방에 들어오지 않게 하고 싶다면, 으깬 토마토 한 그릇을 방구석에 놓아 두어라.
➡ _____

34 곤충들은 토마토 가까이 오지 않을 것이다.
➡ _____

※ 다음 우리말과 일치하도록 빈칸에 알맞은 말을 쓰시오.

Inventions from Plants

1. The Sunflower Battery is a _____ _____ _____ _____ _____ energy.

2. It is a _____ _____ _____ the idea _____ _____ the _____ _____ _____ .

3. _____ sunflowers, it _____ the sun _____ _____ _____ _____ , so it produces _____ _____ _____ _____ _____ _____ .

1. 해바라기 배터리는 에너지를 만드는 좋은 방법입니다.
2. 그것은 해바라기의 특징을 이용한다는 생각에서 만들어진 배터리입니다.
3. 해바라기처럼, 그것은 낮 동안에 태양을 향해서, 다른 배터리보다 더 많은 전기를 만들어 냅니다.

After You Read A Read and Match

1. 1. _____

2. • the _____ of Popeye's _____

3. • _____ _____ _____ _____ _____ _____ _____ _____ on the planet

4. • used _____ sensors _____ _____ _____ _____ _____ in the ground

5. 2. _____

6. • used _____ _____ _____ and bicycles

7. • made _____ a very strong and _____ _____

8. • containing a lot of vitamin A, _____ _____ _____ _____ _____

9. 3. _____

10. • good for _____ _____ _____

11. • considered _____ _____ the 1800s

1. 1. 시금치
2. • Popeye의 초인적인 힘의 비밀
3. • 지구상에서 가장 건강한 식품 10개 중 하나
4. • 땅에 숨겨진 폭탄을 찾기 위해 감지기와 함께 사용된다.
5. 2. 당근
6. • 스노보드와 자전거를 만드는 데에 사용된다.
7. • 매우 강하고 가벼운 물질이 된다.
8. • 많은 비타민 A를 함유하는데, 그것은 정말로 우리 눈을 건강하게 유지해 준다.
9. 3. 토마토
10. • 곤충들이 가까이 오지 못하게 하는데 좋다.
11. • 1800년대까지 독성이 있다고 여겨졌다.

Write

1. Potatoes _____ _____ _____ your health.

2. They _____ _____ _____ _____ _____ because they _____ _____ _____ .

3. They also _____ _____ _____ _____ _____ _____ .

4. Potato juice _____ _____ honey _____ your skin _____ and _____ .

5. _____ _____ , they _____ you _____ _____ _____ .

6. If you eat potatoes, you will _____ _____ _____ _____ _____ _____ _____ .

7. Potatoes _____ you _____ _____ in many ways.

1. 감자는 당신의 건강에 좋다.
2. 감자는 혈압을 낮춰주기 때문에 당신의 심장을 건강하게 지켜준다.
3. 감자는 또한 당신의 피부 문제를 해결해 준다.
4. 꿀을 넣은 감자 주스는 당신의 피부를 부드럽고 깨끗하게 만들어 준다.
5. 게다가, 감자는 당신이 살을 빼도록 도와준다.
6. 당신이 감자를 먹으면, 오랜 시간 배부른 상태를 유지할 것이다.
7. 감자는 여러 가지 면에서 당신을 건강하게 지내도록 도와준다.

※ 다음 우리말을 영어로 쓰시오.

Inventions from Plants

1. 해바라기 배터리는 에너지를 만드는 좋은 방법입니다.
   ➡ _____

2. 그것은 해바라기의 특징을 이용한다는 생각에서 만들어진 배터리입니다.
   ➡ _____

3. 해바라기처럼, 그것은 낮 동안에 태양을 향해서, 다른 배터리보다 더 많은 전기를 만들어 냅니다.
   ➡ _____

After You Read A Read and Match

1. 1. 시금치
   ➡ _____

2. • Popeye의 초인적인 힘의 비밀
   ➡ _____

3. • 지구상에서 가장 건강한 식품 10개 중 하나
   ➡ _____

4. • 땅에 숨겨진 폭탄을 찾기 위해 감지기와 함께 사용된다.
   ➡ _____

5. 2. 당근
   ➡ _____

6. • 스노보드와 자전거를 만드는 데에 사용된다.
   ➡ _____

2. • 매우 강하고 가벼운 물질이 된다.
   ➡ _____

3. • 많은 비타민 A를 함유하는데, 그것은 정말로 우리 눈을 건강하게 유지해 준다.
   ➡ _____

4. 3. 토마토
   ➡ _____

5. • 곤충들이 가까이 오지 못하게 하는데 좋다.
   ➡ _____

6. • 1800년대까지 독성이 있다고 여겨졌다.
   ➡ _____

Write

1. 감자는 당신의 건강에 좋다.
   ➡ _____

2. 감자는 혈압을 낮춰주기 때문에 당신의 심장을 건강하게 지켜준다.
   ➡ _____

3. 감자는 또한 당신의 피부 문제를 해결해 준다.
   ➡ _____

4. 꿀을 넣은 감자 주스는 당신의 피부를 부드럽고 깨끗하게 만들어 준다.
   ➡ _____

5. 게다가, 감자는 당신이 살을 빼도록 도와준다.
   ➡ _____

6. 당신이 감자를 먹으면, 오랜 시간 배부른 상태를 유지할 것이다.
   ➡ _____

7. 감자는 여러 가지 면에서 당신을 건강하게 지내도록 도와준다.
   ➡ _____

※ 다음 영어를 우리말로 쓰시오.

01 greenhouse		22 breathe	
02 harvest		23 destroy	
03 ad(= advertisement)		24 waterfall	
04 exhibition		25 trail	
05 underwater		26 intangible	
06 marine		27 jellyfish	
07 nationwide		28 press	
08 overseas		29 underground	
09 promote		30 suitable	
10 bridge		31 audience	
11 community		32 overwork	
12 moved		33 path	
13 heritage		34 realize	
14 environment		35 wish for	
15 seafood		36 happen to	
16 several		37 walk along	
17 breadwinner		38 a couple of	
18 female		39 get into	
19 volcanic		40 be suitable for	
20 worldwide		41 give a talk	
21 complete		42 a little bit	
		43 be good for	

※ 다음 우리말을 영어로 쓰시오.

01 폭포

02 광고

03 경로, 길

04 과로하다

05 교량, 다리

06 좁은 길

07 지하의

08 세계적으로

09 화산의, 화산 작용에 의한

10 온실

11 파괴하다

12 전시회, 박람회

13 홍보하다, 촉진하다

14 완성[완료]하다

15 몇몇의

16 생계를 책임지는 사람, 가장

17 적합한, 적절한

18 여성의

19 누르다; 언론, 기자

20 지역 공동체

21 무형의, 만질 수 없는

22 수중의, 물속에서

23 해파리

24 해양의, 바다의

25 수확하다

26 청중

27 유산

28 호흡하다

29 전국적인

30 해외의

31 깨닫다, 인식하다

32 단단히. 꽉

33 (북 등을 치는) 소리, (심장의) 고동

34 풍년

35 휴가가다

36 ~에 들어가다

37 우연히 ~하다

38 ~을 따라 걷다

39 ~에 유익하다

40 계속해서 ~하다

41 힘을 북돋아 주다, 격려하다

42 거들어 주다, 돕다

43 발표하다

※ 다음 영영풀이에 알맞은 단어를 <보기>에서 골라 쓴 후, 우리말 뜻을 쓰시오.

1 _____ : to gather a crop: _____

2 _____ : under the surface of the ground: _____

3 _____ : to finish making or doing something: _____

4 _____ : one of a series of regular movements or hitting actions: _____

5 _____ : a place where a stream or river falls from a high place: _____

6 _____ : right or appropriate for a particular purpose or occasion: _____

7 _____ : to take air into your lungs and send it out again: _____

8 _____ : the people who live in the same area, town, etc.: _____

9 _____ : the traditional beliefs, values, customs of a family, country, or society: _____

10 _____ : having value but not existing physically: _____

11 _____ : to or in a foreign country that is across the sea: _____

12 _____ : fish and shellfish that live in the ocean and are used for food: _____

13 _____ : to damage something so badly that it no longer exists, works, etc.: _____

14 _____ : a picture, set of words, or a short film, intended to persuade people to buy: _____

15 _____ : a structure built over something such as a river so that people or vehicles can get across: _____

16 _____ : the member of a family who earns the money to support the others: _____

보기			
destroy	breadwinner	community	suitable
intangible	overseas	harvest	seafood
bridge	complete	waterfall	ad
heritage	breathe	beat	underground

※ 다음 우리말과 일치하도록 빈칸에 알맞은 말을 쓰시오.

해석

Listen & Speak 1 A-1

G: Wow, _____ _____ the _____ in this _____. I wonder _____ _____ _____ _____ _____.

B: That's Gwangandaegyo in Busan.

G: _____ _____ you _____ that?

B: I _____ _____ _____ my family _____ _____.

Listen & Speak 1 A-2

B: _____ _____ there. _____ _____ _____ there are so many people _____ _____ _____.

G: They're _____ _____ _____ _____ _____ the new bakery there.

B: Why? Is it _____?

G: Yes. It was _____ a TV program.

B: Really? We _____ _____ their bread _____.

G: Sure.

Listen & Speak 2 A-1

W: Excuse me, _____ _____ _____ _____ an audio guide.

M: _____ you _____.

W: Could you _____ _____ _____ _____ _____ _____?

M: Sure. _____ this button, and it'll tell you _____ _____ _____.

Listen & Speak 2 A-2

B: _____ you _____ _____ this summer?

G: I'm _____ _____ Jejudo to _____ _____ the Jeju Olle Trail.

B: The Jeju Olle Trail? _____ _____ _____ _____ _____ _____?

G: It's a _____ _____ _____ _____ Jejudo.

B: Oh, I see. I hope you _____ _____ _____!

Communication A

Jaden: Do you hear that? _____ _____ _____ that music is _____
_____.

Yuri: I think it's coming from _____ _____. Do you want to go
and _____ _____ _____?

Jaden: Yes, I love that _____ _____. Is it _____ Korean music?

Yuri: Yes, it's _____ nongak. It's _____ _____ _____ _____
band music.

Jaden: Nongak? _____ _____ _____ _____ _____
more about it?

Yuri: It's _____ used to _____ _____ farmers and _____
_____ a _____ _____.

Jaden: I see. Look! Some people _____ _____ _____ the _____.

Yuri: Yes, that's a big _____ _____ nongak. Dancing together
_____ the music.

Jaden: _____ _____ them.

Yuri: Sure. _____ _____?

Jaden: 저거 들리니? 저 음악이 어디서 오는 것인지 궁금하네.
유리: 저기서 나오는 것 같은데. 가서 확인해 볼래?
Jaden: 그래, 저 강한 비트가 마음에 들어. 그게 한국의 전통 음악이니?
유리: 맞아, 농악이라고 해. 공동체 악단 음악의 한 종류야.
Jaden: 농악? 그것에 대해 좀 더 설명해 줄래?
유리: 그건 전통적으로 농부들의 힘을 북돋아 주고 풍년을 기원하기 위해 사용되었어.
Jaden: 그렇구나. 봐! 몇몇 사람들이 리듬에 맞춰 춤추고 있어.
유리: 그래, 그게 농악의 큰 부분이야. 함께 춤추는 것이 음악을 완성하지.
Jaden: 저들과 함께 하자.
유리: 물론이야. 왜 안 되겠어?

Progree Check 1

W: Look over there. _____ _____ _____ _____ _____
_____ _____ _____ on the road.

M: _____ _____ people are _____ _____ _____ this
weekend.

W: Really? Then, _____ _____ _____ go somewhere, _____?

M: O.K.

W: 저기 좀 봐요. 도로에 왜 저렇게 차가 많은지 궁금하네요.
M: 많은 사람들이 이번 주말에 휴가를 가거든요.
W: 정말로요? 그럼, 우리도 어디 가는 게 어떤가요?
M: 좋아요.

Progree Check 2

B: _____ me, I'd like to use a _____ _____.

W: O.K. You can use this machine.

B: Could you explain _____ _____ _____ _____ _____ _____?

W: Sure. _____ the button for _____ _____, and then _____
the start button.

B: Thank you.

B: 실례합니다, 복사기를 좀 쓰고 싶은데요.
W: 알겠어요. 이 기계를 써도 돼요.
B: 어떻게 양면 복사를 하는지 설명해 주실 수 있나요?
W: 물론이죠. 양면 복사 버튼을 누르고, 시작 버튼을 누르세요.
B: 감사합니다.

대화문 Test **25**

※ 다음 우리말에 맞도록 대화를 영어로 쓰시오.

Listen & Speak 1 A-1

G: _____

B: _____

G: _____

B: _____

G: 와, 이 광고에 나오는 다리 좀 봐. 어디에서 찍은 사진인지 궁금하네.
B: 부산의 광안대교야.
G: 그걸 어떻게 아니?
B: 작년 여름에 우리 가족들과 그곳에 갔었거든.

Listen & Speak 1 A-2

B: _____

G: _____

B: _____

G: _____

B: _____

G: _____

B: 저기 좀 봐. 왜 저렇게 많은 사람들이 줄을 서서 기다리고 있는지 궁금하네.
G: 새로 생긴 제과점에 들어가려고 기다리고 있는 거야.
B: 왜? 유명한 곳이야?
G: 맞아. TV 프로그램에 나왔어.
B: 정말? 그럼 우리 저곳의 빵을 먹어 봐야겠다.
G: 그래.

Listen & Speak 2 A-1

W: _____

M: _____

W: _____

M: _____

W: 실례합니다, 음성 가이드를 대여하고 싶은데요.
M: 여기 있습니다.
W: 어떻게 사용하는지 설명해 주실 수 있나요?
M: 물론이죠. 이 버튼을 누르면, 무엇을 해야 할지 말해 줄 겁니다.

Listen & Speak 2 A-2

B: _____

G: _____

B: _____

G: _____

B: _____

B: 이번 여름에 어디 갈 거야?
G: 제주 올레길을 따라 걸으러 제주도에 갈 거야.
B: 제주 올레길? 그게 무엇인지 설명해 줄래?
G: 제주도 둘레에 있는 긴 하이킹 코스야.
B: 오, 그렇구나. 즐거운 여행이 되길 바랄게!

Communication A

Jaden: _____

Yuri: _____

Jaden: _____

Yuri: _____

Jaden: _____

Yuri: _____

Jaden: _____

Yuri: _____

Jaden: _____

Yuri: _____

Jaden: 저거 들리니? 저 음악이 어디서 오는 것인지 궁금하네.

유리: 저기서 나오는 것 같은데. 가서 확인해 볼래?

Jaden: 그래, 저 강한 비트가 마음에 들어. 그게 한국의 전통 음악이니?

유리: 맞아, 농악이라고 해. 공동체 악단 음악의 한 종류야.

Jaden: 농악? 그것에 대해 좀 더 설명해 줄래?

유리: 그건 전통적으로 농부들의 힘을 북돋아 주고 풍년을 기원하기 위해 사용되었어.

Jaden: 그렇구나. 봐! 몇몇 사람들이 리듬에 맞춰 춤추고 있어.

유리: 그래, 그게 농악의 큰 부분이야. 함께 춤추는 것이 음악을 완성하지.

Jaden: 저들과 함께 하자.

유리: 물론이야. 왜 안 되겠어?

Progree Check 1

W: _____

M: _____

W: _____

M: _____

W: 저기 좀 봐요. 도로에 왜 저렇게 차가 많은지 궁금하네요.

M: 많은 사람들이 이번 주말에 휴가를 가거든요.

W: 정말로요? 그럼, 우리도 어디 가는 게 어떤가요?

M: 좋아요.

Progree Check 2

B: _____

W: _____

B: _____

W: _____

B: _____

B: 실례합니다, 복사기를 좀 쓰고 싶은데요.

W: 알겠어요. 이 기계를 써도 돼요.

B: 어떻게 양면 복사를 하는지 설명해 주실 수 있나요?

W: 물론이죠. 양면 복사 버튼을 누르고, 시작 버튼을 누르세요.

B: 감사합니다.

※ 다음 우리말과 일치하도록 빈칸에 알맞은 것을 골라 쓰시오.

1 _____, _____ _____ of Korea
   A. Divers   B. Female   C. Haenyeo

2 For the past _____ years, the _____ photographer Zin Kim has _____ the culture of Jeju haenyeo _____.
   A. promoted   B. several   C. worldwide   D. underwater

3 Haenyeo are Korean _____ divers who _____ seafood _____ any _____ devices.
   A. without   B. female   C. breathing   D. harvest

4 Their culture _____ UNESCO's _____ Cultural _____ in 2016.
   A. Heritage   B. Intangible   C. made   D. list

5 At her studio _____ week, Zin Kim was _____ about her _____ of _____ pictures of haenyeo.
   A. interviewed   B. taking   C. last   D. experience

6 Q. How did you _____ photos of haenyeo?
   A. interested   B. in   C. become   D. taking

7 _____ _____, I _____ _____ take pictures of a haenyeo.
   A. happened   B. day   C. to   D. one

8 I _____ _____ _____ that she was enjoying her job.
   A. to   B. was   C. find   D. surprised

9 _____ then, I had only _____ black-and-white photos of haenyeo who _____ very _____.
   A. looked   B. until   C. tired   D. seen

10 However, she _____ _____ even after she had _____ in the water for _____ five hours.
   A. over   B. kept   C. been   D. laughing

11 I _____ then that I _____ _____ pictures of haenyeo.
   A. should   B. realized   C. take

12 Q. You take beautiful pictures of them, but _____ _____ _____ take pictures of haenyeo?
   A. to   B. isn't   C. difficult   D. it

13 _____ first, they didn't understand _____ _____ _____ to take their pictures.
   A. wanted   B. why   C. I   D. at

14 They didn't think they _____ _____ their _____.
   A. pretty   B. wetsuits   C. looked   D. in

15 _____, I said to them, "You're _____ _____.
   A. very   B. so   C. special

16 I want to _____ your _____ the _____."
   A. to   B. show   C. culture   D. world

17 They _____ _____ to me _____.
   A. up   B. opened   C. then

18 Of course, I also promised them that I would _____ _____ in my pictures.
   A. them   B. beautiful   C. make   D. look

1 해녀, 한국의 여성 잠수부

2 지난 몇 년 동안, 수중 사진작가 Zin Kim은 제주 해녀 문화를 전 세계에 홍보해 왔다.

3 해녀는 어떤 호흡 장치도 사용하지 않고 해산물을 채취하는 한국의 여성 잠수부들이다.

4 그들의 문화는 2016년에 유네스코 무형문화유산에 등재되었다.

5 지난주 그녀의 작업실에서, Zin Kim과 해녀의 사진을 찍는 그녀의 경험에 대해 인터뷰를 했다.

6 Q. 어떻게 해녀의 사진을 찍는 것에 관심을 가지게 되었나요?

7 어느 날, 저는 우연히 한 해녀의 사진을 찍게 되었어요.

8 저는 그녀가 자신의 일을 즐겁게 하는 것을 보고 놀랐습니다.

9 그때까지, 저는 흑백 사진 속의 아주 지친 모습의 해녀만 봐 왔죠.

10 하지만, 그녀는 다섯 시간이 넘도록 물속에 있은 후에도 계속 웃었어요.

11 저는 그때 해녀의 사진을 찍어야겠다고 깨달았어요.

12 Q. 작가님은 아름다운 해녀 사진들을 찍으시는데, 그들의 사진을 찍는 것이 어렵진 않으신가요?

13 처음에, 그들은 제가 왜 자신들의 사진을 찍으려고 하는지 이해하지 못했어요.

14 그들은 잠수복을 입은 자신들의 모습이 예뻐 보인다고 생각하지 않았으니까요.

15 그래서, 제가 그들에게 말했죠, "여러분들은 아주 특별해요.

16 저는 여러분의 문화를 세계에 알리고 싶어요."

17 그들은 그때 제게 마음을 열었어요.

18 물론, 저 또한 그들에게 제 사진 속에서 그들을 아름답게 보이도록 하겠다고 약속했지요.

19 Q. Could you _____ _____ _____ _____ haenyeo?
A. more   B. tell   C. about   D. us

20 What's _____ _____ _____ them?
A. special   B. about   C. so

21 I _____ _____ _____ three _____ .
A. things   B. tell   C. you   D. can

22 First, haenyeo are a _____ of _____ _____ .
A. strong   B. symbol   C. women

23 Jejudo, which is a _____ island, is not _____ for _____ , so many haenyeo have become the _____ for their families.
A. suitable   B. breadwinners   C. farming   D. volcanic

24 Second, haenyeo _____ their _____ communities and help _____ _____ .
A. each   B. form   C. other   D. own

25 For _____ , _____ haenyeo train _____ haenyeo.
A. example   B. less-experienced   C. more-experienced

26 Third, because they _____ in the water _____ any _____ devices, haenyeo can't _____ a lot of seafood.
A. without   B. stay   C. catch   D. breathing

27 This is _____ _____ the _____ _____ .
A. good   B. environment   C. for   D. underwater

28 Catching too much _____ life at one _____ in one _____ can _____ the ocean.
A. destroy   B. marine   C. place   D. time

29 Q. Lastly, please tell us _____ you're _____ to _____ in the _____ .
A. what   B. future   C. planning   D. do

30 I once _____ an overseas _____ with a couple of haenyeo to give a _____ about their _____ .
A. talk   B. attended   C. lives   D. exhibition

31 When I _____ my talk, one of the haenyeo _____ my _____ _____ .
A. held   B. tightly   C. finished   D. hand

32 She _____ _____ me, "Thank you _____ _____ .
A. much   B. so   C. to   D. said

33 I've never known in my whole life that I was _____ _____ _____ _____ ."
A. special   B. a   C. person   D. such

34 She was _____ _____ _____ .
A. with   B. crying   C. happiness

35 Everyone in the audience _____ _____ _____ .
A. deeply   B. was   C. moved

36 I can _____ _____ that _____ , so I'll _____ to take pictures of haenyeo.
A. continue   B. forget   C. never   D. moment

37 I want to tell _____ _____ _____ them to many more people in the world.
A. beautiful   B. about   C. more   D. stories

19 Q. 해녀에 대해서 더 말씀해 주시겠어요?
20 그들은 무엇이 그렇게 특별한가요?
21 세 가지를 말씀 드릴게요.
22 첫 번째로, 해녀들은 강인한 여성의 상징이에요.
23 제주도는 화산섬이고, 이는 농사에 적합하지 않아서 많은 해녀들이 가족들의 생계비를 버는 가장이 되어 왔어요.
24 둘째로, 해녀들은 그들 자신의 공동체를 조직하고 서로 도와요.
25 예를 들어, 경험이 더 많은 해녀들이 경험이 적은 해녀들을 훈련시키지요.
26 세 번째로, 어떤 호흡 장치도 사용하지 않고 물속에 머물기 때문에, 해녀는 많은 해산물을 채취할 수가 없어요.
27 이것은 수중 환경에 좋은 것이지요.
28 한 번에 한 장소에서 너무 많은 해양생물을 채취하는 것은 바다를 파괴할 수 있으니까요.
29 Q. 마지막으로, 앞으로 계획하고 있는 것에 대해 말씀해 주세요.
30 예전에 두 명의 해녀들과 함께 그들의 삶에 대해 이야기하기 위해 해외에서 열리는 박람회에 참가한 적이 있어요.
31 제가 연설을 마쳤을 때, 해녀 중 한 분이 제 손을 꼭 잡았어요.
32 그분이 말했죠, "너무 고마워.
33 내 평생 내가 이렇게 특별한 사람이라는 걸 미처 알지 못했어."
34 그녀는 행복해서 울고 있었어요.
35 청중들 모두가 깊은 감동을 받았어요.
36 전 그 순간을 절대 잊을 수가 없기 때문에 해녀의 사진을 계속해서 찍을 거예요.
37 저는 그들에 대한 더 많은 아름다운 이야기들을 세계의 더 많은 사람에게 알려 주고 싶어요.

※ 다음 우리말과 일치하도록 빈칸에 알맞은 말을 쓰시오.

1 Haenyeo, _____ _____ of Korea

2 For the past several years, the _____ _____ Zin Kim _____ _____ the culture of Jeju haenyeo _____.

3 Haenyeo are Korean _____ _____ who harvest seafood _____ _____ _____ _____ _____.

4 Their culture _____ _____ _____ _____ _____ _____ _____ in 2016.

5 At her studio last week, Zin Kim _____ _____ about her _____ _____ _____ of haenyeo.

6 Q. How did you _____ _____ _____ _____ photos of haenyeo?

7 _____ _____, I _____ _____ take pictures of a haenyeo.

8 I _____ _____ _____ that she _____ _____ her job.

9 _____ _____, I _____ _____ black-and-white photos of haenyeo who _____ _____ _____.

10 However, she _____ _____ even after she had been in the water _____ _____ _____ _____ _____.

11 I _____ then that I _____ _____ _____ _____ of haenyeo.

12 Q. You take beautiful pictures of them, but _____ _____ _____ _____ _____ _____ of haenyeo?

13 _____ _____, they didn't understand _____ _____ _____ to take their pictures.

14 They didn't think they _____ _____ _____ _____ _____.

15 So, I said to them, "You're _____ _____.

16 I want to _____ your culture _____ the world."

17 They _____ _____ to me _____.

18 _____ _____, I also promised them that I would _____ _____ look _____ in my pictures.

---

1 해녀, 한국의 여성 잠수부

2 지난 몇 년 동안, 수중 사진작가 Zin Kim은 제주 해녀 문화를 전 세계에 홍보해 왔다.

3 해녀는 어떤 호흡 장치도 사용하지 않고 해산물을 채취하는 한국의 여성 잠수부들이다.

4 그들의 문화는 2016년에 유네스코 무형문화유산에 등재되었다.

5 지난주 그녀의 작업실에서, Zin Kim과 해녀의 사진을 찍는 그녀의 경험에 대해 인터뷰를 했다.

6 Q. 어떻게 해녀의 사진을 찍는 것에 관심을 가지게 되었나요?

7 어느 날, 저는 우연히 한 해녀의 사진을 찍게 되었어요.

8 저는 그녀가 자신의 일을 즐겁게 하는 것을 보고 놀랐습니다.

9 그때까지, 저는 흑백 사진 속의 아주 지친 모습의 해녀만 봐 왔죠.

10 하지만, 그녀는 다섯 시간이 넘도록 물속에 있은 후에도 계속 웃었어요.

11 저는 그때 해녀의 사진을 찍어야겠다고 깨달았어요.

12 Q. 작가님은 아름다운 해녀 사진들을 찍으시는데, 그들의 사진을 찍는 것이 어렵진 않으신가요?

13 처음에, 그들은 제가 왜 자신들의 사진을 찍으려고 하는지 이해하지 못했어요.

14 그들은 잠수복을 입은 자신들의 모습이 예뻐 보인다고 생각하지 않았으니까요.

15 그래서, 제가 그들에게 말했죠, "여러분들은 아주 특별해요.

16 저는 여러분의 문화를 세계에 알리고 싶어요."

17 그들은 그때 제게 마음을 열었어요.

18 물론, 저 또한 그들에게 제 사진 속에서 그들을 아름답게 보이도록 하겠다고 약속했지요.

19 Q. Could you tell us _____ _____ haenyeo?

20 What's _____ _____ about them?

21 I _____ _____ _____ three things.

22 First, haenyeo are a _____ _____ _____ _____ _____ _____.

23 Jejudo, _____ is a volcanic island, _____ _____ _____ farming, so many haenyeo _____ _____ _____ _____ their families.

24 Second, haenyeo _____ their _____ _____ and help _____ _____.

25 For example, _____ haenyeo train _____ haenyeo.

26 Third, _____ they stay in the water _____ any _____, haenyeo _____ _____ a lot of seafood.

27 This _____ _____ _____ the _____ _____.

28 _____ too much marine life _____ _____ _____ _____ _____ _____ _____ the ocean.

29 Q. Lastly, please tell us _____ you're _____ in the future.

30 I once _____ an _____ _____ with a couple of haenyeo to _____ _____ _____ about their lives.

31 When I finished my talk, one of the haenyeo _____ _____ _____.

32 She said to me, "Thank you _____ _____.

33 I've never known in my _____ _____ that I was _____ _____ _____."

34 She was _____ _____.

35 Everyone in the audience _____ _____ _____.

36 I _____ _____ _____ that moment, so I'll _____ pictures of haenyeo.

37 I want to tell _____ _____ _____ _____ _____ to many more people in the world.

19 Q. 해녀에 대해서 더 말씀해 주시겠어요?

20 그들은 무엇이 그렇게 특별한가요?

21 세 가지를 말씀 드릴게요.

22 첫 번째로, 해녀들은 강인한 여성의 상징이에요.

23 제주도는 화산섬이고, 이는 농사에 적합하지 않아서 많은 해녀들이 가족들의 생계비를 버는 가장이 되어 왔어요.

24 둘째로, 해녀들은 그들 자신의 공동체를 조직하고 서로 도와요.

25 예를 들어, 경험이 더 많은 해녀들이 경험이 적은 해녀들을 훈련시키지요.

26 세 번째로, 어떤 호흡 장치도 사용하지 않고 물속에 머물기 때문에, 해녀는 많은 해산물을 채취할 수가 없어요.

27 이것은 수중 환경에 좋은 것이지요.

28 한 번에 한 장소에서 너무 많은 해양생물을 채취하는 것은 바다를 파괴할 수 있으니까요.

29 Q. 마지막으로, 앞으로 계획하고 있는 것에 대해 말씀해 주세요.

30 예전에 두 명의 해녀들과 함께 그들의 삶에 대해 이야기하기 위해 해외에서 열리는 박람회에 참가한 적이 있어요.

31 제가 연설을 마쳤을 때, 해녀 중 한 분이 제 손을 꼭 잡았어요.

32 그분이 말했죠. "너무 고마워.

33 내 평생 내가 이렇게 특별한 사람이라는 걸 미처 알지 못했어."

34 그녀는 행복해서 울고 있었어요.

35 청중들 모두가 깊은 감동을 받았어요.

36 전 그 순간을 절대 잊을 수가 없기 때문에 해녀의 사진을 계속해서 찍을 거예요.

37 저는 그들에 대한 더 많은 아름다운 이야기들을 세계의 더 많은 사람들에게 알려 주고 싶어요.

※ 다음 문장을 우리말로 쓰시오.

1 Haenyeo, Female Divers of Korea
➡ _____

2 For the past several years, the underwater photographer Zin Kim has promoted the culture of Jeju haenyeo worldwide.
➡ _____

3 Haenyeo are Korean female divers who harvest seafood without any breathing devices.
➡ _____

4 Their culture made UNESCO's Intangible Cultural Heritage list in 2016.
➡ _____

5 At her studio last week, Zin Kim was interviewed about her experience of taking pictures of haenyeo.
➡ _____

6 Q. How did you become interested in taking photos of haenyeo?
➡ _____

7 One day, I happened to take pictures of a haenyeo.
➡ _____

8 I was surprised to find that she was enjoying her job.
➡ _____

9 Until then, I had only seen black-and-white photos of haenyeo who looked very tired.
➡ _____

10 However, she kept laughing even after she had been in the water for over five hours.
➡ _____

11 I realized then that I should take pictures of haenyeo.
➡ _____

12 Q. You take beautiful pictures of them, but isn't it difficult to take pictures of haenyeo?
➡ _____

13 At first, they didn't understand why I wanted to take their pictures.
➡ _____

14 They didn't think they looked pretty in their wetsuits.
➡ _____

15 So, I said to them, "You're very special.
➡ _____

16 I want to show your culture to the world."
➡ _____

17 They opened up to me then.
➡ _____

18 Of course, I also promised them that I would make them look beautiful in my pictures.
➡ _____

19 Q. Could you tell us more about haenyeo?w
➡ _____

20 What's so special about them?

➡ _____

21 I can tell you three things.

➡ _____

22 First, haenyeo are a symbol of strong women.

➡ _____

23 Jejudo, which is a volcanic island, is not suitable for farming, so many haenyeo have become the breadwinners for their families.

➡ _____

24 Second, haenyeo form their own communities and help each other.

➡ _____

25 For example, more-experienced haenyeo train less-experienced haenyeo.

➡ _____

26 Third, because they stay in the water without any breathing devices, haenyeo can't catch a lot of seafood.

➡ _____

27 This is good for the underwater environment.

➡ _____

28 Catching too much marine life at one time in one place can destroy the ocean.

➡ _____

29 Q. Lastly, please tell us what you're planning to do in the future.

➡ _____

30 I once attended an overseas exhibition with a couple of haenyeo to give a talk about their lives.

➡ _____

31 When I finished my talk, one of the haenyeo held my hand tightly.

➡ _____

32 She said to me, "Thank you so much.

➡ _____

33 I've never known in my whole life that I was such a special person."

➡ _____

34 She was crying with happiness.

➡ _____

35 Everyone in the audience was deeply moved.

➡ _____

36 I can never forget that moment, so I'll continue to take pictures of haenyeo.

➡ _____

37 I want to tell more beautiful stories about them to many more people in the world.

➡ _____

※ 다음 괄호 안의 단어들을 우리말에 맞도록 바르게 배열하시오.

1 (Female / Haenyeo, / of / Divers / Korea)
➡ _____

1 해녀, 한국의 여성 잠수부

2 (the / for / past / years, / several / underwater / the / Zin / photographer / Kim / promoted / has / culture / the / Jeju / of / worldwide. / haenyeo)
➡ _____
_____

2 지난 몇 년 동안, 수중 사진작가 Zin Kim은 제주 해녀 문화를 전 세계에 홍보해 왔다.

3 (are / haenyeo / Korean / divers / female / harvest / who / without / seafood / breathing / any / devices.)
➡ _____
_____

3 해녀는 어떤 호흡 장치도 사용 하지 않고 해산물을 채취하는 한국의 여성 잠수부들이다.

4 (culture / their / UNESCO's / made / Cultural / Intangible / Heritage / in / list / 2016.)
➡ _____
_____

4 그들의 문화는 2016년에 유네스 코 무형문화유산에 등재되었다.

5 (her / at / last / studio / week, / Kim / Zin / interviewed / was / her / about / of / experience / taking / of / pictures / haenyeo.)
➡ _____
_____

5 지난주 그녀의 작업실에서, Zin Kim과 해녀의 사진을 찍는 그녀 의 경험에 대해 인터뷰를 했다.

6 (Q. / did / how / become / you / in / interested / photos / taking / haenyeo? / of)
➡ _____
_____

6 Q. 어떻게 해녀의 사진을 찍는 것에 관심을 가지게 되었나요?

7 (day, / one / happened / I / take / to / of / pictures / haenyeo. / a)
➡ _____

7 어느 날, 저는 우연히 한 해녀의 사진을 찍게 되었어요.

8 (was / I / to / surprised / find / she / that / enjoying / was / job. / her)
➡ _____

8 저는 그녀가 자신의 일을 즐겁 게 하는 것을 보고 놀랐습니다.

9 (then, / until / had / I / seen / only / photos / black-and-white / haenyeo / of / looked / who / tired. / very)
➡ _____
_____

9 그때까지, 저는 흑백 사진 속의 아 주 지친 모습의 해녀만 봐 왔죠.

10 (she / however, / laughing / kept / after / even / she / been / had / the / in / water / over / for / hours. / five)
➡ _____
_____

10 하지만, 그녀는 다섯 시간이 넘 도록 물속에 있은 후에도 계속 웃었어요.

11 (realized / I / that / then / should / I / pictures / take / haenyeo. / of)
➡ _____

11 저는 그때 해녀의 사진을 찍어 야겠다고 깨달았어요.

12 (Q. / take / you / pictures / beautiful / them, / of / isn't / but / difficult / it / take / to / of / pictures / haenyeo?)
➡ _____
_____

12 Q. 작가님은 아름다운 해녀 사 진들을 찍으시는데, 그들의 사 진을 찍는 것이 어렵진 않으신 가요?

13 (first, / at / didn't / they / why / understand / wanted / I / take / to / pictures. / their)

➡ _____

14 (didn't / they / they / think / pretty / looked / their / in / wetsuits.)

➡ _____

15 (I / so, / said / them, / to / very / "you're / special.)

➡ _____

16 (want / I / show / to / culture / your / the / to / world.")

➡ _____

17 (opened / they / to / up / then. / me)

➡ _____

18 (course, / of / also / I / them / promised / I / that / make / would / look / them / in / beautiful / pictures. / my)

➡ _____

➡ _____

19 (Q. / you / could / us / tell / about / more / haenyeo?)

➡ _____

20 (so / what's / about / special / them?)

➡ _____

21 (can / I / you / tell / things. / three)

➡ _____

22 (haenyeo / first, / a / are / of / symbol / women. / strong)

➡ _____

23 (which / Jejudo, / is / volcanic / a / island, / not / is / for / suitable / farming, / many / so / have / haenyeo / the / become / breadwinners / their / for / families.)

➡ _____

➡ _____

24 (haenyeo / second, / their / form / communities / own / and / each / help / other.)

➡ _____

25 (example, / for / haenyeo / more-experienced / less-experienced / train / haenyeo.)

➡ _____

13 처음에, 그들은 제가 왜 자신들의 사진을 찍으려고 하는지 이해하지 못했어요.

14 그들은 잠수복을 입은 자신들의 모습이 예뻐 보인다고 생각하지 않았으니까요.

15 그래서, 제가 그들에게 말했죠. "여러분들은 아주 특별해요.

16 저는 여러분의 문화를 세계에 알리고 싶어요."

17 그들은 그때 제게 마음을 열었어요.

18 물론, 저 또한 그들에게 제 사진 속에서 그들을 아름답게 보이도록 하겠다고 약속했지요.

19 Q. 해녀에 대해서 더 말씀해 주시겠어요?

20 그들은 무엇이 그렇게 특별한가요?

21 세 가지를 말씀 드릴게요.

22 첫 번째로, 해녀들은 강인한 여성의 상징이에요.

23 제주도는 화산섬이고, 이는 농사에 적합하지 않아서 많은 해녀들이 가족들의 생계비를 버는 가장이 되어 왔어요.

24 둘째로, 해녀들은 그들 자신의 공동체를 조직하고 서로 도와요.

25 예를 들어, 경험이 더 많은 해녀들이 경험이 적은 해녀들을 훈련시키지요.

26 (because / third, / stay / they / the / in / without / water / breathing / any / devices, / can't / haenyeo / a / catch / of / lot / seafood.)

➡ _____

_____

27 (is / this / for / good / underwater / the / environment.)

➡ _____

28 (too / catching / much / life / marine / one / at / time / one / in / place / destroy / can / ocean. / the)

➡ _____

_____

29 (Q. / please / lastly, / us / tell / you're / what / to / planning / do / the / in / future.)

➡ _____

_____

30 (once / I / an / attneded / overseas / with / exhibition / a / of / couple / haenyeo / a / give / to / talk / their / lives. / about)

➡ _____

_____

31 (I / when / my / finished / talk, / of / one / haenyeo / the / my / held / tightly. / hand)

➡ _____

32 (said / she / me, / to / you / "thank / much. / so)

➡ _____

33 (never / I've / in / known / whole / my / that / life / was / I / a / such / person." / special)

➡ _____

34 (was / she / with / crying / happiness.)

➡ _____

35 (in / everyone / audience / the / was / moved. / deeply)

➡ _____

36 (can / I / forget / never / moment, / that / I'll / so / to / continue / take / of / haenyeo / pictures)

➡ _____

37 (want / I / to / more / tell / stories / beautiful / about / to / them / more / many / people / the / in / world.)

➡ _____

_____

26 세 번째로, 어떤 호흡 장치도 사용하지 않고 물속에 머물기 때문에, 해녀는 많은 해산물을 채취할 수가 없어요.

27 이것은 수중 환경에 좋은 것이지요.

28 한 번에 한 장소에서 너무 많은 해양생물을 채취하는 것은 바다를 파괴할 수 있으니까요.

29 Q. 마지막으로, 앞으로 계획하고 있는 것에 대해 말씀해 주세요.

30 예전에 두 명의 해녀들과 함께 그들의 삶에 대해 이야기하기 위해 해외에서 열리는 박람회에 참가한 적이 있어요.

31 제가 연설을 마쳤을 때, 해녀 중한 분이 제 손을 꼭 잡았어요.

32 그분이 말했죠. "너무 고마워.

33 내 평생 내가 이렇게 특별한 사람이라는 걸 미처 알지 못했어."

34 그녀는 행복해서 울고 있었어요.

35 청중들 모두가 깊은 감동을 받았어요.

36 전 그 순간을 절대 잊을 수가 없기 때문에 해녀의 사진을 계속해서 찍을 거예요.

37 저는 그들에 대한 더 많은 아름다운 이야기들을 세계의 더 많은 사람들에게 알려 주고 싶어요.

※ 다음 우리말을 영어로 쓰시오.

1 해녀, 한국의 여성 잠수부

➡ _____

2 지난 몇 년 동안, 수중 사진작가 Zin Kim은 제주 해녀 문화를 전 세계에 홍보해 왔다.

➡ _____

_____

3 해녀는 어떤 호흡 장치도 사용하지 않고 해산물을 채취하는 한국의 여성 잠수부들이다.

➡ _____

4 그들의 문화는 2016년에 유네스코 무형문화유산에 등재되었다.

➡ _____

5 지난주 그녀의 작업실에서, Zin Kim과 해녀의 사진을 찍는 그녀의 경험에 대해 인터뷰를 했다.

➡ _____

6 Q. 어떻게 해녀의 사진을 찍는 것에 관심을 가지게 되었나요?

➡ _____

7 어느 날, 저는 우연히 한 해녀의 사진을 찍게 되었어요.

➡ _____

8 저는 그녀가 자신의 일을 즐겁게 하는 것을 보고 놀랐습니다.

➡ _____

9 그때까지, 저는 흑백 사진 속의 아주 지친 모습의 해녀만 봐 왔죠.

➡ _____

10 하지만, 그녀는 다섯 시간이 넘도록 물속에 있은 후에도 계속 웃었어요.

➡ _____

11 저는 그때 해녀의 사진을 찍어야겠다고 깨달았어요.

➡ _____

12 Q. 작가님은 아름다운 해녀 사진들을 찍으시는데, 그들의 사진을 찍는 것이 어렵진 않으신가요?

➡ _____

13 처음에, 그들은 제가 왜 자신들의 사진을 찍으려고 하는지 이해하지 못했어요.

➡ _____

14 그들은 잠수복을 입은 자신들의 모습이 예뻐 보인다고 생각하지 않았으니까요.

➡ _____

15 그래서, 제가 그들에게 말했죠, "여러분들은 아주 특별해요.

➡ _____

16 저는 여러분의 문화를 세계에 알리고 싶어요."

➡ _____

17 그들은 그때 제게 마음을 열었어요.

➡ _____

18 물론, 저 또한 그들에게 제 사진 속에서 그들을 아름답게 보이도록 하겠다고 약속했지요.

➡ _____

19 Q. 해녀에 대해서 더 말씀해 주시겠어요?

➡ _____

20 그들은 무엇이 그렇게 특별한가요?

➡ _____

21 세 가지를 말씀 드릴게요.

➡ _____

22 첫 번째로, 해녀들은 강인한 여성의 상징이에요.

➡ _____

23 제주도는 화산섬이고, 이는 농사에 적합하지 않아서 많은 해녀들이 가족들의 생계비를 버는 가장이 되어 왔어요.

➡ _____

_____

24 둘째로, 해녀들은 그들 자신의 공동체를 조직하고 서로 도와요.

➡ _____

25 예를 들어, 경험이 더 많은 해녀들이 경험이 적은 해녀들을 훈련시키지요.

➡ _____

26 세 번째로, 어떤 호흡 장치도 사용하지 않고 물속에 머물기 때문에, 해녀는 많은 해산물을 채취할 수가 없어요.

➡ _____

_____

27 이것은 수중 환경에 좋은 것이지요.

➡ _____

28 한 번에 한 장소에서 너무 많은 해양생물을 채취하는 것은 바다를 파괴할 수 있으니까요.

➡ _____

29 Q. 마지막으로, 앞으로 계획하고 있는 것에 대해 말씀해 주세요.

➡ _____

30 예전에 두 명의 해녀들과 함께 그들의 삶에 대해 이야기하기 위해 해외에서 열리는 박람회에 참가한 적이 있어요.

➡ _____

31 제가 연설을 마쳤을 때, 해녀 중 한 분이 제 손을 꼭 잡았어요.

➡ _____

32 그분이 말했죠, "너무 고마워.

➡ _____

33 내 평생 내가 이렇게 특별한 사람이라는 걸 미처 알지 못했어."

➡ _____

34 그녀는 행복해서 울고 있었어요.

➡ _____

35 청중들 모두가 깊은 감동을 받았어요.

➡ _____

36 전 그 순간을 절대 잊을 수가 없기 때문에 해녀의 사진을 계속해서 찍을 거예요.

➡ _____

37 저는 그들에 대한 더 많은 아름다운 이야기들을 세계의 더 많은 사람들에게 알려 주고 싶어요.

➡ _____

※ 다음 우리말과 일치하도록 빈칸에 알맞은 말을 쓰시오.

Communicate – B Talk and Play

1. A: I wonder _____ _____ _____.
2. B: They're _____ _____.
3. A: Could you _____ _____ _____ them?
4. B: They're _____ _____ _____ _____.

1. A: 나는 이것들이 무엇인지 궁금해.
2. B: 그것들은 송편이라고 불려.
3. A: 이것에 대해 좀 더 설명해 줄래?
4. B: 그것들은 전통적인 한국 떡이야.

After You Read A

1. A _____ _____ _____ Haenyeo
2. Zin Kim, _____ _____ _____, _____ _____ the culture of Jeju haenyeo _____.
3. She _____ _____ _____ of them _____ _____ _____ a haenyeo _____ _____ _____ her job.
4. _____ was not _____ _____ their pictures _____ _____.
5. _____, when she told them _____ she wanted to show _____ _____ _____, the haenyeo _____ _____ _____.
6. _____ _____ _____, she _____ _____ about the lives of haenyeo.
7. After her speech, _____ _____ the haenyeo _____ _____ _____ _____.
8. Zin Kim said that she _____ _____ _____ _____ pictures of haenyeo.

1. 해녀를 사랑하는 사진작가
2. 수중 사진작가 김진은 전 세계에 제주의 해녀 문화를 홍보해 왔다.
3. 그녀는 자신의 일을 즐기고 있었던 한 해녀를 만났을 때, 그들의 사진을 찍기로 결심했다.
4. 처음에는 그들의 사진을 찍는 것이 쉽지 않았다.
5. 그러나, 그녀가 세상 사람들에게 그들의 문화를 보여주고 싶다고 그들에게 말했을 때, 마침내 해녀들은 마음을 열었다.
6. 한 해외 전시회에서 그녀는 해녀들의 삶에 대해 강연했다.
7. 그녀의 연설이 끝나자 해녀들 중 한 사람은 기쁨의 눈물을 흘렸다.
8. 김진은 앞으로도 해녀들의 사진 찍는 일을 계속할 것이라고 말했다.

Write

1. Kim Minho is a barista. He _____ _____ _____ _____ _____ _____.
2. He _____ _____ after he _____ _____ _____ _____ for coffee.
3. _____ _____ _____ his job is _____ _____ _____ hot milk and _____ his customers _____ it.
4. He is _____ _____ _____ his own coffee shop.

1. 김민호는 바리스타이다. 그의 직업은 커피 음료를 만드는 것이다.
2. 그는 커피에 대한 그의 열정을 발견한 후에 바리스타가 되었다.
3. 그의 직업에서 그가 가장 좋아하는 부분은 뜨거운 우유로 커피를 장식하고 그의 손님들이 그것을 즐기는 것을 보는 것이다.
4. 그는 자신의 커피점을 열 계획이다.

※ 다음 우리말을 영어로 쓰시오.

Communicate – B Talk and Play

1. A: 나는 이것들이 무엇인지 궁금해.
➡ _____

2. B: 그것들은 송편이라고 불려.
➡ _____

3. A: 이것에 대해 좀 더 설명해 줄래?
➡ _____

4. B: 그것들은 전통적인 한국 떡이야.
➡ _____

After You Read A

1. 해녀를 사랑하는 사진작가
➡ _____

2. 수중 사진작가 김진은 전 세계에 제주의 해녀 문화를 홍보해 왔다.
➡ _____

3. 그녀는 자신의 일을 즐기고 있었던 한 해녀를 만났을 때, 그들의 사진을 찍기로 결심했다.
➡ _____

4. 처음에는 그들의 사진을 찍는 것이 쉽지 않았다.
➡ _____

5. 그러나, 그녀가 세상 사람들에게 그들의 문화를 보여주고 싶다고 그들에게 말했을 때, 마침내 해녀들은 마음을 열었다.
➡ _____
➡ _____

6. 한 해외 전시회에서 그녀는 해녀들의 삶에 대해 강연했다.
➡ _____

7. 그녀의 연설이 끝나자 해녀들 중 한 사람은 기쁨의 눈물을 흘렸다.
➡ _____

8. 김진은 앞으로도 해녀들의 사진 찍는 일을 계속할 것이라고 말했다.
➡ _____

Write

1. 김민호는 바리스타이다. 그의 직업은 커피 음료를 만드는 것이다.
➡ _____

2. 그는 커피에 대한 그의 열정을 발견한 후에 바리스타가 되었다.
➡ _____

3. 그의 직업에서 그가 가장 좋아하는 부분은 뜨거운 우유로 커피를 장식하고 그의 손님들이 그것을 즐기는 것을 보는 것이다.
➡ _____

4. 그는 자신의 커피점을 열 계획이다.
➡ _____

01	seafood		22	psychologist	
02	anxious		23	carefully	
03	competition		24	political	
04	enemy		25	supporter	
05	relax		26	apart	
06	graduate		27	chew	
07	actually		28	presentation	
08	helpless		29	solution	
09	professional		30	convenient	
10	instead		31	rare	
11	judge		32	rival	
12	stranger		33	stressful	
13	lucky		34	psychology	
14	relieved		35	get off	
15	famously		36	make a presentation	
16	prepare		37	stop by	
17	mind		38	not ~ at all	
18	nervous		39	by oneself	
19	confident		40	come up with	
20	behavior		41	make a reservation	
21	unique		42	turn A into B	
			43	not only A but also B	

※ 다음 우리말을 영어로 쓰시오.

01	졸업하다	
02	행동	
03	자신감 있는	
04	해결책	
05	결심하다	
06	적	
07	(음식을) 씹다	
08	유명하게	
09	전문적인	
10	실제로	
11	심리학자	
12	드문, 희귀한	
13	스트레스가 많은	
14	휴식을 취하다	
15	지원자	
16	해산물, 해물	
17	정치적인	
18	안도하는	
19	무력한	
20	조심스럽게	
21	심리학	
22	경쟁, 대회	
23	대신에	
24	이어달리기	
25	발표	
26	판단하다	
27	편리한	
28	경쟁자	
29	낯선 사람	
30	독특한	
31	행운인, 운이 좋은	
32	준비하다	
33	빌려주다	
34	추측하다	
35	~에 따르면	
36	A를 B로 바꾸다	
37	발표하다	
38	A뿐만 아니라 B도	
39	혼자서	
40	(해답 등을) 찾아내다, 내놓다	
41	결코 ~가 아닌	
42	예약하다	
43	더 이상 ~가 아닌	

※ 다음 영영풀이에 알맞은 단어를 <보기>에서 골라 쓴 후, 우리말 뜻을 쓰시오.

1 _____ : not common: _____

2 _____ : to cook something using dry heat, in an oven: _____

3 _____ : someone who hates you and wants to harm you: _____

4 _____ : someone that you do not know: _____

5 _____ : to bite food several times before swallowing it: _____

6 _____ : someone who supports a particular person, group, or plan: _____

7 _____ : unable to look after yourself or to do anything to help yourself: _____

8 _____ : useful to you because it saves you time: _____

9 _____ : to complete your education at a college, school, etc.: _____

10 _____ : an event at which you describe or explain a new product or idea: _____

11 _____ : feeling happy because you are no longer worried about something: _____

12 _____ : the study of the mind and how it influences people's behavior: _____

13 _____ : to let someone borrow money or something that belongs to you for a short time: _____

14 _____ : to rest or do something that is enjoyable, especially after you have been working: _____

15 _____ : sure that something will happen in the way that you want or expect: _____

16 _____ : a person, group, or organization that you compete with in sport, business, a fight, etc. : _____

rival	chew	helpless	convenient
graduate	lend	stranger	rare
relax	relieved	psychology	presentation
supporter	confident	bake	enemy

※ 다음 우리말과 일치하도록 빈칸에 알맞은 말을 쓰시오.

해석

Listen & Speak 1 A-1

G: What _____ _____ your shoes? _____ they new?

B: Yes, but my dog _____ them. He does it _____ _____ _____. I'm _____ _____ him.

G: He was probably _____. _____ _____ _____ _____ him more often?

B: O.K., I will. I _____ he will _____ _____ my shoes.

G: 신발이 왜 그래? 새것 아니었어?
B: 맞는데, 내 개가 씹어 버렸어. 항상 그렇게 해. 그 개가 걱정돼.
G: 아마 심심했었을 거야. 개와 더 자주 놀아 주는 게 어때?
B: 알겠어, 그럴게. 그 개가 내 신발 씹는 걸 그만두면 좋겠네.

Listen & Speak 1 A-2

B: You look a bit _____.

G: I'm _____ _____ my _____ _____ this Saturday.

B: Don't _____. You're such a good swimmer. Just _____ and _____ yourself!

G: Thanks. I feel _____ _____ now.

B: 너 좀 긴장한 것 같아 보이는데.
G: 이번 토요일에 있는 수영 대회가 걱정돼.
B: 걱정 마. 너는 수영을 아주 잘 하잖아. 그냥 긴장을 풀고 즐겨!
G: 고마워. 기분이 훨씬 괜찮아졌어.

Listen & Speak 2 A-1

B: Mom, _____ _____ are we going to _____ _____ tomorrow morning?

W: _____ 8 a.m. I'm going to _____ _____ for her before we go.

B: Then, should I _____ _____ _____ to help you?

W: You _____ _____ _____. Your dad will help me.

B: O.K, then. Good night, Mom!

B: 엄마, 우리 내일 아침 몇 시에 할머니 댁에 가나요?
W: 8시쯤에. 가기 전에 할머니를 위해 쿠키를 구울 거란다.
B: 그럼, 제가 일찍 일어나서 도와드릴까요?
W: 그럴 필요 없단다. 아빠가 도와주실 거야.
B: 알겠어요, 그럼. 안녕히 주무세요, 엄마!

Listen & Speak 2 A-2

W: _____ _____ _____ that new Mexican restaurant tomorrow?

M: _____ not? I'll _____ the restaurant to _____ _____ _____ for us.

W: You _____ _____ _____ call them. You can do it _____.

M: Oh, I see. _____ _____!

W: 우리 내일 새로 생긴 멕시코 레스토랑에 가 볼까요?
M: 좋죠! 레스토랑에 전화해서 예약해 둘게요.
W: 전화할 필요 없어요. 온라인으로 할 수 있거든요.
M: 오, 그렇군요. 정말 편리하네요!

Communicate A

Yuri: Hi, Jaden. Sports Day is next Friday. I _____ _____!

Jaden: Really? I'm _____ _____ about it.

Yuri: Why? _____ you _____ _____ sports?

Jaden: Yes, I am, but I'm _____ about the 800-meter _____.

Yuri: _____ do you _____?

Jaden: I'm the _____ _____. _____ _____ our team loses _____ _____ me?

Yuri: I think you're _____ _____ _____ _____ yourself.

Jaden: Really? Don't you think I should _____ every day?

Yuri: No, you _____ _____ _____ _____ that. It's just a school race. It's not about _____ or _____.

Jaden: I guess you're _____, Yuri. I'm _____ to have a friend _____ you.

Progress Check 1

B: You look a bit _____.

G: Well, I'm _____ _____ my _____ in _____ _____.

B: Don't worry. You've _____ _____ _____. You'll _____ a great _____.

G: Thanks. I _____ _____ _____ now.

Progress Check 2

M: Shall we have _____ _____ for dinner?

W: Sure. I'll _____ _____ the store _____ _____ _____ home.

M: _____ _____ _____ _____ do that. We already have _____ we _____.

W: Oh, I see. Then, I'll be _____ _____ _____ 6 to _____ you _____.

※ 다음 우리말에 맞도록 대화를 영어로 쓰시오.

Listen & Speak 1 A-1

G: _____

B: _____

G: _____

B: _____

G: 신발이 왜 그래? 새것 아니었어?
B: 맞는데, 내 개가 씹어 버렸어. 항상 그렇게 해. 그 개가 걱정돼.
G: 아마 심심했었을 거야. 개와 더 자주 놀아 주는 게 어때?
B: 알겠어, 그럴게. 그 개가 내 신발 씹는 걸 그만두면 좋겠네.

Listen & Speak 1 A-2

B: _____

G: _____

B: _____

G: _____

B: 너 좀 긴장한 것 같아 보이는데.
G: 이번 토요일에 있는 수영 대회가 걱정돼.
B: 걱정 마. 너는 수영을 아주 잘 하잖아. 그냥 긴장을 풀고 즐겨!
G: 고마워. 기분이 훨씬 괜찮아졌어.

Listen & Speak 2 A-1

B: _____

W: _____

B: _____

W: _____

B: _____

B: 엄마, 우리 내일 아침 몇 시에 할머니 댁에 가나요?
W: 8시쯤에. 가기 전에 할머니를 위해 쿠키를 구울 거란다.
B: 그럼, 제가 일찍 일어나서 도와드릴까요?
W: 그럴 필요 없단다. 아빠가 도와주실 거야.
B: 알겠어요, 그럼. 안녕히 주무세요, 엄마!

Listen & Speak 2 A-2

W: _____

M: _____

W: _____

M: _____

W: 우리 내일 새로 생긴 멕시코 레스토랑에 가 볼까요?
M: 좋죠! 레스토랑에 전화해서 예약해 둘게요.
W: 전화할 필요 없어요. 온라인으로 할 수 있거든요.
M: 오, 그렇군요. 정말 편리하네요!

Communicate A

Yuri: _____

Jaden: _____

Yuri: _____

Jaden: _____

Yuri: _____

Jaden: _____

Yuri: _____

Jaden: _____

Yuri: _____

_____

Jaden: _____

유리: 안녕, Jaden. 운동회가 다음 주 금요일이야. 너무 기다려져!
Jaden: 정말? 난 사실 걱정돼.
유리: 왜? 너 운동 잘하지 않아?
Jaden: 응, 그렇긴 하지만, 800미터 릴레이가 걱정돼.
유리: 무슨 뜻이니?
Jaden: 내가 마지막 주자거든. 나 때문에 우리 팀이 지면 어쩌지?
유리: 넌 네 스스로에게 너무 많은 압박을 주고 있는 것 같아.
Jaden: 그래? 내가 매일 연습해야 한다고 생각하지 않니?
유리: 아니, 그럴 필요 없어. 그냥 학교 경기일 뿐인걸. 이기고 지고에 관한 게 아냐.
Jaden: 네 말이 맞는 것 같다, 유리야. 너 같은 친구를 둬서 다행이야.

Progress Check 1

B: _____

G: _____

B: _____

G: _____

B: 너 좀 긴장한 것 같다.
G: 그게, 역사 수업 시간에 내가 할 발표가 걱정돼.
B: 걱정 마. 많이 준비했잖아. 잘할 거야.
G: 고마워. 기분이 훨씬 나아졌어.

Progress Check 2

M: _____

W: _____

M: _____

W: _____

M: 우리 저녁으로 해물 스파게티를 먹을까요?
W: 좋아요. 집에 오는 길에 가게에 들를게요.
M: 그럴 필요 없어요. 필요한 건 이미 가지고 있거든요.
W: 오, 그렇군요. 그럼, 6시까지 돌아와서 요리하는 걸 도울게요.

※ 다음 우리말과 일치하도록 빈칸에 알맞은 것을 골라 쓰시오.

1 _____ _____ Your _____
A. Answers B. Questions C. Psychology

2 Do you _____ you _____ a _____ problem?
A. unique B. have C. think

3 _____ are that _____ _____ people have the _____ problem.
A. same B. chances C. other D. many

4 Psychology is the study of the _____ _____ and _____, so it can help you find a _____ to your problem.
A. behavior B. solution C. mind D. human

5 How do I _____ _____ _____ ?
A. less B. become C. nervous

6 It was five minutes before Jisu's big _____ in _____ of the _____ _____.
A. class B. presentation C. whole D. front

7 _____ _____, Jisu was _____ _____ her notes in her chair.
A. carefully B. feeling C. studying D. nervous

8 Then, her teacher _____ _____ and told her to _____ _____ like Wonder Woman.
A. over B. came C. tall D. stand

9 After _____ _____ for a few minutes, Jisu did _____ feel nervous _____.
A. anymore B. tall C. not D. standing

10 _____ _____, she was _____ that she would make a great _____.
A. fact B. presentation C. in D. confident

11 _____ to Amy Cuddy, a famous psychologist, we can become more confident just by _____ _____ for two minutes before _____ events.
A. stressful B. standing C. according D. tall

12 Our _____ change our _____, and our minds can _____ our _____.
A. behavior B. bodies C. minds D. change

13 Do you _____ _____ _____ _____ ?
A. confident B. to C. feel D. want

14 Stand _____ your feet _____, and _____ your hands _____ your hips.
A. place B. apart C. with D. on

15 You will _____ only feel _____ about yourself _____ also look _____ to other people.
A. but B. not C. confident D. sure

16 Who can _____ me _____ _____ ?
A. feel B. help C. better

17 When he _____ _____ high school next year, Taeho wants to _____ a _____ farmer.
A. from B. professional C. graduates D. become

18 _____, he _____ _____ anyone about it.
A. never B. however C. told D. has

1 심리학이 당신의 물음에 답하다

2 여러분은 당신만의 유일무이한 고민을 가지고 있다고 생각하는가?

3 아마 많은 다른 사람들이 여러분과 똑같은 고민을 가지고 있을 것이다.

4 심리학은 인간의 마음과 행동에 관한 연구이며, 따라서 여러분이 문제에 대한 해결책을 찾는 데 도움을 줄 수 있다.

5 어떻게 하면 긴장을 덜 할 수 있나요?

6 지수가 반 전체 앞에서 발표를 하기 5분 전이었다.

7 지수는 긴장이 되어, 의자에 앉아 자신의 필기를 열심히 들여다보고 있었다.

8 그때 선생님이 다가와서는 원더 우먼처럼 꼿꼿이 서 있어 보라고 말했다.

9 그렇게 몇 분을 우뚝 선 후에, 지수는 더 이상 긴장되지 않았다.

10 사실, 그녀는 발표를 멋있게 할 수 있을 것이라는 자신감이 생겼다.

11 유명한 심리학자인 Amy Cuddy에 의하면, 우리는 스트레스를 받는 상황 이전에 2분 정도 꼿꼿이 서 있는 것만으로도 자신감이 더 생길 수 있다고 한다.

12 우리의 몸은 마음을 바꾸고, 마음은 우리의 행동을 바꿀 수 있다.

13 자신감이 생기기를 원하는가?

14 양발을 벌리고, 허리께에 손을 올려 보아라.

15 자신에 대한 확신이 생길 뿐만 아니라 다른 사람이 보기에도 자신감에 차 보인다.

16 누가 내 기분을 낫게 해 줄 수 있나요?

17 내년에 고등학교를 졸업한 이후에 태호는 전문적인 농부가 되고 싶어 한다.

18 하지만, 누구에게도 그것에 대해 한 번도 말하지 않았다.

19 He is _____ _____ his parents or his friends _____ not _____.

A. understand   B. worried   C. will   D. that

20 _____ to _____ his mind, Taeho decided to take a day trip on a train _____ _____.

A. himself   B. wanting   C. by   D. clear

21 On the train, he told a _____ _____ _____ _____ him about his problem.

A. sitting   B. complete   C. beside   D. stranger

22 He had no idea _____ _____ _____ _____.

A. he   B. why   C. it   D. did

23 However, he _____ _____ _____ _____ when he got _____ the train.

A. off   B. much   C. felt   D. better

24 _____ _____, we often tell _____ about our problems just _____ Taeho.

A. enough   B. strangely   C. like   D. strangers

25 That is _____ we do not have to worry about _____ or _____ them again.

A. being   B. because   C. seeing   D. judged

26 If you have a problem that you cannot _____ _____ your family or friends, _____ _____ to a stranger.

A. with   B. talking   C. share   D. try

27 You will _____ _____ _____.

A. much   B. feel   C. better

28 How do I _____ a _____ _____ a friend?

A. rival   B. turn   C. into

29 Benjamin Franklin once had a _____ rival who did _____ like him _____ _____.

A. not   B. political   C. all   D. at

30 Franklin wanted to become _____ _____ _____ him, so he _____ _____ with a plan.

A. came   B. friends   C. with   D. up

31 His _____ had a _____ _____.

A. rival   B. rare   C. book

32 Franklin asked his rival _____ _____ him the book a _____ days.

A. few   B. lend   C. for   D. to

33 When Franklin _____ the book, he _____ him _____.

A. thanked   B. returned   C. deeply

34 _____ that day, his rival became not _____ a political _____ but _____ a good friend.

A. only   B. also   C. since   D. supporter

35 Franklin _____ said, "_____ who do you one _____ will want to do _____."

A. favor   B. famously   C. more   D. enemies

36 If you want to _____ a rival _____ a friend, don't do your _____ a _____.

A. into   B. rival   C. turn   D. favor

37 _____, ask your _____ to _____ you a _____.

A. rival   B. favor   C. instead   D. do

19 그는 부모님이나 친구들이 이해하지 못할까 걱정이 된다.

20 마음을 정리하기 위해서, 태호는 혼자 하루 기차 여행을 떠나기로 결심했다.

21 기차에서, 그는 옆에 앉은 전혀 모르는 사람에게 자신의 고민에 대해서 말했다.

22 그는 자신이 왜 그랬는지 알 수 없었다.

23 그러나, 기차에서 내릴 때 기분이 훨씬 좋아졌다.

24 정말 이상하게도, 우리는 태호처럼 우리의 문제에 대해 낯선 사람에게 말할 때가 있다.

25 그것은 우리가 평가받거나 그 사람을 다시 볼 것이라는 걱정을 할 필요가 없기 때문이다.

26 만약 가족이나 친구들과도 나눌 수 없는 고민이 있다면, 낯선 이에게 말해 보아라.

27 기분이 훨씬 나아질 것이다.

28 라이벌을 어떻게 친구로 만들 수 있을까요?

29 Benjamin Franklin에게는 한때 그를 전혀 좋아하지 않는 정치적 경쟁자가 있었다.

30 Franklin은 그와 친구가 되고 싶어서, 계획을 세웠다.

31 그의 경쟁자는 희귀한 책을 가지고 있었다.

32 Franklin은 그의 정적에게 그 책을 며칠 동안 빌려달라고 부탁했다.

33 Franklin이 그 책을 돌려줄 때, 그는 그에게 진심으로 감사를 표했다.

34 그날 이후로, 그의 경쟁자는 정치적인 후원자뿐만 아니라 좋은 친구가 되었다.

35 Franklin은 "당신을 한 번 도운 적은 더 돕고 싶어 하게 된다."라는 유명한 말을 했다.

36 여러분이 경쟁자를 친구로 만들고 싶다면, 경쟁자의 부탁을 들어주지 마라.

37 대신, 경쟁자에게 부탁을 해 보아라.

※ 다음 우리말과 일치하도록 빈칸에 알맞은 것을 골라 쓰시오.

1 _____ _____ Your _____

2 Do you think you have a _____ _____?

3 _____ _____ that many other people have the same problem.

4 Psychology is the study of the _____ _____ and _____, _____ it can _____ you _____ a solution _____ your problem.

5 How do I _____ _____ _____?

6 It was five minutes before Jisu's _____ in _____ of the _____ _____.

7 _____ _____, Jisu was _____ _____ her notes in her chair.

8 Then, her teacher _____ _____ and told her _____ _____ _____ Wonder Woman.

9 After _____ _____ for _____ minutes, Jisu did _____ feel nervous _____.

10 _____ _____, she was _____ _____ she would _____ a great _____.

11 _____ _____ Amy Cuddy, a famous psychologist, we can _____ more confident just _____ _____ _____ two minutes before _____ _____.

12 Our _____ change our _____, and our _____ can change our _____.

13 Do you want to _____ _____?

14 Stand with your _____ _____, and _____ your hands _____ your hips.

15 You will _____ _____ _____ _____ about yourself _____ _____ _____ to _____ _____.

16 Who can help me _____ _____?

17 When he _____ _____ high school _____ _____, Taeho wants to become a _____ farmer.

18 _____, he _____ _____ _____ anyone about it.

1 심리학이 당신의 물음에 답하다

2 여러분은 당신만의 유일무이한 고민을 가지고 있다고 생각하는가?

3 아마 많은 다른 사람들이 여러분과 똑같은 고민을 가지고 있을 것이다.

4 심리학은 인간의 마음과 행동에 관한 연구이며, 따라서 여러분이 문제에 대한 해결책을 찾는 데 도움을 줄 수 있다.

5 어떻게 하면 긴장을 덜 할 수 있나요?

6 지수가 반 전체 앞에서 발표를 하기 5분 전이었다.

7 지수는 긴장이 되어, 의자에 앉아 자신의 필기를 열심히 들여다보고 있었다.

8 그때 선생님이 다가와서는 원더 우먼처럼 꼿꼿이 서 있어 보라고 말했다.

9 그렇게 몇 분을 우뚝 선 후에, 지수는 더 이상 긴장되지 않았다.

10 사실, 그녀는 발표를 멋지게 할 수 있을 것이라는 자신감이 생겼다.

11 유명한 심리학자인 Amy Cuddy에 의하면, 우리는 스트레스를 받는 상황 이전에 2분 정도 꼿꼿이 서 있는 것만으로도 자신감이 더 생길 수 있다고 한다.

12 우리의 몸은 마음을 바꾸고, 마음은 우리의 행동을 바꿀 수 있다.

13 자신감이 생기기를 원하는가?

14 양발을 벌리고, 허리께에 손을 올려 보아라.

15 자신에 대한 확신이 생길 뿐만 아니라 다른 사람이 보기에도 자신감에 차 보인다.

16 누가 내 기분을 낮게 해 줄 수 있나요?

17 내년에 고등학교를 졸업한 이후에 태호는 전문적인 농부가 되고 싶어 한다.

18 하지만, 누구에게도 그것에 대해 한 번도 말하지 않았다.

19 He is _____ _____ his parents or his friends _____ _____ _____.

20 _____ to _____ _____ _____, Taeho _____ _____ a day trip on a train _____ _____.

21 On the train, he told a _____ stranger _____ _____ him about his problem.

22 He had no idea _____ _____ _____ _____ _____.

23 _____, he _____ _____ _____ when he _____ _____ the train.

24 _____ _____, we _____ _____ _____ _____ about our problems just like Taeho.

25 That is _____ we do _____ _____ worry about _____ _____ or _____ them again.

26 If you have a problem _____ you cannot _____ _____ your family or friends, try _____ to a _____.

27 You will _____ _____ _____.

28 How do I _____ a _____ _____ a friend?

29 Benjamin Franklin once had a _____ _____ _____ did _____ like him _____ _____.

30 Franklin wanted to _____ _____ him, so he _____ _____ _____ a plan.

31 His rival had a _____ book.

32 Franklin asked his rival _____ _____ him the book for _____ _____.

33 When Franklin returned the book, he thanked him _____.

34 _____ that day, his rival became _____ _____ a political supporter _____ _____ a good friend.

35 Franklin _____ said, "Enemies _____ _____ _____ _____ _____ will want to do more."

36 If you want to _____ a rival _____ a friend, don't _____ _____ _____ _____.

37 _____, ask your rival _____ _____ you a _____.

---

19 그는 부모님이나 친구들이 이해 하지 못할까 걱정이 된다.

20 마음을 정리하기 위해서, 태호 는 혼자 하루 기차 여행을 떠나 기로 결심했다.

21 기차에서, 그는 옆에 앉은 전혀 모르는 사람에게 자신의 고민에 대해서 말했다.

22 그는 자신이 왜 그랬는지 알 수 없었다.

23 그러나, 기차에서 내릴 때 기분 이 훨씬 좋아졌다.

24 정말 이상하게도, 우리는 태호 처럼 우리의 문제에 대해 낯선 사람에게 말할 때가 있다.

25 그것은 우리가 평가받거나 그 사람을 다시 볼 것이라는 걱정 을 할 필요가 없기 때문이다.

26 만약 가족이나 친구들과도 나눌 수 없는 고민이 있다면, 낯선 이 에게 말해 보아라.

27 기분이 훨씬 나아질 것이다.

28 라이벌을 어떻게 친구로 만들 수 있을까요?

29 Benjamin Franklin에게는 한때 그를 전혀 좋아하지 않는 정치 적 경쟁자가 있었다.

30 Franklin은 그와 친구가 되고 싶 어서, 계획을 세웠다.

31 그의 경쟁자는 희귀한 책을 가 지고 있었다.

32 Franklin은 그의 정적에게 그 책 을 며칠 동안 빌려달라고 부탁 했다.

33 Franklin이 그 책을 돌려줄 때, 그는 그에게 진심으로 감사를 표했다.

34 그날 이후로, 그의 경쟁자는 정 치적인 후원자뿐만 아니라 좋은 친구가 되었다.

35 Franklin은 "당신을 한 번 도운 적은 더 돕고 싶어 하게 된다." 라는 유명한 말을 했다.

36 여러분이 경쟁자를 친구로 만들 고 싶다면, 경쟁자의 부탁을 들 어주지 마라.

37 대신, 경쟁자에게 부탁을 해 보 아라.

※ 다음 문장을 우리말로 쓰시오.

1 ▶ Psychology Answers Your Questions
➡ _____

2 ▶ Do you think you have a unique problem?
➡ _____

3 ▶ Chances are that many other people have the same problem.
➡ _____

4 ▶ Psychology is the study of the human mind and behavior, so it can help you find a solution to your problem.
➡ _____

5 ▶ How do I become less nervous?
➡ _____

6 ▶ It was five minutes before Jisu's big presentation in front of the whole class.
➡ _____

7 ▶ Feeling nervous, Jisu was carefully studying her notes in her chair.
➡ _____

8 ▶ Then, her teacher came over and told her to stand tall like Wonder Woman.
➡ _____

9 ▶ After standing tall for a few minutes, Jisu did not feel nervous anymore.
➡ _____

10 ▶ In fact, she was confident that she would make a great presentation.
➡ _____

11 ▶ According to Amy Cuddy, a famous psychologist, we can become more confident just by standing tall for two minutes before stressful events.
➡ _____

12 ▶ Our bodies change our minds, and our minds can change our behavior.
➡ _____

13 ▶ Do you want to feel confident?
➡ _____

14 ▶ Stand with your feet apart, and place your hands on your hips.
➡ _____

15 ▶ You will not only feel sure about yourself but also look confident to other people.
➡ _____

16 ▶ Who can help me feel better?
➡ _____

17 ▶ When he graduates from high school next year, Taeho wants to become a professional farmer.
➡ _____

18 However, he has never told anyone about it.
➡ _____

19 He is worried that his parents or his friends will not understand.
➡ _____

20 Wanting to clear his mind, Taeho decided to take a day trip on a train by himself.
➡ _____

21 On the train, he told a complete stranger sitting beside him about his problem.
➡ _____

22 He had no idea why he did it.
➡ _____

23 However, he felt much better when he got off the train.
➡ _____

24 Strangely enough, we often tell strangers about our problems just like Taeho.
➡ _____

25 That is because we do not have to worry about being judged or seeing them again.
➡ _____

26 If you have a problem that you cannot share with your family or friends, try talking to a stranger.
➡ _____

27 You will feel much better.
➡ _____

28 How do I turn a rival into a friend?
➡ _____

29 Benjamin Franklin once had a political rival who did not like him at all.
➡ _____

30 Franklin wanted to become friends with him, so he came up with a plan.
➡ _____

31 His rival had a rare book.
➡ _____

32 Franklin asked his rival to lend him the book for a few days.
➡ _____

33 When Franklin returned the book, he thanked him deeply.
➡ _____

34 Since that day, his rival became not only a political supporter but also a good friend.
➡ _____

35 Franklin famously said, "Enemies who do you one favor will want to do more."
➡ _____

36 If you want to turn a rival into a friend, don't do your rival a favor.
➡ _____

37 Instead, ask your rival to do you a favor.
➡ _____

※ 다음 괄호 안의 단어들을 우리말에 맞도록 바르게 배열하시오.

1 (Answers / Psychology / Questions / Your)
➡ _____

2 (you / do / you / think / a / have / problem? / unique)
➡ _____

3 (are / chances / many / that / people / other / the / have / problem. / same)
➡ _____

4 (is / psychology / the / of / study / the / mind / human / and / so / behavior, / it / help / can / you / a / find / to / solution / problem. / your)
➡ _____

5 (do / how / become / I / nervous? / less)
➡ _____

6 (was / it / minutes / five / Jisu's / before / presentation / big / front / in / the / of / class. / whole)
➡ _____

7 (nervous, / feeling / was / Jisu / carefully / her / studying / notes / her / in / chair.)
➡ _____

8 (her / then, / teacher / over / came / and / her / told / to / tall / stand / Wonder / like / Woman.)
➡ _____

9 (standing / after / for / tall / few / a / minutes, / did / Jisu / feel / not / anymore. / nervous)
➡ _____

10 (fact, / in / was / she / that / confident / would / she / a / make / presentation. / great)
➡ _____

11 (to / according / Cuddy, / Amy / a / psychologist, / famous / can / we / more / become / just / confident / by / tall / standing / two / for / before / minutes / events. / stressful)
➡ _____

12 (bodies / our / change / minds, / our / and / minds / our / change / can / behavior. / our)
➡ _____

13 (you / do / to / want / confident? / feel)
➡ _____

14 (with / stand / feet / your / apart, / place / and / hands / your / on / hips. / your)
➡ _____

15 (will / you / only / not / sure / feel / yourself / about / also / but / confident / look / other / to / people.)
➡ _____

16 (can / who / me / help / better? / feel)
➡ _____

17 (he / when / graduates / high / from / school / year, / next / wants / Taeho / to / a / become / farmer. / professional)
➡ _____

18 (he / however, / never / has / anyone / told / it. / about)
➡ _____

1 심리학이 당신의 물음에 답하다

2 여러분은 당신만의 유일무이한 고민을 가지고 있다고 생각하는가?

3 아마 많은 다른 사람들이 여러분과 똑같은 고민을 가지고 있을 것이다.

4 심리학은 인간의 마음과 행동에 관한 연구이며, 따라서 여러분이 문제에 대한 해결책을 찾는 데 도움을 줄 수 있다.

5 어떻게 하면 긴장을 덜 할 수 있나요?

6 지수가 반 전체 앞에서 발표를 하기 5분 전이었다.

7 지수는 긴장이 되어, 의자에 앉아 자신의 필기를 열심히 들여다보고 있었다.

8 그때 선생님이 다가와서는 원더 우먼처럼 꼿꼿이 서 있어 보라고 말했다.

9 그렇게 몇 분을 우뚝 선 후에, 지수는 더 이상 긴장되지 않았다.

10 사실, 그녀는 발표를 멋있게 할 수 있을 것이라는 자신감이 생겼다.

11 유명한 심리학자인 Amy Cuddy에 의하면, 우리는 스트레스를 받는 상황 이전에 2분 정도 꼿꼿이 서 있는 것만으로도 자신감이 더 생길 수 있다고 한다.

12 우리의 몸은 마음을 바꾸고, 마음은 우리의 행동을 바꿀 수 있다.

13 자신감이 생기기를 원하는가?

14 양발을 벌리고, 허리께에 손을 올려 보아라.

15 자신에 대한 확신이 생길 뿐만 아니라 다른 사람이 보기에도 자신감에 차 보인다.

16 누가 내 기분을 낫게 해 줄 수 있나요?

17 내년에 고등학교를 졸업한 이후에 태호는 전문적인 농부가 되고 싶어 한다.

18 하지만, 누구에게도 그것에 대해 한 번도 말하지 않았다.

19 (is / he / that / worried / parents / his / or / friends / his / not / will / understand.)
➡ _____

20 (to / wanting / his / clear / mind, / decided / Taeho / take / to / day / a / trip / a / on / train / himself. / by)
➡ _____

21 (the / on / train, / told / he / complete / a / stranger / beside / sitting / about / him / problem. / his)
➡ _____

22 (had / he / idea / no / he / why / it. / did)
➡ _____

23 (he / however, / felt / better / much / he / when / off / got / train. / the)
➡ _____

24 (enough, / strangely / often / we / strangers / tell / our / about / problems / like / Taeho. / just)
➡ _____

25 (is / that / we / because / not / do / to / have / worry / being / about / or / judged / them / seeing / again.)
➡ _____

26 (you / if / a / have / problem / you / that / share / cannot / with / family / your / friends, / or / talking / try / a / to / stranger.)
➡ _____

27 (will / you / much / feel / better.)
➡ _____

28 (do / how / turn / I / into / rival / friend? / a)
➡ _____

29 (Franklin / Benjamin / had / once / a / rival / political / did / who / like / not / at / him / all.)
➡ _____

30 (wanted / Franklin / become / to / with / friends / him, / he / so / up / came / a / with / plan.)
➡ _____

31 (rival / his / a / had / book. / rare)
➡ _____

32 (asked / Franklin / rival / his / lend / to / the / him / for / book / few / a / days.)
➡ _____

33 (Franklin / when / the / returned / book, / thanked / he / deeply. / him)
➡ _____

34 (that / since / day, / rival / his / not / became / only / political / a / but / supporter / a / also / friend. / good)
➡ _____

35 (Franklin / said, / famously / who / "enemies / you / do / favor / one / want / will / do / to / more.")
➡ _____

36 (you / if / to / want / turn / rival / a / into / friend, / a / do / don't / rival / your / favor.)
➡ _____

37 (ask / instead, / rival / your / do / to / you / favor. / a)
➡ _____

19 그는 부모님이나 친구들이 이해 하지 못할까 걱정이 된다.

20 마음을 정리하기 위해서, 태호 는 혼자 하루 기차 여행을 떠나 기로 결심했다.

21 기차에서, 그는 옆에 앉은 전혀 모르는 사람에게 자신의 고민에 대해서 말했다.

22 그는 자신이 왜 그랬는지 알 수 없었다.

23 그러나, 기차에서 내릴 때 기분 이 훨씬 좋아졌다.

24 정말 이상하게도, 우리는 태호 처럼 우리의 문제에 대해 낯선 사람에게 말할 때가 있다.

25 그것은 우리가 평가받거나 그 사람을 다시 볼 것이라는 걱정 을 할 필요가 없기 때문이다.

26 만약 가족이나 친구들과도 나눌 수 없는 고민이 있다면, 낯선 이 에게 말해 보아라.

27 기분이 훨씬 나아질 것이다.

28 라이벌을 어떻게 친구로 만들 수 있을까요?

29 Benjamin Franklin에게는 한때 그를 전혀 좋아하지 않는 정치 적 경쟁자가 있었다.

30 Franklin은 그와 친구가 되고 싶 어서, 계획을 세웠다.

31 그의 경쟁자는 희귀한 책을 가 지고 있었다.

32 Franklin은 그의 정적에게 그 책 을 며칠 동안 빌려달라고 부탁 했다.

33 Franklin이 그 책을 돌려줄 때, 그는 그에게 진심으로 감사를 표했다.

34 그날 이후로, 그의 경쟁자는 정 치적인 후원자뿐만 아니라 좋은 친구가 되었다.

35 Franklin은 "당신을 한 번 도운 적은 더 돕고 싶어 하게 된다." 라는 유명한 말을 했다.

36 여러분이 경쟁자를 친구로 만들 고 싶다면, 경쟁자의 부탁을 들 어주지 마라.

37 대신, 경쟁자에게 부탁을 해 보 아라.

※ 다음 우리말을 영어로 쓰시오.

1 심리학이 당신의 물음에 답하다
➡ _____

2 여러분은 당신만의 유일무이한 고민을 가지고 있다고 생각하는가?
➡ _____

3 아마 많은 다른 사람들이 여러분과 똑같은 고민을 가지고 있을 것이다.
➡ _____

4 심리학은 인간의 마음과 행동에 관한 연구이며, 따라서 여러분이 문제에 대한 해결책을 찾는 데 도움을 줄 수 있다.
➡ _____
_____

5 어떻게 하면 긴장을 덜 할 수 있나요?
➡ _____

6 지수가 반 전체 앞에서 발표를 하기 5분 전이었다.
➡ _____

7 지수는 긴장이 되어, 의자에 앉아 자신의 필기를 열심히 들여다보고 있었다.
➡ _____

8 그때 선생님이 다가와서는 원더우먼처럼 꼿꼿이 서 있어 보라고 말했다.
➡ _____

9 그렇게 몇 분을 우뚝 선 후에, 지수는 더 이상 긴장되지 않았다.
➡ _____

10 사실, 그녀는 발표를 멋있게 할 수 있을 것이라는 자신감이 생겼다.
➡ _____

11 유명한 심리학자인 Amy Cuddy에 의하면, 우리는 스트레스를 받는 상황 이전에 2분 정도 꼿꼿이 서 있는 것만으로도 자신감이 더 생길 수 있다고 한다.
➡ _____

12 우리의 몸은 마음을 바꾸고, 마음은 우리의 행동을 바꿀 수 있다.
➡ _____

13 자신감이 생기기를 원하는가?
➡ _____

14 양발을 벌리고, 허리께에 손을 올려 보아라.
➡ _____

15 자신에 대한 확신이 생길 뿐만 아니라 다른 사람이 보기에도 자신감에 차 보인다.
➡ _____

16 누가 내 기분을 낮게 해 줄 수 있나요?
➡ _____

17 내년에 고등학교를 졸업한 이후에 태호는 전문적인 농부가 되고 싶어 한다.
➡ _____

18 하지만, 누구에게도 그것에 대해 한 번도 말하지 않았다.
➡ _____

19 그는 부모님이나 친구들이 이해하지 못할까 걱정이 된다.
➡ _____

20 마음을 정리하기 위해서, 태호는 혼자 하루 기차 여행을 떠나기로 결심했다.
➡ _____

21 기차에서, 그는 옆에 앉은 전혀 모르는 사람에게 자신의 고민에 대해서 말했다.
➡ _____

22 그는 자신이 왜 그랬는지 알 수 없었다.
➡ _____

23 그러나, 기차에서 내릴 때 기분이 훨씬 좋아졌다.
➡ _____

24 정말 이상하게도, 우리는 태호처럼 우리의 문제에 대해 낯선 사람에게 말할 때가 있다.
➡ _____

25 그것은 우리가 평가받거나 그 사람을 다시 볼 것이라는 걱정을 할 필요가 없기 때문이다.
➡ _____

26 만약 가족이나 친구들과도 나눌 수 없는 고민이 있다면, 낯선 이에게 말해 보아라.
➡ _____

27 기분이 훨씬 나아질 것이다.
➡ _____

28 라이벌을 어떻게 친구로 만들 수 있을까요?
➡ _____

29 Benjamin Franklin에게는 한때 그를 전혀 좋아하지 않는 정치적 경쟁자가 있었다.
➡ _____

30 Franklin은 그와 친구가 되고 싶어서, 계획을 세웠다.
➡ _____

31 그의 경쟁자는 희귀한 책을 가지고 있었다.
➡ _____

32 Franklin은 그의 정적에게 그 책을 며칠 동안 빌려달라고 부탁했다.
➡ _____

33 Franklin이 그 책을 돌려줄 때, 그는 그에게 진심으로 감사를 표했다.
➡ _____

34 그날 이후로, 그의 경쟁자는 정치적인 후원자뿐만 아니라 좋은 친구가 되었다.
➡ _____

35 Franklin은 "당신을 한 번 도운 적은 더 돕고 싶어 하게 된다."라는 유명한 말을 했다.
➡ _____

36 여러분이 경쟁자를 친구로 만들고 싶다면, 경쟁자의 부탁을 들어주지 마라.
➡ _____

37 대신, 경쟁자에게 부탁을 해 보아라.
➡ _____

※ 다음 우리말과 일치하도록 빈칸에 알맞은 말을 쓰시오.

Listen & Speak 2 - Think and Talk

1. A: What _____ I _____ _____ _____ on Stress-Free Day?

2. B: You _____ _____ _____ _____ the classroom.

3. C: You _____ _____ _____ _____ _____ _____ _____ 8:30.

1. A: 스트레스가 없는 날에 무엇을 할 필요가 없을까?
2. B: 너는 교실 청소를 할 필요가 없어.
3. C: 너는 8:30분까지 학교에 올 필요가 없어.

Link

1. _____ _____ do you _____ _____ _____?

2. _____ _____ _____ _____ the answer to this question, we _____ _____ _____ about confidence.

3. Thirty students _____ _____ _____. The _____ _____ was nine.

4. Eighteen students _____ _____ _____ _____ _____.

5. _____, sixty percent of the students _____ _____ _____ _____ _____.

1. 당신은 스스로에 대해 얼마나 확신이 있나요?
2. 질문에 대한 답을 찾고 싶어, 우리는 자신감에 대한 검사지를 만들었습니다.
3. 30명의 학생들이 검사를 했습니다. 평균적인 점수는 9점이었습니다.
4. 18명의 학생들이 평균 점수를 넘었습니다.
5. 따라서, 학생들의 60%가 그들 스스로에 대해 꽤 자신감을 갖고 있습니다.

Write

1. _____ _____ _____ in my life

2. The _____ _____ _____ _____ _____ was when my grandmother _____ _____ five years _____.

3. When I was _____, she _____ _____ _____ me _____ _____ the time.

4. _____ _____ _____ _____, I _____ _____ and _____.

5. _____ _____, I _____ my grandmother's diary.

6. She _____ _____ _____ _____ _____ about her memories _____ _____ _____ that I would lead a happy life.

7. _____ _____ _____, I _____ _____ that I should _____ _____ just _____ _____ _____.

1. 내 삶에서 가장 힘들었던 순간
2. 내 삶에서 가장 힘들었던 순간은 5년 전 할머니께서 돌아가셨을 때였다.
3. 내가 더 어렸을 때, 그녀는 대부분의 시간 동안 나를 돌봐 주셨다.
4. 그녀가 곁에 없어서, 나는 슬프고 외로웠다.
5. 어느 날, 나는 할머니의 일기장을 발견했다.
6. 그녀는 그녀의 기억에 대해 많이 적었을 뿐만 아니라, 내가 행복한 삶을 살기를 바랐다.
7. 이 경험을 통해, 나는 그녀가 원했던 것처럼 행복해지려고 노력해야 한다는 것을 배웠다.

※ 다음 우리말을 영어로 쓰시오.

Listen & Speak 2 - Think and Talk

1. A: 스트레스가 없는 날에 무엇을 할 필요가 없을까?
   ➡ _____

2. B: 너는 교실 청소를 할 필요가 없어.
   ➡ _____

3. C: 너는 8:30분까지 학교에 올 필요가 없어.
   ➡ _____

Link

1. 당신은 스스로에 대해 얼마나 확신이 있나요?
   ➡ _____

2. 질문에 대한 답을 찾고 싶어, 우리는 자신감에 대한 검사지를 만들었습니다.
   ➡ _____

3. 30명의 학생들이 검사를 했습니다. 평균적인 점수는 9점이었습니다.
   ➡ _____

4. 18명의 학생들이 평균 점수를 넘었습니다.
   ➡ _____

5. 따라서, 학생들의 60%가 그들 스스로에 대해 꽤 자신감을 갖고 있습니다.
   ➡ _____

Write

1. 내 삶에서 가장 힘들었던 순간
   ➡ _____

2. 내 삶에서 가장 힘들었던 순간은 5년 전 할머니께서 돌아가셨을 때였다.
   ➡ _____

3. 내가 더 어렸을 때, 그녀는 대부분의 시간 동안 나를 돌봐 주셨다.
   ➡ _____

4. 그녀가 곁에 없어서, 나는 슬프고 외로웠다.
   ➡ _____

5. 어느 날, 나는 할머니의 일기장을 발견했다.
   ➡ _____

6. 그녀는 그녀의 기억에 대해 많이 적었을 뿐만 아니라, 내가 행복한 삶을 살기를 바랐다.
   ➡ _____

7. 이 경험을 통해, 나는 그녀가 원했던 것처럼 행복해지려고 노력해야 한다는 것을 배웠다.
   ➡ _____

MEMO

MEMO

MEMO

영어 기출 문제집

적중100

1학기

정답 및 해설

미래 | 최연희

중3

영어 기출 문제집

적중 100

1학기

정답 및 해설

미래 | 최연희

중 3

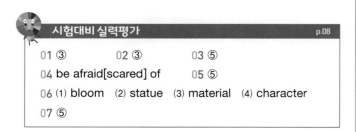

Plants That Feed Us

시험대비 실력평가   p.08

01 ③   02 ③   03 ⑤
04 be afraid[scared] of   05 ⑤
06 (1) bloom   (2) statue   (3) material   (4) character
07 ⑤

01 주어진 단어는 반의어 관계에 있다. 모두 유의어이지만 ③번은 반의어이다. ① 비슷한 ② 필수적인 ③ 진실 – 거짓 ④ 흔치 않은 ⑤ 이점

02 '소수의 사람들에 의해서만 알려진 사실이며 다른 누구에게도 말해지지 않는 어떤 것'은 '비밀(secret)'이다.

03 ⑤ composer라고 쓰는 것이 적절하다.

04 be scared of 혹은 be afraid of: ~을 두려워하다

05 각각 pilot, soak, crush, actor의 영영풀이이다. 따라서 tour가 적절하다.

06 bloom: (꽃을) 피우다, 피다, statue: 동상, material: 재료, 물질, character: 등장인물

07 '~ 옆에'라는 의미의 by는 교통수단과 함께 쓰여 '~로'라는 의미로도 쓰일 수 있으며 동명사와 함께 쓰이면 '~함으로써'라는 의미로도 쓰인다.

서술형 시험대비   p.09

01 inventor
02 (1) expect   (2) statue   (3) insect
03 (1) After graduation, I got a job with NASA as a researcher.
   (2) The interviewer asked me about my future plans.
   (3) I am proud of being a cartoonist.
04 (A) have   (B) keep   (C) take
05 (1) is good for   (2) no longer   (3) In addition
   (4) by making   (5) poisonous material
06 inventor

01 동사에 '-er'이나 '-or'을 붙여서 명사를 만든 것이다. invent는 직업을 나타내는 명사로 쓰기 위하여 '-or'을 붙인다.

02 (1) 어떤 일이 일어날 것이라고 믿다 (2) 돌이나 금속 같은 단단한 재료로 만들어진 사람이나 동물의 이미지 (3) 여섯 개의 다리를 가진 파리나 개미 같은 작은 생물

03 researcher: 조사원, interviewer: 면접관, cartoonist: 만화가

04 have a fever: 열이 있다, have difficulty in Ving: V 하는 데 어려움이 있다, keep ~ a secret: ~을 비밀로 하다, keep a diary: 일기를 쓰다, take medicine: 약을 먹다, take a walk: 산책하다

05 (1) be good for: ~에 유익하다 (2) no longer: 더 이상 ~가 아닌 (3) in addition: 게다가 (4) by Ving: V함으로써 (5) poisonous: 독성이 강한, material: 재료, 물질

06 에디슨이 롤모델이며 무언가를 발명하는 것을 좋아한다고 하였으므로 '발명가(inventor)'를 빈칸에 쓰는 것이 적절하다.

교과서
Conversation

핵심 Check   p.10~11

1 ④
2 What do you think I should do?

01 Bomi에게 약이 있는지 물어보는 것으로 보아 거기에 대한 대답으로 Bomi는 '왜? 무슨 문제가 있니?'라고 다시 물어보는 것이 적절하다. 'Where have you been?'은 '어디 갔다 왔니?'라는 뜻이다.

교과서 대화문 익히기

Check(√) True or False   p.12

1 F   2 T   3 F   4 T   5 T

교과서 확인학습   p.14~15

Listen & Speak 1 A-1
some medicine / something wrong / a stomachache, too much / go for a walk / it a try

Listen & Speak 1 A-2
something wrong, so good / a sore throat, because of / Put, take, in, produce / get a few plants

Listen & Speak 2 A-1
so hard to lose, do you think / walk your dog / it, it help, lose weight / actually exercising, too / think about it

시험대비 기본평가

p.16

01 ④   02 ③   03 ③

04 She has watched a movie on her phone for two hours.

01 빈칸에는 안부를 묻는 말이 들어가는 것이 자연스럽다. 따라서 ④번이 적절하다.

02 밑줄 친 부분은 조언을 구하는 말이므로 ③번이 가장 적절하다.

03 눈이 충혈되었다는 것으로 보아 tired가 가장 적절하다.

04 소녀는 자신의 휴대전화로 두 시간 동안 영화를 보았다.

시험대비 실력평가

p.17~18

01 ③   02 ③   03 ④

04 It's because he has a stomachache.

05 ④   06 ③   07 ②

08 (C)–(A)–(D)–(B)

09 what should I do to say sorry to Mina?

10 She has the tomato pot in the kitchen.

11 ④   12 ⑤

13 He watches a movie on his phone until late at night.

01 조언을 구하고 조언을 제공하는 대화를 나누고 있으므로 ③번이 가장 적절하다.

02 안부를 묻는 말에 '좋다'고 답하고 목이 아프다는 말이 이어지고 있으므로 어색하다.

03 밑줄 친 (A)는 시도해 보겠다는 의미로, 걷는 것이 어떠냐는 소녀의 조언을 시도해 보겠다는 말이다.

04 소년이 소녀에게 약이 있느냐고 물은 이유는 복통 때문이다.

05 (A)는 조언을 구하는 말이므로 ④번이 가장 적절하다.

06 help는 목적격보어로 to부정사나 동사원형을 취한다. 따라서 to lose 혹은 lose라고 쓰는 것이 적절하다.

07 소년의 문제에 소녀는 개를 산책시키라고 조언해 주고 있으므로 ②번을 답할 수 있다.

08 (C) 무슨 일이냐고 묻자 (A) 엄마가 가장 좋아하는 접시를 깼다며 조언을 구하자 (D) 엄마에게 사실대로 말씀드리라며 조언하고 (B) 이에 대한 답이 이어지는 것이 가장 자연스럽다.

09 'What should I do to ~?'는 조언을 구하는 표현이다. '미나에게 사과하기 위해서 무엇을 해야 할까?'라고 묻는 것이 적절하다.

10 소녀는 토마토 화분을 주방에 둔다고 하였다.

11 소년은 소녀에게 조언을 하고 있으므로 ④번이 대화의 내용과 일치한다.

12 눈을 건강하게 유지하는 데 도움을 주기 때문에 당근과 토마토를 먹으라고 권하는 것이 적절하다.

13 수호는 새벽 2시까지 휴대폰으로 영화를 본다고 하였으므로 수호가 요즈음에 종종 하는 것은 밤늦게까지 영화를 보는 것이라고 답할 수 있다.

서술형 시험대비

p.19

01 What do you think I should do?

02 (A) have   (B) take   (C) get

03 the fine dust, sore

04 She is likely to buy a few plants.

05 What's wrong with you?

06 It's because she has watched a movie on her phone for two hours.

07 (C)–(E)–(A)–(D)–(B)   08 is something wrong

01 의견을 묻는 말로 What do you think I should do?를 쓸 수 있다.

02 (A) '~가 아프다'고 말할 때에는 'have+병명'을 쓰는 것이 일반적이다. (B) 'take ~ in'은 '~을 흡수하다'는 의미이며, (C)에서 'get'은 '사다, 구하다'라는 의미로 쓰인다.

03 Jane은 미세먼지가 자신의 목을 아프게 한다고 생각한다.

04 식물을 몇 개 사야겠다고 하였다.

05 무슨 일이 있는지를 묻는 말이다. 'What's wrong with you?'와 그 의미가 같다.

06 소녀가 피곤한 이유는 휴대전화기로 두 시간 동안 영화를 봤기 때문이다.

07 (C) 약이 있냐고 물음 - (E) 무슨 문제가 있는지 되물음 - (A) 약이 필요한 이유를 설명 - (D) 조언 제공 - (B) 조언을 시도해 보겠다고 말함

08 슬퍼 보이는 친구에게 안부를 묻는 말이 들어가는 것이 적절하다. 'What's the matter?'라고 써도 무방하다.

핵심 Check   p.20~21

1 (1) named   (2) broken   **2** (1) did   (2) do

시험대비 기본평가   p.22

01 (1) using → used   (2) called → call
   (3) eats → eating   (4) writing → written
02 ②   **03** ②
04 (1) Most Americans did think that tomatoes were
      poisonous.
   (2) The pictures taken by Lily were impressive.

01 (1) 당근이 전쟁에서 사용될 수도 있다는 수동이므로 used가 적
   절하다. (2) 강조의 조동사 뒤에는 동사 원형을 쓴다. (3) 능동
   의 현재분사가 뒤에서 꾸미는 것이 적절하다. (4) 라틴어로 쓰여
   진 편지이므로, written이 적절하다.
02 주어가 복수이므로 동사를 강조할 때 do를 써야 한다.
03 싫증을 느끼는 것은 능동이 아니라 수동의 과거분사를 써야 한
   다.
04 (1) 주어가 복수이므로 동사를 강조할 때 do를 써야 한다. (2)
   명사를 뒤에서 꾸미는 과거분사의 활용에 유의하여, 단어를 배
   열한다.

시험대비 실력평가   p.23~25

01 ③   **02** ①
03 (1) were many people watching
   (2) built by my grandfather is
04 ②   **05** making → made   **06** ⑤
07 ②
08 Potato juice mixed with honey makes your skin
   soft.
09 ③   **10** ②   **11** ③
12 ①, ④, ⑤   **13** ④   **14** ⑤   **15** ④
16 (1) writing → written   (2) mixing → mixed
   (3) cry → crying
17 ④   **18** ①, ③, ⑤   **19** ③
20 (A) made   (B) known   (C) using   (D) named
   (E) meaning   (F) covered
21 ②   **22** invented, using

01 (1) 꽃을 꺾는 소년(능동) (2) 여행에 쓰인 돈(수동) (3) 두려워
   하는(수동) 등에 적절하게 분사를 활용한다.
02 첫 번째 빈칸은 동사 강조의 does이며, 두 번째 빈칸은 본동사

이다. do the laundry: 빨래를 하다
03 분사가 명사의 뒤에서 꾸며주는 것을 적절히 활용한다. (1)은
   watching the pet contest가 people을 꾸며주고(능동), (2)
   는 built by my grandfather가 the swimming pool을 뒤
   에서 꾸민다.(수동)
04 ② Be로 시작하는 명령문도 Do로 강조 가능하다. ① warned
   → warn, ③ changed → change, ④ believed →
   believe, ⑤ looks → look
05 베트남에서 제조된 셔츠이므로 과거분사가 적절하다.
06 '그는 잃어버린 아이를 정말로 찾아냈다.'라는 문장과 '잃어버린
   아이를 찾을 수 있었다.'라는 문장은 다르다.
07 ②는 try의 목적어로 쓰인 동명사이고, 나머지는 모두 명사를
   앞 또는 뒤에서 꾸며 주는 현재분사이다.
08 분사가 명사 뒤에서 꾸며주는 것을 활용한다. 수동이므로
   mixed를 사용하고, 본동사는 makes를 쓴다.
09 첫 번째 빈칸은 강조의 does 또는 did를 쓸 수 있다. 두 번째 빈
   칸은 시제가 과거이기 때문에 did만 가능.
10 ⓐ 타는 불, ⓑ 노래하는 학생들 모두 '능동'의 의미를 갖고 있으
   며, 명사를 앞, 뒤에서 꾸며주고 있다.
11 강조의 did를 쓰면 동사는 원형이 와야 한다.
12 ① 토마토를 먹고 있는 소녀이므로 eats → eating ④ '거짓
   말을 하고 있었다'는 뜻의 과거진행형이므로 현재분사가 필요.
   lied → lying, ⑤ 그녀의 가족을 만난 것이면, meeting her
   family가, 그녀의 가족이 만난 사람들이면 meeting → met으
   로 하는 것이 적절하다.
13 11년 전 과거의 일이므로 does를 did로 바꿔야 한다.
14 ① 수동의 의미이므로, 과거분사 surrounded가 온다. ② 명사
   를 뒤에서 꾸미는 분사를 활용한다. 능동이므로 sat → sitting
   ③ using → used ④ 남겨진 케이크가 없는 것이므로 leaving
   → left가 적절하다.
15 과거 시제를 강조하는 'did+동사원형'을 이용한다.
16 (1) 쓰인 책(수동) (2) 꿀과 섞인 감자 주스(수동) (3) 우는 아기
   들(능동)
17 동사 강조의 do(does/did)를 찾는다.
18 ① 감동적인 장면들 touched → touching ③ 신나는
   날 excited → exciting ⑤ 시간을 알려주는 shown →
   showing
19 ① do → does ② made → make ④ plays → play ⑤
   called → call
20 (A) 만들어진 (B) ~로 알려진 (C) (당근)을 이용하여 (D) ~라
   고 이름 불리는 (E) ~를 의미하는 (F) ~로 덮인
21 동사 강조의 do(does/did)를 찾는다.
22 어법에 맞게 배열하면, 'This is a battery invented from
   the idea of using the characteristic of sunflowers.'이다.
   invented는 과거분사, using은 동명사이다.

01 (1) Sofia did find her missing cat.

   (2) Gordon does know many K-pop songs.

   (3) Grace did write these essays last week.

02 (1) girl standing across the street

   (2) played by the band on the stage

   (3) wearing a red shirt

03 (1) did build   (2) do think   (3) did write

04 (1) This is the thing placed on the wall.

   (2) Sarah is the one wearing glasses.

   (3) Mary is erasing the scores written on the board.

   (4) I do love Susan, the girl drinking water.

   (5) The news was really shocking.

05 (1) with the crying baby

   (2) the birds flying southwards

   (3) an illegally parked taxi

06 (A) sitting   (B) standing   (C) closed

07 (1) Alex himself called you yesterday.

   (2) It was you that Alex called yesterday.

   (3) Alex did call you yesterday.

   (4) It was yesterday that Alex called you.

08 As Ethan did feel a headache

09 (1) does   (2) hidden   (3) kill   (4) called

10 place a cup of crushed tomatoes

01 수와 시제 등에 유의하여 do/does/did를 활용하되 강조를 위해 사용한 do 뒤에는 본동사의 원형이 와야 한다.

02 명사의 뒤에서 꾸미는 분사 활용 (1) 서 있는 소녀(능동) (2) 연주되는 음악(수동) (3) 셔츠를 입은 사람(능동)

03 수와 시제 등에 유의하여 do를 활용하되 do 뒤에는 동사 원형이 와야 한다.

04 명사를 뒤에서 꾸며주는 분사를 활용한다. 능동/진행은 현재분사, 수동/완료는 과거분사를 쓴다. (1) 벽에 놓이는 물건 placed (2) 안경을 쓰고 있는 사람 wearing (3) 보드에 쓰여진 점수 written (4) 물을 마시는 소녀 drinking (5) 충격적인 뉴스 shocking

05 (1) 울고 있는 아기 (2) 남쪽으로 날아가고 있는 새들 (3) 불법으로 주차된 택시(부정관사 an에 유의한다)

06 (A) 능동 (B) 능동 (C) 'with+목적어' 뒤에 나오는 '현재분사/과거분사' 여부는 목적어의 '능동/수동'을 따진다. 목적어가 eyes이므로, 수동의 과거분사 closed가 적절하다.

07 (1) himself를 문미로 보내도 된다. (2) (대)명사와 부사는 'It ~ that 강조 구문'으로 강조 가능하다. (3) 'did+동사원형'으로 동사를 강조한다. (4) 부사 yesterday는 'It ~ that 강조 구문'으로 강조한다.

08 동사 강조의 'do'를 시제에 맞게 활용한다. 과거시제이므로 did를

09 (1) does로 강조 (2) 땅에 숨겨진 폭탄이므로 hide의 과거분사 hidden이 적절하다. (3) 강조의 did 뒤에는 원형동사 kill이 적절하다. (4) '~라고 불리는'이라는 표현은 call의 과거분사를 쓴다.

10 으깬 토마토가 되려면 crush의 과거분사형이 명사의 앞에서 수식하는 형태가 된다. 명령문이므로 place로 시작하는 것이 적절하다.

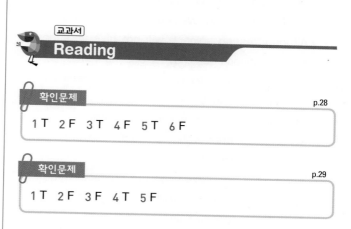

교과서
Reading

확인문제   p.28

1 T   2 F   3 T   4 F   5 T   6 F

확인문제   p.29

1 T   2 F   3 F   4 T   5 F

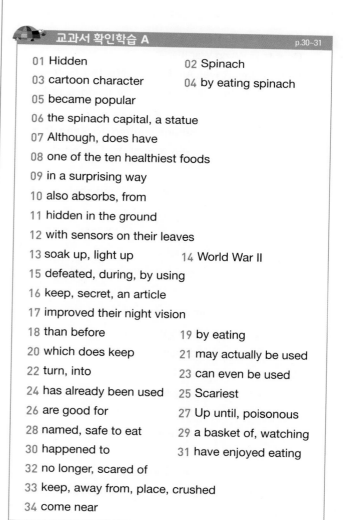

교과서 확인학습 A   p.30~31

01 Hidden   02 Spinach

03 cartoon character   04 by eating spinach

05 became popular

06 the spinach capital, a statue

07 Although, does have

08 one of the ten healthiest foods

09 in a surprising way

10 also absorbs, from

11 hidden in the ground

12 with sensors on their leaves

13 soak up, light up   14 World War II

15 defeated, during, by using

16 keep, secret, an article

17 improved their night vision

18 than before   19 by eating

20 which does keep   21 may actually be used

22 turn, into   23 can even be used

24 has already been used   25 Scariest

26 are good for   27 Up until, poisonous

28 named, safe to eat   29 a basket of, watching

30 happened to   31 have enjoyed eating

32 no longer, scared of

33 keep, away from, place, crushed

34 come near

1 Hidden Stories about Plants

2 Popeye and the Great Spinach

3 Popeye is a world-famous cartoon character.

4 He gets his super power by eating spinach.

5 When Popeye became popular in the 1930s in the United States, a lot of children began to eat spinach.

6 Crystal City in Texas, which is called the spinach capital of the world, even built a statue of Popeye.

7 Although eating spinach will not give us super powers, spinach does have a lot of nutrients.

8 It is actually considered one of the ten healthiest foods on the planet.

9 Spinach can be used in a surprising way.

10 When it absorbs water, spinach also absorbs many other things from the soil.

11 Some scientists have used this characteristic of spinach to find bombs hidden in the ground.

12 They make special spinach plants with sensors on their leaves.

13 When these plants soak up traces from bombs, the sensors light up.

14 Carrots in World War II

15 In 1940, the Royal Air Force defeated German fighters during World War II by using a radar system.

16 The British government wanted to keep this technology a secret, so it published an article in the newspaper.

17 It said that British pilots improved their night vision because they ate a lot of carrots.

18 Everybody believed the story and began to eat a lot more carrots than before.

19 Can we really improve night vision by eating lots of carrots?

20 Not really, but carrots contain a lot of vitamin A, which does keep our eyes healthy.

21 In the future, carrots may actually be used in wars.

22 Scottish researchers have discovered a way to turn carrots into a very strong and light material.

23 It can even be used to make battleships.

24 This new material has already been used to make snowboards and bicycles.

25 Tomatoes, the Scariest Vegetables

26 We all know that tomatoes are good for our health.

27 Up until the 1800s, however, most Americans thought that tomatoes were poisonous.

28 In 1820, a man named Robert Johnson wanted to prove that tomatoes were safe to eat.

29 So, he ate a basket of tomatoes in front of many people watching him.

30 They all expected him to die, but nothing happened to him.

31 Ever since then, Americans have enjoyed eating tomatoes.

32 We are no longer afraid of tomatoes, but some insects are still scared of them.

33 If you want to keep insects away from your room, place a bowl of crushed tomatoes in a corner of your room.

34 Insects will not come near the tomatoes.

시험대비 실력평가 p.34~37

01 ④　　　02 ②　　　03 ④　　　04 ①

05 시금치가 물을 흡수할 때, 시금치는 흙으로부터 다른 많은 것들도 흡수하는 것

06 go out → light up　　　07 ④

08 the British government　　　09 ②

10 carrots may actually be used in wars

11 ②, ④　　12 ③　　13 ⑤　　14 ③

15 (A) crushed tomatoes　(B) scared[afraid]

16 Some / ground　　17 ②, ③, ④, ⑤

18 absorb　19 (A) called　(B) capital　(C) does

20 ③　　　　21 He gets it by eating spinach.

22 tomatoes　23 died → didn't die　24 ④

01 ④번 다음 문장의 It에 주목한다. 주어진 문장의 spinach를 받고 있으므로 ④번이 적절하다.

02 ⓐ와 ②: 캐릭터, 등장인물, ① 성격, ③ 문자, ④ 특징, ⑤ 인격

03 시금치를 먹는 것이 우리에게 초인적인 힘을 주지는 않는다.

04 ⓐ absorb A from B: B로부터 A를 흡수하다, ⓑ with sensors on their leaves: 잎에 감지기가 있는

05 시금치의 이 특성은 바로 앞 문장의 내용을 가리킨다.

06 시금치의 특성을 사용하여 땅에 숨겨진 폭탄을 찾는다고 했기 때문에, 이 특별한 시금치가 폭탄의 흔적을 흡수하면 감지기가 '빛난다'고 해야 하므로 light up으로 고치는 것이 적절하다. go out: (불·전깃불이) 꺼지다, light up: (빛·색으로) 환하게 되다

07 본문 끝 부분에 '실제로 그렇지는 않지만(야간 시력을 높일 수는 없지만), 당근은 많은 비타민 A를 함유하는데, 그것은 정말로 우리 눈을 건강하게 유지해 준다.'라는 말이 있으므로, 야간 '시력'

이라고 하는 것이 적절하다. vision: 시력, 시야, ① (이전의 것·비슷한 종류의 다른 것들과 약간 다른) 판[형태], ② 촉각, ③ 청력 ⑤ 후각

08 '영국 정부'를 가리킨다.

09 이 글은 '영국 공군이 제2차 세계 대전에서 독일군을 패배시킨 레이더 시스템을 비밀로 하려고, 영국 비행사들이 당근을 많이 먹어 야간 시력이 좋아졌다는 신문 기사를 실었는데, 당근이 야간 시력을 높일 수는 없지만 실제로 많은 비타민 A를 함유하고 있어서 우리 눈을 건강하게 유지해 준다.'는 내용의 글이므로, 제목으로는 ②번 '제2차 세계대전에서의 당근'이 적절하다.

10 추측을 나타내는 조동사 may를 사용하여 수동태로 쓰는 것이 적절하다.

11 ⓑ와 ②, ④: 완료 용법, ① 계속 용법, ③ 경험 용법, ⑤ 결과 용법

12 스코틀랜드의 연구원들은 어떻게 당근을 매우 강하고 가벼운 물질로 바꾸는지는 대답할 수 없다. ① Yes. ② A way to turn carrots into a very strong and light material. ④ Yes. ⑤ Yes, it has already been used to make snowboards and bicycles.

13 앞에 나오는 내용과 상반되는 내용이 뒤에 이어지므로 however가 가장 적절하다.① 그 결과, ② 뿐만 아니라, 더욱이, ③ 즉, 말하자면 ④ 예를 들면

14 이 글은 '1820년에 Robert Johnson이 토마토가 먹기에 안전하다는 것을 증명하기 전까지는 대부분의 미국인들은 토마토에 독성이 있다고 생각했던 것과 몇몇 곤충들은 여전히 토마토를 무서워한다.'는 내용의 글이므로, 주제로는 ③번 '토마토에 관한 근거 없는 믿음과 진실'이 적절하다. myth: (많은 사람들의) 근거 없는 믿음

15 몇몇 곤충들은 여전히 토마토를 '무서워해서' 토마토 가까이 오지 않을 것이므로, 만약 '으깬 토마토' 한 그릇을 방구석에 놓아두면 곤충들이 방에 들어오지 않게 할 수 있다.

16 시금치의 놀라운 용도는 '몇몇 과학자들이 시금치의 특성을 사용하여 땅에 숨겨진 폭탄을 찾는 것'을 가리킨다.

17 ⓑ와 ①: 부사적 용법, ②, ③, ⑤: 명사적 용법, ④: 형용사적 용법

18 soak up = absorb: 흡수하다, 빨아들이다

19 (A) 시금치 수도라고 '불린다'고 해야 하므로 called가 적절하다. (B) 시금치 '수도'라고 해야 하므로 capital이 적절하다. capital: 수도, capitol: 미국 국회 의사당, (C) 시금치가 정말로 많은 영양분을 가지고 있다는 것은 일반적인 사실에 해당하므로 현재시제로 쓰는 것이 적절하다.

20 ⓐ와 ①, ③, ④: 동명사, ②, ⑤: 현재분사

21 Popeye는 '시금치를 먹음으로써' 초인적인 힘을 얻는다.

22 '토마토'를 가리킨다.

23 Robert Johnson은 그를 지켜보는 많은 사람들 앞에서 한 바구니의 토마토를 먹었고, 모두 그가 죽을 것이라고 예상했

으나 '그에게는 아무 일도 일어나지 않았다.' against one's expectations: 예상과 달리

24 무슨 곤충들이 토마토를 무서워하는지는 알 수 없다. ① They thought that tomatoes were poisonous. ② He wanted to prove that tomatoes were safe to eat. ③ They have enjoyed eating tomatoes since Robert Johnson proved that they were safe to eat. ⑤ Insects will not come near the tomatoes.

서술형 시험대비

01 As → Although 또는 Though
02 actually considers → is actually considered
03 (A) cartoon character   (B) eating spinach
04 ⓐ be used   ⓑ hidden
05 ⓒ Some scientists   ⓓ special spinach plants
06 (A) sensors   (B) bombs
07 (A) defeated   (B) during   (C) healthy
08 World War Two 또는 the second World War
09 An article
10 (1) 영국 비행사들이 당근을 많이 먹어 야간 시력이 좋아졌다.
   (2) 당근은 많은 비타민 A를 함유하는데, 그것은 정말로 우리 눈을 건강하게 유지해 준다.
11 Ever since then, Americans have enjoyed eating tomatoes.
12 any longer[more]   13 crushing → crushed
14 Because he wanted to prove that tomatoes were safe to eat.

---

01 '비록' 시금치를 먹는 것이 우리에게 초인적인 힘을 주지는 않지만, 시금치는 정말로 많은 영양분을 가지고 있다고 해야 하므로, Although 또는 Though로 고치는 것이 적절하다.

02 '가장 건강한 식품 10개 중 하나로 여겨진다.'고 해야 하므로 수동태로 쓰는 것이 적절하다.

03 시금치를 먹음으로써 초인적인 힘을 얻는 Popeye는 세계적으로 유명한 만화 캐릭터다. Popeye 덕분에, 1930년대 미국의 많은 어린이들이 시금치를 먹기 시작했다. 동사 begin은 목적어로 to부정사와 동명사를 모두 다 사용할 수 있다.

04 ⓐ 시금치는 놀라운 용도로 '사용될 수 있다'고 해야 하므로, 수동태로 쓰는 것이 적절하다. ⓑ 땅에 '숨겨진' 폭탄이라고 해야 하므로 hidden으로 쓰는 것이 적절하다.

05 ⓒ '몇몇 과학자들' ⓓ '특별한 시금치'를 가리킨다.

06 시금치는 흙으로부터 물뿐만 아니라 다른 많은 것들도 흡수한다. 잎에 '감지기'가 있는 특별한 시금치가 폭탄의 흔적을 흡수하면, 감지기가 빛나서 땅속에 있는 '폭탄'을 찾도록 도와준다.

07 (A) 영국 공군이 독일군을 '패배시킨' 것이므로 defeated가 적

절하다. (B) '제2차 세계 대전에서'라고 해야 하므로 during이 적절하다. during+기간을 나타내는 명사, while+주어+동사, (C) keep의 목적격보어에 해당하기 때문에 형용사 healthy가 적절하다.

08 'World War+기수', 또는 'the 서수+World War'로 읽는 것이 적절하다.

09 신문의 '기사'를 가리킨다.

10 영국 공군이 제2차 세계 대전에서 독일군을 패배시킨 레이더 시스템을 비밀로 하려고, '영국 비행사들이 당근을 많이 먹어 야간 시력이 좋아졌다'는 신문 기사를 실었는데, 당근이 야간 시력을 높일 수는 없지만 '실제로 많은 비타민 A를 함유하고 있어서 우리 눈을 건강하게 유지해 준다.'

11 과거의 일이 현재까지 영향을 미쳐 현재와 관련이 있을 때 사용하는 현재완료시제로 쓰는 것이 적절하다.

12 no longer = not ~ any longer[more]: 더 이상 … 아닌

13 토마토가 으깨지는 것이므로 crushed가 적절하다.

14 토마토가 먹기에 안전하다는 것을 증명하기를 원했기 때문이다.

영역별 핵심문제
p.41~45

01 ⑤ 02 ③

03 (1) The magician turned the hat into a rabbit.
(2) What do you advise me to do?
(3) Why don't you get some fresh air?

04 ③ 05 ③

06 (1) the director, the actor, surprising
(2) visitors were scared of

07 ③ 08 ⑤번 → a few 09 ⑤

10 ② 11 move it over to the window

12 ③ 13 ③ 14 ④ 15 ①

16 (1) ate a basket of tomatoes in front of many people watching him
(2) did eat a basket of tomatoes in front of many people who[that] were watching him

17 ④ 18 ②, ⑤ 19 (1) did (2) found

20 ③ 21 ③ 22 ②, ⑤

23 wanting to prove that tomatoes were safe to eat was Robert Johnson

24 ③

25 It is actually considered one of the ten healthiest foods on the planet.

26 (A) spinach (B) nutrients (C) healthiest

27 ② 28 a radar system 29 ④

01 모두 유의어이지만 ⑤번은 반의어로 '이기다 – 굴복하다'라는 의미로 쓰인다.

02 각각 ① interviewer ② meal ③ nutrient ④ ingredient

⑤ flavor를 풀이한 말이다.

03 (1) turn A into B: A를 B로 바꾸다 (2) advise+목적어+to V: 목적어가 V하도록 조언하다 (3) get some fresh air: 신선한 공기를 마시다

04 trace는 '흔적'이라는 명사와 '추적하다'라는 의미의 동사로 쓰인다. 따라서 ③번이 가장 적절하다.

05 주어진 문장의 밑줄 친 부분은 '수도'라는 의미로 쓰였다. capital은 그 외에도 '자본', '대문자의'라는 의미로도 쓰인다.

06 (1) '놀라운'이라는 의미로 쓰이는 것은 surprising이다. (2) '~을 두려워하다'는 'be scared of' 혹은 'be afraid of'를 쓴다.

07 자신의 잘못에 대한 조언을 구하는 말이 들어가는 것이 적절하다.

08 셀 수 있는 명사를 수식하는 'a few'를 쓰는 것이 적절하다.

09 소년은 소녀에게 방 안에 식물을 두라고 권하고 있다.

10 주어진 문장은 조언을 구하는 말이다. 지금까지 토마토를 몇 개밖에 수확하지 못했다는 말을 하며 조언을 구하는 말을 하는 것이 가장 자연스럽다.

11 해석: 토마토 화분이 충분한 햇빛을 얻도록, 소녀는 화분을 창가로 옮길 것이다.

12 소년의 조언에 알겠다며 고마움을 표시하고 있으므로, 한 번 시도해 보겠다는 ③번이 가장 적절하다.

13 ① Popeye라고 '이름이 불리는' 것이므로 named가 적절하다. ② 그 농부들에 의해 '길러진 채소들'이 되어야 하므로 grown을 써야 한다. ④ 비타민 A를 '함유하고 있는' 것이므로 containing이 적절하다. ⑤ 파티에 '초대 받은 사람들'이므로 invited가 적절하다.

14 ① Vegetables가 복수이므로 do make가 적절하다. ② does say가 적절하다 ③ be동사와 상태를 나타내는 look 본동사가 같이 쓰였다. is를 생략하거나 does look으로 강조한다. ⑤ 과거동사 met을 강조할 때는 did meet이 적절하다.

15 첫 번째 문장에서 '사용될 것(수동)'을 뜻하므로 used가 적절하다. 두 번째 문장에서 '두려워하는'(수동)의 내용이므로 scared가 적절하다. be scary of로는 표현하지 않는다.

16 (1) 과거시제이므로 ate를 써야 하고, 명사를 뒤에서 꾸미는 현재분사 watching에 유의하여 영작한다. (2) ate의 강조는 did eat이며, 명사를 뒤에서 수식하는 분사의 앞에 '관계대명사+be동사'를 넣을 수 있다. who를 that으로 써도 된다.

17 do some laundry는 '빨래를 하다'라는 뜻으로 do는 본동사이다. 다른 문장들의 do는 강조를 위해 사용되었다.

18 ② be busy ~ing는 '~하느라 바쁘다'라는 뜻의 동명사의 관용적 표현이며, ⑤는 전치사 by의 목적어로 쓰인 동명사이다. 다른 문장들에서는 모두 현재분사로 사용되었다.

19 (1) 책 '어린 완자'는 3인칭 단수이고, 동사원형 make가 쓰였으므로, 강조의 does 또는 did가 가능하지만, 시제가 과거이므로 did가 적절하다. (2) 이집트의 Giza에서 발견된 pyramids(수동)이므로, 과거분사 found가 적절하다.

20 'with+A+형용사/분사' 형태는 A의 능동/수동 여부에 따라 현재분사 또는 과거분사를 활용한다. ③ with one's legs crossed '다리를 꼰 채로', crossing은 부적절하다.

21 ① (A) 강조 (B) 본동사 ② (A) 본동사 (B) 강조 ③ (A) 강조 (B) 강조 ④ (A) 본동사 (B) 강조 ⑤ (A) 의문문을 만드는 조동사 (B) 본동사

22 ② do likes → does like 또는 likes가 적절하다. ⑤ 강조의 did 뒤에는 동사 원형을 써야 한다.

23 분사가 명사의 앞, 뒤에서 꾸미는 것을 적절히 활용하여 영작한다.

24 ⓐ와 ③: 수도, ① 자본의(형용사), investment: 투자, ② 대문자, ④ 자본금, 자금, ⑤ 사형에 처해야 할(형용사), sentence: 선고하다

25 one of the ten healthiest foods: 가장 건강한 식품 10개 중 하나, 수량형용사 ten을 성상 형용사(사물의 성질, 상태, 종류를 나타내는 형용사) healthiest보다 먼저 쓰는 것이 적절하다.

26 '시금치'를 먹는 것으로 우리가 초인적인 힘을 얻지는 못하지만, 시금치는 정말로 많은 '영양분'을 가지고 있다. 실제로 사람들은 그것을 지구상에서 '가장 건강한' 식품 10개 중 하나로 여긴다.

27 주어진 문장의 It에 주목한다. ②번 앞 문장의 an article을 받고 있으므로 ②번이 적절하다.

28 '레이더 시스템'을 가리킨다.

29 실제로 당근을 많이 먹어서 야간 시력을 높일 수 있는 것은 아니라고 했다.

단원별 예상문제
p.46~49

01 ③　　　　　02 ⑤　　　　　03 ③

04 Do you still keep in touch with your friends?

05 (D)–(A)–(C)–(B)　　　　06 ⑤

07 What about telling her the truth?

08 It's because he broke his mom's favorite plate.

09 ④　　　　　10 ⑤　　　　　11 ③, ⑤, ⑦

12 ①, ②, ⑥, ⑦　　　　13 ③

14 ①, ③

15 eating spinach won't give us super powers, spinach does have a lot of nutrients

16 Although eating spinach will not give super powers to us

17 ⑤

18 (1) 시금치를 먹으면 초인적인 힘을 얻는다.
　　(2) 시금치는 정말로 많은 영양분을 가지고 있고, 실제로 지구상에서 가장 건강한 식품 10개 중 하나로 여겨진다.

19 making → make

20 (A) strong and light　(B) carrots

21 ③　　　　　22 ④

---

23 a man named Robert Johnson wanted to prove that tomatoes were safe to eat

24 ②　　　　　**25** ①

26 (1) 혈압을 낮춰 심장을 건강하게 유지시켜 준다.
　　(2) 피부 문제를 해결해 준다.
　　(3) 살이 빠지도록 도와준다.

01 ①, ②, ④, ⑤는 동사에 '-er'이나 '-or'을 붙여서 사람을 나타내는 명사로 쓰였으나 cooker는 '주방기구'의 뜻으로 사람을 나타내지 않는다.

02 keep away from: ~으로부터 멀어지다

03 '책, 연극, 영화 등에 등장하는 사람'은 '등장인물(character)'이다.

04 keep in touch (with): (~와) 연락하고 지내다

05 (D) 무슨 문제가 있냐고 물음 - (A) 자신의 문제를 말함 - (C) 조언을 제시함 - (B) 조언을 받아들임

06 조언을 구하는 말이 들어가는 것이 자연스러우므로 ⑤번은 적절하지 않다.

07 What about ~?: ~하는 것이 어때?

08 소년이 걱정스러워 보였던 이유는 그의 엄마가 가장 좋아하는 그릇을 깨트려서이다.

09 보미는 소년이 왜 약을 달라고 하는지 궁금해 하고 있으므로 ④번이 대화 내용과 일치한다.

10 Make sure는 that절을 이끈다. 따라서 'Make sure that you take it to the police station.'이라고 말하는 것이 적절하다.

11 명사를 꾸미는 분사가 다른 어구와 결합해서 뒤에서 꾸밀 때는 '관계대명사+be동사'가 생략된 것으로 볼 수 있다. 그러므로, 명사를 앞에서 꾸미거나 서술적 용법으로 사용된 분사를 찾으면, '관계대명사+be동사'가 생략된 것이 아닌 경우에 해당한다. ③, ⑦번은 서술적 용법으로, ⑤번은 명사 앞에서 수식하는 분사로 사용되었다.

12 ① are와 make 두개의 동사가 같이 쓰였다. make만 쓰거나 강조의 do make로 하는 것이 적절하다. ②, ⑥ 강조의 do/does/did 뒤에는 원형동사를 써야 한다. ⑦ 'It ~ that 강조 구문'의 동사는 is와 was 둘 뿐이다.

13 ③번은 전치사의 목적어로 쓰인 동명사이다. 그 외에는 모두 명사의 뒤에서 꾸미는 분사로 사용되었다.

14 분사의 역할이 아니라 종류가 다른 두 개를 찾는 문제이다. ①, ③번만 과거분사로서 ① abandoned dogs, ③ make himself understood이며, 나머지는 모두 현재분사를 써야 한다. ③ smoke coming out, ④ kept him waiting, ⑤ the boy smiling at her

15 has를 강조할 때는 does have로 한다.

16 give는 to를 사용하여 3형식으로 고친다.

17 ⓑ와 ⑤: 강조의 조동사, ① 부정문의 조동사, ② 부사(구) 따위가 문두에 오면서 어순이 도치되는 경우에 쓰이는 조동사, ③

9

~을 하다(본동사), ④ 의문문의 조동사

18 비록 시금치를 먹는 것이 우리에게 초인적인 힘을 주지는 않지만, 시금치는 정말로 많은 영양분을 가지고 있고, 이것은 실제로 지구상에서 가장 건강한 식품 10개 중 하나로 여겨진다.

19 '전함을 만드는 데 사용될 수도 있다'라고 해야 하므로 to부정사의 부사적 용법(목적)이 되도록, make로 고치는 것이 적절하다. be used to ~ing: ~하는 데 익숙하다

20 그것은 스코틀랜드의 연구원들에 의해 '당근'을 재료로 하여 만들어진 매우 '강하고 가벼운' 물질이다.

21 이 글은 '미래에는, 당근이 실제로 전쟁에 이용될지도 모른다.'는 내용의 글이므로, 주제로는 ③번 '미래에 전쟁에서의 당근의 용도'가 적절하다.

22 주어진 문장의 They에 주목한다. ④번 앞 문장의 many people을 받고 있으므로 ④번이 적절하다.

23 safe to eat: 먹기에 안전한

24 1800년대까지 대부분의 미국인들은 토마토에 '독성이 있다'고 생각했다.

25 앞에 나오는 내용에 추가하는 내용이 뒤에 이어지므로 In addition이 가장 적절하다. ② 그러므로, ④ 그에 반해서

26 (3) 오랜 시간 동안 허기를 느끼지 않고 배부른 상태를 유지하게 하여 살이 빠지도록 도와준다. stay full: 허기를 느끼지 않고 배부른 상태를 유지하다

서술형 실전문제 p.50~51

01 It is so hard to lose weight.

02 lose weight

03 is something wrong

04 ⓐ surprising ⓑ leaving ⓒ eating ⓓ covered
ⓔ written ⓕ eating

이유: ⓒ와 ⓕ 두 개는 동명사이고, 나머지는 모두 분사이다.

05 (1) British pilots did eat a lot of carrots.

(2) Do place a bowl of crushed tomatoes in a corner of your room.

(3) People in Hong Kong do love freedom.

06 which does keep our eyes healthy

07 to die

08 (A) named (B) watching (C) happened

09 (1) 토마토에 독성이 있다.

(2) 토마토를 먹는 것을 즐겼다.

10 The British government wanted to keep this technology a secret, so it published an article in the newspaper.

11 British pilots improved their night vision because they ate a lot of carrots.

---

01 가주어 It과 진주어 to부정사구를 이용하여 문장을 쓸 수 있다. lose weight: 몸무게를 줄이다

02 소녀가 소년에게 개를 매일 산책시키라고 제안한 이유는 그렇게 하는 것이 소년이 살을 빼도록 도움을 줄 것이라고 생각하기 때문이다.

03 엄마에게 무슨 문제가 있는지 묻는 말이 들어가는 것이 적절하다. 'what's the matter'를 써도 좋다.

04 ⓐ '놀라운 방법'(능동) ⓑ '7시에 출발하는 기차'(능동) ⓒ '먹음'으로써, 전치사의 목적어로 쓰인 동명사 ⓓ '담쟁이로 덮인 건물 벽'(수동) ⓔ '에머슨에 의해 쓰여진 시'(수동) ⓕ '먹는 것'을 즐겨왔다. enjoy의 목적어로 쓰인 동명사

05 (1) 과거 시제이므로 did eat이 적절하다. (2) 명령문의 강조는 동사 앞에 Do를 쓴다. (3) 주어가 복수이고 현재시제이므로 do love로 강조한다.

06 선행사 vitamin A를 받으며, 접속사 역할까지 하는 관계대명사 which를 사용하고, 동사 keep을 강조하는 does를 이용해서 알맞게 배열한다.

07 expect+목적어+to부정사

08 (A) Robert Johnson이라는 '이름의(~라고 이름 지어진)' 남자라고 해야 하므로 named가 적절하다. (B) 그를 '지켜보는' 많은 사람들이라고 해야 하므로 watching이 적절하다. (C) happen은 수동태로 만들 수 없으므로 happened가 적절하다.

09 1800년대까지 대부분의 미국인들은 토마토에 독성이 있다고 생각했지만, Robert Johnson이 토마토가 먹기에 안전하다는 것을 증명한 이후로, 미국인들은 토마토를 먹는 것을 즐겼다.

10 keep+목적어+목적격보어: ~을 …한 상태로 유지시키다

11 영국 정부가 신문에 낸 기사의 내용을 가리킨다.

창의사고력 서술형 문제 p.52

|모범답안|

01 growing well, she has gotten only a few tomatoes, her advice, where she has the pot, in the kitchen, tomato plants need about 7 hours of sunlight a day, she will move the pot over to the window

02 (1) Unlike the man presenting the plan, the boss is sleeping in a chair.

(2) Unlike my sister reading a book on the sofa, I am cleaning the table.

03 (A) your health (B) lower blood pressure
(C) skin problems (D) soft and clear

단원별 모의고사 p.53~57

01 ④ 02 ④ 03 ④

04 (C)-(A)-(E)-(D)-(B)

05 ④   06 fine dust, put some plants

07 ⑤   08 ③

09 What do you think I should do?   10 ③

11 It's because they are rich in vitamin A, so they'll keep Suho's eyes healthy.

12 ⑤   13 ⑤   14 ③, ⑥   15 ③

16 (1) This new material has already been used to make bicycles.

(2) Some scientists have used this characteristic of spinach to find bombs hidden in the ground.

17 ⑤

18 real person → world-famous cartoon character

19 spinach   20 does keep

21 ②   22 and it

23 ⓐ eighteen hundreds   ⓑ eighteen twenty

24 ①, ②, ④   25 ④   26 ②   27 ③, ⑤

28 By lowering blood pressure.

29 Garlic tea which[that] is mixed with honey makes you get better faster.

01 ① keep ~ a secret: ~을 비밀로 하다 ② keep away: 멀리하다 ③ keep in touch: 연락하다 ④ make use of: ~을 이용하다 ⑤ keep the change: 잔돈을 가지다

02 주어진 단어는 '명사-명사(행위자)'의 관계에 있다. ④번은 '형용사-명사'의 연결이다. economic: 경제의, 경제성이 있는 economist: 경제학자

03 defeat은 '~를 패배시키다'라는 의미이므로 '전투에서 이기는 것에 성공하지 못하다'는 적절한 풀이가 아니다.

04 (C) 체중을 줄이는 것이 힘들다고 말하며 조언을 요청함 (A) 개를 산책시키라고 조언함 (E) 그것이 어떻게 체중을 줄이는데 도움이 되는지 되물음 (D) 이에 대한 설명 (B) 생각해 보겠다고 말함

05 빈칸에는 상대를 걱정하며 안부를 묻는 말이 들어가는 것이 적절하다. ④번은 무엇을 잘못했는지를 묻는 말이다.

06 소녀는 미세먼지 때문에 목이 아프다고 생각하고, 이에 소년은 방 안에 식물을 두라고 조언하고 있다.

07 돈을 저축할 수 없다고 말하며 조언을 요청하고 있으므로 더 많은 옷을 사라는 조언은 적절하지 않다.

08 모두 선생님에게 도움을 요청하라는 의미이지만 ③번은 선생님이 너에게 도움을 요청하는 것을 확실히 하라는 의미이다.

09 조언을 구하는 말로 자주 쓰이는 표현은 'What do you think I should do?'이다.

10 새벽 2시까지 휴대 전화로 영화를 본 결과 눈이 충혈된 것이므로 'that's why'라고 쓰는 것이 적절하다.

11 Anna가 수호에게 당근과 토마토를 많이 먹어 보라고 한 이유는 그것들에 비타민 A가 많아서 눈을 건강하게 유지해 줄 것이기

때문이다.

12 수호가 휴대전화로 영화를 얼마나 오래 보는지는 위 글을 읽고 답할 수 없다.

13 ⑤ included → including

14 ③, ⑥번이 주어진 문장의 밑줄 친 does와 같은 용법인 동사를 강조하는 do/did로 사용되었다. ①, ②, ④번은 모두 조동사로서 각각 ① 의문문, ② 부정문, ④ 명령문을 만들기 위해 사용됐다. ⑤, ⑦번은 본동사로 쓰였다.

15 ③번은 containing(현재분사)이 들어가야 하지만 주어진 문장과 나머지는 모두 수동의 의미로 명사를 뒤에서 꾸미는 과거분사가 들어가야 한다. *repellent: 방충제

16 (1) used는 과거분사의 서술 용법으로, (2) hidden은 과거분사의 한정 용법으로 명사 뒤에서 꾸미는 역할이다.

17 ⑤번만 현재완료시제에 사용되어 동사의 일부가 되었다. 나머지는 모두 형용사적 용법으로 사용된 과거분사이다. *crush: 즙 음료

18 Popeye는 세계적으로 유명한 '만화 캐릭터'다.

19 '시금치'를 가리킨다.

20 조동사 does를 사용하여 고치는 것이 적절하다.

21 (A)와 ②: (신문·잡지의) 글, 기사, ① (같은 종류의 물건 중) 한 개, 한 가지, ③, ⑤: 물품, 물건, ④ (조약·계약 등의) 조항, 조목

22 계속적 용법의 관계대명사 = 접속사+대명사

23 연도는 두 단위씩 끊어서 읽는 것이 적절하다. 단, 2000년이 넘어가면 'two thousand+나머지 숫자'로 읽는 것이 적절하다. ⓐ의 경우는 끝부분을 hundreds로 읽으면 된다.

24 ⓒ와 ③, ⑤: 부사적 용법, ①, ④: 명사적 용법, ②: 형용사적 용법

25 이 글은 '요즘 우리는 토마토를 두려워하지 않지만, 1800년대까지 대부분의 미국인들은 토마토에 독성이 있다고 생각했고, 몇몇 곤충들은 여전히 그것을 무서워한다.'는 내용의 글이므로, 제목으로는 ④번 '토마토, 가장 무서운 채소'가 적절하다.

26 1800년대까지 대부분의 미국인들은 토마토에 '독성이 있다'고 생각했지만, Robert Johnson이 토마토가 먹기에 '안전하다'는 것을 증명하기를 원했다고 하는 것이 문맥상 적절하다. ① harmless: 해가 없는, ③ precious: 귀중한, harmful: 해로운, ⑤ evil: 사악한

27 ⓒ와 ①, ②, ④: 계속 용법, ③, ⑤ 경험 용법

28 '혈압을 낮춤으로써' 심장을 건강하게 유지시켜 준다.

29 mixed 앞에 주격 관계대명사(which/that)와 be동사가 생략되어 있다.

This Is Korea

시험대비 실력평가
p.62

01 lend 02 ⑤ 03 ⑤

04 (1) (w)etsuit (2) (w)orldwide (3) ad (4) bridge

05 (1) is good for (2) wish for (3) Cheer up

(4) walk along (5) get into

06 ②

01 주어진 단어는 반의어 관계이다. lend: 빌려주다, borrow: 빌리다

02 '가치가 있지만 물리적으로 존재하지는 않는'을 의미하는 말은 intangible(무형의)이다.

03 experience: 경험

04 wetsuit: 잠수복, worldwide: 세계적으로, ad: 광고, bridge: 다리

05 cheer up: 격려하다, wish for: 기원하다, get into: ~에 들어가다, be good for: ~에 유익하다, walk along: ~을 따라 걷다

06 주어진 문장에서 press는 '누르다'를 의미하며 이와 같은 의미로 쓰인 것은 ②번이다. 나머지는 모두 '신문, 언론'을 뜻한다.

서술형 시험대비
p.63

01 past

02 (1) (p)ath (2) community (3) (p)romote

(4) jellyfish

03 (1) We had a good harvest last year.

(2) Money does not always bring happiness.

(3) Our national heritage was destroyed by the fire.

04 (1) We walked along the street for an hour.

(2) This book is suitable for elementary school students.

(3) Let's make double-sided copies to save paper.

05 (1) promote (2) realize (3) several

(4) underwater (5) volcanic

01 주어진 단어는 반의어 관계이다. future: 미래, past: 과거

02 path: 길, community: 지역 공동체, promote: 홍보하다, jellyfish: 해파리

03 good harvest: 풍년, happiness: 행복, heritage: 유산

04 walk along: ~을 따라 걷다, be suitable for: ~에 적절하다, make double-sided copies: 양면 복사를 하다

05 realize: 깨닫다, promote: 홍보하다, underwater: 물속의, 수중의, volcanic: 화산의, several: 몇몇의

교과서
Conversation

핵심 Check
p.64~65

1 I wonder where the photo was taken.

2 (C) → (B) → (A)

교과서 대화문 익히기

Check(√) True or False
p.66

1 T 2 T 3 T 4 F

교과서 확인학습
p.68~69

Listen & Speak 1 A-1

bridge, ad, where the photo was taken / How / with, last summer

Listen & Speak 1 A-2

I wonder why, waiting in line / get into / famous / on / try

Listen & Speak 2 A-1

I'd like to borrow / explain how to use it / Press, what to do

Listen & Speak 2 A-2

somewhere / walk along / Could you explain / long hiking path / enjoy your trip

Communicate A

I wonder where / check it out / strong beat, traditional / community / Could you explain / traditionally, cheer up, good harvest / rhythm / completes / Why not

Progress Check 1

I wonder why there are so many cars / going on vacation / why don't we

copy machine / how to make double-sided copies /
Press, press

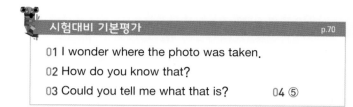
시험대비 기본평가   p.70

01 I wonder where the photo was taken.
02 How do you know that?
03 Could you tell me what that is?   04 ⑤

01 간접의문문 어순으로 '의문사+주어+동사'의 어순이 알맞다.

04 Tom이 구체적으로 제주 올레길에 대한 설명을 요청한 것으로
   보아 Tom이 이미 올레길에 대해 잘 알고 있다는 설명은 일치하
   지 않는다.

시험대비 실력평가   p.71~72

01 (E) → (C) → (B) → (D) → (A)   02 ⑤
03 ⓑ → was taken   04 ⑤   05 ⑤
06 ⑤   07 (C) → (B) → (D) → (E) → (A)
08 ④
09 Dancing together completes the music.
10 ⑤

01 (E) 궁금함에 대한 대답 → (C) 유명한지 질문→ (B) 대답 및
   이유 설명 → (D) 제안 → (A) 동의

02 ⑤번을 제외한 나머지는 모두 설명을 요청하는 표현이다.

03 사진이 찍혔으므로 수동태가 알맞다.

04 소녀가 다리 사진을 찍고 싶다는 내용은 대화를 통해 알 수 없다.

05 (A)는 진행을 나타내는 현재분사 waiting, (B) get into: 들어
   가다, get out: 나가다, (C) TV에 나왔음을 나타내는 on이 적
   절하다.

06 Brian과 수진은 줄을 서 있는 사람들을 보고 있다.

07 (C) 하고 싶은 일 부탁 → (B) 허락 → (D) 양면 복사 방법 질
   문 → (E) 대답 → (A) 감사 표현

08 궁금함을 나타내는 표현으로 ④번으로 바꾸어 쓸 수 있다.

09 complete: 완성하다

10 궁금한 것을 알고 싶다는 말에 노력에 감사하다는 대답은 어색
   하다.

서술형 시험대비   p.73

01 Could you explain how to use it?
02 She gets to know what she should do.
03 (A) waiting in line   (B) the new bakery
   (C) get into   (D) it was on a TV program

04 (1) band   (2) strong   (3) farmers   (4) harvest
05 They are going to join some people dancing to
   the rhythm.

02 버튼을 누르면 여자는 무엇을 해야 하는지 알 수 있다.

03 Brian과 Sujin은 새로 생긴 제과점 앞에 줄을 서 있는 많은 사
   람들을 보았다. 사람들은 그곳에 들어가고 싶어 했다. 새로 생긴
   제과점은 매우 인기가 있었다. 왜냐하면 TV 프로그램에 나왔었
   기 때문이다. Brian과 Sujin은 함께 그곳의 빵을 먹어보고 싶
   어 했다.

05 Jaden과 유리는 대화 후 춤추는 사람들과 함께 할 것이다.

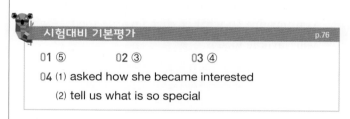
교과서
Grammar

핵심 Check   p.74~75

1 (1) had   (2) visited
2 (1) will she make → she will make
  (2) was Sarah → Sarah was

시험대비 기본평가   p.76

01 ⑤   02 ③   03 ④
04 (1) asked how she became interested
   (2) tell us what is so special

01 기준이 되는 시점이 과거이고, 그 이전에 일어난 동작이므로 과
   거완료시제를 찾는다.

02 의문사가 없는 의문문의 간접의문문은 if 또는 whether가 접속
   사 역할을 한다.

03 ① '지금까지'이므로 현재완료시제로 써야 한다. had lived →
   has lived, ② has → had ③ had found → found, ⑤ 과거
   시점 이전에 일어난 일이므로 had gone이 적절하다.

04 간접의문문을 만들 때, 의문사는 접속사 역할을 하고 '의문사+주
   어+동사'의 어순이 된다. 시제와 수에 유의하여, 동사를 적절히
   쓴다. 의문사가 주어일 때는 순서가 바뀌지 않는 것도 주의한다.

시험대비 실력평가   p.77~79

01 ③   02 ⑤   03 ④   04 ④
05 ⑤   06 had been → has been   07 ⑤
08 ⑤   09 ②   10 ④   11 ③
12 ⑤

13 many customers had spent quite a long time lining up in order to eat pork cutlet

14 Why do you think the temples are famous?

15 (1) asked his sister why people could not fly in the sky

(2) told his friend that he had touched a hive that morning

---

01 ③ 과거시점(Lucy asked) 이전에 발생한 일이다. has broken → had broken이 적절하다.

02 간접의문문의 어순은 '의문사+주어+동사'이다. 원래의 의문문 'What is that?'에서 What은 주어로 쓰인 것이 아님에 유의하여 'what that is' 어순으로 배열한 정답을 찾는다.

03 '의문사+be+there+주어'는 간접의문문이 될 때, '의문사+there+be+주어'의 어순이 된다.

04 ① had read → has read ② 'San Francisco로 이사를 하기 전에 New York에서 살았다'는 문장이므로 'William lived[had lived] in New York before he moved to San Francisco.'가 적절하다. ③ '민수가 보고서를 완성해야 한다고 요구'한 것이므로 had completed → (should) complete ⑤ had not eaten → have not eaten

05 ① what so special is → what is so special ② do I like → I like ③ Do you imagine how old → How old do you imagine ④ what is your favorite food → what your favorite food is

06 과거의 특정 시점 이전에 발생한 일을 과거완료시제로 표현해야 한다. 종속절이 'since+과거시제'이므로, 주절은 과거완료가 아니라 현재완료시제로 표현하는 것이 적절하다.

07 간접의문문의 접속사 역할을 하는 who가 주어로 사용되었으므로, 어순을 바꿀 필요가 없다. 'who took away her kids' toys' 원래 어순 그대로 쓰는 것이 적절하다.

08 <보기>의 had found는 과거완료시제 중 '완료' 용법으로 쓰였다. ①, ③, ④는 '계속', ②는 '경험' 용법이다.

09 <보기> if는 조건의 '부사절' 접속사이며, ②도 그렇다. 나머지는 모두 '의문사 없는 간접의문문을 이끄는 접속사'이다.

10 본동사가 think일 때, 간접의문문의 의문사는 문두로 보내고 어순은 '주어+동사' 순으로 한다.

11 ① 내용상 '내가 사준 것'이 '그녀가 목걸이를 잃어버린 것'보다 먼저이기 때문에 'Cecilia lost the necklace which I had bought for her.'가 적절하다. ② had melted → melted ④ have → had ⑤ has → had

12 ① Do you think where → Where do you think ② what did your action mean → what your action meant ③ did anyone see → anyone saw ④ how the writer of these books old → how old the writer of these books is

13 과거완료시제(had spent)와, 'spend+시간+V-ing'를 활용하

여, 주어진 어구를 적절히 배열한다.

14 간접의문문을 활용하는 문제이다. 생각 동사 think, believe, imagine 등이 주절에 올 때, 간접의문문의 의문사를 문두로 보내는 것에 유의한다.

15 (1) 의문사 why를 간접의문문으로 활용한 문장이다. '지호는 누나에게 왜 사람이 하늘을 날 수 없는지 물어봤다.' (2) 과거완료시제를 이용하여, 어구를 배열하는 문장이다. 'Pooh는 그의 친구에게 그 날 아침에 벌집을 건드렸다고 말했다.'

01 (1) collected many Korean treasures that some French had stolen before

(2) wonders how she can promote the haenyeo worldwide

(3) he found someone had broken into his house

(4) Can you guess where the photographer took

02 (1) how they could get to the meeting on time

(2) which boy the girl next to Jane chose at the blind date

(3) if(또는 whether) Shrek hasn't learned German yet

(4) where Alex found the baby tiger

(5) the new employee looks

03 had only seen black-and-white photos of haenyeo who

04 (1) Can you tell me where the magician was when he disappeared?

(2) Does the young student know how far the hotel is?

(3) Do you know if[whether] I could take pictures of haenyeo?

(4) They didn't understand why the girl wanted to take their pictures.

(5) Tell me what Zin Kim promised the haenyeo.

(6) I wonder why Jejudo isn't suitable for farming.

05 The haenyeo had not thought that she was pretty until the photographer took her picture twelve years ago.

06 (1) Tom wondered how haenyeo could stay in the water for so long without any breathing devices.

(2) They are studying how catching too much marine life can destroy the ocean.

(3) The witch asked the mirror who the most beautiful woman in the world was.

(4) The mother goat did not know when the babies opened the door to the wolf.

01 (1), (3) 과거의 특정 시점 이전에 일어난 일은 '과거완료시제'로 쓰는 것에 유의한다. (2), (4) '간접의문문'의 어순은 '의문사+주어+동사'이다. 특히, (4)번에서 guess라는 생각 동사가 오지만, yes나 no로 대답이 가능한 의문문의 경우 의문사가 앞으로 가지 않는 것에 유의한다.

02 '간접의문문'의 어순은 '의문사+주어+동사'이다. 어순이 바뀔 때는 수와 시제에 유의해야 한다. (5)번에서 think와 같은 생각 동사가 있을 때는 의문사가 문두로 와야 한다.

03 only see를 과거완료시제로 표현하면 had only seen이다. 빈칸 뒤의 looked가 동사이므로 주어 역할의 관계대명사 who를 마지막에 쓴다.

04 (1) was the magician → the magician was (2) how the hotel is far → how far the hotel is (3) could I → if(또는 whether) I could (4) did the girl want → the girl wanted (5) did Zin Kim promise → Zin Kim promised (6) why is Jejudo not → why Jejudo isn't

05 과거의 어느 특정 시점을 기준으로 그 전의 동작은 과거완료시제로 표현한다. 12년 전에 사진작가가 사진을 찍기까지는 자신을 예쁘다고 생각하지 않았으므로, 부정의 과거완료시제를 사용해서 표현하면, 'had not thought that she was pretty'가 적절하다.

06 주어진 단어들 중 동사의 수와 시제에 유의하여, 간접의문문의 어순과 내용에 알맞게 적절한 문장을 영작한다.

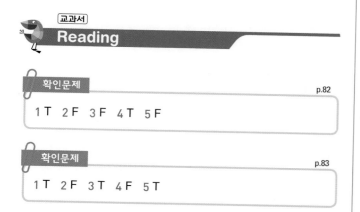

교과서 Reading

확인문제 p.82

1 T 2 F 3 F 4 T 5 F

확인문제 p.83

1 T 2 F 3 T 4 F 5 T

교과서 확인학습 A p.84~85

01 Female Divers
02 underwater photographer, has promoted
03 without any breathing devices
04 made UNESCO's Intangible Cultural Heritage list
05 was interviewed
06 become interested in
07 happened to
08 was surprised to find
09 looked very tired
10 kept laughing
11 should take
12 isn't it difficult

13 why I wanted
14 in their wetsuits
15 very special
16 show, to
17 opened up
18 make them, beautiful
19 more about
20 so special
21 can tell you
22 strong women
23 is not suitable for, the breadwinners for
24 form, each other
25 more-experienced, less-experienced
26 without, can't catch
27 is good for
28 at one time in one place
29 planning to do
30 attended, give a talk
31 held my hand
32 so much
33 such a special person
34 with happiness
35 was deeply moved
36 can never forget
37 more beautiful stories about them

교과서 확인학습 B p.86~87

1 Haenyeo, Female Divers of Korea

2 For the past several years, the underwater photographer Zin Kim has promoted the culture of Jeju haenyeo worldwide.

3 Haenyeo are Korean female divers who harvest seafood without any breathing devices.

4 Their culture made UNESCO's Intangible Cultural Heritage list in 2016.

5 At her studio last week, Zin Kim was interviewed about her experience of taking pictures of haenyeo.

6 Q. How did you become interested in taking photos of haenyeo?

7 One day, I happened to take pictures of a haenyeo.

8 I was surprised to find that she was enjoying her job.

9 Until then, I had only seen black-and-white photos of haenyeo who looked very tired.

10 However, she kept laughing even after she had been in the water for over five hours.

11 I realized then that I should take pictures of haenyeo.

12 Q. You take beautiful pictures of them, but isn't it difficult to take pictures of haenyeo?

13 At first, they didn't understand why I wanted to take their pictures.

14 They didn't think they looked pretty in their wetsuits.

15 So, I said to them, "You're very special.

16 I want to show your culture to the world."

17 They opened up to me then.

18 Of course, I also promised them that I would make them look beautiful in my pictures.

19 Q. Could you tell us more about haenyeo?

20 What's so special about them?

21 I can tell you three things.

22 First, haenyeo are a symbol of strong women.

23 Jejudo, which is a volcanic island, is not suitable for farming, so many haenyeo have become the breadwinners for their families.

24 Second, haenyeo form their own communities and help each other.

25 For example, more-experienced haenyeo train less-experienced haenyeo.

26 Third, because they stay in the water without any breathing devices, haenyeo can't catch a lot of seafood.

27 This is good for the underwater environment.

28 Catching too much marine life at one time in one place can destroy the ocean.

29 Q. Lastly, please tell us what you're planning to do in the future.

30 I once attended an overseas exhibition with a couple of haenyeo to give a talk about their lives.

31 When I finished my talk, one of the haenyeo held my hand tightly.

32 She said to me, "Thank you so much.

33 I've never known in my whole life that I was such a special person."

34 She was crying with happiness.

35 Everyone in the audience was deeply moved.

36 I can never forget that moment, so I'll continue to take pictures of haenyeo.

37 I want to tell more beautiful stories about them to many more people in the world.

시험대비 실력평가
p.88~91

01 ②, ④   02 ⑤   03 ④   04 ③

05 laughing   06 ④   07 ⑤   08 ②

09 they didn't understand why I wanted to take their pictures

10 (A) attended (B) such (C) so

11 ⑤   12 ④   13 ②, ③

14 breadwinners   15 that → which

16 because they stay in the water without any breathing devices, haenyeo can't catch a lot of seafood

17 ②   18 ③   19 ①

20 looking → look   21 ④   22 ③

23 suitable → not suitable 또는 unsuitable

24 ①, ⑤   25 to catch

01 주격 관계대명사 who와 that이 적절하다.

02 ⓑ와 ⑤: ~이 되다, ~의 지위를 얻다; ~으로 승진[승격]하다, 존스는 5년 만에 교수가 되었다. ① 만들다[제작/제조하다], ② (~로 하여금 …하게) 만들다[하다], ③ 선출[임명/지명]하다, ④ (억지로 무엇을 하게) 만들다[시키다]

03 해녀는 어떤 호흡 장치도 '사용하지 않고' 해산물을 채취하는 한국의 여성 잠수부들이다.

04 대답에서 해녀의 사진을 찍는 것에 관심을 가지게 된 이유를 설명하고 있으므로, 빈칸에 들어갈 질문으로는 ③번 '어떻게 해녀의 사진을 찍는 것에 관심을 가지게 되었나요?'가 적절하다.

05 keep -ing: 계속 ~하다

06 (B)와 ②: 계속 용법, ①, ④: 완료 용법, ③: 결과 용법, ⑤: 경험 용법

07 주어진 문장의 then에 주목한다. 그들이 '그때' 제게 마음을 열었다고 했을 때의 '그때'는 ⑤번 앞 문장에서 말한 "여러분들은 아주 특별해요. 저는 여러분의 문화를 세계에 알리고 싶어요."라고 말한 때를 가리키므로 ⑤번이 적절하다.

08 이 글은 '글쓴이가 해녀들을 설득하여 그들의 사진을 찍게 된 과정'을 설명하는 글이므로, 제목으로는 ②번 '와! 해녀들은 내가 사진을 통해 그들의 문화를 알리도록 허락해 주었어!'가 적절하다.

09 why는 의문문의 문두에 쓰이는 의문사이지만 간접의문문에서는 문장 안에 쓰인다. 이때는 보통 주어가 동사 앞에 와서 '의문사+주어+동사'의 순서로 쓰인다.

10 (A) 박람회에 '참가한' 적이 있다고 해야 하므로 attended가 옳다. attend to: ~을 돌보다, 시중들다, (B) 'such+a+형용사+명사'의 순서로 써야 하므로 such가 옳다. 'so+형용사+a+명사', (C) '그 순간을 절대 잊을 수가 없기 때문에 해녀의 사진을 계속해서 찍을 것'이라고 해야 하므로 so가 옳다.

11 중반부의 'She was crying with happiness. Everyone in the audience was deeply moved.'를 통해 'touching'을 찾을 수 있다. touching: 감동적인, ① 혼란스러운, ② 재미있는, 흥미로운, ③ 우울하게 만드는, 우울한, ④ 지루한

12 Zin Kim이 얼마나 오랫동안 해녀들의 사진을 찍어 왔는지는 대답할 수 없다. ① With a couple of haenyeo. ② To give a talk about haenyeo's lives. ③ She said, "Thank you so much. I've never known in my whole life that I was such a special person." ⑤ She wants to tell more

beautiful stories about haenyeo.

13 ⓐ와 ②, ③: 경험 용법, ① 완료 용법, ④ 완료 용법, ⑤ 계속 용법

14 필수적인 것들을 위해 가족이 필요한 돈을 버는 사람들, breadwinner: (집안의) 생계비를 버는 사람, 가장

15 관계대명사 that은 계속적 용법으로 쓸 수 없으므로 which로 바꾸는 것이 적절하다.

16 앞 문장의 내용을 가리킨다.

17 이 글은 '해녀에 대해 무엇이 특별한지'를 설명하는 글이므로, 주제로는 ②번 '해녀에 대한 특별한 점들'이 적절하다. ① subject: (그림·사진 등의) 대상[소재]

18 ⓐ in: '착용'을 나타내는 전치사, ⓑ show는 3형식으로 고칠 때 전치사 to를 사용한다.

19 ①은 Zin Kim을 가리키고, 나머지는 다 '해녀들'을 가리킨다.

20 사역동사 make의 목적격보어이므로 동사원형으로 고치는 것이 적절하다.

21 전반부의 'they didn't understand why I wanted to take their pictures'를 통해 'puzzled'를, 중반부의 'They opened up to me then.'을 통해 'consenting'을 찾을 수 있다. puzzled: 어리둥절해하는, 얼떨떨한, consenting: 동의[승낙]하는, ① nervous: 초조한, ② delighted: 아주 기뻐하는, upset: 속상한, ③ agreeing: 동의하는, ⑤ confused: 혼란스러워 하는, disappointed: 실망한

22 앞의 내용의 예가 나오고 있으므로 For example이 가장 적절하다. ① 그러므로, ④ 게다가, ⑤ 그 결과

23 제주도는 화산섬이라서 농사에 '적합하지 않다'로 고치는 것이 적절하다.

24 (B)와 ②, ③, ④: 동명사(목적, 용도), ①, ⑤: 현재분사(동작의 진행)

25 to부정사를 진주어로 하여 고치는 것이 적절하다.

서술형 시험대비
p.92~93

01 by chance (또는 by accident)

02 have → had

03 (A) enjoying   (B) laughing

04 (A) For   (B) any   (C) Intangible

05 Haenyeo 또는 haenyeo

06 two thousand (and) sixteen 또는 twenty sixteen

07 marine

08 (A) breathing devices   (B) can't catch

09 (1) 해녀들은 강인한 여성의 상징이다.

  (2) 해녀들은 그들 자신의 공동체를 조직하고 서로 돕는다.

  (3) 어떤 호흡 장치도 사용하지 않고 물속에 머물기 때문에, 해녀는 많은 해산물을 채취할 수가 없다.

10 what you're planning to do in the future

11 me   12 touched

13 (A) take pictures   (B) more beautiful stories

01 by chance = by accident = accidentally: 우연히, 뜻밖에, happen to do it = do it by chance[by accident]: 우연히 ~하다

02 Until then이 있으므로 과거완료로 고치는 것이 적절하다.

03 Zin Kim이 우연히 한 해녀의 사진을 찍게 되었을 때, 그녀는 자신의 직업을 '즐겼고' '다섯 시간이 넘도록 물속에 있은 후에도 계속 '웃었다'. Zin Kim은 그것에 놀라서 해녀의 사진을 찍어야겠다고 결심했다.

04 (A) '지난 몇 년 동안'이라고 해야 하므로 For가 옳다. during은 뒤에 기간을 나타내는 명사를 써서, 특정 기간 중의 어느 한 시점을 가리키고, for는 'how long?'에 대한 답을 나타낸다. (B) 부정의 뜻을 가지는 without이 있으므로 any가 옳다. (C) '무형문화유산'이라고 해야 하므로 Intangible이 옳다. tangible: 유형의

05 haenyeo를 복수로 취급했고, 한 명의 해녀는 a haenyeo라고 하는 것이 적절하다.

06 2001년부터 2009년까지는 two thousand (and) ~로 읽는 것이 적절하다.

07 바다 혹은 바다에서 사는 동식물들과 관련된, marine: 바다의, 해양의

08 해녀는 어떤 '호흡 장치'도 사용하지 않고 물속에 머물러서, 많은 해산물을 '채취할 수가 없기' 때문이다.

09 인터뷰 질문에 대한 답 세 가지를 쓰는 것이 적절하다.

10 간접의문문의 순서(의문사+주어+동사)로 쓰는 것이 적절하다.

11 소유격+신체의 일부를 나타내는 명사 = 목적격+전치사+the+ 신체의 일부를 나타내는 명사

12 moved = touched: 감동한

13 Zin Kim은 해녀 중 한 분이 그녀에게 감사를 표했던 순간을 절대 잊을 수가 없기 때문에 해녀의 '사진을 계속해서 찍을' 것이다. 그녀는 그들에 대한 '더 많은 아름다운 이야기들을' 세계의 더 많은 사람들에게 알려 주고 싶어 한다.

영역별 핵심문제
p.95~100

01 happiness   02 ②   03 ⑤

04 (1) go on (a) vacation   (2) a couple of

  (3) cheer up   (4) Give, a call

05 (1) overwork   (2) greenhouse   (3) breathe

  (4) device   (5) heritage

06 He wants to make double-sided copies.

07 He will press the button for double-sided copies.

08 ③   09 ⑤   10 ⓐ → check it out

17

11 beat　　12 ⑤　　　　13 had eaten

14 ①, ②　　15 ③, ④

16 (1) thinking about which university he should go
　　 to

　　(2) wondering when the rain will stop

17 (1) had pulled　(2) was killed

　　(3) had already gone　(4) had been

　　(5) had seen　(6) appeared

18 (1) what time the store opens

　　(2) how we can contact the store manager

　　(3) where the store is located

　　(4) if[whether] there is any subway station near the
　　 store

19 (1) ⓑ　(2) ⓒ　(3) ⓐ　(4) ⓒ　(5) ⓐ　(6) ⓓ　(7) ⓑ

　　(8) ⓓ

20 (1) Vanessa had cleaned the windows and (had)
　　 washed the dishes

　　(2) Sally had given the dog some food and (had)
　　 watered the plant

21 (1) why she had to learn how to cook in another
　　 country

　　(2) if there are any seats left on the plane

22 ③　　　　23 ①, ④　　24 ⑤　　　　25 ②

26 ③　　　　27 ⑤　　　　28 ④　　　　29 ②

---

01 주어진 단어는 형용사와 명사의 관계이다.

02 '가족을 부양하려고 돈을 버는 가족 구성원'을 나타내는 말은 breadwinner(생계를 책임지는 사람, 가장)이다.

03 path: 오솔길, 작은 길

04 go on (a) vacation: 휴가가다, a couple of: 두 서너 개의, cheer up: 힘을 북돋아 주다, 격려하다, give (someone) a call: 전화를 걸다

05 heritage: 유산, greenhouse: 온실, device: 장치, breathe: 호흡하다, overwork: 과로

06 Jack은 양면 복사를 하고 싶다.

07 Jack은 시작 버튼을 누르기 전에 양면 복사 버튼을 누를 것이다.

08 주어진 문장은 구체적인 설명을 요청하는 것이므로 이어지는 문장에서 구체적 제주 올레길에 대한 설명이 이어지는 (C)에 들어가는 것이 적절하다.

09 Tom이 제주도에서 무엇을 하고 싶은지는 대화를 통해 알 수 없다.

10 '동사+부사'로 이루어진 구동사의 목적어가 인칭대명사일 때 목적어가 동사 바로 뒤에 위치한다.

11 '일련의 규칙적인 움직임 또는 치는 동작 중의 하나'를 가리키는 말은 beat(소리)이다.

12 유리는 함께 춤추는 것이 음악을 완성한다고 설명한다.

13 대학 졸업 전에 처음 치즈 퐁듀를 먹었다고 했으므로, 과거완료시제이다. before와 같이 명백한 전후 관계를 알 수 있는 접속사가 있을 때는 과거시제로 써도 괜찮다. 그러나 빈칸이 두 개이므로 과거완료시제를 쓰는 것이 적절하다.

14 ① where the monsters are from ② why 뒤에는 완전한 문장 구조가 와야 한다. in 뒤에 특정한 명사를 덧붙이거나 why 대신 의문대명사 who, which, what 등을 써야 한다.

15 간접의문문에서는 '의문사+주어+동사' 구조를 잘 이해하고, think 동사 등의 예외에 주의해야 한다. ③ when did he leave → when he left ④ Do you think when → When do you think

16 (1) 준호는 어느 대학에 갈지 생각 중이다. (2) 예은이는 비가 언제 그칠지 궁금해 하고 있다.

17 (1), (3), (4), (5) 과거의 어느 특정 시점을 기준으로 그 이전에 시작된 일은 과거완료시제로 표현한다. (2) '역사적 사실'은 주절의 동사 시제와 상관없이 과거시제를 쓴다. (6) when은 '시점'을 표현하기 때문에 의문문 또는 간접의문문에서 완료시제로 표현할 수 없다.

18 의문문이 간접의문문이 될 때는 '의문사+주어+동사'의 어순이 된다. 의문사가 없을 경우 if 또는 whether를 써서 접속사 역할을 하도록 한다.

19 과거완료시제는 완료, 경험, 결과, 계속 등의 용법으로 구분할 수 있으며, 해석을 정확하게 하는 것이 중요하다.

20 우리말에 맞게 과거완료시제를 사용하여 쓴다.

21 (1) 간접의문문의 어순은 '의문사+주어+동사'이다. (2) '의문사가 없는 간접의문문'은 if또는 whether가 접속사 역할을 한다.

22 ⓐ be suitable for: ~에 적합하다, ⓑ the breadwinners for their families: 가족들의 생계비를 버는 가장

23 ⓒ와 ①, ④: 동명사, ②, ③, ⑤ : 현재분사

24 어떤 호흡 장치도 사용하지 않고 물속에 머물기 때문에, 해녀는 한 번에 많은 해산물을 채취할 수가 '없다.'

25 ⓐ와 ②: 감동시키다, ① (몸 등을) 움직이다, ③ (집, 근무지 등을) 옮기다[이사하다], ④ (차·배 따위가) 나아가다, 전진하다, ⑤ (안건 등을) 제안[제출]하다

26 이 글은 'Zin Kim이 앞으로 계획하고 있는 것'을 설명하는 글이므로, 주제로는 ③번 'Zin Kim의 앞으로의 계획'이 적절하다.

27 앞에 나오는 내용과 상반되는 내용이 뒤에 이어지므로 However가 가장 적절하다. ① 즉[말하자면], ② 게다가, 더욱이, ③ 따라서, 그러므로

28 위 글은 '기사문'이다. ① (책·연극·영화 등에 대한) 논평[비평], 감상문, ② 독후감, ⑤ 자서전

29 Zin Kim이 어떻게 해녀들의 사진을 찍었는지는 대답할 수 없다. ① She is an underwater photographer. ③ When she met a haenyeo who was enjoying her job. ④ No. ⑤ Haenyeo's culture.

01 ①　　02 (D) → (C) → (A) → (B)　　03 ②
04 ⑤
05 She wants to borrow an audio guide.
06 She should press the button.
07 I wonder why there are so many cars on the road.
08 how about going somewhere, too?
09 (D) → (B) → (A) → (C)
10 Could you explain how to make double-sided copies?
11 ⑤　　12 ①
13 (1) After Susan had learned the importance of recycling, she promised her teacher not to throw away used batteries.
(2) Before Sunwoo lay in his room all day long, he had sprained his ankle during the basketball game.
14 ⓐ when the shopping mall closes
ⓒ what kind of movie she was watching
ⓓ what she usually does on Sundays
ⓕ what time the show begins
15 ④, ⑤
16 how much he weighed, he had already gained, had often eaten
17 ④　　18 ④　　19 ③
20 She had only seen black-and-white photos of haenyeo who looked very tired.
21 ⑤　　22 ②　　23 ①　　24 ④
25 ②　　26 for　　27 barista
28 It's decorating coffee with hot milk and watching his customers enjoying it.

01 give a presentation: 발표하다, give a hand: 돕다, give a call: 전화를 걸다
02 (D) 궁금한 점 말하기 → (C) 궁금한 점에 대한 답변 → (A) 제안 → (B) 수락
03 농악을 소개하는 문장으로 그것은 한국의 전통 음악인지 묻는 대답으로 적절하므로 (B)가 적절하다.
04 대화를 통해 어떤 종류의 춤이 음악을 완성하는지 알 수 없다.
05 여자는 음성 가이드를 빌리고 싶다.
06 여자는 음성 가이드를 사용하기 위해 버튼을 눌러야 한다.
08 'Why don't we ~?'는 '~하는 게 어때?'라고 제안하는 표현으로 'How about ~?'으로 바꾸어 쓸 수 있다.
09 (D) 궁금한 것 말하기 → (B) 궁금한 것에 대한 설명 → (A) 어떻게 알게 되었는지 질문 → (C) 대답
10 double-sided: 양면의
11 Jack은 양면 복사 버튼을 먼저 누르고 시작 버튼을 눌러야 한

12 'Do you suppose?'와 'What music is Paul listening to?'를 한 문장으로 합칠 때 간접의문문의 의문사를 문두로 보내고 '주어+동사'의 어순으로 정리하면 ①과 같다.
13 과거의 특정 시점을 기준으로 전에 일어난 동작이나 상태를 과거완료로 표현한다. before나 after와 같이 '명확한 전후 관계'를 알 수 있는 경우 과거완료를 쓰지 않아도 되지만, 문제의 조건에 맞게 과거완료를 사용하도록 한다.
14 간접의문문의 어순은 '의문사+주어+동사'이다. 시제와 인칭에 맞게 동사의 형태에 유의한다.
15 과거 이전에 발생한 일은 과거완료시제로 표현한다. ① '그의 가족은 Brian이 전날 열심히 일했지만 결국 병원에 실려갔다는 사실을 우연히 알게 되었다' has worked → had worked ② '우리가 경기장에 도착했을 때, 전반전이 벌써 시작되었다'는 The first half of the match had already started when we arrived at the stadium.이 적절하다. ③ '대부분의 아시아인들은 봉감독이 칸 영화제에서 대상을 수상한 것을 자랑스럽게 느꼈다.' has won → had won 또는 felt → feel로 고쳐도 된다.
16 '불독은 몸무게가 얼마나 될지 알고 싶었다. 그는 저울에 오르기 전에 이미 살이 쪘다는 사실을 알게 되어 놀랐다. 그는 자기 전에 간식을 자주 먹었던 것을 후회했다.'
17 간접의문문 앞에 think, believe, imagine, guess 등 생각, 추측 등의 동사가 있을 때는 의문사를 문두로 보낸다. How old do you guess she is?가 적절하다.
18 앞에 나오는 내용과 상반되는 내용이 뒤에 이어지므로 however가 가장 적절하다. ① 게다가, ③ 즉, ⑤ 그러므로
19 이 글은 '어떻게 Zin Kim이 해녀의 사진을 찍는 것에 관심을 가지게 되었는지'를 설명하는 글이므로, 주제로는 ③번 'Zin Kim이 해녀의 사진을 찍는 것에 관심을 가지게 된 이유'가 적절하다.
20 Zin Kim이 우연히 한 해녀의 사진을 찍었을 때까지, '그녀는 흑백 사진 속의 아주 지친 모습의 해녀만 봐 왔다.'
21 ⓐ와 ⑤: 가주어, ① 가목적어, ② 비인칭 주어, ③ 'It is … that'의 구문으로 문장의 주어·목적어·부사어구를 강조하는 대명사, ④ 그것(앞에 이미 언급되었거나 현재 이야기되고 있는 사물·동물을 가리킴)
22 처음에, 해녀들은 왜 Zin Kim이 자신들의 사진을 찍으려고 하는지 이해하지 못했다.
23 주어진 문장의 my talk에 주목한다. ①번 앞 문장의 a talk를 받고 있으므로 ①번이 적절하다.
24 lastly = finally: (여러 개를 언급할 때) 마지막으로, ① 결국, 마침내, ② 즉시, ③ 극도로, 극히, ⑤ 마침내[드디어]
25 ⓐ와 ①, ③, ④: 부사적 용법, ②: 형용사적 용법, ⑤: 명사적 용법
26 ⓐ for a living: 밥벌이로, 생계 수단으로, ⓑ passion for: ~

19

에 대한 열정

27 barista: 바리스타, 커피 내리는 사람

28 '뜨거운 우유로 커피를 장식하고 그의 손님들이 그것을 즐기는 것을 보는 것'이다.

서술형 실전문제 p.106~107

01 They are waiting to get into the new bakery.

02 Because it was on a TV program.

03 He wants to try the new bakery's bread.

04 ① The film director was tired because he spoke[had spoken] in front of so many people.

05 ④ Where do you think the police officer caught the thief?

06 (1) Because Mary had learned taekwondo before, she fought off a strange man's attack.

   (2) Until Kevin saw a video of himself being a heavy drinker, he had never thought of quitting drinking.

07 prettily → pretty

08 I would make them look beautiful in my pictures.

09 (A) very special   (B) show their culture

10 (A) without   (B) for   (C) destroy

11 (A) Less-experienced   (B) more-experienced

12 Because they stay in the water without any breathing devices.

01 많은 사람들이 새로 생긴 제과점에 들어가려고 줄을 서서 기다리고 있다.

02 새로 생긴 제과점이 TV에 나왔었기 때문이다.

03 Brian은 새로 생긴 제과점의 빵을 먹어 보고 싶어 한다.

04 영화감독이 피곤한 것은 너무나 많은 사람들 앞에서 연설했기 때문이다. 피곤한 상황이 과거완료가 되어서는 전후 관계가 뒤바뀌므로 적절하지 않다.

05 간접의문문 앞에 think, believe, imagine, guess 등 생각, 추측 등의 동사가 있을 때 의문사가 문두에 와야 한다.

06 (1) 'Mary는 전에 태권도를 배웠기 때문에 낯선 남자의 공격을 물리쳤다' (2) 'Kevin이 본인의 주정뱅이 모습을 보기 전까지는 술을 끊는 것을 생각해 본 적이 없었다.'

07 감각동사 looked의 보어로 형용사를 써야 하므로 pretty로 고치는 것이 적절하다.

08 사역동사 make+목적어+목적격보어(동사원형)의 순서로 쓰는 것이 적절하다.

09 해녀들은 '아주 특별하고', 세계에 '그들의 문화를 알리고' 싶었기 때문이다.

10 (A) 어떤 호흡 장치도 '사용하지 않고'라고 해야 하므로 without이 옳다. (B) 이것은 수중 환경에 '좋은' 것이라고 해야

하므로 for가 옳다. be good at: ~을 잘하다, be good for: ~에 좋다, (C) 한 번에 한 장소에서 너무 많은 해양생물을 채취하는 것은 바다를 '파괴할 수 있다'고 해야 하므로 destroy가 옳다. protect: ~을 보호하다

11 '경험이 적은 해녀들'은 '경험이 더 많은 해녀들'에 의해 훈련을 받는다.

12 '어떤 호흡 장치도 사용하지 않고 물속에 머물기' 때문이다.

창의사고력 서술형 문제 p.108

|모범답안|

01 (A) strong beat   (B) where the music came from
   (C) nongak   (D) community band music
   (E) cheer up farmers and wish for a good harvest

02 (1) He wants to know when I fed the puppy.
   (2) Did you check whether the plant is dried?
   (3) Tell me where I should empty the waste bin.

01 거리를 걷다가, 나는 강한 비트가 있는 음악을 들었다. 나는 음악이 어디서 오는 것인지 알고 싶었다. 유리와 나는 그것이 농악이라고 불리는 한국의 전통 음악이라는 것을 알게 되었다. 유리는 그것이 공동체 악단 음악의 한 종류로 전통적으로 농부들의 힘을 북돋아 주고 풍년을 기원하기 위해 사용되었다고 설명했다. 나는 몇몇 사람들이 리듬에 맞춰 춤을 추는 것이 인상 깊었다. 왜냐하면 함께 춤추는 것이 음악을 완성했기 때문이다. 유리와 나는 함께 했고 음악을 완성했다.

단원별 모의고사 p.109~112

01 ①   02 ①

03 (1) I want to be a photographer.
   (2) She was the most suitable candidate.
   (3) He held my hand tightly.
   (4) I'd like to borrow the novel.

04 ⑤

05 He visited Gwangandaegyo in Busan (with his family).

06 I wonder why there are so many people waiting in line.

07 ⑤   08 (C) → (D) → (E) → (A) → (B)

09 Because lots of people are going on vacation this weekend.

10 She suggested going somewhere.

11 ⑤   12 ②   13 ④   14 ⑤

15 if the woman had really put(또는 really had put) the fish

16 (A) after she had gotten 20,000 views

(B) sharing what is special about Korean food

17 ①, ③　　18 ③　　19 ①　　20 ④

21 many haenyeo have become the breadwinners for their families

22 twenty thousand　　23 the thing which[that]

24 ③

01 '사람들이 사도록 설득하려고 의도된 사진, 어구 또는 짧은 영상'을 가리키는 말은 advertisement(광고)이다.

02 주어진 문장에서 beat는 '리듬, 비트'를 가리키며 이와 같은 의미로 쓰인 것은 ①번이다. ②번은 '이기다', 나머지는 모두 '때리다, 두드리다'를 뜻한다.

03 photographer: 사진작가, suitable: 적절한, tightly: 단단히, 꽉, novel: 소설, borrow: 빌리다

04 ⑤번을 제외하고는 궁금한 점을 묻는 표현이다.

05 소년은 (그의 가족들과) 부산에 있는 광안대교를 방문했다.

07 위 대화를 통해 새로 생긴 제과점이 언제 TV에 방영되었는지는 알 수 없다.

08 (C) 이번 여름 계획 질문 → (D) 계획 설명 → (E) 올레길에 대한 설명 요청 → (A) 올레길에 대한 설명 → (B) 바람 표현

09 길 위에 많은 차들이 있는 것은 많은 사람들이 이번 주말에 휴가를 가려고 하기 때문이다.

10 Emma는 어딘가 갈 것을 제안했다.

11 궁금한 것을 묻는 질문에 이해가 가지 않는다는 말은 어색하다.

12 간접의문문의 어순은 '의문사+주어+동사'이다. 의문사를 문두로 보낼 이유가 없다.

13 그가 바이러스에 감염된 것은 그 질병의 중심지에서 3개월간 체류했던 것 때문이며, 과거보다 더 앞선 시점의 일이다. 과거완료 시제를 활용하는 것이 적절하다.

14 모두 '명사절로 사용된 간접의문문'인데, ⑤번만 '관계대명사가 이끄는 형용사절'로 쓰였다.

15 James는 그 여자가 붕어빵에 정말로 붕어를 넣었는지 궁금했다. 부사 really는 'had+p.p'의 중간에 와도 좋고, had 앞에 위치해도 괜찮다.

16 (A) Yori는 WeTube에서 그녀의 첫 비디오가 2만 개의 조회수를 얻었을 때 콘텐츠 창작자가 되었다. (B) 그녀가 자신의 직업에서 가장 좋아하는 부분은 한국 음식의 어떤 점이 특별한지 세계의 많은 사람들과 공유하는 것이다.

17 ⓐ와 ①, ③: 부사적 용법, ②, ⑤: 명사적 용법, ④: 형용사적 용법

18 Zin Kim이 우연히 한 해녀의 사진을 찍기 전에 그녀는 '흑백 사진 속의' 아주 지친 모습의 해녀만 봐 왔다.

19 이 글은 '해녀에 대해 무엇이 특별한지'를 설명하는 글이므로, 빈칸에 들어갈 질문으로는 ①번 '그들은 무엇이 그렇게 특별한가요?'가 적절하다. ④ hold one's breath: 숨을 참다

20 주어진 문장의 This에 주목한다. ④번 앞 문장의 내용을 받고 있으므로 ④번이 적절하다.

21 '되어 왔어요'를 현재완료 시제로 쓰는 것이 적절하다.

22 twenty thousands로 읽지 않도록 조심해야 한다.

23 what 다음의 동사가 is이므로, the things which[that]는 적절하지 않다.

24 Yori가 WeTube의 그녀의 첫 번째 동영상에 대해 언제 20,000 뷰를 돌파했는지는 알 수 없다. ① She is a content creator about traditional Korean food. ② By getting 20,000 views on her first video clip on WeTube. ④ It is sharing what is special about Korean food with many people around the world. ⑤ She is planning to write a cookbook on Korean food.

A Journey into Your Mind

시험대비 실력평가   p.116

01 (r)are   02 ②   03 ④   04 ⑤

05 ⑤

06 (1) apart (2) behavior (3) hips (4) invisible

01 주어진 단어는 반의어 관계이다. common: 흔한, rare: 드문, 귀한

02 사람의 마음과 그것이 행동에 영향을 미치는 방식을 연구하는 학문을 가리키는 말은 psychology(심리학)이다.

03 confident: 자신감 있는

04 주어진 문장에서 judge는 '판단하다'를 의미한다. ① 심사위원을 하다 ② 판사 ③ 추정하다 ④ 재판하다 ⑤ 판단하다

05 come back: 돌아오다, come up with: 떠올리다, come over: (장소에) 들르다

06 apart: 떨어진, behavior: 행동, hip: 엉덩이, 허리께, invisible: 눈에 보이지 않는

서술형 시험대비   p.117

01 careful 또는 careless

02 (1) Chances are that (2) Strangely enough
    (3) stand tall (4) by myself

03 (1) I want to become a professional psychologist.
    (2) Children get bored easily.
    (3) My dog often chews my shoes.
    (4) Believe in yourself, and be confident.

04 (1) judge (2) law (3) loudly (4) rivals (5) seat

05 (1) His drawing skills are almost professional.
    (2) What if she forgets to make a reservation?
    (3) I decided to take a walk to clear my mind.
    (4) Stand with your feet apart and your hands facing upwards.

01 주어진 단어는 명사와 형용사와의 관계를 나타낸다. careful: 주의 깊은, careless: 부주의한

02 chances are that: 아마 ~일 것이다, strangely enough: 매우 이상하게도, stand tall: 당당해 보이다, by oneself: 혼자서

03 professional: 전문적인, psychologist: 심리학자, bored: 지루해하는, chew: 씹다, confident: 자신감 있는

04 rival: 경쟁자, seat: 좌석, judge: 판단하다, loudly: 큰 소리

로, law: 법

05 professional: 전문적인, What if ~?: ~하면 어쩌지?, clear one's mind: 마음을 가다듬다 with one's feet apart: 양발을 벌린 채로

Conversation 【교과서】

핵심 Check   p.118~119

1 I'm worried about him.

2 No, you don't have to. / No, you don't need to.

3 (C) → (A) → (B)

교과서 대화문 익히기

Check(√) True or False   p.120

1 T   2 F   3 T   4 F

교과서 확인학습   p.122~123

Listen & Speak 1 A-1

happened to / chewed, all the time, worried about / bored . Why don't you / hope, chewing

Listen & Speak 1 A-2

nervous / swimming competition / worry, relax, enjoy / better

Listen & Speak 2 A-1

what time / bake cookies / get up / don't have to

Listen & Speak 2 A-2

Shall we try / Why, make a reservation / don't have to, online / convenient

Communicate A

wait / worried / good at / relay / What, mean / last runner, What if / putting too much pressure on / practice / don't have to do / winning, losing / right, lucky

Progress Check 1

nervous / presentation, history / prepared, do, job / feel much better

Progress Check 2

seafood spaghetti / stop by, on the way / You don't have to, what / back, help, cook

01 ⓔ → chewing 　　　　02 ②
03 She's worried about her swimming competition this Saturday.
04 He advises her to relax and enjoy herself.

01 stop+to부정사: ~하기 위해 멈추다, stop+~ing: ~하던 것을 멈추다. 개가 신발을 씹는 걸 그만두길 바란다는 내용이 이어져야 하므로 chewing이 적절하다.
02 Brian은 항상 개가 신발을 씹는다고 이야기했다.
03 소녀는 이번 주 토요일에 있는 수영대회에 대해 걱정한다.
04 소년은 소녀에게 긴장을 풀고 즐길 것을 조언한다.

01 ①, ③
02 How about playing with him more often?
03 ⑤　　　　04 ⑤　　　　05 ①
06 (E) → (C) → (B) → (D) → (A)
07 She suggests trying that new Mexican restaurant tomorrow.
08 Because he can do it online.
09 ②　　　　10 ⑤　　　　11 ⑤

01 걱정을 나타내는 표현으로 ①, ③번과 바꾸어 쓸 수 있다.
02 Why don't you ~? = How about ~ing?: ~하는 게 어때?
03 Brian이 언제 신발을 샀는지는 알 수 없다.
04 이어지는 대화에서 걱정하는 모습이 나타나므로 nervous가 적절하다.
05 수영대회에 대해 걱정했지만 기분이 나아졌으므로 ①번이 적절하다. relieved: 안도된, 안심한, lonely: 외로운
06 (E) 몇 시에 출발할지 질문 → (C) 대답 및 계획 설명 → (B) 일찍 일어나야 하는지 질문 → (D) 대답 → (A) 반응 및 인사
07 Emily는 새로운 멕시코 레스토랑에 가볼 것을 제안한다.
08 레스토랑 예약은 온라인으로 할 수 있기 때문에 Tom은 레스토랑에 전화할 필요가 없다.
09 (A) be concerned about: ~에 대해 걱정하다 (B) because+주어+동사, because of+명사(대명사), (C) 주어와 목적어가 일치하므로 재귀대명사 yourself가 적절하다.
10 대화를 통해 누가 800미터 릴레이에 첫 번째 주자인지는 알 수 없다.
11 영어 수업 시간에 할 발표에 긴장하고 있다는 말에 감사하다는 말은 어색하다.

01 (B) → (D) → (C) → (A)
02 He's going to go to his grandma's place.
03 She is going to bake cookies for her.
04 She doesn't need his help because his dad will help her.
05 (A) last runner
　　(B) my team might lose because of me
　　(C) much pressure　(D) I should practice
　　(E) winning or losing

01 (B) 긴장되어 보임을 언급 → (D) 걱정 표현 → (C) 격려 → (A) 감사 표현
02 Jack은 내일 할머니 댁에 갈 것이다.
03 엄마는 할머니를 위해 쿠키를 구울 것이다.
04 엄마는 아빠가 그녀를 도와줄 것이기 때문에 Jack의 도움이 필요하지 않다.
05 오늘 나는 운동회에 대해 매우 걱정했다. 나는 800미터 릴레이의 마지막 주자로 선정되었다. 모든 학급 친구들은 내가 잘할 수 있을 것이라고 믿었다. 하지만 나는 매우 부담이 되었다. 나는 만약 나 때문에 팀이 지게 될까봐 걱정되었다. 나는 이것에 대해 유리에게 이야기를 했고 그녀는 내가 스스로에게 너무 많은 부담을 주고 있다고 말했다. 사실, 나는 내가 매일 연습을 해야 할지 말지 생각 중이었다. 유리는 내게 하지 말라고 했다. 왜냐하면 이것은 단지 학교 경기일 뿐이며 이기고 지는 것에 관한 것이 아니기 때문이었다. 나는 그녀로 인해 많이 용기를 북돋게 되었으며 정말로 그녀에게 고마웠다.

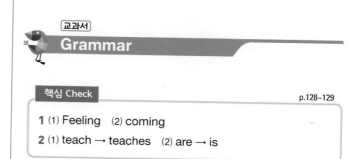

교과서
Grammar

핵심 Check p.128~129

1 (1) Feeling　(2) coming
2 (1) teach → teaches　(2) are → is

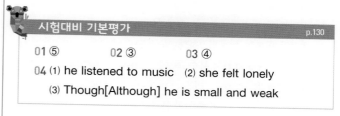

01 ⑤　　　　02 ③　　　　03 ④
04 (1) he listened to music　(2) she felt lonely
　　(3) Though[Although] he is small and weak

01 상관접속사 not only와 but also 뒤에는 문법적으로 같은 것이 들어가야 한다.
02 부사절을 분사구문으로 바꿀 때, 주어가 같으면 주어를 생략하

고 분사를 쓴다. ④의 완료분사구문은 종속절의 시제가 주절의 시제보다 앞설 때 써야 한다.

03 ④ 상관접속사 not only와 but also 뒤에는 문법적으로 같은 것이 들어가야 한다. 동사 writes가 오면, but also 뒤에도 dances가 와야 한다.

04 분사구문은 분사를 활용하여 부사절을 부사구로 줄인 표현이다. 대개 양보, 동시동작, 이유, 시간, 조건 등의 부사절이며, 절과 구의 전환시 동사의 시제 등에 유의해야 한다. (3)은 내용상 양보이므로 Though 외에도 Although, Even though 등의 접속사가 가능하다.

01 ①	02 ⑤	03 ④	04 ③
05 ⑤	06 Exhausting → Exhausted		
07 ②	08 ①	09 ②	10 ④
11 ③	12 ⑤		

13 Having been built of wood and dry grass
14 Not wanting to be late for the meeting
15 (1) standing tall like Wonder Woman for a few minutes
    (2) not only late for school but also hit by

01 ① not only ~ but also에서는 but also 뒤의 명사에 동사의 수를 일치시킨다. have → has가 적절하다.

02 'with+목적어+분사' 구문은 '목적어의 능/수동' 여부가 중요하다. 눈이 '감겨진 것'이므로 closed가 적절하다.

03 부사절로 영작하면, 'Though he had bullied many people, Tom lived well off.'이다. 분사구문 Having bullied에 의미를 명확하게 하기 위해 접속사 Though를 추가한 문장이 ④이다.

04 ① both는 복수 주어(is → are) ② 'not only A but also B'는 B가 주어(have → has) ④ neither ~ nor는 부정문과 함께 쓸 수 없다(don't have → have 또는 neither ~ nor → either ~ or) ⑤ not only가 문두에 오면 주어와 동사를 도치시킨다.(I am → am I)

05 ① speak → speaks ② know → knows ③ is → are ④ she likes to go → where she likes to go

06 '고된 일로 지친 것'(수동)이므로 Being이 생략된 과거분사 형태가 문두에 오는 것이 적절하다.

07 ② Both A and B는 복수 동사를 써야 한다. listens → listen이 적절하다.

08 <보기>와 ①은 '양보' 의미의 분사구문이다.

09 <보기>는 'Josh 뿐만 아니라 Mina도 음주 뿐 아니라 흡연을 좋아하지 않는다.'라는 뜻이다. ① 'Josh와 Mina 둘 다 흡연이 아닌 음주를 좋아한다.' ③ 'Josh 또는 Mina 둘 중 하나는 흡연

도 음주도 좋아하지 않는다.' ④ 문법적 오류 ⑤ 'Josh와 Mina 둘 다 흡연이 아니라 음주를 싫어한다.'

10 완료분사구문과 양보 의미의 부사구가 쓰였으므로, 접속사는 Though, 시제는 came이 적절하다.

11 ① and also → but also ② likes → like ④ the passengers were → were the passengers ⑤ only → not only

12 ① or → and ② nor → or ③ wonder → wonders ④ know → knows

13 종속절의 시제가 앞서 있고, 수동태이므로 완료분사구문의 수동형인 'Having been p.p.'를 활용하여 알맞게 배열한다.

14 분사구문의 부정은 분사 앞에 not이나 never를 쓴다.

15 (1) '몇 분간 원더우먼처럼 꼿꼿이 서 있고 나서, 지수는 더 이상 긴장되지 않았다.' (2) 'Jenny는 학교에 늦었을 뿐만 아니라 도로에서 물벼락까지 맞았다.' *splash: 물이 튐

01 (1) Wanting to clear his mind
    (2) not only feel sure about yourself but also look confident
    (3) Wanting to turn a rival into a friend

02 (1) When he graduates from high school next year
    (2) Though I was sick all day long
    (3) If you have a problem that you cannot share with your family or friends
    (4) While he listened to the radio
    (5) Because we do not have to worry about being judged

03 (1) Having no friends at school,
    (2) She not only helped me but also became a good friend.
    (3) Asking for help, you can make friends.

04 (1) Minju's mom is not only a good doctor but also a great cook.
    (2) Harry not only speaks Spanish but also dances well.
    (3) Seohyun is not only beautiful but also very kind.
    (4) Not only Frank but also his parents are nice.

05 (1) study → studies (2) is → are (3) is → are
    (4) stress → stressful (5) is → are

06 (1) that its food is not only delicious[healthy] but also healthy[delicious]
    (2) Having picked a huge carrot, the farmer donated it

01 (1), (3)은 분사구문을 활용하는 문제이다. 의미에 맞게 단어를 배열하도록 한다. *clear one's mind: 마음을 정리하다 *do one a favor: A에게 부탁을 들어주다[호의를 베풀다] (2)는 'not only A but also B' 구문이다.

02 문제에 쓰인 분사구문은 각각 시간, 양보, 조건, 동시동작, 이유 등의 의미로 쓰였다. (1) 내년에 고등학교를 졸업할 때, Tammy는 전문적인 농부가 되고 싶어 한다.(동사 시제를 현재형으로 쓰는 것에 유의할 것) (2) 비록 하루 종일 아팠지만, 나는 그 힘든 프로젝트를 완수할 수 있었다. (3) 가족이나 친구들과 나눌 수 없는 문제가 있다면, 낯선 이에게 얘기를 걸어보라. (4) 라디오를 들으면서, Henry는 자신의 기타들을 닦았다. (5) 우리가 평가받을 것에 대해 걱정할 필요가 없기 때문에, 우리는 종종 낯선 사람에게 우리 문제를 말한다.

03 (1) not ~ any를 no로 바꾸면, 'As I had no friends at school'이 된다. 분사구문으로 전환하면 'Having no friends at school'이다. (3) 부사절을 활용하면, 'If you ask for help'이며, 분사구문으로 바꾸면 'Asking for help'가 된다.

04 (1) 민주의 엄마는 좋은 의사일 뿐만 아니라 훌륭한 요리사이다. (2) Harry는 스페인어를 말할 뿐만 아니라 춤도 잘 춘다. (3) 서현이는 예쁠 뿐만 아니라 매우 친절하다. (4) Frank뿐만 아니라 그의 부모님 또한 착하다.

05 (1) 그녀는 모든 시험에서 만점을 받아야 한다고 생각할 뿐만 아니라, 잠도 안 자고 공부한다. (2) Both는 항상 복수 동사가 온다. (3) either A or B는 동사와 가까운 주어에 수를 일치시킨다. (4) 'not only A but also B'는 등위접속사이므로 문법적으로 같은 것을 써야 한다. stress는 명사이므로, 형용사형으로 고치는 것이 적절하다. (5) but also 뒤의 주어에 일치시킨다. the islands가 복수이다.

06 (1) 이 식당의 음식은 맛있을 뿐만 아니라 건강에 좋다.(건강에 좋을 뿐만 아니라 맛있다) healthy와 delicious는 서로 자리가 바뀌어도 좋다. (2) 거대한 당근을 수확했기 때문에, 그 농부는 그것을 원님에게 기부했다.

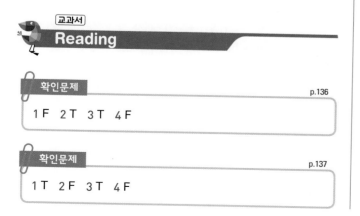

Reading

| 확인문제 | p.136 |

1 F 2 T 3 T 4 F

| 확인문제 | p.137 |

1 T 2 F 3 T 4 F

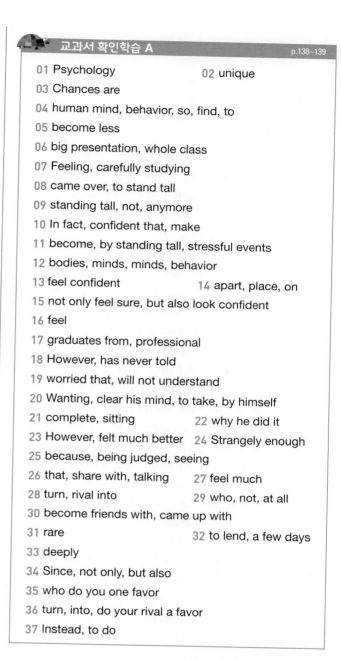

교과서 확인학습 A   p.138~139

01 Psychology   02 unique
03 Chances are
04 human mind, behavior, so, find, to
05 become less
06 big presentation, whole class
07 Feeling, carefully studying
08 came over, to stand tall
09 standing tall, not, anymore
10 In fact, confident that, make
11 become, by standing tall, stressful events
12 bodies, minds, minds, behavior
13 feel confident   14 apart, place, on
15 not only feel sure, but also look confident
16 feel
17 graduates from, professional
18 However, has never told
19 worried that, will not understand
20 Wanting, clear his mind, to take, by himself
21 complete, sitting   22 why he did it
23 However, felt much better 24 Strangely enough
25 because, being judged, seeing
26 that, share with, talking   27 feel much
28 turn, rival into   29 who, not, at all
30 become friends with, came up with
31 rare   32 to lend, a few days
33 deeply
34 Since, not only, but also
35 who do you one favor
36 turn, into, do your rival a favor
37 Instead, to do

교과서 확인학습 B   p.140~141

1 Psychology Answers Your Questions
2 Do you think you have a unique problem?
3 Chances are that many other people have the same problem.
4 Psychology is the study of the human mind and behavior, so it can help you find a solution to your problem.
5 How do I become less nervous?
6 It was five minutes before Jisu's big presentation in front of the whole class.
7 Feeling nervous, Jisu was carefully studying her notes in her chair.

8 Then, her teacher came over and told her to stand tall like Wonder Woman.

9 After standing tall for a few minutes, Jisu did not feel nervous anymore.

10 In fact, she was confident that she would make a great presentation.

11 According to Amy Cuddy, a famous psychologist, we can become more confident just by standing tall for two minutes before stressful events.

12 Our bodies change our minds, and our minds can change our behavior.

13 Do you want to feel confident?

14 Stand with your feet apart, and place your hands on your hips.

15 You will not only feel sure about yourself but also look confident to other people.

16 Who can help me feel better?

17 When he graduates from high school next year, Taeho wants to become a professional farmer.

18 However, he has never told anyone about it.

19 He is worried that his parents or his friends will not understand.

20 Wanting to clear his mind, Taeho decided to take a day trip on a train by himself.

21 On the train, he told a complete stranger sitting beside him about his problem.

22 He had no idea why he did it.

23 However, he felt much better when he got off the train.

24 Strangely enough, we often tell strangers about our problems just like Taeho.

25 That is because we do not have to worry about being judged or seeing them again.

26 If you have a problem that you cannot share with your family or friends, try talking to a stranger.

27 You will feel much better.

28 How do I turn a rival into a friend?

29 Benjamin Franklin once had a political rival who did not like him at all.

30 Franklin wanted to become friends with him, so he came up with a plan.

31 His rival had a rare book.

32 Franklin asked his rival to lend him the book for a few days.

33 When Franklin returned the book, he thanked him deeply.

34 Since that day, his rival became not only a political supporter but also a good friend.

35 Franklin famously said, "Enemies who do you one favor will want to do more."

36 If you want to turn a rival into a friend, don't do your rival a favor.

37 Instead, ask your rival to do you a favor.

시험대비 실력평가　　　　　　　p.142~145

01 ②　　　02 ③　　　03 ④　　　04 ①, ⑤
05 to do　　06 ②　　　07 ①
08 by himself　　　　09 why → because
10 (A) less　(B) confident　(C) apart
11 Chances　　　　12 ⑤　　　13 ④
14 ②　　　15 ⑤
16 his rival became a good friend as well as a political supporter
17 professional　　　18 ④　　　19 ①
20 ③　　　21 ③　　　22 no more → anymore
23 ①, ④

01 이어지는 글의 내용이 긴장하고 있던 지수가 몇 분을 우뚝 선 후에, 더 이상 긴장되지 않았다는 것이므로 '어떻게 하면 긴장을 덜 할 수 있나요?'가 적절하다.

02 psychologist: 심리학자 psychology: 심리학

03 ④ 선생님은 지수에게 다가와서 원더우먼처럼 꼿꼿이 서 있어 보라고 말했다.

04 관계대명사 주격이 필요한 자리이므로 who나 that이 적절하다.

05 ask의 목적격보어로 to부정사가 적절하다.

06 ②번은 Franklin의 정치적 경쟁자를 가리키지만, 나머지는 모두 Franklin을 가리킨다.

07 주어진 문장의 However와 it에 주목한다. However로 앞 문장과 상반되는 내용이 나오며 it이 앞 문장의 내용을 가리키므로 ①번이 적절하다.

08 by oneself: 혼자

09 That is why: 그것이 ~한 이유이다(앞에는 원인이 나오고, 뒤에는 결과가 나옴), That is because: 그것은 ~ 때문이다(앞에는 결과가 나오고 뒤에는 원인이 나옴). 앞 문장의 원인이 이어지므로 That is because가 적절하다. 원인이냐 결과냐를 따지지 말고 해석으로 판단하는 것이 더 좋다.

10 (A) 지수가 원더우먼처럼 꼿꼿이 서 있고 난 후 더 이상 긴장되지 않았다고 했으므로 less가 적절하다. (B) Amy Cuddy를 들어 앞의 내용을 추가 설명하고 있으므로 confident가 적절하다. (C) 원더우먼처럼 꼿꼿이 서려면 양발을 '벌리고' 서야 하므로 apart가 적절하다.

11 Chances are that ~: 아마 ~일 것이다

12 ⓑ와 ⑤번은 분사구문으로 쓰인 현재분사이다. ① 목적격보어로 쓰인 현재분사, ② 진행형에 쓰인 현재분사, ③, ④ 동명사

13 왜 우리의 몸이 마음을 바꾸는지는 대답할 수 없다. ① Amy Cuddy is a famous psychologist. ② By standing tall for a few minutes. ③ She told her to stand tall. ⑤ She stood tall for a few minutes.

14 책을 빌리고 돌려줄 때 진심으로 감사를 표한 후, 경쟁자가 후원자뿐만 아니라 좋은 친구가 되었다는 내용이다.

15 뒤에 days라는 복수 명사가 나오므로 a few가 적절하다. little과 a little은 복수 명사와 함께 쓰이지 않는다.

16 not only A but also B = B as well as A

17 professional: 전문적인, 영영풀이: 전문가는 진보한 교육과 훈련을 요구하는 직업을 갖고 있다.

18 앞에 나오는 내용과 상반되는 내용이 뒤에 이어지므로 However가 가장 적절하다. ① Moreover: 게다가, 더욱이, ③ Therefore: 그러므로, ⑤ In addition: 게다가

19 (A)의 much는 비교급을 강조하는 말로 even, a lot, far, still 등으로 바꿔 쓸 수 있다.

20 ③ 위 글에서 'He had no idea why he did it.'이라고 말하고 있다. ① A professional farmer. ② He has never told anyone about it. ④ Because he wanted to clear his mind. ⑤ By telling a complete stranger about our problem.

21 '선생님이 말씀하신 대로 몇 분을 우뚝 선 후에, 지수는 더 이상 긴장되지 않았다.'고 했으므로 어떻게 하면 긴장을 '덜' 할 수 있나요?가 적절하다.

22 not ~ anymore = ~ no more. 앞에 not이 나와 있으므로 no more를 anymore로 고치는 것이 적절하다.

23 (B)와 ②, ③, ⑤: 동명사, ①, ④: 현재분사

서술형 시험대비   p.146~147

01 a complete stranger

02 Strangely enough

03 we often tell strangers about our problems just like Taeho

04 Because psychology is the study of the human mind and behavior.

05 We can get to be more confident just by standing tall for two minutes before stressful events.

06 Becaus[As, Since] she was feeling

07 with   08 deep → deeply

09 his rival became a good friend as well as a political supporter

10 (A) Wanting   (B) sitting   (C) being judged

11 Taeho wants to become a professional farmer

12 He had no idea why he did it.

13 (A) a complete stranger   (B) much better

01 태호가 옆에 앉은 전혀 모르는 사람에게 자신의 고민에 대해서 말한 후 기분이 훨씬 좋아졌다고 했다.

02 Strangely enough: 정말 이상하게도, 기이하게도

03 앞 문장의 내용을 가리킨다.

04 '심리학은 인간의 마음과 행동에 관한 연구이며, 따라서 여러분이 문제에 대한 해결책을 찾는 데 도움을 줄 수 있다.'라고 하고 있다

05 'Amy Cuddy에 의하면, 우리는 스트레스를 받는 상황 이전에 2분 정도 꼿꼿이 서 있는 것만으로도 자신감이 더 생길 수 있다고 한다.'라고 하고 있다

06 Feeling은 'Because[As, Since] she was feeling'을 분사구문으로 고친 것이다.

07 become friends with: ~와 친구가 되다 come up with: (해답 등을) 찾아내다, 내놓다

08 deep: (깊이가) 깊이, 깊게, deeply: ('매우'의 의미로) 깊이, 철저하게

09 not only A but also B = B as well as A

10 (A) 주어인 태호가 원하는 것이므로 능동의 뜻을 갖는 Wanting이 적절하다. (B) 문장의 동사로 told가 나와 있으므로 sitting이 적절하다. (C) 우리가 평가하는 것이 아니라 평가를 받는 것이므로 being judged가 적절하다.

11 ⓐ의 it은 앞 문장에서 언급된 '태호가 전문적인 농부가 되고 싶어 하는 것'을 가리킨다.

12 why he did it(의문사+주어+동사)의 순서로 쓰는 것이 적절하다. have no idea = do not know

13 태호는 전문적인 농부가 되고 싶어 하지만, 부모님이나 친구들이 이해하지 못할까봐 걱정이 된다. 혼자 하루 기차 여행을 하는 동안, 그는 전혀 모르는 사람에게 자신의 고민에 대해서 말했다. 그는 자신이 왜 그랬는지 알 수 없었다. 그러나, 기차에서 내릴 때 기분이 훨씬 좋아졌다.

영역별 핵심문제   p.149~153

01 successful   02 ①   03 ⑤

04 (1) (p)robably   (2) professional   (3) psychology
   (4) (r)are

05 (1) make a presentation (2) stop by (3) stand tall
   (4) Chances are that (5) get off

06 ①   07 ⓔ → help you cook[to cook]

08 ①   09 ②

10 I'm worried about my presentation in history class.

11 ⑤   12 (C) → (D) → (B) → (A)

13 His dog chewed them.

14 She advises him to play with him[his dog] more often.   15 ④

16 (1) Both the honeybee and the ladybug are in trouble
   (2) neither to go to college nor to get a job

17 ②, ③

18 (1) likes (2) dancing (3) or (4) is (5) appears

19 ⑤   20 ②   21 ①   22 ④

23 ②   24 ②   25 ⑤   26 ⑤

27 ③   28 ③

29 He lent his rare book to Franklin.

01 주어진 단어는 명사와 형용사와의 관계를 나타낸다. successful: 성공적인, traditional: 전통적인

02 '대학, 학교 등에서 교육을 끝내다'를 가리키는 말은 graduate(졸업하다)이다.

03 apart: 떨어져

04 probably: 아마도, professional: 전문적인, psychology: 심리학, rare: 희귀한

05 chances are that: 아마 ~일 것이다, get off: 내리다, stop by: 들르다, stand tall: 당당해 보이다, make a presentation: 발표하다

06 by oneself: 혼자서, stop by: 들르다, by 6: 6시까지

07 help는 준사역동사로 원형부정사 또는 to부정사를 목적격 보어로 취할 수 있다.

08 stop by = drop by: 들르다

12 (C) 제안 → (D) 수락 → (B) 의무 부인하기 → (A) 반응

13 그의 개가 씹었다.

14 그녀는 Brian에게 개와 더 자주 놀아줄 것을 조언한다.

15 '큰 아파트에 혼자 살고 있는 것'과 '거의 외로움을 느끼지 않는 것'은 '역접' 관계이다. '양보' 접속사가 적절하다..

16 (1) 꿀벌과 무당벌레 둘 다 거미줄에서 곤경에 처했다. (2) 지호는 대학 진학도 취업도 하지 않기로 결정했다.

17 ② Both A and B로 고친다. ③ Either A or B로 고친다.

18 (1) 'not only A but also B'는 동사의 수를 일치시킨다.
   (2) 'not only A but also B'는 문법적으로 같은 것을 받으며, 준동사도 그렇다. (3), (4) Either A는 or B와 함께 써서 'A 또는 B 둘 중 하나'를 가리키며, 동사와 가까운 주어에 일치시킨

다. (5) Not A but B는 B에 동사를 일치한다.

19 분사구문의 부정은 분사 앞에 not을 쓴다. 접속사를 쓸 경우, 접속사 뒤에 주어가 오면 분사구문은 쓸 수 없다.

20 분사구문에서의 비인칭 주어 It과 주절의 주어가 다르므로, 'It raining all day' 형태의 독립분사구문이 적절하다.

21 ⓐ a solution to A: A에 대한 해결책, to: [행위·동작·작용의 대상] ~에 대하여 ⓑ told의 목적격보어로 to부정사가 적절하다.

22 ② in fact: 사실(앞 문장에 나온 내용에 대해서 자세한 내용을 덧붙이거나 내용을 강조할 때 사용), ③ 게다가, 더욱이, ⑤ 그러므로

23 이 글은 '만약 가족이나 친구들과도 나눌 수 없는 고민이 있다면, 낯선 이에게 말해 보면 기분이 훨씬 나아질 것임'을 설명하고 있으므로, 주제로는 '고민이 있을 때 기분이 나아지는 법'이 적절하다.

24 밑줄 친 ⓐ는 내용상 이유를 나타내는 분사구문으로 보는 것이 적절하다. ⑤번으로 보면 이후의 진행과 연결이 어색하다.

25 '태호는 옆에 앉은 전혀 모르는 사람에게 자신의 고민에 대해서 말했다. 그는 자신이 왜 그랬는지 알 수 없었다.'라고 되어 있다.

26 앞의 내용에 대안을 제시하고 있으므로 '대신에'가 가장 적절하다. ③ Nonetheless: 그럼에도 불구하고

27 주어진 문장의 the book이 ③번 앞 문장의 a rare book을 받고 있으므로 ③번이 적절하다.

28 ① wicked: 사악한, ⑤ evil: 나쁜, 흉악한

29 Franklin의 정치적 경쟁자는 Franklin에게 그의 희귀한 책을 빌려 주었다.

단원별 예상문제
p.154~157

01 ⑤

02 (1) Don't put too much pressure on yourself.
   (2) Stand with your feet apart.
   (3) I'll call the restaurant and make a reservation.

03 He is going to cook seafood spaghetti (for dinner).

04 It's because Minsu and Emma already have what they need.

05 She will be back home by 6 to help him.

06 (C) → (D) → (A) → (B)   07 You don't have to.

08 ④   09 ⑤   10 ⑤   11 ②

12 ②, ⑤   13 ④   14 ④

15 (1) Using green energy vehicles
   (2) Anne not coming back
   (3) Not having been invited to the final match

16 ③　　　　17 sixty

18 Because[As/Since] we wanted to find the answer to this question,

19 unique

20 Chances are that many other people have the same problem.

21 ③

22 Her teacher advised Jisu to stand tall like Wonder Woman.

23 ⑤

---

01 '당신을 싫어하면서 당신에게 해를 끼치고 싶어 하는 사람'을 가리키는 말은 enemy(적)이다.

02 put too much pressure on: ~에게 너무 많은 부담을 주다, with your feet apart: 양발을 벌린 채로, make a reservation: 예약하다

03 민수는 저녁으로 해물 스파게티를 요리할 것이다.

04 민수와 Emma는 이미 필요한 것을 갖고 있기 때문에 가게에 들를 필요가 없다.

05 Emma는 6시까지 민수를 도우러 집에 돌아올 것이다.

06 (C) 신발에 생긴 일에 대해 질문 → (D) 설명 및 걱정 표현 → (A) 제안 → (B) 수용 및 바람 표현

07 don't have to: ~할 필요 없다

08 ④ Jack의 엄마는 내일 아침에 쿠키를 구울 것이다.

09 주어진 문장은 매일 연습을 해야 한다고 생각하는가에 대한 질문에 대한 대답으로 알맞으므로 (E)가 적절하다.

10 유리는 Jaden이 매일 연습을 할 필요가 없다고 이야기한다.

11 수영대회는 이번 주 토요일이다.

12 ① Opened → Opening ③ Worked → Working ④ Knowing not → Not knowing

13 but also 뒤에 형용사 generous가 있으므로, 부사 truly(진심으로, 진정으로)는 적절하지 않다.

14 not only 뒤에 과거동사가 나왔으므로, 과거시제 동사가 아닌 것을 찾는다. ④ proud는 형용사이다.

15 부사절을 분사구문으로 만들 때, 일반적으로 접속사를 생략한 후 주어가 같으면 주어도 생략하고, 동사를 V-ing 형태로 바꾸는데 Being은 보통 생략한다. 주절보다 시제가 앞서면 Having been 형태가 되고, 부정문에서 not은 분사 앞에 쓰는 것이 적절하다.

16 'not only A but also B'가 주어 자리에 있을 때는 but also 뒤의 B에 동사를 일치시킨다. 주어가 their mom이므로 동사는 likes가 적절하다.

17 30명의 학생들 중에서 18명의 학생들이 평균 점수를 넘었으므

로 60%이다.

18 이유를 나타내는 부사절로 고치는 것이 적절하다.

19 unique: 유일무이한, 독특한

20 chances are that ~: 아마 ~일 것이다

21 주어진 문장의 After에 주목한다. ③번 앞 문장에서 '선생님이 다가와서는 원더우먼처럼 꼿꼿이 서 있어 보라고 말했'으므로 ③번이 적절하다.

22 지수의 선생님은 지수에게 원더우먼처럼 꼿꼿이 서 있어 보라고 했다.

23 not only A but also B = not only A but B = not simply A but (also) B = not just A but (also) B = not merely A but (also) B cf. not A but B: A가 아니라 B

🦉 서술형 실전문제
p.158~159

01 She is looking forward to Sports Day.

02 He is worried that his team may[might] lose because of him.

03 Because she thinks that the 800-meter relay is just a school race and it's not about winning or losing.

04 (1) Walking down the street

(2) Not knowing what her father meant

(3) There being any seats left on the plane

(4) Wanting to clear her mind

05 either / Neither, nor, Not only, but also / both, and

06 Because[As/Since] I didn't have her around

07 Not only did she write a lot about her memories

08 필자는 할머니가 원했던 것처럼 행복해지려고 노력해야 한다는 것을 배웠다.

09 nose

10 (A) getting hotter　(B) rises

11 (A) lying　(B) Not only do they　(C) as if (D) rises

---

01 유리는 운동회를 기대하고 있다.

02 Jaden은 800미터의 마지막 주자로서 그의 팀이 자기 때문에 질까봐 걱정한다.

03 유리는 800미터 릴레이는 학교 경기일 뿐이며 이기고 지고에 관한 것이 아니라고 생각한다.

04 주어진 어휘에 접속사들이 없으므로, 분사구문을 배열하는 문제이다. 각각 (1) 시간, (2) 양보, (3) 조건, (4) 이유 등의 부사절

을 분사구문으로 만든 것이며, (3)의 경우 주절과 종속절의 주어가 다르기 때문에, 유도부사 There 등을 문두에 써야 한다.

05 지나가 지훈에게 엄마의 생일을 묻자, 지훈은 11월 10일인지, 12일인지라고 대답해서 지나를 답답하게 한다. 지나는 아빠뿐만 아니라, 동생도 엄마에게 관심이 없다고 말하고, 미안한 지훈이는 어떻게 할지를 묻는다.

06 이유를 나타내는 부사절로 고치는 것이 적절하다.

07 부정어구(not only)로 문장이 시작되면 의문문 형식으로 도치가 이루어진다.

08 본문의 마지막 부분의 내용을 쓰는 것이 적절하다.

09 Pinocchio Effect(피노키오 효과)를 설명하는 대화로 마지막 부분에서 '코가 더 뜨거워지고 눈 주위의 체온이 올라가는 것처럼 느낀다'라고 하고 있으므로 nose가 적절하다.

10 코가 더 뜨거워지고 눈 주위의 체온이 올라가는 것처럼 느끼기 때문이다.

11 (A) '거짓말하다'라는 의미의 자동사 lie가 쓰일 자리이므로 현재분사 lying이 적절하다. (B) 부정어구(not only)로 문장이 시작되면 의문문 형식으로 도치가 이루어지므로 Not only do they가 적절하다. (C) even if: (비록) ~일지라도, (설사) ~이라고 할지라도, as if: 마치 ~인 것처럼, 흡사 ~와도 같이 (D) 체온이 올라간다는 뜻의 자동사 rises가 적절하다. raise는 타동사로 '~을 올리다, 끌어올리다'라는 뜻이다.

창의사고력 서술형 문제
p.160

|모범답안|

01 (A) Grandma's place   (B) bake cookies
(C) My dad

02 (A) has just moved to a new school   (B) lonely
(C) Having nobody to talk to
(D) showed me her notes but also started to talk about herself
(E) helps you make new friends

---

01 나는 내일 할머니 댁을 방문하는 것을 기대하고 있다. 우리는 내일 8시쯤에 떠날 것이다. 엄마는 할머니를 위해 쿠키를 만들 계획이다. 아빠는 엄마를 아침 일찍 도와주실 것이다. 나는 할머니를 뵙는 것이 몹시 기대된다.

단원별 모의고사
p.161~165

01 (1) came up with   (2) (c)ame over   (3) came back

---

02 (1) text message   (2) anxious   (3) unique
(4) prepare   (5) mind   (6) competition

03 (1) Are you interested in the political issue?
(2) You don't have to prepare your speech every day.
(3) I'm not worried about our presentation at all.

04 ⑤

05 She is concerned about her presentation in history class.

06 It's because she's prepared a lot.

07 ⑤   **08** make a reservation   **09** ②

10 (B) → (C) → (D) → (A)   **11** ④

12 (A) nervous   (B) her swimming competition
(C) this Saturday
(D) just relax and enjoy yourself

13 ③   **14** ④   **15** ④

16 Both Minju[Sam] and Sam[Minju] are interested in joining a club

17 ⑤

18 ④ Having seen him before, Julie decided to make friends with Charles.

19 ⑤ Neither the president nor his secretaries want to know the basic causes of the problem.

20 ② Having, ③ classmates
이유: ② 주어인 I가 친구가 없는 것이므로 능동의 의미로 쓰여야 한다. ③ 'one of+복수 명사'로 쓰인다.

21 ①   **22** ③   **23** ②

24 He took a day trip on a train by himself to clear his mind.

25 ②

---

01 come up with: ~을 떠올리다, come over: (장소에) 들르다, come back: 돌아오다

02 competition: 경쟁 text message: 문자 메시지, prepare: 준비하다, mind: 마음, 생각, anxious: 걱정하는, unique: 독특한

03 political: 정치적인, prepare: 준비하다, be worried about: ~에 대해 걱정하다, not ~ at all: 전혀 ~ 아닌

04 가족이 걱정된다는 말에 서로 이야기할 필요가 없다는 대답은 어색하다.

05 소녀는 역사 시간에 할 발표에 대해 걱정한다.

06 소년은 소녀가 준비를 많이 했기 때문에 잘할 것이라고 생각

한다.

07 엄마가 쿠키를 굽기 위해 내일 몇 시에 일어날지는 대화를 통해 알 수 없다.

10 (B) 긴장한 것 같아 보인다고 이야기함 → (C) 걱정 표현하기 → (D) 격려 → (A) 감사 표현

11 (A) be worried about: ~에 대해 걱정하다, (B) 감정을 나타 내므로 과거분사 bored, (C) stop+~ing: ~하던 것을 멈추다, stop+to부정사: ~하기 위해 멈추다

12 소녀는 긴장돼 보였다. 그녀는 수영대회 때문에 매우 걱정이 되 었다. 대회는 이번 주 토요일에 열릴 것이다. 소년은 그녀가 수 영을 잘한다는 것을 알기 때문에 긴장을 풀고 즐기라고 말하며 그녀를 격려했다. 소년 덕분에 소녀는 안도감을 느꼈다.

13 'not only V-ed but also V-ed' 형태로 영작하는 것이 적절하 다. look은 2형식 동사로서 형용사 보어 confident를 받는다. ④의 경우, feel과 Jisu의 위치를 바꾼다면, 정답이 될 수 있다.

14 'not only A but also B' 구문이 주어가 아닌, 문장을 꾸미는 형태에서 Not only가 문두로 나오면, 주어와 동사는 '도치'되므 로 정답은 ④가 적절하다.

15 '날씨가 춥지만 맑았다'는 내용과, '우리가 소풍을 갔다'는 내용 은 '양보' 접속사 though로 표현하기에 어색하다. '이유'를 나타 내는 Because 또는 As 등이 적절하다.

16 Minju와 Sam 둘 모두 동아리에 가입해서 봉사활동을 하는 것 에 관심이 있다.

17 ①, ③, ④ '주절과 종속절의 주어가 다르므로, 분사구문의 주어 를 쓴다.' ① Watching → Babe watching, ② 주절과 종속 절의 주어가 같으면, 주어를 생략한다. She going → Going, ③ Cutting → You cutting, ④ Being → It being

18 분사구문에서 부사절의 주어와, 주절의 주어가 같을 때 분사구 문에 주어를 쓰지 않는다. 내용상 '전에 그를 본 적이 있기 때문 에, Julie는 Charles와 친구가 되기로 했다'는 것이므로, Julie 와 she는 동일 인물이다.

19 'Neither A nor B'는 동사와 가까운 주어에 수를 일치시킨다. secretaries가 복수이므로 wants → want가 적절하다.

21 도와달라고 부탁했을 때 도와주었을 뿐만 아니라 좋은 친구가 되었다고 했으므로 ①번이 적절하다.

22 'Having no friends at school'이라고 하고 있다.

23 이 글은 '모르는 사람에게 자신의 고민에 대해서 말한 후 기분이 좋아졌다.'는 글이므로, 빈칸에 들어갈 말로는 ②번 '누가 내 기 분을 낫게 해 줄 수 있나요?'가 적절하다.

25 ②번 다음 문장에서 '그는 부모님이나 친구들이 이해하지 못할

교과서 파헤치기

Lesson 3

단어 TEST Step 3   p.04

1 character, 등장인물   2 cartoon, 만화   3 hide, 숨기다
4 prove, 증명하다   5 insect, 곤충   6 publish, 출판하다
7 soak, 담그다, 적시다   8 carrot, 당근   9 spinach, 시금치
10 battleship, 전함   11 secret, 비밀
12 nutrient, 영양분   13 statue, 동상   14 bean, 콩
15 trace, 흔적   16 snowboard, 스노보드

단어 TEST Step 1   p.02

01 증명하다	02 흡수하다	03 출판하다
04 꽃을 피우다	05 수도	06 비밀
07 실제로	08 해결하다	09 발견하다
10 담그다, 적시다	11 지우다	12 기대하다
13 시금치	14 향하다	
15 물리치다, 패배시키다		16 등장인물
17 조각상, 동상	18 기사, 논문	19 전함
20 정부, 국가	21 콩	22 숨겨진
23 고려하다, 여기다	24 일어나다	25 숨다, 숨기다
26 특성, 특징; 특징적인		
27 개선하다, 향상시키다		28 낮추다
29 포함하다, 담고 있다		30 영양소, 영양분
31 세계적으로 유명한		32 으스러뜨리다
33 흔적; 추적하다	34 유독한, 독성의	35 살을 빼다
36 흡수하다, 빨아들이다		
37 ~을 …로부터 멀리하다		38 A를 B로 바꾸다
39 더 이상 ~가 아닌	40 ~을 무서워하다	41 시도해 보다
42 비밀을 지키다	43 게다가	

단어 TEST Step 2   p.03

01 absorb	02 article	03 battleship
04 bloom	05 capital	06 character
07 expect	08 consider	09 defeat
10 characteristic	11 crush	12 poisonous
13 contain	14 hide	15 publish
16 statue	17 improve	18 lower
19 truth	20 trace	21 spinach
22 material	23 hidden	24 nutrient
25 prove	26 world-famous	27 soak
28 planet	29 vision	30 secret
31 solve	32 cartoon	33 researcher
34 government	35 stay full	36 in addition
37 be good for	38 lose weight	39 keep a secret
40 no longer	41 soak up	42 give it a try
43 take medicine		

대화문 TEST Step 1   p.05~06

Listen & Speak 1 A-1
some medicine / something wrong / a stomachache, too much / Why don't, go for a walk / it a try

Listen & Speak 1 A-2
something wrong, look so good / a sore throat, because of, these days / Put, take, in, produce fresh air / get a few plants

Listen & Speak 2 A-1
so hard to lose weight, do you think / walk your dog / it, it help, lose weight / When, walk, actually exercising, too / think about it

Listen & Talk 2 A-2
How are, doing, growing / gotten, a few, so far, I should do / Where / In / need about, a day / move, over

Communicate A
is something wrong, quiet / a bit tired, little / something late / on, until, what I often do these days / that's why, before midnight / getting worse, I should do / eating lots of carrots, rich in vitamin, keep, healthy / see

Progress Check 1
Is, wrong / a little tired, watched, for two hours / why, red eyes, putting, over

Progress Check 2
wrong, look worried / broke, plate, do you think / Tell, truth, understand / hope, right

대화문 TEST Step 2   p.07~08

Listen & Speak 1 A-1
B: Bomi, do you have some medicine?
G: Why? Is something wrong?
B: I have a stomachache. I think I ate too much for lunch.
G: Why don't you go for a walk?

B: O.K. I'll give it a try.

Listen & Speak 1 A-2

B: Is something wrong? You don't look so good.

G: I have a sore throat. I think it's because of the fine dust these days.

B: Put some plants in your room. They take bad air in and produce fresh air.

G: Really? I'll get a few plants right away.

Listen & Speak 2 A-1

B: It's so hard to lose weight. What do you think I should do?

G: Well, why don't you walk your dog every day?

B: My dog would love it, but would it help me lose weight?

G: Sure. When you walk your dog, you're actually exercising, too.

B: O.K. I'll think about it.

Listen & Talk 2 A-2

B: How are your tomatoes doing? Are they growing well?

G: No. I've gotten only a few tomatoes so far. What do you think I should do?

B: Where do you have the pot?

G: In the kitchen.

B: Well, tomato plants need about 7 hours of sunlight a day.

G: Oh, I see. I'll move the pot over to the window.

Communicate A

Anna: Suho, is something wrong? You're very quiet today.

Suho: I'm just a bit tired. I slept very little last night.

Anna: Did you do something late last night?

Suho: Yes, I watched a movie on my phone until 2 a.m. That's what I often do these days.

Anna: Oh, that's why you have red eyes. You should go to bed before midnight for your health.

Suho: I think my eyes are getting worse. What do you think I should do?

Anna: Try eating lots of carrots and tomatoes. They're rich in vitamin A, so they'll keep your eyes healthy.

Suho: I see. Thank you, Anna.

Progress Check 1

B: Is something wrong?

G: I'm just a little tired. I've watched a movie on my phone for two hours.

B: That's why you have red eyes. Try putting a warm towel over your eyes.

G: O.K. Thanks.

Progress Check 2

G: What's wrong? You look worried.

B: Well, I broke my mom's favorite plate. What do you think I should do?

G: Tell her the truth. She will understand.

B: I hope you're right.

본문 TEST Step 1   p.09~10

01 Hidden, Plants   02 Great Spinach

03 world-famous cartoon character

04 gets, by eating spinach

05 When, became popular, lot

06 called, capital, built, statue

07 Although, powers, spinach, nutrients

08 considered, healthiest foods, planet

09 used, surprising way

10 When, absorbs, other, soil

11 characteristic, bombs hidden, ground

12 with sensors on, leaves   13 soak, bombs, light up

14 World War II

15 defeated, during, by using

16 keep, secret, published, article

17 said, improved, vision, ate

18 believed, lot, than before

19 improve, by eating, carrots

20 contain, vitamin, keep, healthy

21 future, may, used, wars

22 discovered, turn, into, light

23 even be used, battleships

24 has already been used   25 Scariest Vegetables

26 are good for, health

27 Up until, however, poisonous

28 named, prove, safe, eat

29 ate, basket, front, watching

30 expected, nothing happened to

31 since, have enjoyed eating

32 no longer, scared of

33 keep, away, place, crushed

34 Insects, come near

본문 TEST Step 2   p.11~12

01 Hidden, Plants   02 Spinach

03 world-famous cartoon character

04 by eating spinach

33

05 became popular, a lot of

06 which, the spinach capital, a statue

07 Although eating, does have, nutrients

08 one of the ten healthiest foods

09 in a surprising way

10 When, absorbs, also absorbs, from

11 to find, hidden in the ground

12 with sensors on their leaves

13 soak up traces, light up   14 World War II

15 defeated, during, by using

16 keep, secret, published an article

17 improved their night vision because

18 a lot, than before

19 improve, by eating

20 which does keep, healthy

21 may actually be used

22 turn, into, light material   23 can even be used

24 has already been used   25 Scariest

26 are good for

27 Up until, however, poisonous

28 named, to prove, safe to eat

29 a basket of, in front of, watching

30 happened to

31 since, have enjoyed eating

32 no longer, scared of

33 keep, away from, place, crushed

34 come near

본문 TEST Step 3   p.13~14

1 식물에 대한 숨겨진 이야기

2 Popeye와 위대한 시금치

3 Popeye는 세계적으로 유명한 만화 캐릭터다.

4 그는 시금치를 먹음으로써 초인적인 힘을 얻는다.

5 Popeye가 1930년대 미국에서 인기를 얻었을 때, 많은 어린이들이 시금치를 먹기 시작했다.

6 텍사스의 크리스털 시티는 세계의 시금치 수도라고 불리는데, 이곳에서는 Popeye의 동상을 세우기까지 했다.

7 비록 시금치를 먹는 것이 우리에게 초인적인 힘을 주지는 않지만, 시금치는 정말로 많은 영양분을 가지고 있다.

8 이것은 실제로 지구상에서 가장 건강한 식품 10개 중 하나로 여겨진다.

9 시금치는 놀라운 용도로 사용될 수 있다.

10 그것이 물을 흡수할 때, 시금치는 흙으로부터 다른 많은 것들도 흡수한다.

11 몇몇 과학자들은 시금치의 이 특성을 땅에 숨겨진 폭탄을 찾는 데 사용했다.

12 그들은 잎에 감지기가 있는 특별한 시금치를 만든다.

13 이 식물들이 폭탄의 흔적을 흡수하면, 감지기가 빛난다.

14 제2차 세계대전에서의 당근

15 1940년, 영국 공군은 제2차 세계 대전에서 레이더 시스템을 사용해 독일군을 패배시켰다.

16 영국 정부는 이 기술을 비밀로 하기를 원했기 때문에, 신문에 기사를 하나 냈다.

17 그것은 영국 비행사들이 당근을 많이 먹어 야간 시력이 좋아졌다는 내용이었다.

18 모두가 그 이야기를 믿었고 전보다 훨씬 많은 당근을 먹기 시작했다.

19 우리는 정말 당근을 많이 먹어서 야간 시력을 높일 수 있을까?

20 실제로 그렇지는 않지만, 당근은 많은 비타민 A를 함유하는데, 그것은 정말로 우리 눈을 건강하게 유지해 준다.

21 미래에는, 당근이 실제로 전쟁에 이용될지도 모른다.

22 스코틀랜드의 연구원들은 당근을 매우 강하고 가벼운 물질로 바꾸는 방법을 발견했다.

23 그것은 심지어 전함을 만드는 데 사용될 수도 있다.

24 이 새로운 소재는 이미 스노보드와 자전거를 만드는 데 사용되었다.

25 토마토, 가장 무서운 채소

26 우리는 모두 토마토가 건강에 좋다는 것을 안다.

27 그러나, 1800년대까지 대부분의 미국인들은 토마토에 독성이 있다고 생각했다.

28 1820년에, Robert Johnson이라는 이름의 남자가 토마토가 먹기에 안전하다는 것을 증명하기를 원했다.

29 그래서, 그는 그를 지켜보는 많은 사람들 앞에서 한 바구니의 토마토를 먹었다.

30 그들은 모두 그가 죽을 것이라고 예상했으나 그에게는 아무 일도 일어나지 않았다.

31 그 이후로, 미국인들은 토마토를 먹는 것을 즐겼다.

32 우리는 더 이상 토마토를 두려워하지 않지만, 몇몇 곤충들은 여전히 그것을 무서워한다.

33 만약 곤충들이 방에 들어오지 않게 하고 싶다면, 으깬 토마토 한 그릇을 방구석에 놓아 두어라.

34 곤충들은 토마토 가까이 오지 않을 것이다.

본문 TEST Step 4-Step 5   p.15~18

1 Hidden Stories about Plants

2 Popeye and the Great Spinach

3 Popeye is a world-famous cartoon character.

4 He gets his super power by eating spinach.

5 When Popeye became popular in the 1930s in the United States, a lot of children began to eat spinach.

6 Crystal City in Texas, which is called the spinach

capital of the world, even built a statue of Popeye.

7 Although eating spinach will not give us super powers, spinach does have a lot of nutrients.

8 It is actually considered one of the ten healthiest foods on the planet.

9 Spinach can be used in a surprising way.

10 When it absorbs water, spinach also absorbs many other things from the soil.

11 Some scientists have used this characteristic of spinach to find bombs hidden in the ground.

12 They make special spinach plants with sensors on their leaves.

13 When these plants soak up traces from bombs, the sensors light up.

14 Carrots in World War II

15 In 1940, the Royal Air Force defeated German fighters during World War II by using a radar system.

16 The British government wanted to keep this technology a secret, so it published an article in the newspaper.

17 It said that British pilots improved their night vision because they ate a lot of carrots.

18 Everybody believed the story and began to eat a lot more carrots than before.

19 Can we really improve night vision by eating lots of carrots?

20 Not really, but carrots contain a lot of vitamin A, which does keep our eyes healthy.

21 In the future, carrots may actually be used in wars.

22 Scottish researchers have discovered a way to turn carrots into a very strong and light material.

23 It can even be used to make battleships.

24 This new material has already been used to make snowboards and bicycles.

25 Tomatoes, the Scariest Vegetables

26 We all know that tomatoes are good for our health.

27 Up until the 1800s, however, most Americans thought that tomatoes were poisonous.

28 In 1820, a man named Robert Johnson wanted to prove that tomatoes were safe to eat.

29 So, he ate a basket of tomatoes in front of many people watching him.

30 They all expected him to die, but nothing happened to him.

31 Ever since then, Americans have enjoyed eating

tomatoes.

32 We are no longer afraid of tomatoes, but some insects are still scared of them.

33 If you want to keep insects away from your room, place a bowl of crushed tomatoes in a corner of your room.

34 Insects will not come near the tomatoes.

Inventions from Plants

1. good way to produce
2. battery invented from, of using, characteristic of sunflowers
3. Like, faces, during the day, more electricity than other batteries

After You Read A Read and Match

1. Spinach
2. secret, super power
3. one of the ten healthiest foods
4. with, to find bombs hidden
5. Carrots
6. to make snowboards
7. into, light material
8. which keeps our eyes healthy
9. Tomatoes
10. keeping insects away
11. poisonous until

Write

1. are good for
2. keep your heart healthy, lower blood pressure
3. solve your skin problems
4. mixed with, makes, soft, clear
5. In addition, help, lose weight
6. stay full for a long time
7. help, stay healthy

Inventions from Plants

1. The Sunflower Battery is a good way to produce energy.

2. It is a battery invented from the idea of using the characteristic of sunflowers.

3. Like sunflowers, it faces the sun during the day, so it produces more electricity than other batteries.

35

After You Read A Read and Match

1. 1. Spinach
2. • the secret of Popeye's super power
3. • one of the ten healthiest foods on the planet
4. • used with sensors to find bombs hidden in the ground
5. 2. Carrots
6. • used to make snowboards and bicycles
7. • made into a very strong and light material
8. • containing a lot of vitamin A, which keeps our eyes healthy
9. 3. Tomatoes
10. • good for keeping insects away
11. • considered poisonous until the 1800s

Write

1. Potatoes are good for your health.
2. They keep your heart healthy because they lower blood pressure.
3. They also solve your skin problems.
4. Potato juice mixed with honey makes your skin soft and clear.
5. In addition, they help you lose weight.
6. If you eat potatoes, you will stay full for a long time.
7. Potatoes help you stay healthy in many ways.

Lesson 4

단어 TEST Step 1 p.21

01 온실	02 수확하다	03 광고
04 전시회, 박람회	05 수중의, 물속에서	06 해양의, 바다의
07 전국적인	08 해외의	
09 홍보하다, 촉진하다		10 교량, 다리
11 지역 공동체	12 감동받은	13 유산
14 환경	15 해산물	16 몇몇의
17 생계를 책임지는 사람, 가장		18 여성의
19 화산의, 화산 작용에 의한		20 세계적으로
21 완성[완료]하다	22 호흡하다	23 파괴하다
24 폭포	25 좁은 길	
26 무형의, 만질 수 없는		27 해파리
28 누르다; 언론, 기자	29 지하의	30 적합한, 적절한
31 청중	32 과로하다	33 경로, 길
34 깨닫다, 인식하다	35 ~을 기원하다	36 우연히 ~하다
37 ~을 따라 걷다	38 두 서너 개의	39 ~에 들어가다
40 ~에 적절하다	41 강의하다, 연설하다	
42 조금, 약간	43 ~에 유익하다	

단어 TEST Step 2 p.22

01 waterfall	02 ad(=advertisement)	
03 path	04 overwork	05 bridge
06 trail	07 underground	08 worldwide
09 volcanic	10 greenhouse	11 destroy
12 exhibition	13 promote	14 complete
15 several	16 breadwinner	17 suitable
18 female	19 press	20 community
21 intangible	22 underwater	23 jellyfish
24 marine	25 harvest	26 audience
27 heritage	28 breathe	29 nationwide
30 overseas	31 realize	32 tightly
33 beat	34 good harvest	35 go on vacation
36 get into	37 happen to	38 walk along
39 be good for	40 keep -ing	41 cheer up
42 give (someone) a hand		
43 give a presentation		

단어 TEST Step 3 p.23

1 harvest, 수확하다 2 underground, 지하의
3 complete, 완성[완료]하다 4 beat, (북 등을 치는) 소리
5 waterfall, 폭포 6 suitable, 적합한 7 breathe, 호흡하다

8 community, 지역 공동체　9 heritage, 유산

10 intangible, 무형의, 만질 수 없는　11 overseas, 해외의

12 seafood, 해산물　13 destroy, 파괴하다　14 ad, 광고

15 bridge, 다리　16 breadwinner, 생계를 책임지는 사람, 가장

대화문 TEST Step 1

p.24~25

Listen & Speak 1 A-1

look at, bridge, ad, where the photo was taken / How do, know / went there with, last summer

Listen & Speak 1 A-2

Look over I wonder why, waiting in line / waiting to get into / famous / on / should try, then

Listen & Speak 2 A-1

I'd like to borrow / Here, are / explain how to use it / Press, what to do

Listen & Speak 2 A-2

Are, going somewhere / going to, walk along / Could you explain what that is / long hiking path around / enjoy your trip

Communicate A

I wonder where, coming from / over there, check it out / strong beat, traditional / called, a kind of community / Could you explain a little bit / traditionally, cheer up, wish for. good harvest / are dancing to, rhythm / part of, completes / Let's join / Why not

Progress Check 1

I wonder why there are so many cars / Lots of, going on vacation / why don't we, too

Progress Check 2

Excuse, copy machine / how to make double-sided copies / Press, double-sided copies, press

대화문 TEST Step 2

p.26~27

Listen & Speak 1 A-1

G: Wow, look at the bridge in this ad. I wonder where the photo was taken.

B: That's Gwangandaegyo in Busan.

G: How do you know that?

B: I went there with my family last summer.

Listen & Speak 1 A-2

B: Look over there. I wonder why there are so many people waiting in line.

G: They're waiting to get into the new bakery there.

B: Why? Is it famous?

G: Yes. It was on a TV program.

B: Really? We should try their bread then.

G: Sure.

Listen & Speak 2 A-1

W: Excuse me, I'd like to borrow an audio guide.

M: Here you are.

W: Could you explain how to use it?

M: Sure. Press this button, and it'll tell you what to do.

Listen & Speak 2 A-2

B: Are you going somewhere this summer?

G: I'm going to Jejudo to walk along the Jeju Olle Trail.

B: The Jeju Olle Trail? Could you explain what that is?

G: It's a long hiking path around Jejudo.

B: Oh, I see. I hope you enjoy your trip!

Communicate A

Jaden: Do you hear that? I wonder where that music is coming from.

Yuri: I think it's coming from over there. Do you want to go and check it out?

Jaden: Yes, I love that strong beat. Is it traditional Korean music?

Yuri: Yes, it's called nongak. It's a kind of community band music.

Jaden: Nongak? Could you explain a little bit more about it?

Yuri: It's traditionally used to cheer up farmers and wish for a good harvest.

Jaden: I see. Look! Some people are dancing to the rhythm.

Yuri: Yes, that's a big part of nongak. Dancing together completes the music.

Jaden: Let's join them.

Yuri: Sure. Why not?

Progress Check 1

W: Look over there. I wonder why there are so many cars on the road.

M: Lots of people are going on vacation this weekend.

W: Really? Then, why don't we go somewhere, too?

M: O.K.

Progress Check 2

B: Excuse me, I'd like to use a copy machine.

W: O.K. You can use this machine.

B: Could you explain how to make double-sided copies?

W: Sure. Press the button for double-sided copies, and then press the start button.

B: Thank you.

---

01 Haenyeo, Female Divers
02 several, underwater, promoted, worldwide
03 female, harvest, without, breathing
04 made, Intangible, Heritage list
05 last, interviewed, experience, taking
06 become interested in taking
07 One day, happened to   08 was surprised to find
09 Until, seen, looked, tired
10 kept laughing, been, over
11 realized, should take   12 isn't it difficult to
13 At, why I wanted
14 looked pretty in, wetsuits
15 So, very special
16 show, culture to, world
17 opened up, then
18 make them look beautiful
19 tell us more about   20 so special about
21 can tell you, things
22 symbol, strong women
23 volcanic, suitable, farming, breadwinners
24 form, own, each other
25 example, more-experienced, less-experienced
26 stay, without, breathing, catch
27 good for, underwater environment
28 marine, time, destory, place
29 what, planning, do, future
30 attended, exhibition, talk, lives
31 finished, held, hand tightly
32 said to, so much
33 such a special person
34 crying with happiness
35 was deeply moved
36 never forget, moment, continue
37 more beautiful stories about

---

01 Female Divers
02 underwater photographer, has promoted, worldwide
03 female divers, without any breathing devices
04 made UNESCO's Intangible Cultural Heritage list
05 was interviewed, experience of taking picutres
06 become interested in taking
07 One day, happened to
08 was surprised to find, was enjoying
09 Until then, had only seen, looked very tired
10 kept laughing, for over five hours
11 realized, should take pictures
12 isn't it difficult to take pictures
13 At first, why I wanted
14 looked pretty in their wetsuits
15 very special   16 show, to
17 opened up, then
18 Of course, make them, beautiful
19 more about   20 so special
21 can tell you
22 symbol of strong women
23 which, is not suitable for, have become the breadwinners for
24 form, own communities, each other
25 more-experienced, less-experienced
26 because, without, breathing devices, can't catch
27 is good for, underwater environment
28 Catching, at one time in one place can destory
29 what, planning to do
30 attended, overseas exhibition, give a talk
31 held my hand tightly
32 so much
33 whole life, such a special person
34 crying with happiness
35 was deeply moved
36 can never forget, continue to take
37 more beautiful stories about them

---

1 해녀, 한국의 여성 잠수부
2 지난 몇 년 동안, 수중 사진작가 Zin Kim은 제주 해녀 문화를 전 세계에 홍보해 왔다.
3 해녀는 어떤 호흡 장치도 사용하지 않고 해산물을 채취하는 한국의 여성 잠수부들이다.
4 그들의 문화는 2016년에 유네스코 무형문화유산에 등재되었다.

5 지난주 그녀의 작업실에서, Zin Kim과 해녀의 사진을 찍는 그녀의 경험에 대해 인터뷰를 했다.

6 Q. 어떻게 해녀의 사진을 찍는 것에 관심을 가지게 되었나요?

7 어느 날, 저는 우연히 한 해녀의 사진을 찍게 되었어요.

8 저는 그녀가 자신의 일을 즐겁게 하는 것을 보고 놀랐습니다.

9 그때까지, 저는 흑백 사진 속의 아주 지친 모습의 해녀만 봐 왔죠.

10 하지만, 그녀는 다섯 시간이 넘도록 물속에 있은 후에도 계속 웃었어요.

11 저는 그때 해녀의 사진을 찍어야겠다고 깨달았어요.

12 Q. 작가님은 아름다운 해녀 사진들을 찍으시는데, 그들의 사진을 찍는 것이 어렵진 않으신가요?

13 처음에, 그들은 제가 왜 자신들의 사진을 찍으려고 하는지 이해하지 못했어요.

14 그들은 잠수복을 입은 자신들의 모습이 예뻐 보인다고 생각하지 않았으니까요.

15 그래서, 제가 그들에게 말했죠, "여러분들은 아주 특별해요.

16 저는 여러분의 문화를 세계에 알리고 싶어요."

17 그들은 그때 제게 마음을 열었어요.

18 물론, 저 또한 그들에게 제 사진 속에서 그들을 아름답게 보이도록 하겠다고 약속했지요.

19 Q. 해녀에 대해서 더 말씀해 주시겠어요?

20 그들은 무엇이 그렇게 특별한가요?

21 세 가지를 말씀 드릴게요.

22 첫 번째로, 해녀들은 강인한 여성의 상징이에요.

23 제주도는 화산섬이고, 이는 농사에 적합하지 않아서 많은 해녀들이 가족들의 생계비를 버는 가장이 되어 왔어요.

24 둘째로, 해녀들은 그들 자신의 공동체를 조직하고 서로 도와요.

25 예를 들어, 경험이 더 많은 해녀들이 경험이 적은 해녀들을 훈련시키지요.

26 세 번째로, 어떤 호흡 장치도 사용하지 않고 물속에 머물기 때문에, 해녀는 많은 해산물을 채취할 수가 없어요.

27 이것은 수중 환경에 좋은 것이지요.

28 한 번에 한 장소에서 너무 많은 해양생물을 채취하는 것은 바다를 파괴할 수 있으니까요.

29 Q. 마지막으로, 앞으로 계획하고 있는 것에 대해 말씀해 주세요.

30 예전에 두 명의 해녀들과 함께 그들의 삶에 대해 이야기하기 위해 해외에서 열리는 박람회에 참가한 적이 있어요.

31 제가 연설을 마쳤을 때, 해녀 중 한 분이 제 손을 꼭 잡았어요.

32 그분이 말했죠, "너무 고마워.

33 내 평생 내가 이렇게 특별한 사람이라는 걸 미처 알지 못했어."

34 그녀는 행복해서 울고 있었어요.

35 청중들 모두가 깊은 감동을 받았어요.

36 전 그 순간을 절대 잊을 수가 없기 때문에 해녀의 사진을 계속해서 찍을 거예요.

37 저는 그들에 대한 더 많은 아름다운 이야기들을 세계의 더 많은 사람들에게 알려 주고 싶어요.

1 Haenyeo, Female Divers of Korea

2 For the past several years, the underwater photographer Zin Kim has promoted the culture of Jeju haenyeo worldwide.

3 Haenyeo are Korean female divers who harvest seafood without any breathing devices.

4 Their culture made UNESCO's Intangible Cultural Heritage list in 2016.

5 At her studio last week, Zin Kim was interviewed about her experience of taking pictures of haenyeo.

6 Q. How did you become interested in taking photos of haenyeo?

7 One day, I happened to take pictures of a haenyeo.

8 I was surprised to find that she was enjoying her job.

9 Until then, I had only seen black-and-white photos of haenyeo who looked very tired.

10 However, she kept laughing even after she had been in the water for over five hours.

11 I realized then that I should take pictures of haenyeo.

12 Q. You take beautiful pictures of them, but isn't it difficult to take pictures of haenyeo?

13 At first, they didn't understand why I wanted to take their pictures.

14 They didn't think they looked pretty in their wetsuits.

15 So, I said to them, "You're very special.

16 I want to show your culture to the world."

17 They opened up to me then.

18 Of course, I also promised them that I would make them look beautiful in my pictures.

19 Q. Could you tell us more about haenyeo?

20 What's so special about them?

21 I can tell you three things.

22 First, haenyeo are a symbol of strong women.

23 Jejudo, which is a volcanic island, is not suitable for farming, so many haenyeo have become the breadwinners for their families.

24 Second, haenyeo form their own communities and help each other.

25 For example, more-experienced haenyeo train less-experienced haenyeo.

26 Third, because they stay in the water without any

breathing devices, haenyeo can't catch a lot of seafood.

27 This is good for the underwater environment.

28 Catching too much marine life at one time in one place can destroy the ocean.

29 Q. Lastly, please tell us what you're planning to do in the future.

30 I once attended an overseas exhibition with a couple of haenyeo to give a talk about their lives.

31 When I finished my talk, one of the haenyeo held my hand tightly.

32 She said to me, "Thank you so much.

33 I've never known in my whole life that I was such a special person."

34 She was crying with happiness.

35 Everyone in the audience was deeply moved.

36 I can never forget that moment, so I'll continue to take pictures of haenyeo.

37 I want to tell more beautiful stories about them to many more people in the world.

Communicate – B Talk and Play

1. what these are
2. called songpyeon
3. explain more about
4. traditional Korean rice cakes

After You Read A

1. Photographer Who Loves
2. an underwater photographer, has promoted, worldwide
3. decided to take pictures, when she met, who was enjoying
4. It, easy taking, at first
5. However, that, their culture to the world, finally opened their minds
6. At an overseas exhibition, gave a talk
7. one of, was crying with happiness
8. would continue to take

Write

1. makes coffee drinks for a living
2. became a barista, had found out about his passion
3. His favorite part of, decorating coffee with, watching, enjoying
4. planning to open

Communicate – B Talk and Play

1. A: I wonder what these are.
2. B: They're called songpyeon.
3. A: Could you explain more about them?
4. B: They're traditional Korean rice cakes.

After You Read A

1. A Photographer Who Loves Haenyeo
2. Zin Kim, an underwater photographer, has promoted the culture of Jeju haenyeo worldwide.
3. She decided to take pictures of them when she met a haenyeo who was enjoying her job.
4. It was not easy taking their pictures at first.
5. However, when she told them that she wanted to show their culture to the world, the haenyeo finally opened their minds.
6. At an overseas exhibition, she gave a talk about the lives of haenyeo.
7. After her speech, one of the haenyeo was crying with happiness.
8. Zin Kim said that she would continue to take pictures of haenyeo.

Write

1. Kim Minho is a barista. He makes coffee drinks for a living.
2. He became a barista after he had found out about his passion for coffee.
3. His favorite part of his job is decorating coffee with hot milk and watching his customers enjoying it.
4. He is planning to open his own coffee shop.

단어 TEST Step 1   p.41

01 해산물, 해물	02 불안해하는	03 경쟁, 대회
04 적	05 휴식을 취하다	06 졸업하다
07 실제로	08 무력한	09 전문적인
10 대신에	11 판단하다	12 낯선 사람
13 행운인, 운이 좋은	14 안도하는	15 유명하게
16 준비하다	17 마음, 정신	18 불안해하는
19 자신감 있는	20 행동	21 독특한
22 심리학자	23 조심스럽게	24 정치적인
25 지원자	26 (거리·공간·시간상으로) 떨어져	
27 (음식을) 씹다	28 발표	29 해결책
30 편리한	31 드문, 희귀한	32 경쟁자
33 스트레스가 많은	34 심리학	35 내리다
36 발표하다	37 ~에 들르다	38 결코 ~가 아닌
39 혼자서	40 (해답 등을) 찾아내다, 내놓다	
41 예약하다	42 A를 B로 바꾸다	43 A뿐만 아니라 B도

단어 TEST Step 2   p.42

01 graduate	02 behavior	03 confident
04 solution	05 decide	06 enemy
07 chew	08 famously	09 professional
10 actually	11 psychologist	12 rare
13 stressful	14 relax	15 supporter
16 seafood	17 political	18 relieved
19 helpless	20 carefully	21 psychology
22 competition	23 instead	24 relay
25 presentation	26 judge	27 convenient
28 rival	29 stranger	30 unique
31 lucky	32 prepare	33 lend
34 guess	35 according to	36 turn A into B
37 make a presentation		
38 not only A but also B		39 by oneself
40 come up with	41 not ~ at all	
42 make a reservation		43 not ~ anymore

단어 TEST Step 3   p.43

1 rare, 드문, 희귀한 2 bake, 굽다 3 enemy, 적
4 stranger, 낯선 사람 5 chew, (음식을) 씹다
6 supporter, 지원자 7 helpless, 무력한
8 convenient, 편리한 9 graduate, 졸업하다
10 presentation, 발표 11 relieved, 안도하는
12 psychology, 심리학 13 lend, 빌려주다
14 relax, 휴식을 취하다 15 confident, 자신감 있는
16 rival, 경쟁자

대화문 TEST Step 1   p.44~45

Listen & Speak 1 A-1
happened to, Aren't / chewed, all the time, worried about / bored, Why don't you play with / hope, stop chewing

Listen & Speak 1 A-2
nervous / worried about, swimming competition / worry, relax, enjoy / much better

Listen & Speak 2 A-1
what time, Grandma's place / About, bake cookies / get up early / don't have to

Listen & Speak 2 A-2
Shall we try / Why, call, make a reservation / don't have to, online / How convenient

Communicate A
can't wait / actually worried / Aren't, good at / worried, relay / What, mean / last runner, What if, because of / putting too much pressure on / practice / don't have to do / winning, losing / right, lucky, like

Progress Check 1
nervous / worried about, presentation, history class / prepared a lot, do, job / feel much better

Progress Check 2
seafood spaghetti / stop by, on the way / You don't have to, what, need / back home by, help, cook

대화문 TEST Step 2   p.46~47

Listen & Speak 1 A-1
G: What happened to your shoes? Aren't they new?
B: Yes, but my dog chewed them. He does it all the time. I'm worried about him.
G: He was probably bored. Why don't you play with him more often?
B: O.K., I will. I hope he will stop chewing my shoes.

41

B: You look a bit nervous.

G: I'm worried about my swimming competition this Saturday.

B: Don't worry. You're such a good swimmer. Just relax and enjoy yourself!

G: Thanks. I feel much better now.

B: Mom, what time are we going to Grandma's place tomorrow morning?

W: About 8 a.m. I'm going to bake cookies for her before we go.

B: Then, should I get up early to help you?

W: You don't have to. Your dad will help me.

B: O.K, then. Good night, Mom!

W: Shall we try that new Mexican restaurant tomorrow?

M: Why not? I'll call the restaurant to make a reservation for us.

W: You don't have to call them. You can do it online.

M: Oh, I see. How convenient!

Yuri: Hi, Jaden. Sports Day is next Friday. I can't wait!

Jaden: Really? I'm actually worried about it.

Yuri: Why? Aren't you good at sports?

Jaden: Yes, I am, but I'm worried about the 800-meter relay.

Yuri: What do you mean?

Jaden: I'm the last runner. What if our team loses because of me?

Yuri: I think you're putting too much pressure on yourself.

Jaden: Really? Don't you think I should practice every day?

Yuri: No, you don't have to do that. It's just a school race. It's not about winning or losing.

Jaden: I guess you're right , Yuri. I'm lucky to have a friend like you.

B: You look a bit nervous.

G: Well, I'm worried about my presentation in history class.

B: Don't worry. You've prepared a lot. You'll do a great job.

G: Thanks. I feel much better now.

M: Shall we have seafood spaghetti for dinner?

W: Sure. I'll stop by the store on the way home.

M: You don't have to do that. We already have what we need.

W: Oh, I see. Then, I'll be back home by 6 to help you cook.

---

01 Psychology Answers, Questions

02 think, have, unique

03 Chances, many other, same

04 human mind, behavior, solution

05 become less nervous

06 presentation, front, whole class

07 Feeling nervous, carefully studying

08 came over, stand tall

09 standing tall, not, anymore

10 In fact, confident, presentation

11 According, standing tall, stressful

12 bodies, minds, change, behavior

13 want to feel confident

14 with, apart, place, on

15 not, sure, but, confident

16 help, feel better

17 graduates from, become, professional

18 However, has never told

19 worried that, will, understand

20 Wanting, clear, by himself

21 complete stranger sitting beside

22 why he did it

23 felt much better, off

24 Strangely enough, strangers, like

25 because, being judged, seeing

26 share with, try talking   27 feel much better

28 turn, rival into   29 political, not, at all

30 friends with, came up   31 rival, rare book

32 to lend, for, few

33 returned, thanked, deeply

34 Since, only, supporter, also

35 famously, Enemies, favor, more

36 turn, into, rival, favor

37 Instead, rival, do, favor

p.50~51

01 Psychology Answers, Questions

02 unique problem

03 Chances are

04 human mind, behavior, so, help, find, to

05 become less nervous

06 big presentation, front, whole class

07 Feeling nervous, carefully studying

08 came over, to stand tall like

09 standing tall, a few, not, anymore

10 In fact, confident that, make, presentation

11 According to, become, by standing tall for, stressful events

12 bodies, minds, minds, behavior

13 feel confident

14 feet apart, place, on

15 not only feel sure, but also look confident, other people

16 feel better

17 graduates from, next year, professional

18 However, has never told

19 worried that, will not understand

20 Wanting, clear his mind, decided to take, by himself

21 complete, sitting beside

22 why he did it

23 However, felt much better, got off

24 Strangely enough, often tell strangers

25 because, not have to, being judged, seeing

26 that, share with, talking, stranger

27 feel much better

28 turn, rival into

29 political rival who, not, at all

30 become friends with, came up with

31 rare

32 to lend, a few days

33 deeply

34 Since, not only, but also

35 famously, who do you one favor

36 turn, into, do your rival a favor

37 Instead, to do, favor

p.52~53

1 심리학이 당신의 물음에 답하다

2 여러분은 당신만의 유일무이한 고민을 가지고 있다고 생각하는가?

3 아마 많은 다른 사람들이 여러분과 똑같은 고민을 가지고 있을 것이다.

4 심리학은 인간의 마음과 행동에 관한 연구이며, 따라서 여러분이 문제에 대한 해결책을 찾는 데 도움을 줄 수 있다.

5 어떻게 하면 긴장을 덜 할 수 있나요?

6 지수가 반 전체 앞에서 발표를 하기 5분 전이었다.

7 지수는 긴장이 되어, 의자에 앉아 자신의 필기를 열심히 들여다보고 있었다.

8 그때 선생님이 다가와서는 원더우먼처럼 꼿꼿이 서 있어 보라고 말했다.

9 그렇게 몇 분을 우뚝 선 후에, 지수는 더 이상 긴장되지 않았다.

10 사실, 그녀는 발표를 멋있게 할 수 있을 것이라는 자신감이 생겼다.

11 유명한 심리학자인 Amy Cuddy에 의하면, 우리는 스트레스를 받는 상황 이전에 2분 정도 꼿꼿이 서 있는 것만으로도 자신감이 더 생길 수 있다고 한다.

12 우리의 몸은 마음을 바꾸고, 마음은 우리의 행동을 바꿀 수 있다.

13 자신감이 생기기를 원하는가?

14 양발을 벌리고, 허리께에 손을 올려 보아라.

15 자신에 대한 확신이 생길 뿐만 아니라 다른 사람이 보기에도 자신감에 차 보인다.

16 누가 내 기분을 낫게 해 줄 수 있나요?

17 내년에 고등학교를 졸업한 이후에 태호는 전문적인 농부가 되고 싶어 한다.

18 하지만, 누구에게도 그것에 대해 한 번도 말하지 않았다.

19 그는 부모님이나 친구들이 이해하지 못할까 걱정이 된다.

20 마음을 정리하기 위해서, 태호는 혼자 하루 기차 여행을 떠나기로 결심했다.

21 기차에서, 그는 옆에 앉은 전혀 모르는 사람에게 자신의 고민에 대해서 말했다.

22 그는 자신이 왜 그랬는지 알 수 없었다.

23 그러나, 기차에서 내릴 때 기분이 훨씬 좋아졌다.

24 정말 이상하게도, 우리는 태호처럼 우리의 문제에 대해 낯선 사람에게 말할 때가 있다.

25 그것은 우리가 평가받거나 그 사람을 다시 볼 것이라는 걱정을 할 필요가 없기 때문이다.

26 만약 가족이나 친구들과도 나눌 수 없는 고민이 있다면, 낯선 이에게 말해 보아라.

27 기분이 훨씬 나아질 것이다.

28 라이벌을 어떻게 친구로 만들 수 있을까요?

29 Benjamin Franklin에게는 한때 그를 전혀 좋아하지 않는 정치적 경쟁자가 있었다.

30 Franklin은 그와 친구가 되고 싶어서, 계획을 세웠다.

31 그의 경쟁자는 희귀한 책을 가지고 있었다.

32 Franklin은 그의 정적에게 그 책을 며칠 동안 빌려달라고 부탁했다.

33 Franklin이 그 책을 돌려줄 때, 그는 그에게 진심으로 감사를 표했다.

34 그날 이후로, 그의 경쟁자는 정치적인 후원자뿐만 아니라 좋은 친구가 되었다.

35 Franklin은 "당신을 한 번 도운 적은 더 돕고 싶어 하게 된다."

라는 유명한 말을 했다.

36 여러분이 경쟁자를 친구로 만들고 싶다면, 경쟁자의 부탁을 들어주지 마라.

37 대신, 경쟁자에게 부탁을 해 보아라.

1 Psychology Answers Your Questions

2 Do you think you have a unique problem?

3 Chances are that many other people have the same problem.

4 Psychology is the study of the human mind and behavior, so it can help you find a solution to your problem.

5 How do I become less nervous?

6 It was five minutes before Jisu's big presentation in front of the whole class.

7 Feeling nervous, Jisu was carefully studying her notes in her chair.

8 Then, her teacher came over and told her to stand tall like Wonder Woman.

9 After standing tall for a few minutes, Jisu did not feel nervous anymore.

10 In fact, she was confident that she would make a great presentation.

11 According to Amy Cuddy, a famous psychologist, we can become more confident just by standing tall for two minutes before stressful events.

12 Our bodies change our minds, and our minds can change our behavior.

13 Do you want to feel confident?

14 Stand with your feet apart, and place your hands on your hips.

15 You will not only feel sure about yourself but also look confident to other people.

16 Who can help me feel better?

17 When he graduates from high school next year, Taeho wants to become a professional farmer.

18 However, he has never told anyone about it.

19 He is worried that his parents or his friends will not understand.

20 Wanting to clear his mind, Taeho decided to take a day trip on a train by himself.

21 On the train, he told a complete stranger sitting beside him about his problem.

22 He had no idea why he did it.

23 However, he felt much better when he got off the train.

24 Strangely enough, we often tell strangers about our problems just like Taeho.

25 That is because we do not have to worry about being judged or seeing them again.

26 If you have a problem that you cannot share with your family or friends, try talking to a stranger.

27 You will feel much better.

28 How do I turn a rival into a friend?

29 Benjamin Franklin once had a political rival who did not like him at all.

30 Franklin wanted to become friends with him, so he came up with a plan.

31 His rival had a rare book.

32 Franklin asked his rival to lend him the book for a few days.

33 When Franklin returned the book, he thanked him deeply.

34 Since that day, his rival became not only a political supporter but also a good friend.

35 Franklin famously said, "Enemies who do you one favor will want to do more."

36 If you want to turn a rival into a friend, don't do your rival a favor.

37 Instead, ask your rival to do you a favor.

Listen & Speak 2 - Think and Talk

1. don't, have to do
2. don't have to clean
3. don't have to come to school by

Link

1. How confident, feel about yourself
2. Wanting to find, created a test
3. took the test, average score
4. scored above the average score
5. Thus, felt quite confident about themselves

Write

1. The hardest time
2. hardest time in my life, passed away, ago
3. younger, took care of, most of
4. Not having her around, nfelt sad, lonely
5. One day, found
6. not only wrote a lot, but also wished
7. From this experience, have learned, try to be happy, as she wished

Listen & Speak 2 - Think and Talk

1. A: What don't I have to do on Stress-Free Day?

2. B: You don't have to clean the classroom.

3. C: You don't have to come to school by 8:30.

Link

1. How confident do you feel about yourself?

2. Wanting to find the answer to this question, we created a test about confidence.

3. Thirty students took the test. The average score was nine.

4. Eighteen students scored above the average score.

5. Thus, sixty percent of the students felt quite confident about themselves.

Write

1. The hardest time in my life

2. The hardest time in my life was when my grandmother passed away five years ago.

3. When I was younger, she took care of me most of the time.

4. Not having her around, I felt sad and lonely.

5. One day, I found my grandmother's diary.

6. She not only wrote a lot about her memories but also wished that I would lead a happy life.

7. From this experience, I have learned that I should try to be happy just as she wished.

MEMO

MEMO

적중 100

영어 기출 문제집

정답 및 해설

미래 | 최연희